D1623784

The Just Polity

The Just Polity

Populism, Law, and Human Welfare

Norman Pollack

University of Illinois Press

Urbana and Chicago

This book is printed on acid-free paper.

Library of Congress Cataloging-in-Publication Data

Pollack, Norman.
  The just polity.

  Bibliography: p.
  Includes index.
  1. Populism—United States—History.   I. Title.
JA84.U5P63   1987   320.5'0973   86-11433
ISBN 0-252-01348-4 (alk. paper)

To my family
NANCY *and* PETER
Whose goodness and beauty
Provide a shelter of love

Contents

Acknowledgments

I gratefully acknowledge the influence of my teachers in the shaping of my intellectual growth and personal identity. Frank Freidel has been special in this regard, providing me for more than three decades a fixed point by which to gain my historical and ethical bearings. The integrity and permanence of his scholarship have lifted my spirit about what it was possible to accomplish, and his absolute devotion to free inquiry has encouraged me, like his other students, to pursue an independent path, without fear that our mistakes would reflect on him. His greatness as a teacher lies in his serenity and confidence about his lifework. I shall never be able to repay his wisdom, instruction, and kindness. I was guided by four superb teachers at the University of Florida: Manning Dauer, William G. Carleton, and Alfred Diamant, in political science, and Arthur Thompson, a gifted historian who was tragically cut down in his prime. At Stanford I benefited from the faculties of anthropology, psychology, and philosophy, but I particularly recall the graciousness of the historian George Knoles. From 1956 to 1961, Harvard was the center of the universe to me. In addition to renewing my studies with Frank Freidel, I was privileged to work with two brilliant yet remarkably dissimilar men, Barrington Moore and Louis Hartz. Hartz's recent passing saddens all who knew him and his delight in the unfolding of pure mind. In graduate school I also formed close friendships with Gordon Levin and Gabriel Kolko; I look back fondly to the hours of protest and magnificent intellectual discussion. Yet Harvard was also Cambridge and a community of scholars, some having fled Nazi Germany, who were not affiliated with the university. One of the major forces on my life was Fritz Pappenheim, a gentle man, deeply learned, who shared with me his knowledge of social theory and his concern about the prospect for democratic man. He was a wise counselor and friend whom I greatly miss.

There is, of course, life after Harvard. C. Vann Woodward, without realizing it, continued my education at Yale. I count myself among his devoted followers. From this time, Jesse Lemisch has been a lasting friend, he whose original mind and humane vision never ceases to amaze me. Since the early 1960s, I have derived continuous intellectual stimulation from my students. For almost two decades, Stanley Vittoz has given more than he has received in our theoretical discussions about the nature of capitalism. From the beginning, he has been a valued colleague rather than student. I also anticipate with pleasure the fine careers of Richard Oestreicher, Ronald Edsforth, and Clifton Fox, each of whom from diverse angles of vision has strengthened my grasp of the American social structure. I here record my simple thanks to three friends, Gerald Weintraub, Gerhard Magnus, and James Adley, each outstanding in their respective fields of medicine, aesthetics, and painting, whose cultivated approach to life and concern with essential values have provided me with a clearer sense of purpose and continuity in my work. My debt is great to the John Simon Guggenheim Memorial Foundation, not only for the award of a fellowship but also for the meaning I associate with this particular fellowship: the mandate to transcend one's previous development; the opportunity for a rebirth. My fellowship studies in London during 1968–1969 were divided between concrete historical investigations and the fashioning of an aesthetic mode of consciousness.

None of the foregoing persons has read a single word of this book in manuscript form. They are wholly free from responsibility for its contents. That honor inevitably and properly falls to the author. I have, however, had the invaluable assistance of three highly skilled editors in bringing this work to publication. The basic challenge was to untangle my knotted prose. Jeanine Rosenberg gave my penultimate draft of the manuscript a line by line review and through her queries and perceptive comments about word choice made a vast improvement in the text. Lewis Bateman copy edited the manuscript for the press, transforming a routine task into a creative enterprise. I felt as I turned the pages that I had found my hypothetical reader, who would persist in the face of technical and sometimes lengthy analyses because he had a sure command of structure and evidence. His suggested alterations were few but to

decisive effect. Lawrence J. Malley presided over the scholarly review of the manuscript, made excellent recommendations about its
final form, and, most important, expressed the warm interest for
which even the most austere and remote author is inwardly
moved. He has been the good shepherd, taking my book into the
light of day.

"Plain song"
May 1986

The Just Polity

Introduction

Populism was a remarkably varied movement. The conventional wisdom about its nature can be contradicted at every turn. While the original scholarly framework led to searching questions, the half-century since the publication of John D. Hicks's *The Populist Revolt* represents only the initial stage of inquiry, in which the characteristics of Populism's organizational development, ideological perspective, and social composition were tentatively identified. In the last two decades, Populist scholars have come to a humbling realization of their own ignorance: Today they are aware of how little they know about the movement's internal contours because, in fact, they know so much more.

In retrospect, even disputes during the Cold War that rendered Populism synonymous with protofascism have their positive aspect. They directed subsequent scholarship to a renewed search for primary evidence and required greater conceptual sophistication. Because Populism had not been exempted from the conformist pressures of the Cold War era, its historical identity was more clearly revealed and our understanding of it was greatly enriched. Indeed, Populism became a focus of historical and even popular discussion, suggesting to observers that a key to the social contexts of both the present and the past had been discovered. A dialogue between past and present began to dramatize basic issues concerning business structure, governmental obligation, and the conditions necessary to human satisfaction.

Although at first indirectly, the discussion of Populism stimulated more open speculation on the character of American modernization. The issues were momentous, investing the movement with renewed interest. When fully delineated, Populist ideology called for the separation of business and government. Moreover, Populists demanded that industrialism become a neutral force susceptible to democratic political controls. These features suggest the possibility that Populism advocated an alternative mode of governance and development. Thus, simplistic generalizations about class make-up, political demands, and regional traits are no longer acceptable. Populism became significant because it was closely related to the political and structural formation of modern capitalist society in the United States.

The recognition of Populism's importance in clarifying the nation's growth during and after the late nineteenth century, and in analyzing the patterns of reform and dissent that resulted from modern capitalist development, should determine the next stage in the investigation of the movement. Fundamental studies have to be continued and extended, even to the careful reconstruction of already familiar sources. A synthesis of previous scholarship and the discovery of new material are of less importance presently than an examination of central questions: What position did Populism occupy on the ideological spectrum? How fundamentally did the movement understand and address capitalism and its attendant social problems? Was the factor of class operative in shaping Populists' political identity? Did the movement surmount racism, whether through intrinsic respect for man's welfare, political exigency, or a realistic assessment of the South's economic foundations? For the individual Populist, and for the movement as an expression of a collective process, what were the dynamics in the formation of an active political consciousness? Did Populism exhibit increasing radicalization? Was its ideology founded on a rational, as opposed to a perfunctory, or rote, means of acceptance? Finally, did Populism prescribe limits for its reforming impulse? Did it stay within internally derived political and ideological boundaries? Did such boundaries prevent any progression beyond a certain doctrinal or programmatic point?

In seeking to reorient the investigation of Populism, I have employed a decidely traditional methodology and thematic emphasis: the textual analysis of the Populist moral and legal framework. My purpose is to ascertain from such discourse the essentials of a public philosophy that would be appropriate to democratic government. This focus was also Populism's own. The movement's thought, and its political means of expression, were restrained by constitutionalism and by the assumption that private property was a central feature of the social order. Yet, these ideas were associated with a far-reaching critique of capitalism. In my study, Populists viewed the political economy as a system of emergent monopolism that had altered the character of American law, removed basic safeguards to personal and political liberty, and denied the autonomous existence of the state as the custodian of individual security and the nation's welfare.

The question of sovereignty is central to my interpretation. Populists feared that sovereignty would reside in the private realm and that this would lead to a class-state under the dominance of business. They believed that this process had already begun. Their response was to insist that the locus of sovereignty be an independent public realm. Government would have an autonomous role; it would be granted potentially extensible powers that emanated from and were exercised on behalf of the people. Populists favored a restoration of the founding principles of governance. Concomitantly, they sought to restructure economic and class relations, in order to secure a new social balance. The corporation was to be brought into proper alignment with and subsumed within the jurisdiction of government; more important, it was to be made amenable to the rule of law. Finally, Populists aimed to create the requisite conditions for democratic opportunity. This entailed the public ownership of monopolist enterprises on the ground that they were hindrances to free economic activity. This merging of ethical and structural elements enlarged the political analysis within Populism. Though concentrating on the supervisory powers of the state, Populism maintained its respect for a propertied social order, however democratized this order became in its practice.

Populists intended, therefore, to construct an economy and a supportive culture of democratic capitalism, which would reject, alternatively, monopolism and socialism. This goal included the conservation of institutions and values associated, as if by an act of faith, with America's democratic heritage. But ensuring the survival of these institutions and values required a fundamental rearrangement of the public and private spheres of power. The ownership of private property was accepted, but it could not be permitted to encroach on the rights of the community. Individualism also could not be allowed to destroy its actuating principles, thus degenerating into an anarchic economy ripe for pervasive monopolistic organization. The individual was more sacred than law, even than popular rights, in the Populist cosmology; and the individual, more than property, was the antecedent source of sovereignty. The essential condition for the individual's free existence, which simultaneously affirmed capitalism and attacked its prevailing mode, was the attainment of some measure of economic and social independence. The ownership of a home, which designated a secure anchor, came to represent this independence in Populism's recurrent imagery.

Property was only a threat when it became integrated with mechanisms of domination. In Populist discourse one hears the refrain, "the workman is worthy of his hire." This principle was extended by a strict interpretation of producers' values to include reasonable expectations of profit for the lesser capitalist. Yet this view of property resulted in implacable opposition to corporate wealth. Intracapitalist differences reached to the marrow of the Populist struggle. When property was concentrated, Populists viewed it as taking on a politicized form. Wealth accumulation depended less on internal economic generation than on the private control of the state. Corporate organization, seemingly impersonal, signified a new magnitude of power that obstructed normal economic processes and was impervious to popular controls. Economic concentration denied the promise of an equitable distribution of property. It was a shift from a principle of fair entitlement, in which the producer received the benefits of his labor, to widespread degradation, in which the small holder of property and the nonpropertied suffered expropriation at the hands of dominant economic groups.

There were previous situations in which the defense of property had resulted in a reformist configuration. In Populism's case, this outcome required substantive modifications of the existing stage of capitalism that exceeded the expectations of reform. Yet the starting place for analyzing Populism *is* its reformist character—its retention of property, the wage-relation, and capitalism per se. Populists' dedication to, and immersion deeply within, an idealized American construct provided additional reinforcement for this reform identity. It symbolized the possibilities for transforming society that Populists believed resided in the national heritage. While nonprivileged capitalism may seem a misnomer to modern political sensibilities, Populists gave it a specific referent: depoliticized economic processes. Activation of the economy was to stem from the marketplace. As a corrective to orthodox laissez-faire, the state would enhance competition where practicable by means of antimonopolist activities; otherwise, public ownership would follow in economic sectors affecting the general interest or where natural monopolies had taken form.

In making governmental responsiveness the linchpin of the Populist structure of capitalism, Populists necessarily emphasized a constitutional perspective. They relied on the Constitution to stipulate the state's powers and responsibilities, to adduce proofs for its sovereign capacity and interventionist role, and to create a statement of rights originating from the literalist application of American political tenets. The combination of law and economy led to an exceptional, and historically still untried, capitalist framework. Modernity was embraced (though distinguished from, and not simply equated with, the prevailing stage of capitalism) because it liberated technological and economic energies; but monopolist restriction and the private control of government had to be removed.

To determine whether or not Populism offered an alternative pattern of modernization, I have emphasized its moral and legal premises as the forces shaping its protest. This philosophic baseline enables one to gauge the nature and scope of Populism's challenge to existing capitalist arrangements. Populists sought to modify emergent monopolism by according greater status and powers to the state; in addition, this governmental framework had to embody a pervasive ethical content if structural change was to be meaningful. Yet despite the relatively advanced thinking and humaneness of its critique, Populism applied basic correctives to the organization of business power without simultaneously transcending capitalism. Populists maintained a propertied consciousness; beyond the mere consciousness of property, this referred to a mode of perceiving the world through categories based on the total political culture of capitalism. It acted as a boundary for their social and economic vision. To paraphrase the state of tension often ascribed to the Puritans, and superbly used by N. Gordon Levin in his analysis of the Wilsonian framework: To be *in* but not wholly *of* American capitalism created ideological ambiguities at the heart of Populism.

These ambiguities were rooted in the structural and ethical possibilities that Populists saw inhering in a democratization of capitalism. Capitalism and democracy existed in alliance and in partial antagonism with each other. A categorical answer to the question of whether or not Populism created an alternative modernizing pattern in American history would be difficult. The Populist challenge extended beyond the customary limits of reform. It set in motion impulses having a transformative character. But the recognizable features of a market economy appeared in the movement's ideology, because Populists believed that propertied institutions should be retained. For Populists, the essential changes were to involve an alteration of values and social relations, the formation of a public standard, and the redistribution of power. They considered these objectives attainable in a society that still preserved property.

My earlier focus on Populism's progressive historical orientation indicated the movement's rational and democratic underpinning, and its receptivity to industrialism. Additional factors, not fully perceived at the time, now demand notice. The inclusion of propertied consciousness requires that judgment be suspended on "radical" as a fit designation for Populists. On the other hand, the role they assigned to the state calls attention to elemental propositions of just governance. For this reason my study is philosophically cast. If the term *radicalism* is not accurate, greater precision of analysis, corresponding to Populism's complexity, serves to enhance the strength of the reformist dimension.

This study is intended to be a comprehensive account of how Populists viewed capitalism as a political economy and as a system of power. Intracapitalist differences provide the analytic basis for reconstructing the movement's public philosophy. I am treating a new range of topics—property, law, government—because this area of inquiry matches the Populists' own preoccupation with the requirements of a democratic state. This concern gave impetus to their political and ideological development. My interpretation reflects wider interests, greater distance from the scholarly debates over Populism, and continued study of political philosophy and comparative social history. I have sought a fruitful reconceptualization of Populism.

This volume is centered on the Populist conception of a just polity. It employs the method of textual exegesis to a body of Populist writings, in order to explore such topics as individual rights, the rule of law, the obligations of government, and the foundations of sovereignty, all of which are directed toward the moral and social construction of a democratic state. A second work, *The Humane Economy,* describes an internal progression from polity to macroeconomics that is centered on the Populist variant of capitalism. Its method involves a theoretical examination of political economy, which leads to the further exploration of such topics as alternative modes of capitalism and the reconciliation of property and democracy. There I view Populist economic thought specifically in relation to modernization. Chapter 1 of the present volume, which discusses political consciousness and the restraints on Populist ideology, may be taken as a bridge to both works.

This volume does not purport to be a general history of Populism. It is a highly focused, technical discussion of intellectual history. Even as intellectual history I have confined the genre to topics of political philosophy and economic theory, and I have further narrowed its scope to the analysis of ideas and their interrelationships, without particular attention to the material context or to specific political events. Narration and chronology were not decisive to my purpose; what carries the development of the book forward is the cumulative weight of the evidence and the clarification of basic themes. I have intended textual exegesis as a replacement for narration and chronology. I want method to coincide with content: Exegesis becomes an alternative means of apprehending historical reality. It can best reveal the more subtle features of a given universe of discourse that I want to look at, such as imagery, implicit assumptions, internal consistency, and it can also make possible, when the text is sufficiently extensive, the re-creation of a total position, neither of which is easily accomplished by the use of historical snippets and their narrative organization. Textual exegesis, as in the present work, provides an example for an analytical school of history, and becomes inseparable from my idea of what a reconceptualization of Populism entails.

I have further departed from a general history of Populism by minimizing the historiographical dimension of such histories. Both my method, textual exegesis, and my purpose, a reconceptualization of the topic, indicate my intention to write on Populism as if it were being approached from a new beginning, a disciplined search for meanings and implications that were not derived from, nor in response to, the existing literature. I have devoted little space to Populist historiography, not out of blindness to its merits, but because I regard my work as, literally, a starting over: to *re*conceptualize the subject from the evidence. I have clear differences with the reigning interpretation of Populism. They center on what I believe are issues of secondary importance to the study of Populism, such as the comparative radicalism of western and southern Populists, the character of midroadism, and the potential impact of the subtreasury plan. But I had rather these differences take form in the reader's mind from the evidence and not divert the analysis from its task of reconstruction. It is unavoidable, however, that they arise in specific contexts. I have also integrated several points of controversy in the introduction to chapter 6, which forms the transition from Tom Watson to Ignatius Donnelly, and which is about the powers of government.

I detect, in my book, an apparent severity with southern Populism. The reason for this impression lies in the nature of the inquiry; it does not reflect a lack of sympathy with southern Populists or with the South. To face the problem serves to clarify a more basic, although hitherto not articulated, interpretive difference I have with scholars of southern Populism. Two features of the inquiry are pertinent here. I have closely studied both principal regions of Populism, and my broader findings on the movement's ideological and political development rest, in part, on this comparative perspective. Second, the questions I have chosen to explore (which were not designed to bring out invidious regional comparisons) center on the political and economic dimensions of Populist thought: the disposition for and against the expansion of governmental powers; the receptiveness to, and the construction placed on, public ownership (and its possible connection to a framework of laissez-faire); and the moral and legal rationale for the support of a doctrine of the general welfare. In each case, the emergence of a public principle, as the basis of political society and the democratization of industry, is involved. My seemingly negative position consists of my view that the regional culture of the South imposed greater restrictions on Populist thought than was the situation in the West. I do not see this as a matter of assessing blame, but of trying to understand what happened. It is mean to blame the victim for his difficulties. It is also mistaken to regard the critical analysis of culture and institutions as a sign of hostility. The issue of which section was more radical is too simplistic. It does not, as previously formulated, explain anything, not least because the criteria for establishing what radicalism means have not been satisfactorily presented.

In two additional respects, I have narrowed the scope of this study. I have not given formal consideration to the religious factor—and more particularly, evangelical Protestantism—as a motivating force in Populist thought. Evangelicalism permeated and helped to define the social experience of Populism, not only in the South but also in portions of the West. It provided the original categories for perceiving the world, categories of understanding and social articulation that could be readily converted to secular and political ends. Yet the movement's evangelical background, while crucial to a social history of Populism, is less relevant to my discussion. Moreover, I find that the religious factor had greater bearing on the organizational mode of expressing protest than on the content of the ideology. I approach the whole topic in a different way. My main reason for not dealing directly with religion is that my interest lies specifically in the moral, legal, and ethical realms of Populist thought, because these realms have concrete application to the subject matter of the state and economic development. I have not excluded religion; my evidence, beginning with the quotation "the workman is worthy of his hire," fairly abounds with statements that are religious in their origin. But the reader, provided with this material, is free to develop his own analysis of the religious factor. In the case of two Populist writers, however, I have been more explicit. My treatment of Ignatius Donnelly and Thomas L. Nugent has emphasized their religious orientation. Their social Christianity exemplified in content if not doctrinal sources the expression of evangelical social ethics in Populism.

For different reasons, I have not discussed the intellectual origins of Populism in this book. Although intellectual history should embrace both ideas and their antecedents, I have sought to achieve a specificity of analysis of Populism as absolutely necessary before looking to an enlargement of scope. The topic of Populism's intellectual roots might well require a drastic expansion and recasting of my study, but this consideration is irrelevant to the more basic point—what the topic would mean for this study in the context of current emphases in American historiography. The theme of "republicanism" is now on practically everyone's lips, and interpretations based on it no doubt possess significant historical value. But to subsume Populism under the framework of republicanism would be to prejudge the former in terms of characteristics ascribed to the latter, especially its presumed anticapitalist dimensions. I want the specificity of analysis, not abstractly to preserve the historical integrity of Populism, but concretely to prevent the attribution of ideological traits and directions of intent to the movement before they have been verified in their own right.

The construction of an intellectual tradition is a difficult process. It requires a strict correspondence of ideas, including, in this case, the full contextual meaning of such terms as *capitalism, property,* and *democracy.* I am not persuaded that the well-known candidates for having had an influence on the formation of Populist thought, such as antebellum reform movements, Radical Republicanism, and latter nineteenth-century labor radicalism, would satisfy a standard of accuracy when it came to salient issues of state power, economic organization, and political doctrine. It is precisely because Populism bears a resemblance to other reform experiences, and because analyses of republicanism may seem in places identical to my own, that I want to resist fitting it prematurely into a larger tradition. If, as I believe, Populism showed a more uncritical attitude toward capitalism than I earlier supposed, this may also have been true of republicanism. It is hard for me to see how an acceptance of the property right, whether in Populism or in republicanism, still qualifies as an expression of anticapitalism. In practical terms, my development of the idea of democratic capitalism is quite close to recent discussions of anticapitalist republicanism, except for the fact that I insist on designating Populists as capitalists. I do not define what Populists understood by capitalism in a single formulation; just as their conception of democracy was expressed as a totality of traditional rights, enlarged powers of government, and ethical principles, which requires the entire book to elucidate, so too their conception of capitalism has to be permitted to unfold as a complex of historical, structural, and moral elements.

In the nature of the case, Populists had to draw from somewhere—including, possibly, agrarian republicanism and labor radicalism—in forming the basis of their thought, although to a surprising extent I find their thought to be self-created through the experience of social protest: a specific response to a specific historical context founded on specific economic and political grievances. That context, as I once brought out, also meant for them the alteration of the industrial economy and the deprivation of working people. They did not require the cultural diffusion of labor radicalism to confirm insights they already may have possessed. But the larger point is not what a movement draws on, but what it does with it—the creative uses to which the borrowing has been put. Perhaps a distinctive mark of Populism was its ability to take established ideas and press them to their ideological limits in forming a social vision of democratic society. While I have not discussed the movement's intellectual roots, my analysis suggests the presence of a wider, more diversified, and earlier formative context of ideas than is commonly supposed. Populists were not strangers to a preceding age of constitutionalism.

I have not written a general history, or even a general intellectual history, of Populism. This volume is based on a small number of Populist writings, ranging from treatises on politics and economics to imaginative novels, editorial opinion, the speeches and moments of reflection of political leaders, and the more discursive literature of social agitation. I have placed the depth before the scope of my coverage. My purpose is to study the discourse of Populism, which required, in each case, a sufficiently extended text that I might be enabled to explore the inner world of the writer. The Populist writers I have examined do not necessarily comprise a sample of Populism; their quality of representativeness was not my primary consideration. Although I chose them for wholly unscientific reasons, following no specific principle of selection, several points can be made about them: They do not, as a group, incline the analysis toward a particular ideological position, political faction, or geographical social base, nor do they express a single thematic emphasis, such as monetarist, agricultural, or industrial policy; individually, no two writers were the same, and each one had achieved a degree of distinction or visibility within the movement to make him recognizable, both to contemporaries and historians, as a Populist. The evidential deck has not been stacked. My emphasis is on their diversity of views: shadings, rather than a uniform social perspective. Why were they chosen? I found them challenging; they provided me with texts which afforded a greater opportunity than snippets of evidence to reconstruct premises, values, and imagery; above all, I chose them because I was looking for nothing in particular, and needed room to find my way, sentence by sentence, thought by thought.

Intellectual activity is synonymous with a willing suspension of judgment. The method of textual exegesis has value because it forces the historian into closer contact with his sources. It rivets his attention to the specificity of the text and the individual. I am not troubled about the representative character of my evidence, because I believe that a first step toward understanding a movement is to know its individuals, whether they are placed high or low, and whether they appear to have a representative quality or were adventitious choices gathered up in the historian's net. I have deliberately left out of this study the most important individual to it. In the early 1960s, I undertook a painstaking study of Marion Butler of North Carolina, which by the end of the decade resulted in a manuscript exceeding fifteen hundred pages. I did not care then, nor do I now, about its eventual publication, because it was a training experience. (Indeed, the present volume merely amplifies the first pages of its preface.) Already restive under the canons of narrative history, I realized that I could not pursue the kinds of questions I sought answers to until I had made more direct contact with the bedrock of Populism, the intensive analysis of a single mind. I traced Butler week by week through his editorials, speeches, and political activities, during the Populist years, observing in the most concrete way the dynamics of political consciousness, including the formation of a Populist identity, the unselfconscious statement of assumptions about property and the social order, and the perception of the political process, its challenges, and the traits of character necessary to the growth of Populism as a protest movement. Populist thought became a living reality: It was possible to see the timing and development of issues, the construction placed upon them, their interrelations and consequent evolvement into a unified political position. Butler is not a microcosm of the Populist world; but the factor of representativeness recedes in importance, because one has entered that world on a more secure footing, and because correctives can be made when features unique to an individual perspective have been discovered. In the present work, I have at times drawn inferences from the texts about the Populist movement at large, and the reader should be wary of all such generalizations, particularly when they are not derived from the explication of a given text. Yet I am not troubled about the representative character of my evidence and the statement of generalizations because I seek to foster an analytical tension between the specific text and all that I have learned about Populism from a quarter-century of studying the movement. Scattered references to Butler are made in this work, when in particular contexts the discussion of his career served to make concrete, in my own mind, a range of political and conceptual problems. But his main influence has been as a sounding board, enabling me to clarify my ideas on a two-tiered economic structure and the framework of democratic capitalism, which I initially formulated in the middle stages of my analysis of him.

My study provides approximately equal coverage, in substantive terms, if not actual numbers, to both principal regions of Populism. I have devoted primary attention to three western Populists, William A. Peffer, James B. Weaver, and Ignatius Donnelly, and to four southern Populists, W. Scott Morgan, James H. Davis, Thomas E. Watson, and Thomas L. Nugent; and, because of the abbreviated nature of the texts, I have examined more briefly several other westerners, including Lorenzo D. Lewelling and Frank Doster. Henry Demarest Lloyd is also discussed. For many of the basic texts, the reader is invited to consult my compilation *The Populist Mind* (Indianapolis, 1967), and, of course, to return to the original works.

This book is only in small part a discourse on method. It is appropriate that we now return to substance: Populism expressed the struggle to be within, yet rearrange the elements of, America's propertied foundations. The issue of an alternative pattern of modernization summarizes the affirmations and doubts that Populists experienced, and never resolved, in defining their protest. Yet they cut a wide ideological swath through capitalist society, even when accepting its basic features. Their integration of moral, political, and economic factors possessed an integrity and a cumulative force that could not be readily absorbed into the prevailing structure of capitalism. The Populist vision of the public welfare had to be removed from the historical agenda. It was subsequently eclipsed by the dominance of large-scale enterprise.

CHAPTER ONE

Consciousness and Restraint

Populism was atypical of third-party movements in its authentic search for a political identity; it actively created its foundations of protest through a process of self-definition that depended on more than the existence of widespread privation. Populists recognized that collective modes for engendering awareness were necessary before grievances could be articulated and outrage could be translated into a coherent force. The emphasis on political education gave Populism a unity that partially offset its particular origins and variegated ideology. In shaping a political consciousness, it went through clear developmental stages, from a social to a political formation, from a movement to a party. The sequence was not predetermined; nor did it have entirely beneficial results. Populists made an overrefined adjustment to the requirements of electoral politics by disciplining a sense of anguish that was capable of taking more militant form.

The preparatory work, such as the economic diagnosis, was unhurried. There was a gestational period in which the Farmers' Alliance, in the main, comprised the prepolitical beginnings of the People's party. Through this connection, the Alliance proposed a reform agenda and was a matrix of yearning and reason that imparted vitality and substance to Populist demands. Where the connection did not hold, the fact of large-scale agrarian mobilization nevertheless both set in motion the political direction and steeled the will for resistance among those who had been similarly disaffected from the contemporary structure. Thus, Populism experienced a gradual momentum; it built itself from the ground up historically, if not also by design; and it incorporated political education into its growth pattern as the source of its intended longevity. Populists believed that it was possible to achieve the permanent status of a major party. They attempted to precipitate an ideological realignment of the party system because they viewed this to be indispensable to their survival and political fulfillment.

Populists reversed the conventional expectations of third-party behavior in the United States. The general pattern has been to focus on single issues, engage in short-term if intense agitation to compel their acceptance by the major parties, but in the process neglect to establish a grass-roots organizational base. In contrast, Populism had a manifold program. It sought power directly, in the pursuit of goals that did not depend on outside forces for their recognition. Its localism was mirrored in the development from a social to a political movement: Populist organization was endowed with the values of community that had been a part of the Alliance experience. It maintained a decentralized structure, contesting elections at all political levels, but with a primal source of allegiance resting in the state parties. Finally, although its period of protest was quite brief, a single decade including the Alliance phase, Populism sustained a remarkable political energy that was not simply determined by electoral rhythms. Because protest was a matter of continuous involvement, a subtle influence was at work, transforming political opposition into a way of life. Populism was out of phase with "normal" standards of political comportment; traits of passivity that depended for their reinforcement on the synchronizing powers of the dominant political culture became weakened. If Populists had mobilized solely for elections, they would have ruined the prospects for long-term ideological growth; but their mobilization, because it involved continual political education, had an organic quality. A perpetual state of readiness enlivened the feelings of disaffection, and the hostility encountered by Populism compounded the sense of being a movement apart.

When historians dichotomize Populism into its constituent parts, the Farmers' Alliance and the People's party, they introduce an artificial division which not only ignores the integrated character of Populist growth, and with it the possibility that a pattern of increasing radicalization occurred, but also dismisses the significance of political consciousness as the critical element in analyzing protest. The major phases, though distinct, defined a complementary relationship. To pose the implicit question of which phase best represented Populism's informing force, its historical personality, and even its concrete existence creates a standard of orthodoxy that denies the legitimacy of whichever phase the historian does not favor. For Theodore Saloutos, political action killed the farmers' movement. His emphasis on the Alliance sought to divorce agriculture from class politics, a spirit of confrontation, and broader social issues.[1] Seeming to radicalize the perspective of business agriculture, Lawrence Goodwyn also presented a restricted conception of Populism, employing a monetarist paradigm to suggest the movement's deterioration following the Alliance stage.[2] Among those who have stressed this phase, only Robert C. McMath has explored the richness and diversity of the Alliance, showing the continuities of ideology and practice that made the transition to politics appear plausible.[3] And finally, to concentrate on the People's party, at the expense of its Alliance roots, was also to fragment what was a unified experience. John D. Hicks was clearly aware that the Alliance provided the formative context, but because he gave undue attention to the electoral process he was unable to appreciate the running start that this context afforded to the political phase, and, more broadly, the importance of ideological growth as a dynamic factor in shaping protest.[4]

Additional examples would merely reinforce the point that political consciousness has been neglected or remained unidentified. Yet, each phase of development was necessary to Populism. The phases intersected when the Alliance demonstrated its inadequacy further to sustain the gathering protest, as in the way that Alliance-dominated legislatures in the South continued to express opposition to agrarian demands following the 1890 election. Membership in the Alliance and in the People's party, simply, posed different circumstances of political mobilization. One was not a sign of greater commitment than the other, unless the second could be regarded as more demanding, given the Alliance's failure to announce a clean political break with the existing forces of order. I view Populism as describing an ascending curve of radicalization. This process was halted abruptly at a quite late stage, when demoralization set in during the presidential campaign of 1896. Ideology became the politically integrative agent defining the movement's contours.

Populist scholars have been little given to theoretical probing, especially in tracing ideological currents in order to gauge the depth and peculiarities of Populist radicalism.[5] The term *radical* was applied indiscriminately to cover all sorts of opposition. The movement's growth likewise was more the province of voting tabulations than of an inquiry into the inner propelling elements of political and social conviction. To gain the necessary perspective on Populism, I have turned to English and French social historians who have conceptualized areas of study that identified a separable political culture of laboring people.[6] Although these writings have had an impact on labor studies in America since the mid-1960s, they have not affected Populist scholarship as well.

One serious problem facing American historians is that the nation's historical development lacks the structural complexity and ideological breadth that would permit discriminations both within and beyond capitalism to stand out. The notion of a consensus is patently exaggerated, in light of the undoubted protest occurring in practically every period, and especially in the latter nineteenth century. Yet the counterthrust to the institutions and values of property has been remarkably weak. Broadly, there has been a nondialectical pattern in which social hardship and even actual brutality have not been a sufficient stimulus for attacking capitalism's essential features. That America may have been unique among Western capitalist democracies in not having experienced a revolution that democratized its social foundations helps to account for this narrow ideological range and lineal historical flow. Barrington Moore's comparative analysis of modernization, because not fully crediting the transformative force of the American Civil War, when studied in relation to the Puritan and French Revolutions, lends indirect support for this contention.[7] A failure of protest to transcend capitalist boundaries, while hardly denying the existence of political and structural deprivation, cannot be explained by a recourse to the conventional mixture of repression, false consciousness, and the presumed benefits of accommodation to the prevailing order. The problem was also rooted in the ideological foundations of American society, a topic associated with the seminal ideas of Louis Hartz that I cannot hope to treat adequately in the present book.[8] For now it has to be mentioned that internal restraint, founded in the affirmation of a Lockean configuration of values, was of critical importance to Populism as well as to other protest movements. The confinement within a propertied society has tended to magnify dissent into a more consequential force than it actually was, for participants and historians alike. For Populism, to recur to the ascending curve, one begins with the distinction between radicalization and radicalism, between the process of a deepening awareness, marked by an increasing comprehension of capitalist structure, and the destination that was not attained or perhaps even desired by Populists, a wholly transformed social order no longer centered on property. Where these factors met, in which a cumulative ideological growth threatened to surmount the walls of property, the movement collapsed. Populism did not decline gradually. It fell over a precipice, to some extent a situation of its own making.

A sensitivity to mental texture is helpful in approaching Populism. The historian, interacting with his evidence, can create the tension between theory and history, and between present and past, which might lead, as E. H. Carr showed, to the continuous revision of ideas and search for new questions.[9] But he also requires a different temperament, a willing suspension of arrogance when it comes to the lower classes, in order to be able to listen for the movement's sonorities and indeed the pulse-beat itself. Political narrative becomes debilitating to historical scholarship when the topic has been covered many times, particularly at the expense of detecting inner currents of aspiration and direction. In Populism, the salient feature of historical reality was a striking disproportion between individual misery and collective restraint. An integral part of protest was the limits placed on its expression.

Nearly three decades ago I discovered a letter that has continued to influence my views on the role of political consciousness in analyzing Populism. It was written by Susan Orcutt of western Kansas to Lorenzo D. Lewelling, the Populist governor, in June 1894, and it began: "I take my Pen In hand to let you know that we are Starving to death [.]" The understated desperation, as well as the matter-of-fact delight taken in the land, conveys an authenticity of feeling, the simple eloquence of untapped reserves of inner strength from which movements are constructed and perhaps ignited: "It is Pretty hard to do without any thing to Eat hear in this God for saken country   we would of had Plenty to Eat if the hail hadent cut our rye down and ruined our corn and

Potatoes   I had the Prettiest Garden that you Ever seen and the hail ruined It and I have nothing to look at [.]" Initially, nature appears responsible for her hardship. Yet the larger cycle of unemployment and degradation formed the decisive background of the Orcutts's world. She further confided to Lewelling, whose executive proclamation came to symbolize the Populist concern for the unemployed, that her husband was among those who were compelled to wander in search of work: "My Husband went a way to find work and came home last night and told me that we would have to Starve   he has bin in ten countys and did not Get no work   It is Pretty hard for a woman to do with out any thing to Eat when She dosent no what minute She will be confined to bed   If I was In Iowa I would be all right   I was born there and raised there   I havent had nothing to Eat today and It is three oclock [.]"[10] Beneath the plaintive surface lay an implicit condemnation of a society that permitted the industrious to starve and that was callous to their fate. A pervading loneliness, only partly the result of isolation, heightened the feeling. It was as though the Orcutts, like the countryside, had been forsaken, not by God, but, in light of the knowledge that something better once existed, by man and his ways. Her wistfulness for Iowa becomes heartbreaking.

Mrs. Orcutt was legion. Her name would be "Million" in the Populist vernacular; she expressed a basic element of the movement that each one, in his memories of security, his future hopes, and his present anguish, was able to recognize in himself. There was an irreducible discontent founded in common impoverishment. Yet despite the open provocation, multiplied over countless human lives, Populism contained rather than liberated primordial impulses toward political and social change. The disproportion between misery and restraint occurred in the very anatomy of Populism. The promptings that arose from economic hardship could not be completely unfettered. Protest had a measured quality, even when casting off the mask of composure. The movement first awakened and then focused political energies, its educational function in both major phases providing the basis for a collective sense of membership. But it did not seek to press the development of consciousness beyond this point to a new plateau. Populism failed to actualize the potential residing in its popular base or in an ideology that mirrored advanced sentiments and deeply rooted yearnings. The passion manifestly present was simultaneous with a line of safety, within the political process, that was not trespassed.

The label "reformist" only partially accounts for this inner tension. Had the pertinent factors—the individual, movement, and principles—been closely synchronized in Populism, each reinforcing the element of moderation, the use of "reform" would not present a problem. It would also follow that, as a reformist movement, Populism would be dedicated to modest improvement within the existing structure. Its political agenda would contain no burning questions, and certainly no structural prescriptions that required a basic alteration of society. Presumably, its temperament would be sensibleness itself, and if geniality was not dominant, then at least there would be a reasonable contentment. The full range of fundamental assumptions concerning the values and institutions of property would be preserved.

This description, however, bears little resemblance to Populism. Its constituent parts were not synchronized, and indeed, Populism may have comprised less than the sum of its parts. Its own forward thrust helps to explain a diminished vigor, because of the way that politics and ideology tended to work at cross purposes. To the reformer, Mrs. Orcutt's plight would be unsettling, if not incomprehensible. For her part, the bottom had dropped out, and she with it, placing the assuring tone of reform peculiarly at variance with her single-minded absorption in the elemental aspects of life: starvation, crops, work, birth, return, starvation. The two levels of social reality were incommensurable. Her statement was not political in character or intent. It became invested with political meaning because of the reservoir of pain that might be readily tapped, and because of the society's inability, as constituted, to satisfy her unfulfilled needs—hers and the many others similarly fixed.

Populism was built on unassimilable dreams. Here the disproportion between misery and restraint, as a first approximation, assumed concrete form. Populism's deepest instinct was to reconcile the foregoing levels of social reality, without surrendering either its adversative ground, the demands that had not been and perhaps could not be met in the absence of major structural changes, or the more primal quality that gave rise to the movement, the feelings that derived from a raw state of economic and social deprivation. These purposes were contradictory, even though they were pursued together. Although Populists such as Tom Watson frequently stated that there had to be a revolution at the ballot box, they seldom detected the patness of their formula, the pulsations of excitation and confinement. At a critical point in what purported to be a radical discussion, Watson held: "For in the revolution we seek to accomplish, there shall be Law and order preserved in-violate."[11] In the context of "combatting monopoly," Thomas L. Nugent, a Texas midroad leader, cautioned his Populist audience: "Let us remember that we ought above all others to set ourselves against anarchy in every form, against every measure calculated to break down the security which the laws afford to private property, and in favor only of those lawful and orderly methods which can always be successfully defended, and the observance of which will never fail to enlist for the workingman the sympathies of the good and worthy people of every class."[12] The feelings that were summoned in Populism also underwent not a blunting so much as a domestication of instinct, in order to meet the requirements of political legitimation in society. The apparent disjunction of radicalism and moderation was integrated through the value ascribed to legitimation.

Gaining election was secondary. In a disquieting way, Populists approached the political system with an air of detachment. They adopted what I would term a suprapolitical orientation, largely guided by their moral elaboration of a proper social order. Power and party organization were not self-justifying. Populists refused to emulate the major political parties by pursuing the conventional indices of achievement. Lewelling spoke to more than the absence of a centralized leadership structure in Populism when he stated: "Men are nothing in a great contest of the people like this. It matters not who is the leader so that all the people stand together united for the great principles of humanity."[13] Organization and purpose had to be fused. This position expressed a central tenet of previous Alliance teachings, the combined ethical and political ranking of principle above party. The effect was to imbue politics with an ideological content; the concentration on issues took precedence over the mere attachment to party, and party itself was conceived as the custodian of a creed. Partisanship for its own sake violated the entire ordering of social and ethical priorities. This was a line of reasoning that drew, at times explicitly, on a Madisonian suspicion of factionalism, but more nearly resembled the Puritan doctrine of weaned affections in its unwillingness to give full devotion to prevailing forms. Populists regarded party as a vehicle, in the same way Ignatius Donnelly compared government to a "cooking-pot," the utility of which lay in its instrumental character.[14] It would help to realize the movement's principles, which were themselves viewed not as specific demands but as an encompassing statement of political democracy. Finally, political engagement occurred within a protracted time span. If Populists acted from a sense of urgency, they also maintained a frame of reference in which principled conduct became the basis for overcoming successive hurdles. The perspective was one that encouraged sobriety and earnestness; each stage, in what Populists took to be an uphill struggle, would result in a consolidation of the movement's ideology and support, in turn opening the way for additional issues and wider recruitment. Through the power of their example, Populists sought to gather the awakening forces of protest. James B. Weaver superbly captured the sense of mission running through Populist thought: "It is glorious to live in this age, and to be permitted to take part in this heroic combat is the greatest honor that can be conferred upon mortals."[15]

These traits illumine the disproportion between misery and restraint, for it was precisely the emphasis on a moral posture, in which disciplined striving and rational discussion lent dignity to the movement's principles, that made all forms of unsublimated activity appear harmful. The lessening of constraints also had ideological significance. It would permit unformed dreams to reach the surface without adornment, casting doubt on ballot boxes, political processes, and perhaps even the social framework. Nugent expressed this tension when he pointed to the subterranean currents of feeling in Populism: "In the popular heart 'deep is calling unto deep,' and the social brotherhood is slowly evolving and growing among the people as breast after breast thrills responsively to the sound of that 'calling.' " Yet he added that it was necessary "to recognize the supremacy of the individual in matters of private concern, to restore to the commercial and social world the lost ideas of equity and justice, thus to untrammel legitimate industries and skill and leave them to pursue in freedom the beneficent work of producing wealth," all indicating a resolution of the tension by channeling these feelings into express support for competitive capitalism.[16]

Populism had succeeded quite well as a stage for the primary mobilization of the agrarian masses, the lesser- and middle-propertied as well as the landless and dirt poor. If its social composition tended to blur the dimension of class,[17] it still transformed an amorphous constituency into a people's movement, discovering within itself the necessary skills of articulation and a gradually solidifying world view that nevertheless possessed class implications. When the question of Populism's radical potential is raised, however, one finds concomitant affirmations of social and political order at the very essence of its democratizing urge. A further example of undeniable social misery that encountered restraint, in this case deriving from the individual himself, rather than from Populism, can be seen in the letter of a Minnesota farmer to Ignatius Donnelly. Halvor Harris, like Susan Orcutt, wrote of elemental matters: desolation, work, sickness, the fear of dispossession. In both cases, the workings of capitalism formed the specific background: "In the minds of the forlorne and the unprotected Poor People of this and other states I might say I am one of those Poor and unprotected. One of those which have settled upon the so-called Indemnity Land of the Minn St Paul and Manitoba now the great Northern. I settled on this Land in good Faith   Built House and Barn Broken up Part of the Land. Spent years of hard Labor in grubing fencing and Improving   are they going to drive us out like trespassers wife and children a sickly wife with Poor Health enough Before and give us away to the Corporations [?]" This letter, in the interval of almost three decades, has also affected my thinking on political consciousness. Harris, in questioning the uneven relations of power, offered a political indictment of corporate dominance. He transformed basic hardship into a broader denial of rights, a process of expropriation covering the land, security, and their very lives, all that would define an independent existence. There was a sense of outrage, mixed with a kind of resignation not unknown to an earlier century or social order: "how can we support them. When we are robed of our means. they will shurely not stand this   we must Decay and Die from Woe and Sorow [.]" This was the same solidity of conviction that one found in Mrs. Orcutt, a hidden strength in the social base from which the movement could derive its sustaining force. Yet Harris then revealed the inner brake on political consciousness that would characterize the whole of Populism, an antecedent separation of corporate abuse from capitalism as a system. Even at the social base, restrictions, quite apart from the collective issue of political legitimation, were evident: "We are Loyal Citicens and do Not Intend to Intrude on any R. R. Corporation   we Believed and still do Believe that the RR Co has got No Legal title to this Land in question   We Love our wife and children just as Dearly as any of you But how can we protect them give them education as they should wen we are driven from sea to sea [?]"[18]

In Populism, the spark was ignited, but no conflagration ensued. Ideological powder kegs were, perhaps consciously, set out of reach. Populists accepted a set of fundamental assumptions that was never seriously examined, centering on the supposition that the nation's heritage was devoted to the achievement of democratic rights and equitable arrangements. Indeed, prevailing conditions represented the temporary derangement of an essentially well ordered system of economy, law, and governance. Within this democratic heritage, property and freedom had been, and could once more be, brought into congruity. The conditions necessary to this harmonious state included the supremacy of the rule of law, the absence of economic privilege, and the maintenance of opportunity in all social strata. For Populists, these conditions were a faithful description of the original context of political development. Populism was profoundly American in self-conception.

Although this identity drew the movement more deeply within the ideological universe of property, it worked as well to confirm Populists in the ultimate justice of their protest, a legitimacy derived from an association with the nation's first principles. In 1890, the Lincoln *Farmers' Alliance* portrayed the existing struggle in terms of social and economic polarities, which nevertheless came to an orthodox rest: "It is a conflict between plutocracy on the one hand and the people on the other. Between millionaires and the masses. Between the money bags of the east and the corn and wheat and beef and pork of the west. Between the insatiable greed of organized wealth and the rights of the great plain people, as vouchsafed by the constitution." Despite its characterization of the prevailing system as "a lie and an imposture" that was leading to "hopeless pauperization," the paper reaffirmed its primal American starting point: "Too plain is it to the patriotic vision that our country is fast going the way of Egypt, of Greece, of Rome, that is, to the certain death that awaits all nations alike when the wealth of all falls into the hands of the grasping few." The very love of country, cast as a general defense of rights, propelled the movement forward: "The impending struggle, then, not only involves the safety of our homes, but the cause of liberty as well; the preservation of our free institutions, the very existence of our beloved country." But while occupying advanced ground, Populism conceived of its "duty" in ways that subtly confined its action to approved channels: "It is to check by every lawful means the future concentration of wealth, and to destroy forever the iniquitous domination of railroad and other corporate power in the politics of our state and nation."[19] Populists thought that to abandon the legal and political order was to offend the notion of democracy. It would deny the promise that a sovereign people could shape the practices necessary to its welfare, a principle that Populists located in the nation's historical development, constitutional structure, and value system.

America, property, and social change were reciprocally linked. Yet, this compound did not preclude militance or blur the clarity of the Populists' intended transformation. Populism's ideological and political wellspring lay in its literalist approach to America. America, as represented by the charter documents, was a positive matrix that asserted the primacy of the general welfare and mandated limits on the claims of property. The right of property commanded respect, but it was not a Lockean abstraction or an absolute right. It was in principle capable of being democratized, and if this result was not achieved, it followed that property had to be made democratic in fact. Populists espoused an unashamed patriotism (though hardly of the customary variety), in which America became the source of a permanent standard. The love of country was fashioned into an argument for the democratic control of economic affairs.

James H. Davis of Texas, equating civil liberty with individual initiative and a government that did not show partiality to business, used the imagery of American rights to attack the corporate structure: "I believe that civil liberty is in jeopardy when the aspirations of men are suppressed or exercised by the sufferance of these artificial creations, controlling almost boundless wealth, whose influence is vast enough to shape the laws of the government which created them, and which, knowing no such thing as humanity or patriotism, recognize no duty except that of increasing their wealth and power."[20] The omnipresence of such imagery in Populism affords a striking clue to the way in which the affirmation of a propertied society could serve as the basis for a general indictment of its monopolistic phase. W. Scott Morgan of Arkansas joined the rule of law to the liberation of economic activity in presenting an essentially patriotic defense of antimonopolism: "The root of the evil lay in the laws. Monopolies exist by law, are chartered by law, and should be controlled by law. A trust is a conspiracy against legitimate trade. It is against the interests of the people and the welfare of the public. It is demoralizing in its influence, inconsistent with free institutions and dangerous to our liberties. To participate in a trust should be a crime subject to severe punishment. Trust is only another name for monopoly. Monopoly is wielding a greater power in the government than the people."[21] The Lincoln *Farmers' Alliance* similarly drew support for protest from an American perspective: "At no period in the history of the United States has there been such an uprising of the agricultural and wage-earning people of the country to assert their rights and regain their waxing liberty of shaping the laws and affairs of state and national government." Through class legislation, after the Civil War, "a plutocracy of cruel, unfeeling millionaires have grown up and are attempting to seize the government and reduce the sovereign people to a state of vassalage."[22] A county paper in Nebraska so completely fused the attack on corporations and the plea for individual initiative, within the broader context of American rights, that the capitalistic element practically disappeared from view—a classic instance in which Populist militance encouraged self-deception. Populists believed themselves to be more consistently radical than they were:

No matter for what corporations were organized, nor what they have or may have accomplished in the past, all men today know that they are great engines of oppression. They have crushed individual efforts and hopes for a competent and independent living; they lift up the rich and crush down the poor. They will tolerate but two kinds of people—millionaires and paupers. They believe in but two kinds of homes—palaces and hovels. They have annulled the natural laws of supply and demand. They are fast monopolizing every avenue of industry or employment. . . . They are everlastingly at war with the spirit of our republican form of government.[23]

The social polarization gave renewed legitimacy to a structure of competitive capitalism.

The disproportion between misery and restraint, particularly on the individual plane, raises the seldom discussed matter of popular sublimation. The analyst of Populism does not require an arbitrary standard of radicalism to see that the movement was more temperate politically than was strictly consistent with its primal impulses: the sadness, anger, and inchoate murmurs of disaffection that were pervasive, contagious, and decisive to its formation. If this intensity of expression had been left in an unformed state, but still politicized in the process, it would have undoubtedly possessed millenarian elements of an uncontrollable nature. Yet exactly the absence of chiliasm distinguished Populism from European movements in which a similar mental set, under not terribly divergent circumstances, prevailed. Susan Orcutt was not a stranger to Edward Thompson's or Eric Hobsbawm's world, nor was she less hard pressed than the Parisian housewives who demanded bread in 1789. Populism had checked the dynamics of incipient radicalism in its social base; the primal impulses were not internally sanctioned, brought to a convergence, and permitted to take on a cumulative force.

Preconscious rage was not at issue. Nor is it likely that a movement directed to structural change (which supposes a degree of political consciousness) would be able to subsist exclusively on emotional factors, or that such factors constituted a presumption of radicalism.[24] Rather, Populism had denied itself a crucial impetus: Its politically implosive force might have energized and extended the specifically rational features of its protest. The movement proved sufficiently capacious to include both the emotional and rational aspects of protest, although the balance that it struck was significant. The problem was rooted in the process of expressing protest, which inevitably affected the content of the protest as well. Populism had already defined its political parameters on the substructural level; the effect was less to hamper ideological growth than to chart more precisely what it would find acceptable. It is not necessary to transform Mrs. Orcutt into Rosa Luxemburg to recognize that Populism had failed to invest its otherwise vibrant ideology with the sustaining power to precipitate, still within its own terms, a greater confrontation in American politics.

If Populist ideology has been patently reformist and nothing more, the question of restraint would be a false issue. But in fact the ideology, in addition to expressing primordial yearnings for security, advanced in seminal form the idea of public ownership. This was a critique of structure that surpassed the conventions of reform in a highly property-oriented society. The statement of an apparent puzzle moves the discussion of the disproportion between misery and restraint to a second approximation of meaning: The movement had generated an ideology which continually pressed beyond the confines of the movement's political orientation. Although Populism drew inspiration from its popular base and the segments of its ideology concerned with the principles of government sovereignty and public welfare, it partially nullified these principal sources of enrichment by a political course of measured pacing that was almost circumspect. Populists had not caught up with, or provided adequate mechanisms to achieve, their informing vision of a democratic polity.

Marion Butler of North Carolina illustrated a pattern of growth that fairly typified the formation of political consciousness in the movement.[25] He had patiently to tread his way; he experienced Populism less as a sudden, fully realized mode of personal identification, than as a protracted, deepening, open-ended journey of self-discovery. The inner dynamic of consciousness was based on a collectively reinforced process of political education, but it was also the product of active choices at every step in the development of protest, particularly as the penalties attached to an independent stand became clearer. The solidity of Butler's attachment to Populism was a function of his thorough grasp of reform principles, his growing recognition of the changes to the social structure that would be entailed by the proposed measures, and his painful awareness of the magnitude of the task that would be required to reconstruct American society. A common thread here was the realism of his perspective; he continually closed the gap between the mere words and the substance of the ideology. This was simultaneous with his attempt to extricate himself from the dominant regional, if not also national, political culture. For Butler, ideological growth went beyond simple affiliation to an acutely felt sense of mission.

His search for political identity had an existential quality; he himself constructed a series of turning points that resulted in incremental advances toward a nonracial politics increasingly concerned with national issues.[26] Butler was always standing at the proverbial crossroads. He exhibited fears that the radicalization of Populism was proceeding too rapidly, and yet, because the result of this process was to clarify the nature and potentialities of the institutional structure, he felt less fearful about advocating specific changes, which renewed the stimulus to further investigation and involvement. Several factors had assisted in the unfolding of a more defined consciousness: the general setting of political and social repression; the movement's evolving solidarity as a community that created a haven within the larger society for shaping autonomous goals; and the individual's own persistent will to comprehend and support the cause of reform. While moving forward was perceived as a burden in light of the difficulties of separating from the dominant political culture, the more basic point was the presence of the volitional factor in guiding the individual's conduct. No one compelled Butler or others to become Populists and thus to go against the political and ideological grain. The conscious acts of individuals underpinned the broader process of organization; each one had to make a decision to stand in opposition that was articulated through struggle rather than passively endorsed.[27]

Yet by 1896, the political and psychological strain on Populism was telling, in some measure because its very pattern of growth had threatened to carry the movement outside of its framework of reform. Butler was unusual in his grasp of the situation, seeing

Watson's candidacy and the total midroad position as a reversion to Populism's essentially regional foundations of an earlier stage. In political terms, this was a restrictive sectionalism which shrank from the challenge of mobilization on more avowedly national and class lines. Despite the conventional wisdom, Butler viewed the campaign as a summary of the preceding ideological trends, in which a concentration on the federal government appeared to be consistent with basic demands that in fact were national in scope. This concentration also entailed a reconstituted political base, and he envisioned, as the party chairman, the addition of a northern working-class constituency to complement the movement's previous strongholds. The potential fusion of ideology and politics in this plan, which seemed beyond Populism's resources to execute, raises again the matter of a disproportion. An atrophied development, political more than ideological in nature, had prevented the effective union of these parts.

The measured pacing discouraged a facile acceptance of doctrine, and resulted in an intact ideology. But the single-minded devotion to ideology also made it a self-propelled force, as the transformative content of Populism that exceeded its political manifestations. The disproportion was rooted in the failure to achieve a synthesis of ideology and politics. Butler's conception threatened an impending rupture, for throughout the movement's history, Populists had not devised a creative political mode that would express the cumulative intensity of the ideology. It was as if Populism had been dichotomized. Within its ideology, the cutting edges that represented the possibilities of fundamental change vied for attention with middle-range proposals for remedial legislation, adaptable to the existing society. Although Populists directed their thoughts, at times fervently, to the first plane, their political behavior was consonant with the second, involving the more prosaic level of normal institutional channels.

Incipient radicalism, which fortified the will to act, was preserved as a statement of purpose. But the choice to take America as a given signified the intention to honor the established boundaries of society, and at best attempt to work evolutionary changes in their structural make-up. The distinction between thought and conduct became a Populist notation for the commitment to reform. This acceptance of reform was tantamount to an irrevocable pledge, not because Populists viewed human freedom as a function of property, but because they viewed America as having inherently redemptive, if presently blocked, features, so long as the people were prepared to act. Because their ideology appeared to them radical, they could look to politics as a separate realm that derived a coloration of radicalism from the ideological plane, without inquiring too closely into the absorptive character of political activities. If Populists' ideological conviction produced a euphoric state, their suspension of judgment revealed the desire to screen, while persisting in, nearly ritualized procedures of change.

Populism has to be seen as more subdued. Layers of restraint were evident not only in the movement's political comportment but also in its most advanced ideas. Thought and conduct alike reflected a pulling inward to the institutional core of America. Yet the trend toward immersion in the cultural and political framework affected ideology and behavior in different ways. An immersion in America was a stimulus for transcendent aims that could shake the structure Populists so clearly affirmed, but it was, on matters of conduct, just the reverse: a deadening of resistance that had verged on affirmation for its own sake. The second outcome, a practical ethos of voluntary pacification, stemmed not merely from an acceptance of the electoral context but from the willingness to consider it the exclusive determinant for social protest. Populism's "revolution" at the ballot box was thought to be the only criterion of efficacious action. Even when Populists were flagrantly cheated, they complied with the results, finding no recourse except to return again in greater number.

If the standard of revolutionary violence is wholly inapplicable to reform movements, the absence of this form of violence or any other from Populism nevertheless alerts one to hitherto unnoticed traits and inner strains. The Populists' dependence on a political process that they experienced to be unresponsive and fraudulent was a basic source of demoralization, particularly when a pattern of repeated losses had once been established.[28] Anger had no outlet; high expectations were turned back on to the movement, resulting in a curious torpidness inside the ongoing agitation. The political orientation had a still more damaging effect on the factor of volition. Populists demonstrated a conscious and conscientious opposition throughout the course of the movement that revealed a collective portrait strongly at odds with customary notions of reform. Although Populism had not released the unsublimated energies that would have resulted in mass upheaval, it manifested an equally nonreformist quality of durability, as distinct from simple hardness, that could best be characterized as an ascetic bearing. The axiom of principle over party dictated a stance of this kind, and indeed more. Mission, abnegation, the long-range view, all of these traits, pointing to an absolutist dedication, comprised the sensibility of the movement, coexisting with, and generally surmounting, fits of despair and lassitude. Paradoxically, these traits could apply to the revolutionary psyche as well, which is one reason the disproportion between misery and restraint appears so unnecessary and even pathetic. Populism, however, frequently suffered because of its own best instincts. Its very rectitude invited the violence and vote-manipulation practiced against it, because its opponents knew that these actions would not be reciprocated. It also led to the Democratic party's strategy of absorption in 1896. Populists could be relied on to forego immediate party advantage when there was a ground swell for reform and basic issues stood a chance of wider acceptance. In larger terms, it was because the complex of discipline and asceticism had entailed a one-way relationship to the political process that the volitional factor was ultimately weakened. To be confined to the prescribed channels for expressing protest supposed a faith either that they were open, or that, according to Populism's literal perspective on institutions, they could be democratized in the process of using them. The result was a confusing state of militant supplication. The Populists' disciplined endeavor to advance the principles of the movement led to a headlong involvement in which their energy was placed at the disposal of an electoral mechanism that potentially nullified dissent. Their position was quite different from one involving an autonomous conception and articulation of protest. That society's ground rules were affirmed was of lesser consequence than that Populists' own expectations for reform were shifted from the movement's province to the dominant framework. The pulling inward to America thus became equivalent to the surrender of political initiative.

Populism's attempt to democratize the foundations of property, especially given the traits of durability it brought to this task, defines the movement as more than reformist. Within the American ideological spectrum, it was located on the line between reform and radicalism, an otherwise uninhabited range. This position indicated a growth of political consciousness, but also a limit on its full expression. Populists subjectively viewed reform in more limited terms than its objective consequences appeared to promise, for it created the basis for a more significant alteration of capitalism than they had initially favored. The peculiar dilemma of Populism, which helps to account for its element of restraint, was that it generated forces that exceeded the bounds of its self-identity. When it seemed that the premises of reform might be transgressed, a pronounced antiradicalism occasionally surfaced: Watson's stridency in this regard, from at least 1894, was a heightened instance of Populists' attempts to maintain a delicate balance of internal forces. Still, many others affirmed reform in puristic terms, and not at the expense of radical currents within and outside of the movement. This resilience, more than its particular stands, was Populism's underlying strength, defining its groping as an existential process of becoming. There was a painful search for more encompassing solutions to the original problem, the reconciliation of capitalism and democracy. The Populist scales tipped increasing toward democracy.

Finally, the assessment of restraint in Populism has to take into account the effect of external factors, including contemporary repression, on the development of political consciousness. Scholars of Populism have generally adopted a narrow view that, while crediting the existence of protest, has rendered the movement a self-contained experience, to be subsumed within a pattern of modernization that was seemingly inevitable and unmodifiable. Populism, by implication, was marginal to industrialism, an anachronism that, despite its well-defined grievances, could be analytically separated from the historical framework of American capitalism. Populists themselves would not concede this structural and temporal isolation. They viewed American modernization as a stage of unprecedented brutality in which the small holder of property and the laboring poor bore the costs of economic growth, provided a major source of capital accumulation, and faced in common a process of expropriation that destroyed the independent standing of the lower and middle classes. They perceived not an inevitable pattern but a consciously wrought policy of social impoverishment, specific practices that had little to do with the exigencies of growth and that were inexplicable without a political matrix of business dominance.

The Populist generation knew at firsthand at least two decades of unremitting deprivation. The long-term agricultural decline meant not only falling prices but also mortgage indebtedness, landed concentration, increased tenantry, and, in the South, a furnishing system that converted sharecropping into peonage and strengthened the hold of a one-crop economy on the region. The industrial analogue of this exhibition of class power was the shattering of an inchoate labor movement, unemployment, wage cuts, company towns, scrip, and the introduction of women and children into the workforce to replace adult males. Malnutrition and armed strikebreakers were symptomatic of the pervasive reality. For the coercion of a landed and industrial populace, one would probably have to look to Japan, among the modernizing nations in this period, to find a comparable instance of severity.[29] It is hardly necessary to say that in England, following Peterloo, shooting workers was not considered an accepted method for settling labor disputes, and the Continental working class, however difficult its formation, had also established at least a defensive base; in neither case did a private industrial guard enjoy, as it did in America, quasi-legitimate authority.[30]

The widespread incidence of collective disturbances, beginning with the railroad strikes of 1877, suggests that social discord gathered intensity in the late nineteenth century. Working people, including a broad stratum of the unemployed, had challenged the society's image of classless harmony (contemporary accounts of 1877 dwelt on a supposed loss of innocence in which America had been suddenly transformed into Europe), creating a precedent on which subsequent protest was able to draw for support. A distinctive culture of protest, stemming from these events and continuing through the Pullman strike of 1894, had been imperfectly realized. Strikes and demonstrations, because they often were spontaneous and affected such a diversity of trades, took on the character of a mass awakening; they expressed an underground tradition of resistance, deeds, and political slogans that sustained momentum and fostered greater consciousness. This building process was not a match, however, for the more systematic response of upper groups, in which a different kind of precedent had been created: The initial shock over taking human lives gave way to an inurement to the loss of life *and* rights where strikers and the unemployed were concerned. Americans were becoming habituated to suppression as it was used more frequently and as its rationale—the maintenance of order at all costs—assumed the status of an ideological dogma. Even in 1877, disorder was considered a form of insurrection, making the presumed "crimes" against property an attack on the state itself and thus justifying military and legal intervention.[31] If lower groups did not achieve a fully matured consciousness of class during this entire period (and, if anything, moved back still further from a separate identity in the twentieth century), their protest ironically served to unify the dominant industrial and commercial interests on questions of ideology. This accelerated a class consciousness among upper groups that preceded a comparable organization of the business structure. On labor matters, a common outlook was articulated, the indispensable ties to government were secured, and industrial strategies such as the lockout were perfected. The use of psychological terror, manifested in the Haymarket Affair of 1886, but foreshadowed in the somewhat contrived atmosphere of crisis that had steadily increased since 1877, had the effect of discrediting radicalism, driving a still nonaligned middle class into the arms of upper groups, and fashioning a more rigorous consensus around the values of property. The community drew inward through purging its dissident elements, as though all outstanding class issues had now to be settled with finality. Haymarket, by removing any liveliness that remained in the middle registers of society, had narrowed the range of public sympathy for labor *or* agrarian protest; it contributed to a decisive rightward shift in the ideological spectrum, promoted internal divisions within the labor movement, and became the rallying point for opposing the converging forces of specific unrest: the eight-hour movement, the Knights of Labor (which carried the principle of industrial unionism), and the broader questioning by the lower classes of political and social deference. Although strikes would continue thereafter, the confidence of the American worker had been visibly shaken. With

Homestead and Pullman in the early 1890s, the tightening of the corporate structure became more overt. The barbed wire that was strung around the Homestead Works at the start of the lockout, more than the use of Pinkertons, epitomized the closing world of modernization. Private armies were replaced by public armies in two short years, when federal troops were sent to Chicago, this progression hastened by the intervening depression.[32]

The South had not been exempted from the national pattern; it was atypical in having been assigned a subordinate place in the framework of capitalist development, but not in its emphasis upon a businessmen's government and the containment of social dissent. Racism, as the equivalent of antiradicalism on the national plane, furnished the context of stability for imposing a condition of economic backwardness on the region. Modernization required the systematic ordering of social relations to facilitate this process of capitalist penetration. It also meant the absolute political control of indigenous elites; in seeking to consolidate their own position, they administered the South as a colonial appendage of northern industry and finance.[33] The limited industrial growth that occurred was carefully regimented; there were pastoral versions of the company towns already familiar in northern mining and manufacturing. Moreover, its impact did not spread to other sectors: Capitalistic activity failed to liberalize basic arrangements on the land, leaving in place a predominantly agricultural order that had modified in only superficial ways the previous economy of plantation slavery. The result was a form of decentralized internment in which a peasantry had been attached to the land through conditions of tenure that differed from premodern Europe merely in the legal methods employed to extract a surplus, without the consequent obligations or security of a reciprocal bond.[34] Millhand, tenant, and sharecropper edged precariously near informal servitude, a seemingly color-blind system of capitalism apportioning hardship with fine impartiality among the members of the bottom strata, although at the same time it promoted racial dissension to forestall the political coalitions of a biracial character. Southern culture was readily adaptable to a particular set of capitalistic dynamics: Hierarchical principles of social organization were fixed on a moneyed base; the forces of domination—not bound by contractual rights and nonmaterial restraints—sought to achieve political compliance; and outside investment in railroads, mines, textiles, and natural resources was given full protection and support, including subsidies, public subscriptions, tax abatements, and the use of convict labor. Thus, modernization became a precisely constructed network of economic dependence, a source of protracted and agonizing impoverishment for the region.

When the historical background has been restored, its pertinence to an analysis of Populism appears unmistakable. The movement in its genesis was not divorced from the material setting. Its existence rested on the premise, derived from experience, that America, particularly since the Civil War, was undergoing an antidemocratic transformation. For Populists, this period of upheaval, far from being unfamiliar, comprised the historical fabric of their own time. The breadth of repression and social misery in the country exacted a psychological toll on them as it did on industrial workers, the formidableness of capitalism serving, along with other factors, to narrow Populism's boundaries and to encourage political restraint. Confronting repression alternately stimulated and checked the growth of consciousness; this tension had its source in their sense of the enormity of the tasks of reconstruction and of the forces that were opposed to social change.[35] The larger background also suggests, however, the positive impetus toward reform. Populism was not simply the product of the internal political development of agrarianism, a sequential process of mobilization transmitted directly from the Granger and Greenback movements. Although the earlier demands reappeared (because the original grievances had not been removed but only compounded) and reform veterans assumed positions of leadership, there had nevertheless been a departure from previous organizations because America itself had changed. By the mid-1880s, the problems that once were thought to be of a political character and amenable to finite efforts began to seem structural in nature, entailing more extensive mobilization and more comprehensive solutions. If the movement's social perspective in its specificity bore the memories of an anguished generation, the appreciation of the difficulties to be surmounted invested the Populist consciousness with a greater acuity at whatever level it had reached. Populists were not wholly intimidated by contemporary repression; even when their consciousness was checked, it possessed a broad-gauged vision that was lacking in previous social unrest. The spontaneous growth of suballiances from 1887 to 1890, numbering in the thousands, revealed a generality of concern (and a disposition to organize) that could not be explained solely in terms of the farmers' immediate condition. Nor were the industrial demands of the platforms merely intended to enhance the movement's appeal; they identified the wider context of abuses in which final responsibility for prevailing conditions was fixed on government and corporate power. Populism did not overcome its localism, it did not actualize collective elements that were promised but latent in its ideology, and did not, manifestly, transcend a capitalist framework. But it clearly embraced more than its social base of agrarianism. Populists held that the future character of society, including the preservation of its democratic institutions, now weighed in the balance.

Populism had one "advantage" over earlier and subsequent protest. It emerged when repression had taken a clear-cut form, in contrast to the preliminary stages of the 1870s and the more regularized repression, institutionalized in the political structure, of modern times. Populists viewed the existing repression as marking a fundamental change that was abhorrent to the principles of the Republic and that had no precedent except for slavery in the nation's past. That it derived primarily from private sources made concrete for them the nature of this change: Corporate usurpation had developed at the center of the social system, aided by a government that failed to prevent the rise of monopolism. Their mental comparisons, because Populists were historically close enough to a less repressive context, carried conviction for them. This in turn heightened, particularly among the older generation of Populist leaders, the special features of the age in which they did live. I once speculated that the movement's structural placement helps to explain the prescience so noticeable in its critique. Conceivably, Populism could not have mounted its protest in the specific ideological form it took at any other time. It was not marginal to industrialism in the sense of being irrelevant. But it did appear as an agrarian movement on the periphery of the industrial order, which permitted it to comprehend these developments without becoming engulfed by them.[36] In addition, Populism also appeared when basic social features, not only repression but also the *process* of corporate ascendancy, were still detectable. The social framework had not yet become self-enclosed and self-legitimated. If Populists did not accomplish a break from the existing society, they attained a sufficient ideological distance from it to begin to grasp its systemic contours. Because they rejected the inevitability of business consolidation, they were not submerged, like later reform movements, by the forces they sought to oppose.

CHAPTER TWO

The Corporate Order:
Peffer and Weaver

Populism transcended the limits of agrarian discontent. Its richly textured ideology revealed a cogent analysis of late nineteenth-century American capitalism. The movement's basis in the agricultural sector did not prevent it from identifying monopolistic trends in the industrial economy as the source of a wider social dislocation. The consolidation of industry promoted a new political order; capitalism in its prevailing structure raised serious obstacles to democratic government. Although conditions within agriculture were sufficiently depressed to warrant protest confined to this sector, Populists recognized that such a perspective would be inadequate to the situation they, and the entire nation, were facing.

In their view, farmers were part of a broader stratum of working people, a growing class of the dispossessed that had been created through contemporary industrial organization. This process of impoverishment, in turn, reflected the more pervasive human condition in America, which was characterized by a deterioration in social values, the weakening of constitutional rights, and the abuse of political institutions. Economic privation was symptomatic of a more alarming configuration of change. Populists spoke with feeling about the loss of identity and perceived that their being farmers hardly granted exemption from this predicament. The problem was not merely psychological or even economic; they traced its roots to the individual's basic powerlessness, which determined his place in society. Behind impoverishment was the alteration of political relationships. A structure of private domination was displacing the historic principles of governance.

The social landscape was one of unrelieved Lockean drabness. Modernization, despite its technological promise, was being achieved through the imposition of power by dominant economic groups, fostering the growth of harsh social discipline. Laboring people had become forcibly habituated and subordinated to the rigors of factory production and business authority. Populism was not an isolated expression of protest. Perhaps because it originated on the agricultural periphery, it could discern the broader contours of industrial consolidation without being engulfed by change. The overt harshness of industrial capitalism, as evidenced in sustained labor unrest, dramatized for Populists the inclusive character of social and economic deprivation. A sense of having common grievances with industrial workers revealed a whole system of exploitation; the corporate structure controlled the principal sectors of economic life. This stage of capitalism represented a qualitative shift from past experience. There was a degree of repression unparalleled in earlier periods (or even in the memories of the older Populist generation). But more, the change was indicative of the private arrogation of functions and power normally residing in the state. For Populists, business had become the new locus of sovereignty in America. Government had abdicated its responsibility for the public welfare. They saw in contemporary trends a loss of liberty as well as a loss of identity.

Populism expressed a diversity of positions about capitalism. This was consistent with its own varied character as a movement, its internal complexity of loosely drawn class affiliations, regional differences, and the interaction between dissent and American political values. Yet the movement was not chaotic. Its underlying principles provided political and ideological integration. Additionally, because a gradual phase of political education had preceded its formation, the People's party had at its inception an articulate ideology, necessary political skills, and an extensive press. Populism was distinctive in the history of American reform, establishing firmer local roots and formulating more comprehensive grievances than was typical of third parties.

To achieve cohesion, Populism had to surmount its particular origins and patterns of growth. Its stress on political education, apparent from the onset of the Farmers' Alliance, suggests the importance of volition, a search for identity as a movement, an identity that could not be assumed but that had to be gained through struggle. In helping to lay an ideological foundation, political education also provided a basis for the further radicalization of thought. The developmental process reflected a maturing political consciousness. The participants had actively fashioned their own collective identity as a dissenting movement. This social paradigm is familiar to historians of collective political formations.

The omnipresence of propertied institutions in America must be considered in the American case, where studies of the dynamics of political consciousness have not been sufficiently applied. The acceptance of the right to private ownership of property tended to sublimate dissident energies, even when these energies retained the form and appearance of militancy. The result was to work against a fundamental reconstruction of the polity. Despite common experiences of severe economic deprivation, protest movements did not readily question property as such. To maintain a systemic conception of change was equally difficult. Adopting a class perspective seemed a heavy burden, given its potential for dismounting more of the social structure than reformers ordinarily thought desirable. Although its overall make-up was reformist, Populism moved toward the borderline of radicalism on these matters of property, system, and class. It halted abruptly only when it was in danger of passing outside the capitalistic framework. At that point, the movement began to betray a fear of upheaval destructive to a putatively democratic social order that it was its mission to revitalize and conserve.

Not unlike European social movements, Populist reformism faced toward both political directions. Primarily, it strongly opposed the existent stage of capitalism, mounting in particulars an indictment perhaps as compelling and vociferous as that of labor and/or socialist critics. However, on an underlying level, it also sought to stave off what it perceived as a threat of revolution, emanating from unchecked capitalist practices and social power. But Populism was not centrist or mainstream. The correctives it proposed, and the substance of its structural diagnosis, demonstrate the advanced nature of its reformism. The center it occupied was on a wider ideological spectrum than has ever been present in America. In American terms, the radical label may appear justified. Yet this valuation merely indicates America's diminished ideological horizons. Capitalism has not been the defining issue of ostensibly radical protest; rather, the presence of social activism, in opposition to the prevailing structure, has sufficed as the practical test.

If Populism had revealed a hitherto unsuspected Left dimension in its reasoning on government and the public sector, this would still leave intact, as we shall see, its basic acceptance of property. In addition, it retained notions of balance, order, and political gradualism. Most important, one must consider the American construct; this represented the political and historical symbolization for a precedent constitutional framework and legal norms adequate to the realization of democratic rights. Populism's internal restraint derived from this affirmation of, and immersion within, a national political culture which had traditionally posited the connection between capitalism and freedom. Criticism of a specific stage of American capitalism reinforced Populists' restorative urge and blinded them to how little the essential categories of structure and knowledge had actually been dismounted. To comprehend Populism involves one in the epistemology of protest.

1. Agriculture and Modernization

This brief commentary serves to introduce a discussion of the Populist evidence. We begin with a nonsensational, quite typical work. William A. Peffer, the Populist senator from Kansas, was not an incautious man. He had been a Republican until the eve of Populism, a successful lawyer, and the editor of a leading agricultural paper, the *Kansas Farmer*. His book, *The Farmer's Side, His Troubles and Their Remedy* (1891), bore all the earmarks of one who enjoyed a reputation for moderation and legalistic thinking in previous decades. The presentation of numerous tables on trends in farm income, land valuation, production, and commodity prices, along with extensive use of Treasury reports, added up to a meticulous statistical and political analysis of the deteriorating condition of society. Within this framework, stated so matter-of-factly as to suggest a set of assumptions shared with his readers, he nonetheless presented a thesis of widespread political and economic expropriation. This underlying theme, more than separate practices that Peffer himself would not discuss separately, best addressed the repressive context and expressed the unifying character of Populist thought.

Peffer captured the discrepancy between potential abundance and actual poverty which appeared to characterize American society:

Briefly, while the world has been moving ahead with long and rapid strides, while invention has multiplied machinery a thousand fold, giving every worker ten hands and increasing wealth at marvelous rate; while the country has advanced without parallel in the history of nations; while statisticians flood reports with bewildering figures; while politicians grow big with patriotic conceptions and eloquent with fervid speech, the men and women who do the manual work are growing relatively poorer, and the few who live off of the profits of other men's labor, or off of the interest on money, or rent on buildings and land, and they who gamble in labor's products and play with the fortunes of men as if they were foot-balls or dice, and to whom the toil and sweat of the poor have no more value than the drip of the roof, are growing richer.

Clearly, his account was not hostile to industrialism, but to the way the forces of production had been appropriated. Progress had turned sour. Peffer, while not abandoning capitalism, focused on the disparities in the distribution of wealth. He believed that the roots of the problem were in the principal capitalist sources of profit: labor, interest, and rent (as well as speculation). More relevant to his statement of underlying conditions was the haunting reference to men's lives as footballs and dice. There was an implicit callousness in this system of operations. For Peffer, such a system occurred within the basic relations of class and power: "Advances in wages, real though they are, have not kept pace with the growing necessities of the working people. Is not the workman worthy of his hire? Ought not the producer to be first paid? Who may rightfully despoil him?" Economic questions were moral questions in Populist thought. In this case, expropriation was occurring on the primary, individual level. Men were depersonalized, tossed about as objects of sport and chance. They had been divorced from their own livelihood. Their worth was determined by seemingly capricious outside forces.[1]

Peffer had not forgotten the farmer (however, it is interesting to see how easily he moved back and forth from the industrial to the agrarian sector). He found in agriculture situations which were parallel to those in industry: increased work, diminished income, and a loss of personal direction. After presenting consecutive tables showing the long-term decline in crop prices, he observed that "the progress of agriculture, compared with other industries, has been less and less marked every decennial period since 1860." And he continued: "Farmers now need the use of ten dollars for one that was sufficient forty years ago. Then, when little was required, there was enough; now, when much is required, little or none is to be had." This was not an entrepreneurial lament; Peffer's thought led him to a very different problem, the widening breach in class relations. "Farmers are poor, while manufacturers and bankers and railroad managers are rich. The wealth of the country is fast passing into the hands of a few rich persons, while the number of impoverished grows alarmingly larger every year."[2]

Peffer's examination of census data on mortgage indebtedness brought him to the central issue facing the lesser propertied stratum of society (for whom he, and perhaps Populism itself, spoke). He believed that it was not simply a matter of declining returns for this group but of their survival. He was concerned about expropriation in its most explicit and familiar form, dispossession of land: "Summarized, then, the situation is this: Farmers are passing through the 'valley and shadow of death'; farming as a business is profitless; values of farm products have fallen 50 per cent since the great war, and farm values have depreciated 25 to 50 per cent during the last ten years; farmers are overwhelmed with debts secured by mortgages on their homes, unable in many instances to pay even the interest as it falls due, and unable to renew the loans because securities are weakening by reason of the general depression; many farmers are losing their homes under this dreadful blight, and the mortgage mill still grinds." Unrelieved economic pressure, accompanied by the collapse of a whole sector, transformed personal insecurity into social oppression. Notwithstanding the ideal image of the independent homestead, which represented capitalistic values and recurred frequently in Populism, a collective sense of deprivation emerged. It was expressed as a systemic indictment: "We are in the hands of a merciless power; the people's homes are at stake."[3]

Peffer's analysis of economic and social dependence extended beyond the agrarian sector. He focused his discussion on labor for several reasons. Most evident, he pursued both the labor and agrarian dimensions to suggest that farmers and laborers had common experiences. Because they represented two branches of the same trunk, productive work and values, there was a basis for mutual help and support. Peffer, by emphasizing labor, also shifted the discussion to the foundations of the contemporary economic system. It was not simply that the agrarian order no longer predominated, but inferentially that the problems of agriculture were caused by the functioning of the larger capitalist structure. As a power center it determined money and banking policy, controlled transportation, and in general regulated exchanges. Lastly, Peffer's emphasis on labor helped him to define the dependent relation of working people to the capitalist structure as a qualitative change. It presaged the direction that American society was taking.

He expressed this in an epigram: "We are steadily becoming a nation of hired men." Here Peffer, like other Populists, tended not to question the wage system as such. Yet he found its current state to be not only exploitative but also in open violation of a widely held standard of producer values: "It is time to recall the statement which no one disputes, but which most large employers ignore, 'the workman is worthy of his hire.' And 'hire' means a fair, just, equitable reward for his toil. If he does all the work, surely he is entitled to a large share of the profits." This repeated formulation was intended as a universal principle applying to farmers as well as to laborers. Its abrogation testified to the inequitable premises of an increasingly more rigid class structure. "To value a machine higher than a man or a woman because it can work cheaper, is to place money above muscle, and to place money and labor in competition is to perpetuate the rule of caste." A further comment, prefacing one of the more perceptive analyses of wage labor in this period, again indicated the parallelism between the circumstances of farmers and laborers: "In many respects the same facts which apply to changes that have taken place in the condition of farmers apply to mechanics and to wage workers."[4]

Turning to that analysis, one encounters what at first seems a preindustrial scene that is derived from, and largely restates, Adam Smith's description of the division of labor: "Going back half a century, those of us who have lived that long remember distinctly that in every rural neighborhood the principal lines of mechanical work were represented by persons generally owning their own shops and dwellings. The wagon-maker, the blacksmith, the carpenter, the shoemaker, the tailor, the bricklayer, the stone-mason—all scattered about among the farmers. Now nothing of that kind is seen in the travel of a month over the country, but, in-stead thereof, in the cities we find mechanics for every grade massed in large numbers, where each one works separately at a particular part of the machine which he is making." These simple words were free of sickly nostalgia and the desire to return to the past for its own sake. Peffer sketched the mechanical process of production in a wagon factory, detailing its many operations, and described the interchangeability of parts: "In a pile of a thousand or five thousand of these separate pieces any one of them will fit in its proper place in any one of the wagons made at that establish-ment."[5]

But whereas Adam Smith discussed the division of labor as a self-completing economic fact, divorced from its political ramifica-tions, and especially from its specific effect on class relations, Peffer's main interest was in the importance of these ramifications. Peffer uncovered the essence of private coercion, the regimenta-tion which was founded on the compulsions of the workplace: "These people, from 500 to 3,500 at a place, go to their work at the blowing of a whistle or the ringing of a bell; they go to their meals and return by the same signs at stated times every working day. They are practically as much machines as the unconscious mechanical combinations to which they attend." And he contin-ued: "By this process of absorption in large manufacturing estab-lishments the individuality of the separate workers is virtually lost." The laborer, "once an individual citizen among the farmers," now does his work "with the same precision, the same regularity, the same method that an inanimate implement does."[6]

Here the Populist world opens considerably. To the reader ac-customed to thinking of Populism as narrowly agrarian, even when it became broad enough to include a penetrating treatment of monetary and transportation matters, the line of inquiry that Peffer followed, in a book called *The Farmer's Side*, seems strange-ly out of place. It is as though he had made a heavy-handed appeal to labor, or that his analysis was at best tangential to his own and Populism's main concerns. In fact, Populism's largely agrarian origins did not preclude its cogent response to industrialism, or to the specific form that capitalist development had assumed. Populists recognized not only that an older way of life was being destroyed but also that the one which replaced it was in its basic features prejudicial to a democratic framework.

They did not believe that the choice lay between an agrarian and an industrial order. They perhaps were better developmental theorists than those in our own generation are. This was not because they experienced at first hand this crucial stage in the modernizing process, but because they grasped the *political* as well as the technological character of modernization. My usage of "political" is broad and goes beyond electoral politics. It is both Harringtonian and Populist: that which deals with the phenomenon of power, the class relations derived from its organization and distribution, and the implications its exercise has for control of the state. Peffer strongly implied that the industrial transformation had been traumatic. It had been a wrenching and poignant episode that had fashioned men who resembled the inanimate implements they tended, and had forced them to conform to a regime of set times and factory whistles. This strict scheduling was in contrast to the freer conception of time of the independent producer, as well as to the deeper seasonal rhythms of the agrarian world.[7] Yet it was neither the segmentation of work-tasks nor the routinization of workers' lives that elicited his most critical response.

He saw that there was a choice between two forms of development. On the one hand, there could be a humanely effected transition. Both the industrial and agricultural orders could be integrated into a political economy in which the exigencies of the new mode would not be used as the basis for repression over and above what machine production itself required. On the other, there was the contemporary reality of a politicized modernizing course. Here agriculture was impoverished for the sake of higher profits in the advancing sectors of banking and railroads. Additionally, agriculture suffered from a deflationary monetary structure which facilitated basic capital investment in heavy industry and which fostered a cheap-wages policy that was combined with lowered food prices.[8] In turn, industry became the nucleus of increasingly concentrated wealth and power through its ownership of economic resources. Peffer, like other Populists, understandably deplored the work discipline associated with the advent of modern industry, because it portended loss of the worker's independence and obliterated his pride in his workmanship. But the more serious problems, because they were entirely arbitrary and gratuitous, were the antidemocratic consequences of these changes. Ownership had led to the elaboration of prerogatives on capitalism's behalf that extended the meaning of expropriation to fundamental class relations. Men were depersonalized. Worse still, they were disconnected from the social process as meaningful participants.

Peffer, after describing the laborer as an "inanimate implement," addressed the working people's eroding political autonomy: "One of the necessary results of this change is that the mechanic and the wage worker have become largely dependent upon the business of his employer." Where there are differences between the two, over wages or any other matter, "the employer has the advantage." And should times be dull, wages reduced, and conflict impending, the "circumstances" of control "breed a relation between the owner and the workers at the factory which in times of great excitement give to the employer a practical ownership of his work-people."[9]

Peffer then took up the loss of autonomy in its more subtle form, the pressures inviting workers to identify their interests with that of employers. (Veblen would later write about this as the inculcation of ideology from above, and the consequent surrender of a separable consciousness in favor of sharing in the exploits of the economic rulership.)[10] Peffer sketched the dynamics of the process: "When an economic question, in political discussions, is held up before the people as involving the rights of labor, and particularly in respect to their wages, it is a logical effect of the conditions that the workers should be appealed to to stand by the employer, because it is said whatever is to the interest of the employer will be to the interest of the employé, on the supposition that a good business for the owner of the factory will make more work and better wages for the men and women who do the work." Social control was manifest: "In this way the manufacturer in charge of a large establishment wields a powerful influence over the persons in his employ."[11]

Peffer believed that individual control was rooted in systemic decisions. Exploitation of the worker resulted not from the employer's whim, but from the collective motivation of employers dictated by considerations of profit maximization. "Aside from all this, it has been the rule ever since the relation of employer and employé was first established that the interest of the employer is for himself and not for his workman; that while he admits that the workman is worthy of his hire, yet he believes it to be his privilege to obtain labor at the lowest price." The complement of the worker as hostage to the successful establishment was the conception of labor as a commodity. The depersonalization of the worker had been carried to its logical conclusion. The workforce was but one of the factors of production: "Labor has always been a commodity in the market for which employers bid just as dealers at an auction of dry goods—every one anxious to get what he desires at the lowest possible figure."[12]

The reduction of men and women to the status of commodities served to cheapen human existence and in turn engendered resistance. This was the final step in its social proportions away from a democratic polity. Peffer's statement about the laboring classes is moving: "So it is that work-people in all communities are nearly always within a few days, or at most a few weeks, of starvation; and it is probably because of this great and crushing fact that working men and women have united in organizations for their mutual protection." He found that the use of imported contract-labor, as a mechanism to ensure subsistence living, was a main cause of organization and strikes. And he added that "while these strikes have set on foot an extended investigation of the complaints of our working people, and their rights as citizens of the republic, their condition, compared with that of those who really control social and political affairs, is no better than it was at the beginning of the century."[13]

The obverse side of this loss of autonomy was the formation of a structure of power. Peffer saw the period as one piece, an interweaving of Populism's and labor's struggle; each confronted a political context that was shaped through monopolistic trends and power. He began the last phase of his discussion with this statement: "The employer still has the advantage, and he has it with practical completeness." He attributed this condition to industrial consolidation. Not only did it enlarge the realm of worker dependency, but it also prevented the benefits of greater productivity from being distributed to workers. The merging of these themes revealed the cumulative dominance of ownership:

The tendency is to concentrate still more and more in large establishments. By reference to the census reports of 1850, 1860, 1870, 1880, and 1890, it will be seen that while the number of manufacturing establishments has increased, there has been a gradual absorption of smaller ones into the larger; that, while more persons are employed in them, the number in each one has been greatly increased; that, while the amount of wages in the aggregate paid to employés has increased, compared with the amount of work that they do their wages is not as great now as it was at any former period. Besides that, it appears that every year the individuality of the working man is growing less and less distinct; he is becoming merged into the business of his employer; practically he is out of view.

The worker who was "out of view" was powerless as well as anonymous. The dependent state thus indicated an increasingly fixed class and political relation. It was an inverse relation; the loss of independence for working people translated into a gain in power for a ruling stratum. "While he produces wealth in enormous amounts, it is found that his share of it, from some cause or other, is growing less and less relatively as the years come and go, while his employer grows richer and his influence in social and political affairs continually increases."[14]

Peffer described the dynamics of business hegemony in a succinct sentence: "Not only does the rich man to-day rule at home among his neighbors, but he rules in our national affairs." The important point raised by worker dependence was not loss of prestige but determination of policy; business held the veto over national legislation. Through the repeated use of "power," Peffer tentatively identified the construction of a class-state: "Money controls our legislation, it colors our judicial decisions, it manipulates parties, it controls policies. Manufacturers, bankers, railroad builders, and other capitalists dictated our present financial methods, and to-day their combined opposition is strong enough to defeat any measure proposing a change. It is that power which defeated the free-coinage bills that were proposed in the Fifty-first Congress; it is that power which defeats the reduction of excessive tariff duties; it is that power which holds within the hollow of its hand all the financial interests of the people. Wall Street is king."

The last comment was a flash of defiance intended to expose the imbalance of power: "All of this makes the condition of the wage worker more and more dependent every year."[15]

Populism was not confined to a narrow agrarianism. Nor did it conform to a further stereotype. When it voiced its concern over loss of independence through industrial development, it did not follow the expected course, the one taken, for example, by the German peasantry. Populism's resistance to dependence is not to be confused with a fear of becoming proletarized. This fear is the ideal psychological ground, as Hans Speier has shown for the German case,[16] for protofascistic behavior and ideology. Populism's response totally contradicted these expectations. It chose to join with the workers rather than fight to preserve the ideological separation from them. The anxiety to maintain social distance, which is at the core of the expression of status-deprivation, did not exist in Populism, because Populists perceived hardship as indivisible.

Peffer shared this perception: "He is beginning to see that the same influences which have brought bankruptcy to the farmer's door is taking away from him his home and preventing his neighbor from securing one." Then, commenting on how difficult it was for a worker to obtain a home, more so "than it has been at any time within the reach of memory," he closed the discussion with a statement about the convergence of farmer-labor interests. This was given added plausibility because he had traced in the book the conditions of each: "The farmer and the wage worker are traveling the same road; they are both brought face to face with a perilous condition; they are both confronted with a merciless power which has brought disaster upon them both alike."[17]

2. A Breakdown of Authority

James B. Weaver's *A Call to Action* (1892) was the analysis of a seasoned practitioner of reform politics. His work more specifically criticized business's involvement in the legislative process. He was the candidate of the People's party in 1892 and of the Greenback party in 1880, and he was thrice elected to Congress from Iowa in the years 1878 to 1887. With this political background, complemented by his theoretical acuity, Weaver was able to present his own specific issues from an insider's point of view. He was interested in the interrelated themes of corporate usurpation and the decline of public responsibility. His book contained the kinds of documentation (observation, committee reports, congressional investigations) which other Populists tended to overlook and which fixed the discussion concretely on national affairs.

It may be doubted that Weaver merits a hearing as an authentic Populist voice in light of his presumed identity as an extreme fusionist in the 1896 campaign. This position is thought to entail the narrowing of the platform to silver alone, and the uncritical support of William Jennings Bryan. I cannot accept existing categories which, in essence, divide Populism into pristine mid-roadism and nefarious fusionism.[18] On the immediate matter, Weaver continually attacked corporate encroachment on the public lands. He mapped the political geography of railroad influence, and he stood closely with the labor movement, as, for example, in warning the House about the coercive implications of armories. He is certainly entitled to a hearing.

The first sentence of Weaver's book announced that he would employ a constitutional standard; he would discuss an impending loss of liberty in the present American setting: "The author's object in publishing this book is to call attention to some of the more serious evils which now disturb the repose of American society and threaten the overthrow of free institutions." The broad-gauged approach was essentially political and legal in conception. It took as its premise a prevalent feeling among Populists, that the polity was being torn asunder: "We are nearing a serious crisis. If the present strained relations between wealth owners and wealth producers continue much longer they will ripen into frightful disaster. This universal discontent must be quickly interpreted and its causes removed." Then in bold, quick brush strokes he painted what can be termed an inversion of political democracy. Governmental functions devolved upon the corporation, and the state itself became merely its outer fabric: "The sovereign right to regulate commerce among our magnificent union of States, and to control the instruments of commerce, the right to issue the currency and to determine the money supply for sixty-three million people and their posterity, have been leased to associated speculators. The brightest lights of the legal profession have been lured from their honorable relation to the people in the adminstration of justice, and through evolution in crime the corporation has taken the place of the pirate; and finally a bold and aggressive plutocracy has usurped the Government and is using it as a policeman to enforce its insolent decrees."[19] The approximately 440 pages that followed were an amplification of this passage. For our purposes, what emerges is the shifting of sovereignty to business, widespread political and structural corrosion, and the decline of a public spirit.

For Weaver, corporations were highly evolved pirates, interlopers in the realm of the public interest, fashioning a plutocratic government. Lawyers and jurists, charged with upholding principles of justice, served instead as the technicians of corporate rule. (Throughout his book he was critical of the bench for not maintaining canons of impartiality.) Plutocracy, he continued, "filled the Senate with its adherents," and through the Speakership also controlled the House. He meant, as was clear from later portions of his book, not that a conspiracy existed, but that organized wealth possessed self-reinforcing political power. He next pictured the nation's state of disrepair, and he used, as did Peffer, the imagery of a home as the concrete symbol of independence: "The public domain has been squandered, our coal fields bartered away, our forests denuded, our people impoverished, and we are attempting to build a prosperous commonwealth among people who are being robbed of their homes—a task as futile and impossible as it would be to attempt to cultivate a thrifty forest without soil to sustain it." The devastation was political as well as physical. Society's basic relations had been altered. In the process, the state had surrendered one of its main constituent elements: "The corporation has been placed above the individual and an armed body of cruel mercenaries permitted, in times of public peril, to discharge police duties which clearly belong to the State."[20]

This sense of private usurpation was the distinguishing characteristic of Weaver's analysis. The corporation had supplanted the community as the supreme concern of government. Then it had hedged in its advantageous position by "pleading to be let alone." This was surely a good assessment of the function of laissez-faire ideology, which allowed privileges to be conserved and renewed, while potentially unfavorable interference was fended off. His response to such pleas from corporations was caustic: "They cry out, 'You will disturb the peace, unsettle business and violate our vested constitutional rights.' The world has heard similar lamentations before. The same spirit has lurked in the pathway of progress and hissed its sinister protests from behind the Constitution and from beneath the very altars of our holy religion, from the beginning until now." It presently served "corporation usurpers and tyrants." There was evident resistance to change: "They have nothing to gain by change. On the contrary everything to lose." But he made a further point. Industrial dynamism had left the social structure intact. In essence, capitalist development had defined its own contours. It had nullified the democratizing possibilities of productive growth, in favor of existing class differentials and a rigid definition of order. Thus, he wrote: "Their Juggernaut must move and the car of progress stand still."[21]

Weaver found the Senate to be the particular bastion of "corporate influence." After discussing the powers it gathered from other branches of government and charging that critics of business were denied reelection, he added that even the founding fathers, most concerned with checking the lower house, had not contemplated "that is should become the stronghold of monopoly, nor that it should hedge up the way to all reform and make impossible the peaceful overthrow of conceded abuses." It was not that the Senate was abstractly conservative but that, "this body has come to represent both the evil and the inertia of government." Weaver's description of political reaction was masterful: "When you visit the Senate chamber you are at once reminded of antiquity. You feel that you are not far removed from that period when the changeless laws of the Medes and Persians were in force. If, without diverting your attention, you could be suddenly transported to an Egyptian charnel-house filled with mummies, you would be likely to mistake it for a Senate cloakroom. The very foot-falls of the Senators, as they walk across the tessellated floors, sound like a constant iteration of statu quo! statu quo! statu quo!" But the social composition, not the atmosphere, of the Senate was important: "If wealthy Senators were few in number they would still wield a dangerous influence over legislation. But when you add numbers to wealth, the danger is frightfully increased."[22] And beyond their wealth there lay the more decisive question of the senators' actual conduct.

Weaver's conception of public duty carried his discussion beyond the issue of conflicts of interest to the dynamics of practical power. Men of wealth directly superintended their holdings, or, as corporate retainers, dealt at first hand with the interests under their care. What later writers might term the circulation of elites (or the revolving-door principle) suggested a loss of the distinction between business and government, as men moved freely from one to the other sphere.[23] This pattern openly violated the public's rights and denied the functions that an autonomous government was designed to perform. It was the source of one of Populism's principal complaints. Weaver first outlined the problem: "The immense volume of legislation relating to land grants, internal and external commerce, railway subsidies, excise taxes and import duties, contracts for carrying the mails, purchase of Indian lands, private land grants, steam ship subsidies, and a thousand and one other matters, have given rise to a flood tide of litigation unequaled in any age or clime. A large number of the contentions rising out of this legislation involve the construction of acts of congress, and not unfrequently their constitutionality also. In many cases the collection and proper disbursement of public moneys are called directly in question . . . . " The principle stated in the remainder of the final sentence deserves added emphasis. Legislators were bound to the populace by a sacred trust. The government was obligated to place the general welfare before the interest of special claimants: "and as long as Senators stand in the relation of law makers to the public, a proper appreciation of their high office should restrain them from appearing as attorneys, either for corporations or individuals, in cases involving the proper interpretation of statutes which they themselves have made."[24]

Such self-evident propositions of democratic governance sometimes have a shockingly innocent quality. This was particularly so in the way that Weaver invested "law maker" with positive meaning. The lawmaker was a trustee of the people's weal, whose "high office" was predicated on the disavowal of personal interest and class enrichment. Weaver added immediately: "The practice, however, is just the reverse." One hears "the very foot-falls" of the senators when private and public distinctions have broken down.

"When the Supreme Court is in session it is a common thing to see the leading Senators leave their seats and pass into the court room, there to act as counsel for the leading corporations." Further, "Many Senators are annually retained by corporations and other moneyed interests." If Weaver rode the theme hard, it was not out of fascination for things shabby. Rather, he intended to introduce a major Populist contention: "Such things are incompatible with the faithful discharge of public duty."[25]

The Populist ideal of the democratic state is suggested by this statement. At the outset, "public duty" has the same ring of *civitas* that one finds in the headiness of revolutionary experience and in tightly knit structures affirming the rights of the community. This represented a full inhabitation of the social order, as it were, in which pride in the nation was not necessarily statist or nationalistic in spirit, but referred to a prior value of commonwealth. Specifically, the state was distinguished by its essential neutrality, defined as a dedication to charter rights of freedom as against exploitative class aims that encompassed less than the whole. For Populists, the ideal was not only workable but also had largely characterized America before corporate power became dominant in the nation. Business denied the state's neutral complexion, setting up the contradiction between prevalent and realizable practice that had prompted the Populist elaboration of governmental functions in the first instance.

The critique was not conceived in a vacuum. Moreover, public duty, as the implied message of the passage, helps one to understand why "public" and "people" were central to Populist nomenclature. Populists used these terms as political notations to signify the body politic, which in turn became equated with the nation, particularly in its implementation of what Weaver termed "free institutions." In light of the weight given to the state's democratic responsibilities, how incumbent on the legislator faithfully to discharge his duties! It becomes clear that the discussion involved more than the role of individual senators and was in reality a case study of the fundamental encroachment of the corporation on traditional liberties. We will turn later to further observations on the neutrality of the state, and here proceed to Weaver's final passage on public duty.

The hallowed nature of public service logically followed from the preceding conception of political obligation: "It is true that the salaries and lawful emoluments of Senatorial life are meagre and uninviting; but no one is compelled to accept them. When once accepted, however, the privileges of the lawyer should cease just where the duties of the public servant begin." The line that Weaver drew between private and public life had less to do with separable moralities, each appropriate to a particular realm, than it did with a fixed standard determined by the nature of the constituency to be served. The public was more than a populace. It became the repository of final resort, embodying the nation's putative heritage of political and social welfare. This criterion of public service required the shift from privilege to duty, an ironclad resolution among those who conducted the affairs of the public and spoke in its name. This passage is more important than the specific details of protest, because it provided the framework within which Populist demands were conceived: "At this point his relation to the public changes entirely. The Nation then becomes his client and he should appear in his place and plead the cause of the whole people without mental reservation or self-evasion. No other rule is compatible with public duty or private honor. Public sentiment which will knowingly tolerate the infraction of such rule is utterly demoralized, and law makers who insist upon such indulgence should at once be permitted to return to the practice of their profession and to private life."[26]

A stern, uncompromising tone emerged when vital principles were stated. Here, even the notion of a self-legitimated public, one that could do no wrong, came under scrutiny. Populists consistently applied the standard of social welfare as part of a broader political obligation that defined relations between government and governed. Social welfare took precedence over the people, who were themselves obliged to share responsibility for its maintenance. One seldom finds within Populism the conception of the people as the voice of God. Populists would see this idea as a demagogic appeal, and it was so used from outside the movement to attract political support. Merely idealizing the people would undercut the importance of political education and minimize more than was warranted the obstacles to successful protest. The sternness one frequently encounters in Populism was not the same as, or a mask for, arrogance. It was in fact self-deprecation, admonishing participants in the movement to strive harder, to organize better, and to know more. In the context of mission, especially where this attitude predominated, claims were made not for the people, but for the principles of the movement. Populists willingly acknowledged this distinction as the correct statement of priorities. Weaver's chiding remark about sentiment that was "utterly demoralized" both recognized the people's fallibility and revealed something of the more severely critical perspective that Populists wanted. Finally, he posited the connection between the nation and social welfare, to indicate how far short the contemporary Senate had fallen in meeting the high expectations that were associated with a public trust: "There is not a single great leader in the Senate of today, not one who is abreast of the times, or who can be truthfully said to be the exponent of American civilization or the active champion of the reforms made necessary by the growth and changed relations of a century, and which are now struggling for recognition."[27]

The book's unifying theme was the permeation of corporate power through the social order. At one point, Weaver suggested a historical explanation for the static lines of American development. The incompleteness of democratization in the Civil War's aftermath demonstrated that political and business elites considered only limited change in the wake of accelerated capitalist growth. The failure to achieve democratic gains also permitted unimpeded business consolidation. This passage elaborates the analogy that Populists sometimes drew between chattel and industrial slavery, to point out the persistence and the antidemocratic nature of ruling groups in the society:

The moral, intellectual and political leaders during the twenty years immediately following the war, with the single exception of Wendell Phillips, failed to comprehend the problems which confronted them. They stopped with the overthrow of the outward form of slavery. Through the strength and suffering of the great army of the people they succeeded in breaking the chains of chattel slavery and prepared the way for the complete triumph of man over those who lived by the enslavement of labor. All that was necessary was one more forward movement of the column, and the victory would have been complete. But they failed to make it and surrendered to a handful of task masters of another type, whose triumphs in the slave trade have never, in all the ages, been limited by distinctions of race or complexions of skin.

The analogy was implicitly broadened, as if to describe the proportions of the present conflict, by making the enslavement of labor the modus operandi of dominant forces. The struggle was being recapitulated on contemporary lines: "They have plied their cruel vocation among all the families of men. To overthrow them is the grand work of the new crusade. Confederated labor has proclaimed the new emancipation."[28]

Populists, at least in the West, consciously identified themselves as the new abolitionists (the mention of Phillips is striking). This identity affected the way that they thought of the industrial elite. Attributing merciless acquisitiveness to the planter and the modern capitalist alike served to lessen the deference shown to the latter. Weaver perceived that the planter and the capitalist had the same fundamental motive: "The unholy and lawless determination to acquire wealth and personal comfort at the expense of a weaker and less fortunate race, was the underlying spirit of slavery." Later he noted that "in the very midst of the struggle for the overthrow of the slave oligarchy, our institutions were assailed by another foe mightier than the former, equally cruel, wider in its field of operation, infinitely greater in wealth, and immeasurably more difficult to control." And he added: "It will be readily understood that we allude to the sudden growth of corporate power and its attendant consequences." The analogy thus served to emphasize the converse statement of emancipation. His words "our institutions were assailed" expressed his feelings of outrage at a loss of liberties.[29]

Weaver traced the "extension of corporate life" into fields that were relevant to national power. He was especially concerned about the legal profession and dated its reorientation, as have scholars recently, to opportunities that had been provided in corporate service. This pattern of recruitment, enlisting men "as fast as they rise above the dead level of mediocrity," defined the avenue to subsequent legal eminence. The pool had been created from which to fill the federal and state bench, men thus enjoying position "by the power of their clientage." Weaver's discussion of corporate influence took in as well the administration and the faculty of universities and law schools.[30] After extended treatment of the Supreme Court, he concluded: "The corporation has submerged the whole country and swept everything before it." The imagery was that of glaciated upheaval: "The corporation glacier is now sweeping over this country and lifting out of place the solid granite of our Judiciary and threatening to carry away the very pillars of the Republic." The Court, when free to speak impartially, uniquely symbolized constitutional liberties. He further observed that, like the sun which melted glacial ice, "the light of unclouded public opinion" would, it was hoped, melt the iceberg, "and our great Court be permitted to settle back upon the pedestal of the Constitution, to remain forever as the hope and refuge of the people."[31]

3. Fear of Social Upheaval

Weaver's declaration of a legalist faith has striking importance. Populists believed that the Court had shown a partiality to business in the post–Civil War era (beginning with the early 1880s and the appointment of Stanley Matthews), and hence they felt free to criticize strongly its decisions. Yet Populists would not work outside the Constitution. Rather, they saw the existing Court as representing the negation of essential constitutional doctrines. Unlike mid–twentieth-century critics, they attacked the Court for moving in a rightist direction. They did so not out of cynicism or a disregard for the Court's function, but because they had a deep respect for its potentiality as the bulwark of popular rights. (Marion Butler exemplified this disposition when he introduced legislation, after the imprisonment of Eugene V. Debs, to provide for jury trials in contempt cases. One finds charges of judicial tyranny, based on a similar wish to serve the Constitution, expressed at large in the movement.) Still, the dedication to the American institutional setting was evident here. The more Populists spoke in opposition to the Court, the more they cast themselves as the defenders of legal processes and constitutional principles. By this seeming paradox, they were consciously and unconsciously driven to regard their protest and their larger sense of mission as peculiarly restorative. There had to be a purging of corporate power and the elimination of its "attendant consequences" in order to reinstate the previously realized democratic foundations to a condition of supremacy.

This position also helps to explain the movement's political orientation; its protest was largely, if not exclusively, confined to the channels that the society had established to neutralize dissent. One perhaps takes for granted, as Populists themselves did, the emphasis on a political approach. It was difficult for Populists to recognize the moderating effects which came from seeking legitimation in this manner. Other and possibly more militant strategies had been precluded. (The narrower construction of the term "political" is used here.) To engage in politics, albeit outside the major-parties' frame of reference, nevertheless reaffirmed internal processes that had been directed to the stabilization of the polity. Most important, the political orientation merely restated the Populist dedication to the plane of fundamental law. It entailed the pledge to observe prescribed ground rules, and became synonymous with carefully paced (that is, constitutional) methods of change. This commitment to the law partially accounted for another Populist trait, the virtual absence of violence within the movement. In this case, the connection between law and nonviolent means of protest was fortified through Weaver's belief that the courts not only represented a "hope" and a "refuge," but the sole avenue to the pacific settlement of social conflict.

From this vantage ground, one moves to Populism's explicitly nonrevolutionary dimension. Stated conversely, "nonrevolutionary" meant for Populists the affirmation of a democratic legal and political order. Weaver, like many others, appeared most radical when he was stating a profoundly conservative point. The second sentence of his book reads: "We are nearing a serious crisis. If the present strained relations between wealth owners and wealth producers continue much longer they will ripen into frightful disaster. This universal discontent must be quickly interpreted and its causes removed." He added to this: "It is the country's imperative Call to Action, and can not be longer disregarded with impunity." The presumed radicalism lay in the identification of a social crisis; the further recognition that a fissure between the classes had occurred; the conclusion that disaster was immanent, should the situation remain unchanged; and finally in Populism's role as the democratic protagonist, determined to remove the sources of discontent. These elements formed a paradigm of the rationale for protest. They were repeated with surprising frequency throughout the movement's literature, usually to the same effect.

Ignatius Donnelly, the Minnesota Populist, expressed these sentiments in his novel *Caesar's Column* (1890). The work portrayed a catastrophic upheaval in the late twentieth century. It was a prophecy of what would occur if the contemporary context was not changed. Donnelly early dissociated himself from this disastrous outcome: "It must not be thought, because I am constrained to describe the overthrow of civilization, that I desire it. The prophet is not responsible for the event he foretells. He may contemplate it with profoundest sorrow."[32] More dramatically than most, as in his famous preamble to the Omaha Platform in 1892, Donnelly provided the imagery of sharpened contrasts between wealth and poverty in his writings. Despite his artistic liberties, he distilled in the novel the current fears of a looming, and perhaps irreconcilable, struggle.

"Who is it," he asked, "that is satisfied with the present unhappy condition of society?" Apparently no one was: "The rich, as a rule, despise the poor; and the poor are coming to hate the rich. The face of labor grows sullen; the old tender Christian love is gone; standing armies are formed on one side, and great communistic organizations on the other; society divides itself into two hostile camps; no white flags pass from the one to the other." He spoke of "an acceleration of movement in human affairs" as conditions worsened, and he ominously declared: "The dead missile out of space at last blazes, and the very air takes fire. The masses grow more intelligent as they grow more wretched; and more capable of co-operation as they become more desperate." This was not a loving portrait. If Donnelly saw capitalist oppression as igniting the spark (after posing his quesiton, he stated, "the many are plundered to enrich the few," and "vast combinations depress the price of labor and increase the cost of the necessaries of existence"), one begins nonetheless to ask, what was the Populist attitude toward the masses? The answer is in their network of allegiances, which in turn afford an opportunity to state a provisional definition of Populist thought.[33]

Donnelly's statement that he contemplated the overthrow of civilization with "profoundest sorrow" represented the view of all Populists. While Populists came largely from what could be described as the working poor, regardless of the origins of Populist leadership, they nevertheless had an evident fear of upheaval and even of the lower classes. Since I shall discuss elsewhere the movement's sober-mindedness, which was consistent with its internal political restraint and a general absence of the kind of chiliastic currents that might have been found in England, I can resist the temptation to say that in reality they displayed a fear of themselves. This fear was evident only in their sublimation of that volatility in themselves that so alarmed them in others. Basically, Populists did not need to fear themselves because they had tacitly drawn the distinction between the working poor and an undifferentiated mass, the already "sullen" and brutalized. This self-image depended on the belief that they still *could* act, and were connected to society; they retained a measure of hope for constructive social change.

The question becomes: What function did the distinction serve in affirming the Populists' own sense of identity? Critics of Populism have suggested that the movement exhibited a strong inclination to conspiratorial thinking. They have cited, in support, Donnelly's utterances about "vast combinations," the frequent appearance of "Wall Street" in Populist writings, and other euphemisms which might be taken to designate ruling groups. (While Weaver has been seen only as a misplaced Jacksonian, if more industrious research had uncovered his use of "corporate power," this no doubt would also have qualified as conspiratorial thinking.) Today the reasons for resisting this interpretation seem even sounder than earlier, when controversy depended essentially on counting the number of symbols employed rather than searching beneath the movement's surface expression. While symbols can reveal underlying content, it has not been demonstrated that Populist symbols, including such examples as "shylock" and "money power," were surcharged with dangerous referents. Nor has it been shown that these symbols inspired Populists to persecute others or substituted for hard analysis. Indeed, they were by no means as conspicuous as the undoubted democratic symbolism representing human liberties and political concepts ascribed to the Constitution, such as public duty, impartial justice, and a general-welfare creed. The Constitution was itself a preeminent symbol.

Historians have failed to take the measure of Populism; they have not looked beyond the movement's organization and political demands to its foundations, where the practical development of political consciousness began. Here the vein of conspiratorial thought was lacking. This mode of thought was contrary to the Populist spirit, taken not as an abstraction, but as the principle of the movement's growth, its slow progression upward, in which sustained discussion was essential to political education. The basis of Populism's ideological growth, and the means by which individual Populists came to identify themselves, was in making specific the structure of power. Populism sought to combat vagueness. This helps to explain Peffer's statistics, Weaver's extensive case studies, the detailed editorials in literally hundreds of agrarian newspapers, the interminable speeches, three and four hours long, built on the body of information patiently gathered and circulated, and not least, the platform drafting, from county conventions and suballiance meetings to the national gatherings.

For Populists, this renaissance of popular understanding was a living assertion of citizenry. For purposes of making it better, they wanted to comprehend the framework of society. Despite the provocations offered, their goal was not to rend, but to prevent the rending of, the social fabric. The act of focusing had an ideological significance; the passion for specificity was related to the more expected passionate entry into the political fight. By naming names (as when Marion Butler discussed the policies of Western Union in his call for the public ownership of the telegraph), describing specific existing practices, and analyzing patterns of income distribution, Populists indicated their desire to establish a structural closeness and relevancy to America. There was to be a selective correction of abusive practices in order to conserve the remainder of society.

The exactitude of Populism's economic and political design carried the movement beyond the customary boundaries of reform. This was largely due to the confidence that Populists gained from having isolated with some precision the sectors to be altered, and in having partly revealed the anatomy of political and economic dominance. In both cases, they were able to counter the sense of hopelessness which would have resulted from confronting a nameless, self-generative system of power, necessitating in turn a revolution. Yet this affirmative trait also served to ensure that the movement would remain within a reformist context. It was not that exactitude per se logically implied a circumscribed form of ac-

tion, but that Populist exactitude, however critical it was to animating protest, was predicated on the retention of what Populists
considered permanent, sound, and historically democratic. For all
his dire warnings, Donnelly finally pleaded for political and social
reconciliation; his message was preventive as well as restorative:
"Believing, as I do, that I read the future aright, it would be criminal in me to remain silent. I plead for higher and nobler thoughts
in the souls of men; for wider love and ampler charity in their
hearts; for a renewal of the bond of brotherhood between the
classes; for a reign of justice on earth that shall obliterate the cruel
hates and passions which now divide the world."[34] A primitive
Christianity informed the vision. It depended for its efficacy, however, on a mutual forbearance; the social bond would overcome
the forces of class warfare.

The earlier debates negligently focused on Populists' use of
symbols, and in fact only those believed to contain a conspiratorial
element. But a further, if unintended, limitation was to focus only
on Populism's response which pointed upward—to ruling circles, thus removing from consideration the other half of the
movement's potential experience. This is a common failing in the
analysis of popular forces. Whether historians view these forces as
radical, progressive, and democratic, or in the case of critics of
Populism, as the retrogressive and irrational protest of expectant
capitalists, the difficulty in conceiving of a response extending
downward is apparent. It is as though protest by definition cannot
also be mounted at the expense of, or directed equally against,
groups at the bottom of society. I raise the point only as a theoretical possibility for Populism because it did not in fact mount such
a protest. Rather, there must be an opening of the Populist perspective in a downward direction before I attempt a further
clarification.

The advocates of a conspiracy theory, because they confined
their attention to the Populists' response to upper groups, did not
think to look at their response to other groups; or, in strict terms,
looking at all of society would have been to acknowledge in principle the existence of widespread discontent, outside the political
process, in a presumably consensus-oriented framework. The
scholarly criticism was ambivalent: Populism had to be viewed as
a mainstream movement, however disparaged its democratic repu-

tation, in order to leave intact the preconceived historical pattern of which it formed a part. Populism was represented as a misguided reformism that, because it was so thoroughly committed to capitalism, was still dimly respectable. It could not be radical, but neither, by the same reasoning, could anybody else. Once the perspective is enlarged, it becomes clear that Populists did not adopt a conspiratorial view of the lowest social groups.

Yet a search of this kind would not be fruitless, because greater precision about this issue is essential to understanding Populism's reformist limitations. It is one of several factors, once Populists' anticorporate credentials are also established, that has to be included in the discussion. An opposition to monopolism, however, is not sufficient, for one wants to know the shadings of this opposition; there needs to be a sense of the changes they contemplated, how far these changes were intended to proceed, and to what end. Populists' exactitude, finely calibrated in delineating the face of upper capital, all but disappeared when they shifted to lower groups. This vagueness demands our notice. There are three basic points to be made.

Populists did not seek to persecute those below them and in fact did not know who specifically composed the lowest stratum or even whether it had yet come into existence. What they perceived was that the presence of undisciplined masses in society would create social demoralization. Their own conception of democracy in this context was associated not with the Lockean exclusion of the poor but with the element of hope. Their one tendency toward conspiratorial thinking, beyond their general concern with upheaval, arose from the need for some method, unplanned at this deeper level, to differentiate themselves from potentially disintegrative or amorphous social forces. This need had little to do with whether or not revolution seemed imminent, strong as would be their opposition to revolutionary violence on ideological and political grounds. Rather, they viewed any violent process of change as premonishing tides of nihilism and uncontrollable wrath to which there would be no adequate opposition. In addition, this violence would undermine Populism's reason for existence, because the belief on which its cohesion and self-esteem was founded was that it could determine where actions were meaningful and that they would be. Yet more than prestige was involved.

Populists' need to differentiate themselves from nihilistic forces was based on their projection of what was nowhere evidenced in reality: unsettled conditions, nearing the flash point of horrendous destruction. While capitalist elites bore final as well as proximate responsibility for these conditions, their record was known, their actions were predictable, and hence they did not pose, for Populists, an indeterminate threat. For the same reason, they did not pose an immediate threat. When Donnelly spoke of the contemplated havoc, he conjured up a numerically large nether world, and all reference to the justice of the case was summarily dropped. Even for Weaver, who never descended below a realistic plane, "wealth owners" and "wealth producers" were equally party to the strained relations, ripening into disaster. Donnelly, when he mentioned "great communistic organizations," envisioned a specific form of social disorder, in which the victims organized, resisted, and presumably were driven by a desire for retribution. Viewed from the standpoint of the Left, the imagery that had negative meaning for Donnelly would take on positive value because it would represent the nonsubmissive response of the lowest social groups. But this does not confirm Populism's reformist dimension. Instead, it suggests how basically unsympathetic Populists were to self-protective measures, whether or not extraconstitutional, that could entail a rectification of social injustice through the unmediated action of the lower classes. For such action would bypass not only the political process, and the movement itself, but also what both of these were meant to convey: the still retrievable framework of democratic government. If the social system were attacked, it was self-evident that the framework would not survive.

Second, Populists found themselves in an ideological predicament. They clearly recognized oppression and the oppressed, and when not invoking notions of a social polarization, they numbered themselves emphatically among the unfortunate. Most of the time, when they focused on their program, a problem did not arise. Yet even then, their emphasis on hope for constructive change revealed secondary misgivings because of the strength of business opposition. The whole question of unstable masses was related to the need to bolster their courage. Hope became obligatory to stave off the collapse of Populism. The distinction that Populists raised between themselves and the amorphous masses was a helpful mechanism by which to resolve, if not the matter of overwhelming power, then at least that of Populism's rightful association with America. This attitude recalls their basic need for political legitimation, for ties with America reflected an assurance that there was a line below which Populists could not sink, in political and psychological if not also economic terms. Because their affirmation was edged with a thin border of doubt, Populists required evidence of belonging and of sharing, even indistinctly, in the flow of power.

It appears that the idea of a rock-bottom stratum of society, although it was nebulously conceived, was a necessary support but not for reasons of programmatic exclusion or to gain a social advantage over the dispossessed classes through making them scapegoats. This search for scapegoats especially is a true instance of conspiratorial thinking that is focused on lower social groups; it was present in Germany and in the dynamics of racism generally. But this kind of thinking would have been a repudiation of the Populists' vision of political and economic democracy, and a violation of their principle of an inclusive membership, recruited from the ranks of the hard-pressed. Instead, Populists constructed this foil to certify and enable them to attest to each other all of the movement's distinctive characteristics. These characteristics could be summarized as the disciplined striving within a framework that was both capitalistic and American for limited, if still basic, structural alterations. Their primary intent was to democratize the internal make-up of the business system, remove its powers over public policy, and end its ideological hegemony in defining the polity's values and systemic course; only derivatively were the proposed alterations designed to prevent social conflict. Such conflict, Populists feared, throve on the yet unmodified dominance of capital in the complete range of political and social relations. Although the construction of a rock-bottom social stratum was not entirely harmless, because it was indicative of psychological strains, the traits of disciplined striving were principally a sign of the restorative nature of the Populists' conception of America, their mission, and the work to be done. Social change became for them the imperative political means to arrest monopolism. The end to monopolism would in turn free orderly processes already present in the national heritage; there would be a more equalitarian interpretation of constitutional rights, economic opportunity, and the social obligations of government.

I mean, then, by "ideological predicament" the Populists' inability to confront oppression frankly without invoking external factors. They saw that oppression and the oppressed were intermixed. Yet because they found unmodulated change that went beyond their own framework to be unacceptable, the tendency was to refrain from a full condemnation of oppression, at least more so than when the perception of a social crisis did not govern their thinking. The crosscurrents within Populism, between hope and doubt, oppression and oppressed, did not permit Populists to view the existing social misery positively, as an actual or potential class force. Nor were they inclined to render oppression so explicitly systemic that the sources of danger would receive less evenhanded treatment, and responsibility would have been ascribed mainly to dominant groups. Social goals and political criticisms alike were blunted by filial piety toward America.

If the assault on oppression had required an unqualified embracement of the oppressed, Populists would probably have wanted to narrow their range of action. It was not a case of their accepting poverty, but of their fearing social breakdown. This fear of anarchic conditions gave to their projection of class strife the effect of a safety valve and suggested a certifying of another kind: not simply Populism's self-affirmation, but America's possibilities when free to liberate its orderly processes. In essence, America could not be allowed to deteriorate to the point where social forces that were *not* already present could come into existence. The result was a tidy prefigurement of democratization in which the energies of upheaval not only could not be harnessed but also had to be sanitized and placed within the movement's confines. In political terms, Populism's mission implied a claim to be the democratic protagonist guiding the emergent forces of reform.

Third, the striking point about the rationale for protest was not the forecast of a class struggle, a seemingly radical element in Populist discourse, but the meaning that was placed on the necessary response to this forecast, what Weaver referred to as removing the causes of discontent. The hope for change was successively qualified: First, there was all too human concern over apparently insurmountable power; then, the belief arose that mass action might destroy the social order, of which democracy was an essential part; finally, the unstable masses were used as a contrast to confirm Populists' close relationship to America. Throughout the portrayal of crisis, the reason for removing the causes of discontent was to stabilize a democratized form of capitalism.

Populism, in its desire to avert an impending conflict, performed a mediative role in society. It marked the political culmination of an age of protest. While its own ideological development had been hastened by the precedent period of social turmoil, it nevertheless sought less to extend than to clarify, and in the process to moderate or to contain, the forces of discord. Despite the changes it proposed, its emphasis on a peaceful resolution of basic problems was singularly conservative, seeking to contain, after culminating, protest at an acceptable level. Here, veneration for the law, predicated on the polity's soundness, is best read as a forthright nonrevolutionary position.

Populism's mediative role was not that of a buffer between the business community and the laboring poor, a function that would have preserved unequal shares of power; rather, it involved a grander strategy, based on the principle that a just polity would not have extremes. Like Peffer, who advanced the notion of the worthiness of labor, Populists sought a modernizing alternative which would be built on the industrious men of middling ranks. This course would steer between the intransigence of contemporary industry and social revolution, and obviate a resort to the solutions of either one. When Populists posited a middle-class standard, they, with the possible exception of Watson, did not have in mind the present-day concept of classless plenitude. Instead, the whole of society had to be reconstituted along lines that would retain property while severing the power that derived from organized capital. A people's government concretely embodied the mediative role. It would be empowered to realize more lasting values, centered not on property as such, but on a decent competence, humane conditions of work, and individual security. Populists' aversion to social crisis indicated a strong attachment to the

American institutional framework. Populism's love affair with America is my implicit theme in much that follows.

4. Law and the Republic

Returning to Weaver, one is struck by the tension within his essentially moderate position. Law was sacrosanct, but it was also peculiarly vulnerable to outside depredation. This suggested to Weaver and other Populists a last line of defense, but their "legalist faith" was hardly a statement of acquiescence. We note a paradox here. What appeared radical, particularly the language of struggle, was at bottom conservative in its restorative intent and its premise that the structure of society was sound. By contrast, what seemed and *was* highly conservative, the general veneration for law, actually proved a stimulus to Populism's comparatively more radical features. First, there was the determined cast to protest, founded on a sense of fundamental rightness; and second, as its substantive accompaniment, there was the heightened attention given to corporate power chiefly responsible in Populist thinking for undermining the nation's legal foundations. The duality of veneration and struggle was but another within the movement. These elements figured prominently in the remainder of Weaver's analysis.

After commenting that the Court must be returned to "the pedestal of the Constitution," he traced the circumstances of the Stanley Matthews appointment a decade earlier: Matthews's nomination had lapsed under one president, had been resuscitated by another, and finally had been rammed through the Senate by one vote. Weaver added that "This is a representative case, and it affords the reader a clear view of the influences which shape and control the most important affairs of our Republic." He was emphatic about the existing imbalance: "It is clear that there is some power in this country which is above the Government and more authoritative than public opinion, and which can exert itself successfully at critical moments in high places. A child can tell what that power is." If any single criticism, for Populists, was beyond refutation, it was this one. "It is the omnipresent, omnipotent corporation." Again he presented the slaveholder qua ruling-group analogy: "It is the same old malevolent, insidious influence of organized oligarchy—of plutocratic power—and it is now asserting itself for the second time within the memory of the present generation."[35]

Yet more important to Weaver was the normalization of private power which occurred under the aegis of a compliant government. His thesis was that spoliation was regularized. More precisely than before, he discussed the nature of business-government ties. He described not a takeover of government by business, but an evolving similarity of purpose. The context in which business privilege was likened to criminality implied usurpation, extending to state conduct as well: "The pirate plunders by violence. The burglar enters your house prepared to take life if he cannot otherwise escape. But the corporation plunders by the permission or through the agency of the State, and to cut off all hope of redress they seize upon the courts, which constitute the only hope and refuge of an oppressed people this side of revolution."[36]

The phrase "through the agency" conveyed more than simple favoritism by the state. A structural connection had been made; the state was legitimating, and lengthening the reach of, corporate activity. Still more germane, "this side of revolution" fairly jumps from the page. These words encapsulated the burden of the preceding discussion. Cumulative discontent had found no outlet; respect for the law was the only basis of a peaceful resolution. Including the corporation within the operation of the law would confirm this respect.

Weaver was as concerned about the silent operation of corporate power as about its permeation of society. He stated further: "[T]he people seem to be unmindful of everything pertaining to their welfare, and they suffer uncomplainingly until peaceful redress becomes well nigh impossible."[37] He later expanded this observation to indicate the sweeping dimensions of private influence. Weaver's contention was not that the corporation worked outside the polity, confronting it, or locked in combat with the public. Instead, the corporation was already at the center of the polity, and it was coming to define America's institutional life.

Thus, he elaborated this additional concern: "Slavery was restricted within narrow geographical limits and the visible manifestations of the evil were repulsive and hateful to all who were removed from its immediate influence. Not so with the present foe of justice and social order. It assails the rights of man under the most seductive guise." Corporate influence reflected not suppressed attraction, but overwhelming dominance; this itemization of control suggested the possible means for obliterating the memory of fundamental rights:

You meet it in every walk of life. It speaks through the press, gives zeal and eloquence to the bar, engrosses the constant attention of the bench, organizes the influences which surround our legislative bodies and courts of justice, designates who shall be the Regents and Chancellors in our leading Universities, determines who shall be our Senators, how our legislatures shall be organized, who shall preside over them and who constitute the important committees. It is imperial in political caucuses, without a rival in social circles, endows institutions of learning, disburses monthly large sums of money to an army of employés, has unlimited resources of ready cash, is expert in political intrigue and pervades every community from the center to the circumference of the Republic.[38]

These denotative words, especially because they referred to consequential areas, provided a compelling delineation of monolithic power. For Weaver, as evidenced in the recurrent use of "Republic," the nation itself was threatened.

Beyond that threat lay the destruction of the individual: "For a full quarter of a century the individual, as such, has been lost sight of in a mad rush for corporate adventure." He continued: "The corporation and the wealth which it brings have become the chief concern of society and the State." Business predominated over public and individual rights, and this imbalance had a deeper significance. The legal structure, in its contemporaneous workings, sanctioned corporate ascendance as a systemic process. The concern with the individual did not harken back to an agrarian past, but rooted the discussion in a capitalistic present: "The man and the family have been driven to the wall, the weak trampled under foot and the choicest opportunities of the century showered upon chartered combinations. Wealth, already possessing great advantages, is not satisfied, and incorporates in order that it may have still greater power." Legal privilege suggested a broader organizational matrix, not only multiplying the possibilities of enrichment but also weakening the defenses of the poor. There was cohesion in the dominant groups and fragmentation of the lower classes which left the poor isolated in living according to traditional beliefs: "Every class of business, every calling, everything except poverty, operates under a charter. The poor must defend themselves as best they can, single-handed and alone. Competition and personal responsibility, except with the remaining multitude of the poor, are literally and absolutely annihilated by these monstrous combinations."[39]

Weaver then documented concrete instances of "corporate rapacity." The economic landscape was so strewn with human wreckage that he was moved to say: "One scarcely knows where to begin the story, and having once begun, it seems like mis-prison of a felony to withhold a single fact from an outraged public. But the field is illimitable and the desolation indescribable." There followed examples of starvation, lockouts, Pinkerton intervention. Invariably, the holdings were large, the policies were coordinated, and the display of force was merciless. This was notably the case at Spring Valley, Illinois, in the late 1880s. The struggle at Spring Valley was the subject of a well-documented book by Henry Demarest Lloyd, which Weaver termed "the Iliad of the battle now raging between man and the corporation in America."[40]

Weaver's conclusion, under the heading "Strike Now!", was emphatically affirmative: "We have challenged the adversary to battle and our bugles have sounded the march. If we now seek to evade or shrink from the conflict it will amount to a confession of cowardice and a renunciation of the faith. Let us make the year 1892 memorable for all time to come as the period when the great battle for industrial emancipation was fought and won in the United States." The content of this passage is more instructive than its spirit. Weaver's social vision extended to the future. Industrial emancipation signified the freedom still to be attained, and it was conceived by Populists as their especial burden: "It is glorious to live in this age, and to be permitted to take part in this heroic combat is the greatest honor that can be conferred upon mortals." Appropriately, he closed on the clarion note of mission. The burden was willingly, perhaps even joyously, accepted, because of its momentous consequences for the growth of human liberties. Until nearly the end, this sentiment was the distilled irreducible source of Populist optimism in an otherwise pessimistic setting: "Throughout all history we have had ample evidence that the new world is the theater upon which the great struggle for the rights of man is to be made, and the righteous movement now in progress should again forcibly remind us of our enviable mission, under Providence, among the nations of the earth."[41]

CHAPTER THREE

Public Rights and Individual
Liberties: Morgan and Davis

Populists considered it to be axiomatic that sufficiently aggregated private holdings constituted a system of power which
menaced the foundations of a democratic society. This power had
to be countered by a superseding governmental authority whose
sovereign prerogative extended to the reorganization of economic
life. Although Populists favored competition, they advocated nonmonopolistic relations in which market control no longer obtained and business enterprise was denied inordinate access to the
state. Populists directly sanctioned the property right; yet there
were adumbrations in their conception of property that suggested
a unique capitalist formation. This formation was opposed to an
unmodified laissez-faire structure, because laissez-faire failed to
provide adequately for the collective thrust of an autonomous
state-framework. It was equally opposed to contemporary capitalism, because of *its* more serious deficiencies. Systemic abuses
within capitalism created stagnation and poverty, while conferring
on private ownership real and informal powers of domination
over the populace and government alike.

1. Competition and Community

To provide a regional balance, I now turn to the works of two
southern Populists. The first, W. Scott Morgan's *History of the
Wheel and Alliance, and the Impending Revolution* (1889), displays,
contrary to the agitational promise of its title, the spirit of an oppressed lesser bourgeoisie. It exemplified that curious blend,
within Populism, of antimonopolism and entrepreneurial liberation that one associates with the most progressive phase of the

English middle-class ascent. Morgan himself was aware that the theories of Adam Smith had to be qualified, given the apparent similarity of the Populist and Smithian structures. More important, entrepreneurship, if assigned different emphases within Populism, was never a negligible factor. It in fact energized the movement's more collectivist features. Thus, the foregoing association with the English case is only partially correct. For Populists, with Morgan an excellent illustration, made such liberation contingent on widespread changes in the contemporary (and in the Smithian) order that affected the structure of capitalism. One again finds the conservative-radical paradox. It depends for its solution on the way that property, while confirming the movement's reform dimensions, had been put to more democratic ends. Property was not a goal in its own right.

Early on, Morgan was among the more ideologically advanced southern Populists. He was a politically active, well-informed editor from Hardy, Arkansas, who had a following in the Southwest. Internal evidence suggests a tendency to racial moderation. Additionally, Morgan performed yeoman service in helping to organize the National Reform Press Association, which was a key educational mechanism for upgrading and unifying Populist discussion across state and regional lines. Indeed, to read him is to forget his origins: more western than southern, more national than both, even if also, unlike Peffer and Weaver, predominantly agricultural.

Morgan treated the question of monopoly specifically in relation to the farmer. The cadences of his Donnelly-like indictment were closer to the pulse of his constituency than other statements we have examined:

The agricultural masses, the most numerous and important of any class of people forming the great body of the republic, and whose interests are identical, are kept divided upon the great issues which affect their welfare. They are robbed by an infamous system of finance; they are plundered by transportation companies; they are imposed upon by an unjust system of tariff laws; they are deprived of their lands and other property by an iniquitous system of usury; they are fleeced by the exorbitant exactions of numerous trusts; they are preyed upon by the merchants, imposed upon by the lawyers, misled by the politician and seem to be regarded as the legitimate prey of all other classes. Monopoly names the price of what they have to sell, and charges them what it pleases for what they are compelled to buy.[1]

At every point of contact with capitalism there was a sense of being victimized. But this was not an appeal to an injured folk; it was a bill of particulars addressed to systemic operations. Morgan portrayed a closed market economy that had been realized through the pervasiveness of monopolistic power. The result was harmful to the agrarian sector.

"The farmer," he continued, "may hold his crop in vain, for when he does put it on the market he finds that the same manipulators govern and fix the price of his products." Basic capitalist structure was supposed throughout; restrictions on economic activity were not. He succinctly noted: "Individual effort is fruitless. The relentless, remorseless and unyielding grasp of monopoly is upon every avenue of trade and commerce." The situation was likened to the criminality and arbitrary force of an earlier period: "Extortion is demanded with an audacity that was never surpassed by the Dick Turpins or Jack Ketches of English highways. They lay tribute with as much authority as the vassal lords and princes of feudal times. If they are asked what right they have to do this, their answer would be the same as the highwayman's: 'Because we can. It is a private affair of our own.' "[2] The feudal comparison, often found in Populist sources, became economic shorthand for the rigidity and degree of restraint that was attendant on the concentration of wealth. Equally pertinent was the stress on lawlessness—or more precisely, on the insufficiency of prevailing law to furnish impartial protection.

First he observed: "The organization of farmers is the outgrowth of an invasion of their natural rights." While economic disadvantage has political ramifications, so that it would not do to interpret "natural rights" too narrowly, one nonetheless is struck by the intended entrepreneurial construction. Morgan had asked shortly before, "when these modern barons are levying tribute on everything the farmer sells and all that he buys, is it to be wondered at, that the law of self-preservation is forcing him to unite with his fellow sufferers to repel these encroachments upon his rights?"[3] In Morgan's context, the concept of "rights" turned on transactions in the marketplace; his message possibly contained the same unintended coding that one gathers from the more ingenuous literature of the American Revolution from which Morgan occasionally drew inspiration.

The foregoing does not vitiate his statement on law; rather it helps us to see its import: "The root of the evil lay in the laws. Monopolies exist by law, are chartered by law, and should be controlled by law." Law was impartial and encompassing in scope. Moreover, it testified to a prior sovereignty. Still, in almost Wilsonian fashion, Morgan (and he is by no means an exception) could tacitly link trade and welfare: "A trust is a conspiracy against legitimate trade. It is against the interests of the people and the welfare of the public."[4] What furnished the practical exemption from later Wilsonianism was the latent radicalism in bringing the small-entrepreneur vision to fruition in a monopolistic world. Morgan not only represents the anticorporate bias of Populism but also provides the typical strictures on a legal framework which failed to administer effectively what it summoned into existence. Virtually all Populists who spoke on the matter argued that the power to charter necessarily carried the powers to revoke and to supervise, to force conformance with public objectives.

Morgan's extension of his analysis from the economic to the political realm (however rooted in implicit assumptions such as the propertied basis of freedom) did not stretch the argument to the breaking point. Entrepreneurial rights notwithstanding, there remained an anterior community interest which resided in, and was expressed by, government. Taking aim at the trust, Morgan made the extension without interruption: "It is demoralizing in its influence, inconsistent with free institutions and dangerous to our liberties. To participate in a trust should be a crime subject to severe punishment. Trust is only another name for monopoly." He decisively concluded: "Monopoly is wielding a greater power in the government than the people." As Morgan's own variation on the theme of the imbalance between private and public spheres, this reasoning permitted, and for Populists justified, complete attention to liberties as such. Barely started with the analysis, he had already joined Weaver on the mission barricades: "The independent manhood of the country is rising up in defense of its liberties. An army of oppressed producers are organizing for victory. They are marshalling their hosts on the hilltops of freedom." But the words hardly suggested a violent overthrow: "Let us fondly hope that their mission may be accomplished, and peace, prosperity and happiness may be the inheritance which they bequeath to future generations."[5]

Morgan now reapproached more systematically a statement of grievances, beginning from the seemingly unambiguous ground of producer values: "The natural law of labor is, that the laborer is entitled to all the fruits of his toil. There is no variation to this rule. It is fixed upon the universal law of nature, and any infringement upon it is not only repugnant to the laborer but is dangerous to the welfare of the State." Few within Populism would have denied this assertion or the place accorded it. It took on a natural-law complexion from which basic political and economic deductions might follow. This represented the moral/economic fusion that I have noted throughout the discussion, leading to the principles of just governance. Peffer's notion of the laborer's worthiness was of the same character. Yet, as with Peffer, Morgan's was not a puristic labor theory of value. He clouded at its source the scope and critical force of whatever deductions his theory could have elicited. Labor, if antecedent to capital, must also make way for capital's presumed contribution. Also, the term "fruits" has a Lockean ring. Entitlement was as much concerned with freedom of opportunity as with fair remuneration of labor-power for the wealth it creates. Qualifications followed immediately upon this statement: "There is, however, a difficulty arising in the application of the rule where labor becomes mixed with other forms of capital, such as material, machinery, etc. To properly and equitably eliminate it and fix a just reward for the laborer, is a problem that should commend itself to all who would reach the bottom of the 'labor question.' "[6] Since "there is no variation to this rule," one assumes that its application opens the door to the full set of capitalist social relations, though modified in this singular respect: that capital must not be allowed undisputed control, whether over society or its workforce. The foregoing affords us a proximate sense of Populist economic outlines: The basic acceptance of capitalism was qualified by the attempt to mitigate its harshness and to reground its foundations in order to permit competitive practices. There would be a transformation of the existing economy, to render it compatible with a democratic political order.

Preserving the rule, while allowing for other factors in production, required a new and attenuated formulation: "The true principle, and one that would forever settle strikes, riots and all differences between labor and capital, is, that the laborer should be rewarded according to that that he does, and not according to what the employer can get the labor performed for."[7] This fit nicely with the sense of mitigating harshness. It implicitly called for checks on capital's absolutist power to cheapen labor. One might also infer a provision for unionism and for the right to look to the state for protection (both of which Morgan included at a later point). Yet, stated baldly, reward for "that that he does" introduced a relative scale that made labor-power only one among several productive factors and production costs. In weakening labor's separable identity, it denied the moral basis of labor as the primal factor in organizing the structure of the political economy.

Morgan's defense of the narrowing of principle, the appeal to self-evident grounds, was feeble. No defense became necessary when all already agreed that capitalism, as a system, could be placed within the terms of a labor theory of value. He continued: "We are aware of the fact that when we make this remark we are treading on debatable ground, but if it is necessary, in order to sustain our position, we can fall back upon that universal natural law, 'The laborer is entitled to all the fruits of his toil.'" No duplicity was intended. He sought to place restrictions on capitalism in order to facilitate its more equitable functioning. He combined this goal, which was, at bottom, the system's retention, with assurances that in no other way might grievances be corrected and social violence prevented. The alternative was brute force: "A universal violation of this rule would culminate in the adoption of the barbaric one that 'might makes right,' and the weak would be compelled to succumb to the strong."[8] The Hobbesian reminder could theoretically be the basis for announcing a clear departure, a full-scale democratization, where, in the coalescence of sovereign power, strong and weak would be eliminated as meaningful categories. Instead, under the sway of Lockean principles, Morgan opted to maintain settled arrangements, save, importantly, that might must no longer confer a presumption of rightness. It was to be replaced by the rule of law.

Morgan pursued this second point quite far. Like Weaver, he tied a capitalist transformation to a pride in, and the need for,

Populist nonviolence and the pacific settlement of disputes. In the process, the American Revolution became the inspiration for opposition to revolutionary action: "For certain reasons which we have neither time nor space to discuss here, men are better than the laws they live under. If we are asked why, we simply reply it has always been, and for certain physiological and moral reasons, will ever be so. Were it not a fact, the selfishness of those who have unjustly, though legally, acquired capital in our own country, coming in contact with the interests of, and robbing labor of its profits, would have ere this produced a revolution. But a spirit of forbearance born of the fathers of the Revolution, and an instinctive dread of the horrors of war have often averted such a catastrophe."[9]

One sympathizes with Morgan's attempt again to plead self-evident grounds for the argument, because in fact it was necessary to explain *two* interrelated and seemingly insoluble problems. First, there was the matter of an acquiescent stance. This problem was obliquely faced even this early (1889), before an organized political movement had taken form, but when provocation was perhaps as great as later. While the solution appeared to consist in the praising of forbearance, his ranking of men above "the laws they live under" was more than a convenience to that end. Also because Morgan was forced to sanction capitalism under natural law, he had to confront the second problem, the conflict between law and justice. He therefore made a careful distinction concerning capital accumulation; wealth has been in practice acquired unjustly, if legally.

Morgan's constraints were complex, because, in his analysis, wealth remained unimpeachable from the standpoint of law and still could not excite rebellion; the only serviceable criterion was the one he provided: a condemnatory standard of justice. If nonenforceable, it yet exhorted to right conduct, which would ultimately elevate law to the same plane as human capabilities. The common element was the legal hedgerow enclosing capitalism and the threat of upheaval looming in the background. Morgan was more openly critical of law per se than the previous writers we have noted. Yet he was driven to adopt the overriding Populist conclusion, that the social temple could not be shaken from its foundation. Natural law perhaps now stood for law itself. If law

and justice had not been in opposition to each other, verbal eva-
sions would have been unnecessary. The more striking point, of
course, is that either way forbearance was a positive or even
categorical virtue.

This position did not preclude a strongly felt antimonopolist
militance. Concern over disturbance was present. The burden,
however, was on those who refused to concede the existence of a
problem—one that Morgan, like other Populists, saw as a world
phenomenon, marked by the advent of industrialism: "But he who
closes his eyes to the fact that the world is approaching a crisis
without a parallel, in some respects, in all its past history, must be
either influenced by a spirit of selfishness which has characterized
tyrants of all ages, or densely ignorant of the ominous import of
such widespread dissatisfaction among the producing classes
throughout the world. The fires of discontent are burning on both
continents." There was no ambivalence toward labor: "Where the
freedom of speech is denied the foundation of governments are
honey-combed with secret societies," and where permitted, "labor
organizations under various names, but all having the same
object—self-protection—in view, are springing into existence."
This growth, he added, had no parallel. Yet, as the phrase "ominous import" suggests, uneasiness remained over the failure to
resolve discontent: "To assume that there is no just cause for all
this uprising on the part of labor would be equivalent to courting
national suicide."[10]

Morgan's brief excursion into theory, motivated in part by a
perceived crisis, led him to clarify in a major way the different levels of competition which Populist economics had to address.
There was obvious significance, if not in the effort, then in the
recognition that it should be made. Had Populists honored competition, as some of their statements indicated, and let the matter
rest at that, no basis would have remained for distinguishing their
own from what became the dominant construction (and ideological linchpin) of the age. The latter was a rationale for continued
business consolidation. This construction, simply by inverting
meanings, served to blur critical discussion. Louis Hartz has
described its counterpart in political thought by the epigraph, "the
Whig discovery of America," which suggests that conservatives
had appropriated highly charged democratic symbols.[11] On the

level of political education, the general climate presented an obstacle to developing a *selective,* reformist critique in which the retention of capitalism did not need to preclude its alteration. Unless the differentiation of meanings was sought, Populists were semantically disarmed. Given the ideological saturation, the setting merely compounded the broader problem of extrication from cultural attachments.

The tightly integrated character of contemporary ideology was particularly important. This meant that Populists had to contend against a predefined formulation of capitalism in which the choice was reduced to total dismemberment of the capitalist structure or abject capitulation to it. To the degree that competition had assumed ideological, indeed mythic, proportions, it was mandatory for Populists to demonstrate its lack of correspondence with reality. Even more basic, they had to establish a foothold within the seeming monolith. They had to invest the central notion of competition with a specificity of their own. In this way, it would be possible to work outward toward elucidating key concepts—property, government, capitalism itself—which had been used to keep an entire generation in line.

Their reexamination never completely shattered the reductionist dilemma posed by the dominant ideology. Capitulation to the contemporary system was repudiated. But the suspicion still lurked, so difficult was the struggle against a pervasively sanctioned political-economic symbolism, that change might question more of society than they intended. Possibly worse, it might flow into, and quicken, the primordial currents of dissatisfaction from which they sought escape. Nor was the more pressing task accomplished for inaugurating their own departure. They had not substituted for the present mode their own full conceptualization of the political economy; their concepts still depended upon prevailing usages. If their modifications were confined within capitalism, Populists also utilized constituent parts or categories integral to the system's development. Nothing (except for monopoly) was scrapped; everything had to be made better. And yet "making better," the achievement of democratization from within, was both intellectually and politically trying, when the opposition retained command of the state apparatus, economic processes, and the mechanisms of repression.

Morgan observed: "Some will contend that competition will correct all inequalities arising in the various conditions of labor."[12] Whatever the shortcomings of their critique—hardly that, given the movement's reformist nature—their attempts at clarification suggested that Populists had attained a certain distance from both mythology and contemporary practices. Not surprisingly, Morgan, when looking at the corrective powers attributed to competition, made direct reference to Adam Smith. Not only did Smithian elements form a sturdy component of the general political culture, but also Populists, certainly within the leadership, revealed a reasonably high degree of literacy. They were acquainted with the standard political literature and, as a group, may have surpassed their major parties' counterpart in their motivation to learn and in the successful weaving of texts into their arguments. Unlike the practitioners of spread-eagle politics, Populists had no incentive to obscure the discussion of issues.

Speaking, then, of competition, Morgan took a basic passage as his point of departure: "Adam Smith says, 'it is the great regulator of industrial action. It is beneficent, just and equalizing. In the market of the world it is what gravitation is in the mechanism of the heavens, an all-combining and balancing and beneficent law. Any invasion of this principle is contrary to the law of nature and of sound political economy.' " Significantly, Morgan did not quarrel with the sentiment as an economically desirable goal. Rather, he demurred on the consistency of application. He sensed that a major deficiency from the standpoint of Populism was that competition historically had not been able to maintain its own equilibrium, culminating instead in further concentration of wealth. While it may have yielded salutary results in the market, other areas remained unaffected. Labor-capital relations became exacerbated to the detriment of working people. In commenting on the passage from Adam Smith, he discriminated between the attractiveness of international free trade and the domestic failure to achieve a balance through practical implementation. Capitalistic operations exhibited little of the flexibility Adam Smith had counted on:

This might perhaps be true if we had, or it were possible to have, like competition in all things; and while it will apply to the markets of the world in the sale of the products of labor there are various conditions in the sphere of expenditure of wages which it cannot affect; and as to the things which might be affected by it, it is injurious or has a trick of failing at the moment something is expected of it. Taxes, to which every man owning property is liable, is not affected by competition. . . . Rents are practically unaffected by it, as also a number of other things to which the laborer is subject and over which competition exerts no influence. Competition in wages, when based upon necessity, is decidedly injurious and signifies an unhealthy condition of the industrial interests of the country.[13]

Though rent and taxes are perhaps niggling matters when one is taking the measure of a laissez-faire framework, Morgan's more incisive point was the partial and differential nature of the principle's impact: It neither organized the totality of relations, nor produced an impartial and uniform result across class lines. Thus, the salient criticism: "Competition in commerce, trade and transportation fails 'at the moment something is expected of it,' because it leads to combination." And Morgan added: "In proof of this theory we have only to point to the numerous trusts that have sprung up in our country within the past ten years, and to the consolidation of numerous railroad companies." This was not a complete break from Adam Smith; it was the playing off of an idealized aspect of the framework in opposition to systemic realities. "In the latter part of Dr. Smith's proposition, however, we most heartily concur; 'Any invasion of this principle (competition) is contrary to the law of nature and of sound political economy.' "[14]

This represented a plateau from which more advanced probes could be ventured. As an emendation to the preceding discussion, Morgan stated that "the violation of this principle is one among the many causes which are responsible for the present condition of American labor."[15] Though calling for a more resilient mechanism, in the name of capitalism, he did not dodge the class implications of labor's condition: "Competition is killed by combination, and the laws of trade are perverted to the end that the few are enabled to enrich themselves at the expense of the many." Populists subsequently radicalized this early commentary on Smithian principles (1889), abandoning faith in automatic market forces for stringent governmental action. Yet the larger outlines were kept remarkably intact. There was a continued dedication to idealized competition. But more, one notes a consequent tunneling inward in which the absence of combination became an adequate bridge to the renewal of support for capitalistic society. Implied in Morgan's statement was the sigh: "If only the laws of trade were no longer perverted!" The next step, however, did not quite follow: If this should be the case, the process of class-enrichment to which he referred could be expected to cease. Morgan was after bigger theoretical game. For he looked forward, as did other Populists, to a more equitable distribution, once the economy cast off what were held to be artificial restrictions. In addition, he wanted safeguards for this improved distribution in natural-law terms. Later he too stressed public intervention, and even here he laid the basis for an appeal to government.

The summary served partly to chastise Adam Smith and partly to encircle him, so that competition could be turned to Populist ends:

Having briefly considered some of the elementary principles relating to labor we are enabled to make the following general deductions.

First.—Man is naturally disposed to take pleasure in remunerative employment.

Second.—He is justly entitled to the fruits of his own labor.

Third.—Any violation of this natural law will breed social disorder, and an universal violation will bring national calamity. Add to this that labor creates all wealth and provides not only the necessities of life, but all the comforts and luxuries; that wealth is only past labor—power over nature—crystal[l]ized into tokens of value, called money, and controlled in many cases by those who have performed but little labor themselves. The wealth of the Vanderbilts, Roth[s]childs and Goulds is but the accumulated labor of millions who have received but a part of a just reward for their services.[16]

As Morgan proceeded to indicate, wealth (and its appropriation) was a central *social* question in that it defined fundamental relations of dominance.

But first, it must be noted that even in the preceding statement the natural-law cast was circumscriptive. The potentially radical insight that wealth was "past labor" was not a condemnation of wealth per se, but of its parasitic or unjust accumulation. A clue to Populist limitations can be found in the first law Morgan cited. Pleasure was derived, not from creative or autonomous work (labor as fulfillment, stemming from socialist and communal-utopian ideologies which denied the wage system), but from "remunerative employment." To be sure, this implied a standard of fairness, and yet the issue of the wage system itself disappeared in the quantitative determination of what constituted a proper share for the laborer. Labor conveyed all too readily the notion of future capital. As the creator of wealth, it not only required just reward but also equally reinforced wealth-gathering as a principal activity (provided rules of entitlement were observed), thus preserving a fundamental capitalist premise. Vanderbilt was reduced in scale and very much diminished in reputation, but brought down to manageable proportions, he was free to pursue wealth in noninjurious ways.

Combining the social and circumscriptive elements of the treatment of wealth did not result in a movement comprised of mere expectant capitalists. If Populists had been only that, the issue of domination need never have arisen; they would have construed the principle of just reward as all the traffic would bear and would have stripped competition of its full, antimonopolist possibilities. Expectant capitalists would have taken the system as they found it, only petitioning for admittance. This would have been a largely unmodified capitalism stormed by aspirants of lesser standing. Instead, Populists proposed a qualitatively discrete change in structure, what I might provisionally identify—consistent with Morgan's natural-law cast—as "nondominating capitalism" with both terms meriting emphasis.

After describing wealth as the "accumulated labor of millions" Morgan added: "The individual laborer is not the master of his own actions. He must work or suffer and is therefore compelled to submit to the exactions of his employer who is also his master. He is but an integral part of the society or community which 'fixes the condition of his life.' " One thinks of the preindustrial masterless man, but Morgan's vision was fuller, less narrowly individualistic. To live in society, he reasoned, was a reciprocal process. This reciprocity was the basis for the appeal to government. "Society is the State or government in which he lives. He must therefore appeal to the State for that relief which he has tried in vain to reach through the instrumentality of strikes. An associated effort on the part of the community—or State—of which the laborer is a part may go far towards correcting the evils to which he is subject."[17] Workers might seek relief from the state; yet consider the several major concessions tendered to reach that position!

Morgan curiously abstracted the state from any class foundations, whether dominant capitalists' or the Populists' own; this pursuit of neutrality, as will be seen, linked the state and the community as an impartial voice for betterment. It is not surprising, then, that the state also became an alternative to and a substitute for direct action, as in the resort to the instrumentality of strikes. Not only did the latter not avail, but it identified a specifically class remedy, which would have negated the nonclass associated effort. Finally, Morgan's prescription was most conservative precisely when the collective element, seemingly most radical, had been raised. The laborer was one component of the mutual effort, and the solution was for the community to heal itself. Taken literally, the injunction came down to a plea for classless participation and the submergence of identity. There was a pervading restraint in the analysis of social improvement.

Defining the importation of contract-labor as the workers' "just grounds of complaint," and a question threatening "the very foundations of our social and political structures," Morgan observed: "The community is a sick man suffering from the anti-social disorders of ignorance, selfishness and unlimited competition. The hypocritical philanthropists have thought it a good practice to give the patient fresh doses of ignorance and barbarism. They seem to be charmed with the near dollar to be made out of cheap labor, but utterly ignore the inevitable degradation of the community, and its peril to the estate of those who are fortunate enough to accumulate anything, and to the future of the Republic."[18] The reason that the collective element was disappointing, as a potential source of radicalism, was that he placed complete trust in the community when it was functioning smoothly. The purpose was that of peaceful reabsorption. Discontent was to be abated through society-wide will and activity, leaving the laborer hostage to the good intentions of other classes and the success of nonclass appeals. Equally, the community was cast as the bulwark against disorder. Here, a more basic hostage image was consciously invoked: When the community had been degraded, all property and place were threatened. Populists were often most eloquent and convincing when they fell back on the simple aphoristic vein so reminiscent of and probably drawn from earlier English workingclass plaints: the "peril," as Morgan stated, "to the estate of those who are fortunate enough to accumulate anything." They inhabit, and are uniquely dependent on, the community from which all enjoyments flow.

One must not forget that this was still early in the development of Populist protest. While community never quite took on a class character in subsequent Populist expression, nevertheless it did convey a clearer meaning of social transformation. The emphasis on community was brought into sharper focus as the goal to be reached, rather than the plane of existing battle. Paradoxically, community represented a forward-looking orientation by restoring the older notion of commonwealth. Communities, to be such, must be founded on principles of justice and human respect. Henry D. Lloyd, in particular, argued that only then did they become the repository of higher moral standards. The individualism of the community served to counteract that of dissociated, antagonistic men.

In this important respect, Morgan was very like Marion Butler and, I believe, many other Populists. Once he had fully satisfied himself that his most extensive theoretical probings were still compatible with America, that in effect no anticapitalist skeletons had turned up in the ideological closet, he then felt free to go on the attack against concrete abuses. (This again reflected an interplay of conservatism and radicalism, that made self-legitimation indispensable before venturing outward.) Morgan was particularly critical of the railroads. Symbolically, they were the leading instance of monopolistic power; operationally, they were the nerve center for market closure; and morally, they were the corrupting influence which had set the law at defiance.

He began a later portion with a discussion of the railroads' general lack of accountability to society: "For many years the country has been suffering from evils of which all have been conscious, but which it would seem none have had the courage or wisdom to correct. Prominent among these are the burdens that have been fastened upon the people by the reckless and unscrupulous course of the great railroad monopolies that have sprung up in our midst." The imagery was that of confrontation (gathering intensity as the abuses were protracted) with forces that had acted capriciously and intruded on a hitherto tranquil setting. We see the integration of moral and material concerns. The implicit theme of lost liberties was equated with market freedom: "These vast and powerful corporations have established a series of abuses which have gradually and almost effectually undermined the solid basis upon which our internal commerce was supposed to rest." There followed a single-sentence catalogue of abusive practices one associates with Populist writings, in which everything was listed, lest the details of oppression somehow escape. Yet Morgan also remained focused on the violations of law by monopolistic power:

They have debauched and demoralized our Courts and Legislatures; have bribed and taken into their pay the high public officials charged with the making and execution of our laws; have robbed the nation of a domain sufficient to constitute an empire; have flooded the land with worthless stocks and other so-called securities; have established a system of gambling at our financial centres that has resulted in a financial crisis which covered the whole land with ruin and suffering; have set at defiance the laws of the land and have trampled upon individual and public rights and liberties, openly boasting that they are too powerful to be made amenable to the law; and not content with all this, not satisfied with the ruin they have wrought, they continue to petition the law making power to give them still greater means of robbing and oppressing the people.[19]

The cumulative effect of the passage is that the nation was coming apart at the constitutional seams. The specifics of depredation counted for less than the seeming helplessness of the body politic, as institution upon institution became corrupted. There was blight, contemptuous treatment, and a system of law eroded at its periphery (courts, legislatures, the land itself) and at its heart (the very spirit of compliance). Corporate greed proceeded without foreseeable limit. The potential for constructive service only heightened the disparity: "As public benefactors the railroads take their place first among the great discoveries of the nineteenth century; but they should not be used as a means of oppression." Morgan, however, did not censure individual entrepreneurs. Perhaps because he wished to guard against charges that the Populists engaged in ad hominem attacks, or because he found the analysis of structure more fruitful, he drew a distinction which served to root the railroad problem in the systemic features of monopolism. Thus, in speaking of Gould, Russell Sage, and others, he noted, "we have no personal fight to make. They were perhaps only actuated by the instinctive desire possessed by most men—to become rich and powerful." Even here shading was introduced, "most men" giving way to incumbents of a specific role: "They are perhaps no worse than other men would be occupying the same position." And he continued: "But they are the representatives of the worst system of despotism in existence, and they are shrewd enough to regard the interest of their roads as paramount to that of the public."[20]

If he did not condemn the profit motive outright, he nonetheless perceived a conflict between self-directed corporate firms and the larger public needs and interest. Not only was business privilege connected to market closure, but it threatened to abridge governmental sovereignty. Morgan elaborated the antidemocratic implications of the conflict:

The constitution gives to Congress the power to regulate commerce between the States, but for years the presidents of the trunk lines between the East and West have been exercising that power, and fixing the price that the farmer shall have for the products of his farm. It is certainly inconsistent with free institutions to lodge such power in the hands of a few men who have every incentive to abuse it, and it remains for the people to say how long such a state of affairs shall continue. This power is used against the interests of the people. This despotism in common with that of other monopolies threatens them in every relation of their national life.[21]

Were one to search out an underlying theme in the genesis of Populism, it would reflect the foregoing sentiment. Verifiable exactions by railroads (the book is filled with statistics on, as well as personal accounts of, freight charges) pointed to straitened economic circumstances. In turn, this immediate complaint drew attention to the legal and political context that had failed to inhibit the assertion of private controls or, conversely, to promote within government the necessary public safeguards. Morgan thus constructed a baseline for generalizing on societal corrosion and the need for a mass awakening.

Throughout the book, these and correlative themes were discussed at length. A few passages suffice. On protest as such, after declaring that "in vain has the farmer pleaded," and that forbearance was no longer a virtue, Morgan envisaged a "counter combination" of farmers and workers in response to combination in the business world. Yet, inevitably, he restricted the scope to an electoral permutation of such forbearance: "They are preparing to move upon the enemy. Not in the gaudy trappings of war . . . accompanied with all the horrors of physical contest; but silently, peaceably, and by force of reason and the potent influence of the ballot do they expect to accomplish this mighty revolution in behalf of oppressed labor."[22]

Restraint is perhaps the more apt characterization. For in commenting on "the coming storm," he warned—as had his colleagues—of impendent crisis, the hardening of lines, with "intolerable oppression" and "popular indignation" both increasing. Inferentially, the plea was to avoid collision; nevertheless a suitable alarm had been sounded. Responsibility for deteriorating conditions now rested squarely on corporations in general, and on railroads in particular: "It is worse than idle to talk about measures being unconstitutional. Constitutions may be changed as well as laws, and if the policy of the gigantic corporations is to utterly ignore the popular will, setting every principle of justice at defiance, until the indignation of the people is wrought to such a pitch that the day of spoliation of railways will come, and neither vested rights nor common honesty is likely to obtain a hearing, they may console themselves with the reflection that they were the transgressors."[23] This was not an extraconstitutional appeal, despite an intriguing Rousseau-like reference to the popular will as a precedent standard of authority. Morgan called for widening the Constitution's application to property. The appeal was to greater constitutional vitality, so that corporations would not hide behind the law, which had been construed in terms of absolute property rights and governmental noninterference.

Morgan addressed this theme with a rhetorical question some five hundred pages later: "Do we believe what we say in the preamble to our constitution and the declaration of our principles?" He answered, "Then we are threatened with a multiplicity of monopolies that menace our liberties. No country in the history of the world has ever been cursed with so many and such gigantic monopolies as free (?) America." The question mark inserted after "free" appears frequently in later Populist writings (Morgan's may have been the earliest usage). It effectively spoke to the sense of outrage, the perspicacity of the criticism, and the desire to realize basic changes. He continued: "Free, only in name. Free, only in the fact that we still have a glimmering hope of crushing this monstrous system of robbery by an intelligent use of the ballot; that failing, all hope is lost, except that last fearful resort—revolution." The significance of the ballot, as the affirmation of lawful processes and means of averting chaos, was nowhere more concisely put. Of revolution, Morgan added: "May the God of our fathers prevent it."[24]

Then he asked: "What are the natural results of railroad monopolies?" Here he included a more direct charge of exploitation. Corporate growth had been achieved at the expense of the populace: "Like all other soulless corporations, their only ambition is gain; and that gain must come from the producer. With this sole object in view, they are blind to the true principles of government, and, like all other tyrannical powers, regard not the rights of the people." No effort, he noted later, had been made to furnish protection of popular rights. The Interstate Commerce Commission (he made this observation only two years after its founding) was possibly railroad-inspired, and wholly ineffectual: "But the provisions of the law are worded so intricately, and its operations are so inadequate to the demands of the existing evils, that it is a question whether the bill was got up and passed in the interests of the people or the railroad corporations."[25] Concrete grievances, irresponsible conduct, the failure or nonexistence of regulation, grave constitutional violations, all these factors suggested the need for entertaining more far-reaching solutions.

Populists appeared driven to support public ownership, and they were aware that this reflected a break with contemporary values: "There seems to be but one remedy for the evils growing out of our present railroad system. It is for the government to take absolute supervisory control of the roads, or, by right of eminent domain to become the owner of the roads by gradual purchase. In advocating this remedy we are not unaware of the fact that it is stoutly opposed by the adherents of the two great political parties in the country, and by the subsidized press. . . . The roads are public highways and of right ought only to be operated for the public good." The passage was cautiously phrased. (Populists vacillated on the issue of public ownership or control until at least 1891, though ownership was present in Alliance platforms before that.) Yet the principle stated in the final sentence, the public's jurisdiction in areas invested with a public character, engendered confidence in the broader announcement of governmental sovereignty. This was followed by an implied restriction of the property right: "Any system that is not for the public good—that is detrimental to the public welfare—is and of right ought to be subject to public control."[26]

The issue was not merely that of private dominance over commerce, on which the state, in its constitutional obligation to regulate, had defaulted. One detects the extension of public governance as a vital standard wherever detrimental conduct could be shown. The argument left the property right intact, yet still qualified what Populists took to be its excrescent powers: "Men talk about 'Chartered Privileges' and 'Vested Rights.' If a 'vested right' becomes a nuisance—a public wrong—it is no longer a 'right,' vested or otherwise; for a right can not exist in a wrong. If such was a fact a man's right to carry on a slaughter house within the confines of a densely populated city could not be questioned, provided he held a deed to the property." Lockean possessory rights were no longer sacrosanct. For as Morgan concluded (anticipating the crux of Populist economic analysis), the public was the paramount realm for the determination of rights: "No man has a right to operate against the public welfare and against their expressed will."[27]

2. Regional Modes of Protest

James H. Davis's *A Political Revelation* (1894) was the work of a Texas Populist whose political stance had been associated with midroad orthodoxy through at least the latter part of 1895. Davis was a born dissenter, a self-made lawyer, and an orator of astonishing power, who traveled the country extensively in organizing the Alliance movement. His book uniquely showed—because it was the most comprehensive statement extant—the influence of Jeffersonianism in the movement's thinking, particularly as found in the South. For our purposes, the regional emphasis is less important. Writing five years after Morgan, Davis, as perhaps the most narrowly constitutionalist in his approach, could treat the notion of public right and governance as a Populist commonplace, so ingrained had its usage become. His vantage point, what might be termed an obsession with Jefferson, did not materially alter the broader ideological pattern: a collective thrust harnessed to quite moderate ends. Yet among those who stressed Jefferson, Davis was singular in his ability to bridge the gap from a strict-constructionist outlook to the acceptance of public ownership. He did not seem intimidated by the prevalent view that this supposed paternalism violated cherished regional values.

I raise the matter because one frequently hears the assertion that southern Populism was comparatively more radical than western Populism. This is stated generally by historians whose research has been confined to the South and who understandably take the difficulties in mounting protest as evidence of aggressively formulated political and economic demands.[28] Yet, notwithstanding a regional gift for hyperbole and a luxuriant dispersion of mental activity (that W. J. Cash beautifully captured for the nineteenth century in *The Mind of the South*), the South created what remained essentially a cultural strait jacket. This restricting culture was centered, of course, on the maintenance of racial institutions; but it had a catastrophic effect, for Populists as well as other southerners, on receptivity to intellectual currents from without.[29] Populists in their actions did question the foundations of orthodoxy. This was the case in the matter of race; they called, by and large, for the inclusion of blacks in the political community. More directly, they opposed the one-party state governments, which they viewed as self-perpetuating regimes enforcing conformity and uniting landed and business groups into cohesive local elites who formed welcoming committees for northern capitalist, especially railroad, penetration. This questioning, however, failed to introduce for themselves the ideological latitude that westerners could take as the starting place of protest.

Southern Populists labored under a tremendous handicap, psychological as well as political in nature. Every original thought had to surmount encrusted layers of social habit. We must speak here not of the textbook inertia of development economics, but of continuously reinforced pressures toward uncritical submission. The objective of this context was as much to cheapen labor as to neutralize dissent. It was backed, in time that must be measured by decades, by the full arsenal of formal and informal coercion that began with press indoctrination and rigged elections in which the Democratic party was the sole voice of legitimacy; and it did not cease until all opposition was silenced, driven underground, or otherwise dispatched in ways local chroniclers have been reticent to describe.[30]

It hardly detracts from southern Populism to suggest that its principal task was one of cultural divestment. It had to delegitimate an encompassing political existence that had been equated with regional (including but extending beyond racial) loyalty and identity. And that task was preparation for what proved still more arduous, to compel a hearing from a political framework structured to prevent autonomous dissent. These steps were necessary even before the ideological and political offensive could be taken.[31] In the South, Populists had to struggle for that rudimentary expression matter-of-factly assumed elsewhere. (The one-party, Republican, bloody-shirt West did not pose comparable difficulties. Less orthodoxy was demanded of western Populists, intimidation was not as successful against them, and they did not experience the same psychological drain in the act of disengagement from their culture.) There had to be the breaking of mere democratic surface, epitomized by free and honest elections, and put into practice as the composure to present increasingly advanced demands. Great energy was expended to justify political independence, and with it the biracial factor, as germane and perhaps integral to the challenge. Whatever energy remained was given over to securing a free ballot. Quite literally, the southern phase of Populism, only partly through its own doing, lacked the inner resources and vibrancy to go beyond a perfunctory statement of the movement's comprehensive ideology.

But exoneration for southern Populists cannot follow automatically. There were self-imposed restrictions which partially diluted their vision. Populists were a creation of the southernism they had to combat. Plausibly, a suffocative political matrix had exacted its toll and with consistency on all fronts. If western Populists did not have to face the race issue, those in the South did so ambiguously. One finds in them an irreducible social decency which placed them well above their non-Populist white contemporaries, who were racially motivated in both ideology and practice. (The attempt to eliminate the racial issue from politics and, for the most part, to avoid stereotypic appeals was a step forward, marking at least partial extrication from the regional frame of reference.) Yet beyond that there was a manifest unwillingness to accord racial betterment high priority in its own right. Southern Populists equivocated on the scope of political equality. They consciously sought to confer suffrage on, and simultaneously deny meaningful participation to, blacks.

An inability to transcend considerations of race precluded the imperative speculation on the deeper function of racism, which was to stabilize a political economy founded on agricultural dependence and outside investment. This had the effect of imposing greater limits on economic demands than would have been the case if labor and its needs were perceived entirely as a biracial unit. The more articulated dimension of class had been weakened by a racial factor not present in the West. The class dimension became further altered through the long-term institutional habituation to a politics of deference. Even when the opposition was castigated, it was mainly for betrayal—the departure of the Democratic party from its pristine, Jeffersonian, and, sometimes associated with these, southern cultural origins. The full-scale critique of an exploitative social order in which the dominant party was only a concrete representation had been minimized.

Southern Populists often contributed to their own immobilization. The language of defiance—the bravado of revolution, never matched by deeds and invariably confined to the electoral process—was actually a way of discharging emotion. It served only to confirm old habits of deference. Since this deference could not be shaken, it had to be countered safely through excesses of exuberance which then led easily to disillusionment. (Again, this was unlike the texture of western Populist thought in which, if there was more sobriety, the underlying desire to "prove" militance, as a compensating impulse and means of assuaging doubt, was not only *not* felt, but gave place to an evenness of focus on programmatic lines.) The preoccupation with defeat and for mid-roaders, who in 1896 were located primarily in the South, with purity suggested the resort to rationalization, when Populists did not possess the self-assurance to break cleanly from, or to achieve on their own terms a favorable reconciliation with, southern cultural patterns. There was, then, a curious blend of earnestness, not to be denied, and considerable posturing and uncertainty. Defeat, as in Tom Watson's case, was used to ennoble the struggle. It conveyed a sense of renewal, and yet it also imparted to the everyday experience a siege mentality. For Watson, this raised the further prospect of martyrdom.

In taking up the case of Davis, therefore, one finds that the affirmative treatment of Jefferson stands apart precisely because, though remaining a cultural symbol, he had not been explicitly southernized. This permitted at least some connection with a national plane of discourse. Other southern Populists, Morgan for one, had made a similar breakthrough, but not through a reliance on Jefferson as the primary vehicle. In the West, less interest was shown in appropriating this symbol. Rather, Populists turned directly to existing grievances and proceeded from there. They invoked a broader heritage of reform for support. In contrast, the South appeared as though sealed off from the richness and diversity of national and international currents; Populists themselves were able (no mean achievement) to distill maximum import from certifiably respectable sources. The range of reform ideas, however, spoke volumes for the comparative ferment and elasticity of discussion in the respective Populist segments.[32] Here I make note of Marion Butler's ideological bridge to the West. For he too nationalized Jefferson. But by 1894–1895, he had stepped further outside regional lines of thinking than had Davis. He had a becoming prosaicism that deflated heroics and allowed for the unselfconscious regard for a public standard.

3. Principles of Economic Democracy

Davis revealed his ideological skeleton at the beginning. The Declaration of Independence, the Constitution, and the Populist national platform together "contain all the requisite provisions for the grandest and most perfect civilization."[33] This statement indicated the degree of Populism's immersion in the American political heritage, a return to an organic national expression of rights. Populism became integrated with, and was in subtle ways directed toward, the purposes and structure of fundamental law. Even assuming Populists' need for prior justification of their ideology (and their willingness to interpret freely the first two documents to that end), one notes also their purposeful construction of a framework of political moderation. They did not so much traditionalize revolt as subdue it. Davis's constitutionalist world was dedicated to realizing the conditions for industriousness, a vocal yet limited antimonopolism, that would assure equality before the law in leading a normal capitalistic life.

His concern was that systemic bottlenecks had frustrated the goal of attaining a home. The latter was treated as the primal image for designating the social basis of economic independence, gainful labor, and a society of just rewards. If Jefferson was securely fixed, there remained, despite Smithian overtones, significant support for the idea of public ownership to unblock the channels of trade. In theory, this amalgam was not altogether improbable (though Davis, as a derivative, haphazard thinker, used disparate elements to lurch, as it were, to his desired conclusion). For it was not the governmental sphere per se, but the function to be served, that made possible the combining of nationalization and Jeffersonian-propertied aspirations. Public ownership, potentially a step toward a mixed economy, was somehow eviscerated here. The underlying processes of capitalism were rehabilitated through this course so long as they did not lead to restraints on individual effort.

Davis differed from other Populists to be examined here in his conception of the significance and direction of state activity. In an important way, he assisted the ongoing discussion of an interventionist role for government. The analysis continued to the point which insisted on the public takeover of such crucial areas as banking and transportation. The position, within the mainstream of Populism, implied serious reservations about capitalism in its prevailing form. With the generality of Populists, he subscribed to the goal of universalizing competition, rendered synonymous with democratic opportunity. He similarly departed from strict laissez-faire in order to nurture, through governmental supervision, a capitalistic formation that was reconcilable with the principles of a superseding public interest. Yet Davis's analysis lacked any sense of the potentiality for a social transformation, which others in the movement had accorded to the state.

Capitalism would be purified, but not shaped into a qualitatively different arrangement. Davis did not hint that such intervention as he welcomed might become the foundation for a more indeterminate context in which the cumulative force of antimonopolism could materially alter class relations, enlarge still further the public sector, and lead to a broadened vision of welfare. For Davis, return to a constitutionalist world had the purpose of conserving the basic social order. This return signified more than the restoration of premonopolist outlines: The framework became self-completing *before* subsequent democratization could take hold or could even be envisioned. When he stated that "all the requisite provisions" were to be found in the three documents, it was not to discount the very real vitality of a premonopolistic configuration. (Return was to previously honored ideological and developmental principles, not to an antecedent historical or productive stage.) In Davis, such a configuration still raised as the paramount issue the question of an imbalance of power between public and private spheres. But a predefined standard for change, the Jeffersonian spirit, nevertheless acted to encase such vitality in a mold of structural finitude. Once private control over sensitive economic sectors was removed, public ownership, which Davis thought of as an assertion of political sovereignty rather than as an alternative mode of organizing the economy, ceased to have further value.

When discussing the sources of monopolism, Davis tended to move from one practice to another without pause. He introduced a circularity that appears to vary from the ordinary Populist approach in which some one area of the Omaha Platform's triad—land, transportation, money—was first developed. For all Populists, while monopoly reflected a series of interrelated developments, their differences in approaching the problem are instructive. Davis was less interested in examining capitalist structure, using a specific zone of abuse as the basis for extending the critique beyond immediate grievances, than in showing the problems (perforce on a uniform, more measured plane) as they affected the small producer. The words were there. They did not add up to a wider diagnosis. Rather, they focused on a particular stratum of society and the infringement on its rights. Referring to the three documents, he began the analysis by touching all bases:

If put into action there could be no monopoly in our landed interests. There could be no corporate or foreign control or influence over our finances, neither in coinage volume, distribution, or rate of interest. These would all be under government service, and exercised for the good of the whole people. There could be no foreign or corporate control or interference in the management of our highways. Thus the people, through their national government would coin money for their own use, and would coin enough to transact the business of the country with ease, security and safety. Having coined the money for their own use, they would see that it got into the channels of trade without foreign interference or franchised bank toll gates, charging them toll on the money they, through their government, had coined.[34]

The common element was the loosening of restrictions on enterprise. The pairing of "foreign" and "corporate," beyond indicating concern over international bankers and American investment, suggested an intrusion on the people's own activities. Both words stood for the economic stranglehold that government alone had the power to break. The performance of vital functions was to be kept in public hands; government was to express the will of the people. Yet what was deemed vital was contingent on the freeing of commerce. This indicated Populists' definition of liberty, which was both political and economic. "Toll" therefore became an unwarranted tax or abridgement, levied where there was no right, on the public's business.

Land especially was threatened, Davis continued, for "banking, railway and telegraph companies," through profits from the public, had been able to "buy up and absorb our lands" by reinvesting the money. Coinage, though, was at the heart of the matter, because it affected security on the land and, therefore, an independent existence. We see here the linkage of sovereignty, home, and entitlement to the fruits of individual effort: "The government [by the operation of these documents] would exercise its full sovereign power to coin money, would coin enough money for the needs of the people, and they would not be forced to borrow foreign money and mortgage their lands, and with a reasonable limit of individual ownership and possession, each industrious individual would have the privilege of a home where he could produce and enjoy the comforts of life." In turn, railroads were treated as avenues of commerce. Public ownership would facilitate the exchange of private production. This capitalistic rationale narrowed large-scale governmental intervention to a convenience. "The government being in charge of the great highways, all men would be on an equal footing in the distribution of their wares, products or merchandise."[35] The issue was stripped of political meaning. It was as if this massive transference of property to the public sector were only a question of expediting economic transactions. Only on this ground, as opposed to a direct attack on property, could Davis accept the denial of the property right.

One finds a shared central assumption among Populists that public ownership would activate, and render more equitable, the remainder of capitalism. This would be brought about by making competition practicable in all sectors that were restrictively organized. Yet there was a manifest disposition in the movement to go beyond the stand of Davis and to view the serviceability of government as itself affecting the foundations of the polity. More than aid to the producer was involved. This was considered necessary in its own right. It was the most short-term, self-interested aspect of public intervention; through government activity a decent livelihood and the economic viability of the lesser propertied class were to be safeguarded. It would be foolish to deny the capitalistic dimension, which was equivalent to Populism's reformist boundaries, but such aid to the producer also had a deeper significance for reform. It was considered necessary for the economic implementation of political democracy. It served to redress the balance between unequal shares of wealth, and the degree of cohesion and power resulting from this inequality, politically as well as in the marketplace.

The benefit from government, however, could not be distilled into simple terms of economic advantage, even for a broadly submerged class, and still engender the convictions and enthusiasm displayed throughout the movement. Public ownership ratified the people's capacity to define the social course, unbeholden to capitalist upper groups. The operational bases of legitimacy would be shifted downward. The effect would be to establish government as the guarantor of a widened conception of welfare. Government would become the protector of the weak and the deserving poor. (This statement of generalized responsibility to those who were defenseless against corporate power and to those who faced conditions of depression had been voiced frequently in the western phase.) But also, as so charged, it would be the structural locus of regenerative political and social relations, in which the valuing of human worth would have little explicit capitalistic reference.

Davis continued to delineate the sweep of government: "The government by virtue of its constitutional power would coin money for the people at cost of coinage. The government, through a natural operation of the national and state government, would carry traffic and mails, transmit telegraphic news, and transport the people themselves over the country at actual cost, or if above cost the excess over cost would go into the treasury and relieve taxation that much." There were problems that required efficient solutions; public service had to be cost-effective. But no matter how extensive the government's reach, one searches hard for the qualitative edge which could move the analysis from lesser-entrepreneurial freedom to social freedom. Davis's succeeding sentence encapsulated the whole: "Then there would be no monopoly in lands; all persons would have to rely on their own industry for support and comforts; one could not go to the government and ask it to aid him by giving a charter on some avenue of industry or public necessity, hence there could be no monopoly in the production of wealth."[36]

Special advantages conferred by the state, including for example, "franchised bank toll gates," had to be abolished. The proposition was basic to Populist thought. But what also appeared to follow, and this idea was undoubtedly present as a strand in the movement, was that the purpose of removing obstructions was to throw individuals on their own mettle. They would not be so many Horatio Algers, but individuals still prepared to embark in life under the canons of equal opportunity. Once monopoly was dispelled, activities would proceed at a modulated if steady pace: "There being no monopoly in transportation there would be no monopoly in the distribution of wealth. No monopoly in the coinage and distribution of money being possible all men would be in a manner equal before the law in the privilege to secure a home as well as in production and distribution of wealth."[37]

Davis turned to constitutional exegesis to demonstrate the authorization for public regulation. He took the preamble as the essential political formula from which the enumerated powers of Congress flowed. These powers had to be utilized in their entirety; none could be selectively dropped if government were to adhere faithfully to the broad statement of intent. Whether this reflected strict or loose construction (usually a false dichotomy in any event) was immaterial here. For the literal reading extended the state's jurisdiction precisely by adhering closely to the text—a paradox of American practice, as many Populists had observed, because creedal professions were so rarely implemented. There was a disparity between the literal text and its practical application; culturally sanctioned principles were not realized in the making of policy. Davis's commentary therefore had an impetus toward transforming society otherwise absent when the context of the industrious producer was introduced.

After stating the importance of the preamble, he remarked: "We are not to presume that Congress can do anything and everything it chooses to think would secure the purposes named in the preamble, but it can and must do everything named in the Constitution." If a mere listing of powers had followed, the effect—however promising such phrases in the preamble as to "establish justice" and "promote the general welfare" might be—would be uninspiring. Instead, he first proposed a seemingly mechanical point (italics in the original): "And in every one of these powers we contend that it is the duty of Congress *to act directly on the people and for the people,* and not through the States, counties or any other subdivisions of government, *much less through corporations or syndicates.*"[38] The proposal "to act directly," if self-evident, was also Davis's most valuable contribution to Populist ideology. The activist reading of the phrase enjoined government from sharing its constitutional authority with private bodies, that is, with business, as in the informal but nonetheless real power of railroads to regulate commerce.

This became a prohibition on the general pattern of business-government partnership, which was in violation of the state's positive obligation to uphold the social welfare. But it pertained as well to the historical specifics of private control in areas which, constitutionally, had been invested with a public nature, such as coinage and commerce. According to Davis's reasoning, corporations, far more consequentially than states, had intervened between the people and government. Further, this interposition of power and authority made a shambles not only of the enumerated powers but also of sovereignty itself. He continued: "Where a power of legislation is given Congress it is by the 'Rules of Nations' and the common law complete within itself, and carries with it the logical right to make all laws necessary for carrying it into effect. Without it constitutional governments of all kinds would be failures." The conclusion of this thought no doubt grated on southern ears: "Again, we must consider that this Constitution was formed by the representation of sovereign States, and they conveyed their own rights of sovereignty to the United States in every one of the powers they gave."[39]

The argument clearly invoked the spirit of John Marshall (to enhance Jeffersonian purposes), so far as formal lines of authority were concerned. But the more basic result, beyond the nature of the federal relationship, was to demand for government preclusive as well as indivisible powers. Private parties should not encroach on the public's domain. This was to abstract Hamilton from Marshall, and then to discard him. It left a statist doctrine, freed of business connotations, that stated the characteristic Populist position on the constitutional question.

When Davis itemized the general powers found in the Constitution, he used the mandate "to act directly" as his measure of their valid application. Where this practice was already followed and was regarded as the accepted procedure, the precedent was set for a consistent administration to the more controversial areas in which business had dominated or had made inroads. To say, therefore, that *all* powers must be implemented, with like intensity, was not an innocuous point. Congress acted directly when laying and collecting "tax duties, imposts and excises," and when borrowing "on the credit of the United States"; but, in regard to the commerce clause, Davis asked: "Reader, please inform me what Congress is doing to carry this power into effect, or what has ever been done?" Davis continued on the theme of uniformity. He assigned particular historical significance to the commerce power, contending that it predated the Constitution and was the initial reason for its existence (italics, original):

Now why not apply the same reasoning to this clause that is applied to the others? Why not declare the government to be in possession of this power for the same purposes that she possesses the others, with equal power to carry it into effect? Certainly our forefathers intended this should be done; they intended that the government should act direct on and for the people in this matter just the same as in every power; yea, ten thousand times more urgent is this power, for it was this power that served as a mainspring to build up our government; it was a violation of this power that led us to war with King George; it was a disregard for rights of shippers by the States and a want of some power that could act *on the people to protect the trade,* that gave birth to this Constitution, and do you for one moment suppose that they intended it should lie dormant for a hundred years?[40]

In fathoming the intent of the founders, Populists revealed, particularly in their self-confidence, more than the search for precedents to justify current demands. They felt themselves to be authentic interpreters, if not indeed, in the purposes they hoped to achieve, a second generation of founders. They used history to leap the intervening century of presumed disregard for ideas and experiences shaping the national heritage. The fact that these ideas had been dormant did not negate their essential rightness. Moreover, this aspect of return to the American past furnished the basis for projecting forward. The historical bridge operated in both directions.

Populists, including Davis, reasoned that in order to comprehend the formative constitutional setting, it was necessary to apply it to modern productive forces. Principles were not fixed by the technology in existence. Rather, they marked functional areas of constitutional power wherein governmental supremacy not only had to keep pace with circumstances of change but also had to assert control over new developments, as these came into being, to fulfill the original mandate. Marion Butler argued thus in support of public ownership for the telegraph. If the state was to be charged with responsibility in transmitting information, a duty founded on the power to establish the postal system, all effective agencies to that end should be utilized, whether or not present in the initial context. Otherwise, the public interest would not be served. This particularly affected innovations. If they were allowed to remain privately organized (not to say monopolized), the result would be to hamper government in the expeditious discharge of its obligations. In turn, this would create a rival power in the public arena. Perhaps of greater concern, it would subject what was by right simultaneously a sovereign prerogative and a necessary requirement of the people's daily existence to the fact and criterion of profitmaking. A vital conception of public duty and its enlarged scope would thus be undermined.

Davis's treatment of constitutional power lacked the full articulation of a publicly infused structure and spirit which might strengthen the belief in an alternative standard of performance. Yet he shared the same Populist view of constitutional adaptability to technological advances. The foregoing passage, in its italicized portion, gives one grounds for pause. His emphasis on commercial rights—a Beardian insight before Beard—underscored the way that public ownership became a means to the attainment of economic liberty. Still, despite the moderate objective, the purpose of adapting to modern developments was cleanly stated: "Why not put this power into execution by owning the railways and operating them, by sworn officers, for the good of the people? It is the only reasonable and logical manner of carrying the power into execution."[41]

He mentioned other powers (including those affecting naturalization, counterfeiting, and patents), where the government acted directly; but in speaking of coinage, where it did not act, he captured the salience of private interposition in a fairly standard Populist treatment of the corporation. The term "sworn officers" was intended for contrasting effect. Service was rendered as a public trust, as opposed to the self-defined conduct of business units divorced from a moral and political obligation to the society. For Populists, to favor the capitalistic producer was not at the same time to sanction large-scale business enterprise: "To make the matter short, this is one of the most important powers in the Constitution. In this Congress should act directly on, and for the people as in other matters. In the exercise of this power, like the power to regulate commerce, Congress allows, yea even charters, licenses a lot of cold, faithless, soulless, heartless, merciless corporations, to stand between the government and the people, and usurp the blessings conferred by this power, forcing the people to look to these conscienceless beings for money and transportation to carry on their commerce."[42]

The term "soulless" was frequently used to describe corporations, because, in addition to their size and the impersonality of their operations, they had the freedom to act without scruples or restraint. The latter was thought particularly odious, for this freedom was provided under the aegis (and served practically as the extension) of government, investing business actions with quasi-authoritative power. Davis correctly sensed that such distribution of power within the public realm—as compared with a strictly private sector, where no constitutional claims could be advanced—seriously compromised the integrity of government. This represented the explosive potential of a literal reading of the Constitution. One could be capitalistic and still maintain (even pleading the founders' political logic) that designated powers, if they were to be carried out, could not be lodged in private hands. The conclusion entailed public ownership as the consistent course over and above the economic advantages, Populism's distinctive point, accruing to the small producer.

Davis, examining the right "to establish postoffices and postroads," reasoned: "The word 'establish' is used to give them the right to build and own postoffices in the name of the government, and under the same they can build and own railroads. A double purpose would be served and two objects of the Constitution met, for here is a specific grant given to establish a road and when established it can be used as a means of regulating commerce also." He later affirmed the indivisibility of sovereignty: "We believe in State rights, but only such rights as do not conflict with the rights of the United States as named in the Constitution." Citing Madison, he continued: "[W]e believe the Constitution means what it says when it declared that the laws of the United States, made in pursuance of the Constitution, shall be the supreme law of the land, and we boldly announce that in every power it is a Nation and is expected to act through its own officers, and must so act, and act directly on the people." Nationhood and, inferentially, constitutional democracy depended on preventing the devolution of authority: "To 'farm out' or delegate its powers to anyone is to betray the trust of the people." Unintentionally, the words conjure up a picture of prerevolutionary France (save that the taxgatherers now include major industries). The statement also expressed a more generalized criticism of the contemporary economy; it implied that modern capitalism retained feudal principles. Davis had commerce and coinage in mind when he concluded: "All we, as Populists, ask, is that each power in the Constitution shall be treated with the same regard and respect that is given to others."[43]

Davis's lengthy quotations from Jefferson's collected works

were prefaced by words of high praise: "Certainly no patriot can refuse to listen to Jefferson; all men of all countries acknowledge his wisdom, patriotism and love of universal liberty." The purpose of the Jeffersonian component was to furnish broader statements of direction, for example, the impermissibility of one generation binding the next, or to suggest principles of constitutional construction. It was not to provide a specific guide to legislation and policies. Taking one of many such passages, Davis sought to demonstrate the wider meaning of adaptability. Beyond keeping pace with technology, the intent of the preamble was always to be furthered. He quoted a letter (from 1807) in which Jefferson said that " 'even in judiciary cases, where the opposite parties have a right and counter right in the words of the law,' " emphasis should be placed on " 'the intention of the law' " with the judge giving " 'to all the parts and expressions of the law, that meaning which effects instead of defeating its intentions.' " Jefferson's extension of this method within the public sphere comprised the salient portion: " 'But laws, merely executive, and where no private right stands in the way, and the public object is the interest of all, a much more free scope of construction in favor of the intention of the law ought to be taken, and ingenuity should be exercised in devising constructions which may save to the public the benefits of the law. Constructions must not be favored which go to defeat instead of furthering the principal object of the law.' "[44]

A close relationship existed between the writings and the ideas under discussion. The selections, if not entirely apt (private rights of ownership, in this case, did become modified), were not adventitious. They indicated an intentional emphasis that determined which passages were borrowed. As a rule, Populists did not simply hide behind either the basic documents or the founders. Nor, on the other hand, were the precepts treated as gospel and made the basis for ironclad deductions to be applied in the construction of their own framework. The Populist literalism required in practice a more tentative process of extrapolation. The process was founded on the disposition to accept and identify as peculiarly American the earlier ideological context. Yet in demanding sufficient leeway for themselves, Populists also brought forward only what was particularly relevant to contemporary problems. A segment of the work of the founding generation was enlarged, partially reinterpreted, and made to do service symbolically for the whole. Property was not challenged thereby. In fact, it became a cornerstone of the new edifice. But significantly, the conception of property was that prevalent in Jefferson's time—or, more accurately, that associated with individual ownership and the absence of the market control later attained through major aggregations of wealth.

The animus toward corporations—as representing an excrescent formation—was loosely derived from that strand of eighteenth-century thought which Populists drew upon. Yet it was grounded specifically in their own experiences in equal if not greater measure. Again an admixture of affinity and independence determined their borrowing. Studying Davis's application of the quoted passage, one notes that it does not reveal a blind reliance on the past. To be sure, assumptions about the property right had been retained. But the antagonism toward corporations provided a shift in emphasis that historically Populists perhaps alone have supplied. Antimonopolism was mounted on behalf of property. In turn, because industrialism was never doubted, they had to accord to government (in the form of public ownership) a precedent role, wherever the original conception had been threatened. The stage desired was less precorporate than extracorporate in character. Large-scale organization was not abandoned. Rather, it was rendered compatible with the needs of—and, above all, was not permitted to destroy—the small producer.

Davis thus continued to explain the principles of application: "Now read the clause of the Constitution which says that Congress shall have power to regulate commerce among the several States, apply Jefferson's manner of constructions to it." Setting the method beside the "objects" to be served (justice, domestic tranquility, and so on), he stated the connection between public ownership and opportunity: "Now if the government owned and operated the railroads and telegraph lines it would certainly establish justice, for then all would have to pay the same price for freight and travel. The poor could ship and travel as cheaply as the rich." Labor also would benefit. Wages would be higher. Payment would not be months in arrears. Men would not be turned out by the thousands, "as was done this summer in the West and South," when profits slipped, and employment under the government would be regularized and made more secure. "The government would keep a sufficient number of men at all times to keep the roads in good fix and operate them well. The operatives would have a term of service and regular work under civil services laws."* Such antisocial corporate behavior as blackmailing towns to vote bond issues in order to have rail facilities would also be checked. Davis added: "Surely you do not have to 'exercise your ingenuity' to see that all these would follow a proper construction and application of the principle, and justice be established throughout the Union." On the constitutionality of the range of Populist demands, he observed, still with Jefferson in mind, "consider first the objects of the Constitution, and remember that constructions 'must not be favored which go to defeating instead of furthering the object' of the Constitution."[45]

If the methodology and outlines appear bold, this is less so on the plane of political-economic goals. Antimonopolist capitalism enhanced the role of industriousness, as the basis of propertied democracy, through heightened governmental powers. Reviewing the Omaha Platform, Davis explicitly paired state intervention and individual property as defining characteristics of the platform. He stated in explanation: "Our demands may be classified into three parts, viz: Land, Highways and Money"; then he offered a view of the whole of Populism, finding no inconsistency in the elements that had been combined: "The object of our platform is to set down ways and means by which a monopoly of either of these great blessings [above parts] so necessary to civilization can be abolished and prohibited, and to establish a system of laws and regulations that will prevent all kinds of monopoly and all kinds of aristocracy of wealth, and at the same time encourage individual industry in the acquisition of property and the enjoyment of the

---

*For Populists, government would invert the corporate system. It would be not merely a model employer, but, lacking an exploitative motive, the exemplar of responsible service in the conduct of enterprise. Profits were not questioned when cast as remunerative labor, or when they were the direct outgrowth of productivity in competitive industry. Yet the suspicion remained strong that, quite apart from the social desirability of denying entrance to profitability in the public realm, a profit-standard for major holdings was incompatible with sustained maintenance and humane labor practices. There was no incentive in either aspect beyond that of maximizing returns. Discussions of public ownership in the Populist literature were studded with references to the converse situation obtaining under private monopolistic conditions in which the workforce and basic plant alike were routinely allowed to deteriorate as part of an economic regimen of cheapening costs.

same; establishing an aristocracy of industry, merit and honor, instead of an aristocracy of wealth, arrogance and idleness."[46]

Given this emphasis on structural alteration, one can be pardoned for overlooking the obvious. The transformation to be effected, with concrete demands on three broad fronts (of which two require a fundamental shift from the private to public sector), has for its purpose "the acquisition of property." These words, under any construction, bear a capitalistic imprint. Such a phrase should leap from the page. Historians and Populists themselves have labored under a preconception that opposition to major property holdings and intervention in economic arrangements were by definition advocacy of a radical position. Public ownership was placed under serious constraint. Davis here exemplified the self-deception, however unwitting, that Populists practiced in separating means which were unorthodox for America from quite traditional ends. The former imparted a more advanced character to the latter than a propertied destination warranted.

For he then invoked socialism as integral to the Populist synthesis. In the process, the specific component of property became clouded. Property had been invested with a radicalism that the available means, even in the form of public ownership, could not achieve. Additionally, in Davis's treatment, socialism had become sufficiently diluted to lose its collective force. Though western Populists frequently started from the same general meaning of socialism, they gave greater latitude to its operation. It figured independently in the make-up of their demands and, for that reason, was not confined exclusively to the level of means. The constituents of the synthesis remained, but the proportions had been altered. A public area, distinct from the mere attainment of propertied goals, assumed intrinsic political value.

Davis's emphasis was on unfair advantage: monopolistic property and state franchises which conferred exclusive privileges. He noted that "the object of our platform is to prevent monopolies or government powers being used in the acquirement of property for individual gain." This consideration set the tone. There was a blending of seeming opposites, to ensure that functions indispensable to the lesser propertied classes were performed by government. These could not be left in private monopolists' hands, where they presented restrictions on widened acquisition and, particularly in the cases of transportation and money, became the means of economic oppression. If capitalism became equated with democracy in the discussion of polarities, socialism was also contracted in meaning so that it was consistent with the ideological center. It was as if all objective conflicts between them had been removed. At first, Davis appears to have presented a muddled but curiously good-natured rendering of socialism: "Here let us lay down a text which must serve as the key to this book, the line of demarkation that divides a Democratic or Republican government from a socialism. A Democratic government recognizes the rights of the individual to own, use, produce and enjoy property. While socialism recognizes no private right to property, but forms the government into one vast partnership, all labor and all property being public, held in trust for public good. All civilized governments are more or less a socialism."[47] Despite the categorical denial of the property right within the definition, no hostility toward socialism was evident; the final sentence attested to its nearly universal presence, including its presence in America.

Davis's reconciliation of democracy and socialism was based on keeping two parallel structures intact and separate within the same framework. Each possessed validity within its own sphere of application. Gradations of property determined which sphere should apply. Democracy and socialism became complementary parts of antimonopolist capitalism; they were separated figuratively by a horizontal line drawn across the formation. What occurred below the line was the province of the former, above, of the latter. Thus, property had been divided. It operated on private and individualistic principles, conceived as the dominant mode, wherever competition was or could be realized. This was a universe of independent production and/or fair reward for one's labor without restrictions on opportunity and with the security of the home the moral and economic indicator of equitable systemic development and internal social harmony. It operated alternatively on what were deemed principles of socialism, to assure the public trusteeship of the social wealth held in common, and of economic sectors by nature noncompetitive. This also included whatever, if entrusted to private control, would thwart the prospects for independence, opportunity, and security in the remainder of society. Socialism was simply changed into the public as such, limited to the necessary tasks for replenishing capitalistic energies. It was denied the total implementation that, in its own right, would lead to a differently organized social structure.

When he spoke of public property, following the phrase "all civilized governments," he assigned a restricted, not to say vapid, meaning to socialism—the context for sovereignty, rather than political-structural collectivism: "The courthouses are all owned and held in trust for the public, the poor and the rich being alike interested. Our public schools are owned and held in trust for the public. Our public school systems contain many extreme features of socialism and paternalism."[48] While it is true that an archetypal right can be formulated from small beginnings, these examples—more than the gas-and-water variety of socialism, which, if reformist, affected concrete services and addressed the property right—suggest self-deception. Davis conveyed a sense of having experimented with forbidden doctrines which, domesticated, had then been turned to American purposes. In fact, from the start, the socialism in question was entirely abstracted from all political and class matter. It signified the performance of neutral social duties, leaving poor and rich "alike interested," and hence also still intact as categories.

Further citation of socialism again shied away from controversial matter: "Our roadways, rivers, streets and commons are held in trust and owned by the public." The notion "held in trust" related to what Davis termed a "vast partnership," taken as identical with self-government and as a denial of monarchy. With courthouses, schools, and commons public, it followed that "the dividing line between socialism and Democracy is the right and recognition of private property." The combination was effected in a stroke: "We favor a Democracy and stand by the principle that governments are organized to perform for the whole people at cost, that service which the citizen and family in their own right cannot best perform for themselves." The hierarchy of values was unmistakably set forth: a society which was founded on property, but which could not safely dispense with putative socialism. Such socialism was almost mechanistic, because it was not specifically directed to leveling *within* the private-competitive sphere, and it serviced a capitalistic polity where individual efforts could not avail. Socialism became a public extension of, and the social equivalent for, predominantly individualistic premises and a value system based on the property right. Davis continued: "Thus we have civil courts to settle the business matters between persons who fail or refuse to settle among themselves. And we have criminal courts holding censorship or paternal care over society, naming certain things the individual shall and shall not do, a violation of which is pronounced criminal." Having reduced socialism to a platitude—social organization itself—he not surprisingly concluded: "Thus running through all our public affairs, National, State, county or municipal, we are paternalistic, socialistic or communistic; therefore these terms need not alarm you."[49]

Nor did they give cause for alarm. Nowhere is the need to investigate the complete field of discourse more evident. If the preceding statement stood alone, it would be a heady brew indeed, evidencing a Populist radicalism that, when actually present, would require careful qualification. I have indicated something of the mental reservations and implicit assumptions that hampered an ideological breakthrough in relation to capitalism, and conversely, that tended to confirm the movement's reformist proportions. Still, it is instructive to follow Davis several paces further. For if he were moderate (as I believe the Texas-midroad economic position to be, once it moved beyond the greenback-versus-silver preference to issues of capitalism and socialism), he nevertheless was fairly representative on themes which have to do with existing capitalist practices.

The term "usurpation" comes to mind; it marks the direction that Davis's analysis was pointed. Socialism (by his construction) did not alarm because it signified the legitimate powers of government. This characterization accomplished a twofold purpose. First, *as* government, in a constitutional democracy, he reasoned, there were limitations to power set forth. Second, because the same limitations were not binding on private bodies (recall his contrasting use of "sworn officers"), which did not exist within or acknowledge a political obligation to the populace, the powers assumed would operate without safeguards and probably without restraint. The public's business was not to be privately transacted; this in itself would compromise the essentials of sovereignty.

More consequential, the areas involved in this transference of power became precisely the sources of greatest economic abuse because they touched all facets of common exchange and individual livelihood.

Despite the private supplanting of government, collective principles of organization would still be retained through what Davis expressed in the remarkable and consistent phrase, a "communism of capital." But rather than a legitimate authority, deriving its power from the formula of consent, there would be a despotism of consolidated wealth. In this light, the Constitution may be read as an ethical diagram that established for Populists the foundations of political consent. For such consent to be operative, private intermediaries had to be eliminated from the process of governance. This is a return to his previous defense of the sovereign right to act directly. Also, to be inferred here, the realm of economic governance had to be decollectivized in order to ensure that where the state was not specifically involved, a private formation would not arise to assert the prerogatives of authority in its own name and by virtue of its own strength. Simply, power was transferred, but consequent responsibilities were not, leaving the populace vulnerable. Such a condition would lead to the disintegration of the bond cementing government and people.

The emphasis on security of home was perhaps the most elemental sign of underlying social conservatism because it focused aspiration on the acquirement and protection of property. Paradoxically, it led to Populists' most thoroughgoing attack on capital. For within the cherished notion of a stable social order—in which the home figured prominently, marking, more than steady employment, safety of both place and rights—was the constitutional paradigm of political democracy. The ultimate measure of society's well-being became the prevention of despotic economic power, a corporate hegemony engendering pressures toward instability that Populists feared the polity could not bear. Davis proceeded in a singular way through these various stages, including the association of home and a stable order, implicitly placing the Constitution and organized capitalism at cross-purposes. Going beyond the earlier undifferentiated view of upheaval in which blame was not clearly assigned, the present criticism envisioned a systemic disintegration with or without rebellion (though certainly encouraging it). Capitalist power fragmented the democratic precepts of consent, obligation, and legitimacy.

Thus, after asserting that seemingly radical language "need not alarm," he indicated his reason for believing that the public-collective dimension was not a threat: "There is a proper limit at which government should stop." Limit was synonymous with constitutional observance. It represented a confinement of power to the public, and on behalf of the private, sphere. As further protection, the collective dimension would also be mediated through the people's own consensual desires—the bypassing of private channels, as befitted a political democracy: "But in a government which is organized as ours, by the people for their own good, there need be no fear so long as the power is kept in the hands of the people and a constitutional limit recognized."[50] In contrast, when power having political magnitude was lodged in the private sphere, the result was an open invitation to a system of monolithic controls. This meant the conversion of power into economic oppression.

Suggesting parallels to earlier political oppression, Davis stated in a single explosive burst the Populist case against private collectivism. It was as though the constitutional bottom had dropped out. More than faithless relations were involved; there was total separation from the historical purposes and current needs of the society:

But when the power is taken from the people and placed in the hands of a few, and those few chartered into corporations with almost unlimited power over lands, highways, and money, and under no oath of office, obligation or bond to the people, who toll without conscience the tillers of the soil for the use of the earth, either for home or tillage; assessing a rent roll from the laborers of our cities with more greed and avarice than ever an English lord or duke manifested towards his vassals; laying a tariff on the distribution of life's comforts that pass over our highways which prostrates and impoverishes the producer on the one hand and the consumer on the other; and with the Bible-cursed, but government-chartered hand of the usurer, taxing every element of labor, industry and enterprise throughout our country by demanding tribute for the use of every dollar that passes from the mints of our government into the commerce of our people, we find today a "communism of capital," a despotism of aristocracy unknown to our Constitution, foreign to our theory of government, repulsive to our ideas of justice, and which, if not arrested in its devastating sway, must soon result in the complete vassalage of the masses and the aristocracy of the classes.[51]

Private-economic liberties and constitutional liberties had been melded in the critical analysis, to be contrasted with the negation of both through the workings of the contemporary structure. The term "aristocracy" designated a private government inside, and antithetical to, the democratic state.

He was describing a privileged caste, which had legally conferred rights denied the general public and enjoyed immunities because it was free to follow self-appointed norms of conduct. Particularly galling was this dual standard: Corporations were created under law and then given license to step outside the founding source through government charters. These charters served as the means of effecting the transfer of power. For the people, such a transference represented more than a surrender of power. It brought the entire democratic schema into question. Davis had those who were specially favored in mind when he wrote: "Now, before we go further, let us agree that the government of the United States is not a separate thing from the people, geared up and held in the hands of a royal family or aristocracy. The people here constitute their royal family; every man is just as much a sovereign, or is just as much a king as any other man." That government belongs to the people was vintage Populist doctrine. Self-government was also what Davis meant by socialism, if his recurrent phrase on partnership can be taken as our guide: "The government is the organized agency through which the people rule themselves, and in all governmental affairs we are a great partnership, every person's rights being equal."[52]

Whether or not these rights have capitalistic referents is of less importance than that government has been charged, as spokeman for the people, with guarding the provision for equality. This was an overarching superintendence; for Populists, it made the state uniquely the guardian of popular liberties. The term "self-government," although often repeated to the point of glibness, had assumed a vibrancy in Populist discourse, because phrases like Davis's "the people rule themselves" were invested with a constitutional literalism, and derived in contradistinction to private government. The public-collective factor, equated with government, and in turn, with the people themselves, also provided, again at the expense of private controls, a working definition of justice.

Essentially, justice was that political condition which kept the lines of legitimate authority intact. "Legitimate" here signified the conservation of the first principles on which government rested. Conversely, injustice originated in the failure to implement a public structure of governance based on, and geared to, political consent. This is not the place to speculate on whether Populists devised an informal compact theory, indications of which appear from time to time in the evidence presented. Yet consent was never intended as a lifeless formality. Conditions were attached, even if only in the realm of an idealized vision and even if their abrogation did not automatically furnish the right of revolution. There was a sufficiency of Locke (though democratized) in Populism to cloud the issue, with the same ambiguity over the limitations to be observed: a dedication to stable propertied arrangements and yet pugnacity when rights were trespassed. The main point, however, is that consent and with it justice became unthinkable in a private governmental frame. For there by definition and in practice the people could not rule themselves.

Davis proceeded exactly in this manner. He combined the Declaration of Independence (including the phrase "deriving their just powers from the consent of the governed") and the caption clause of the Constitution ("to establish justice") to indict specifically private government. Of the former he said: "It meant a new theory of government in which there should be no royalty, no nobility, no special classes, either born as nobility or titled by law." And combining the two, he continued: "Hence we must infer that the framers of our Constitution did not mean to contradict the principle that all power of government is derived from the people who are to be governed."[53] This was the salience of justice. It was established through government by consent in which the governed, because sovereign, existed, or were presumed to exist, as politically equal. In turn, this made impermissible, as contradicting the governed's antecedent status, all bestowals of privilege. If the concept of nobility was a red herring (leading, in the Revolutionary generation, as well as later, to an inflated view of republican classlessness), to be "titled by law," when broadly interpreted, was not.

Like other Populists, Davis clearly saw the existence of private government as an economic phenomenon:

Hence, when a traffic association consisting of railway managers meet and issue orders, tariff or tax rates that control the commerce of eight or ten States (sometimes the whole United States), they are governing the people, and under this government they have thousands of officers with more power over the people than the President of the United States. Many of these officers appoint more officers under his government, and distribute more patronage and more money than the governors of half a dozen States. Yet his power is not derived from the people; it is a usurpation, a species of royalty, because he exercises a power independent of and without the consent of the people.[54]

The obverse of independence here was arbitrariness, in both its discretionary and absolutist guises.

Populists were not troubled that a rival government might actually dislodge the formal political structure. (In speaking next of annual bankers' conferences as "representing the same kind of a government that the traffic association does," Davis pointed, perhaps unintentionally, to a loose collection of capitalist upper groups, each dominant in its own sector and having in microcosm autonomous powers similar to those commonly attributed to government.) Rather, there was concern that key decisions affecting people's lives and political in their consequences were removed from the public realm, and made the prerogative of a ruling stratum aided by, but beyond the reach of, the state. Severed from the populace, such power became a self-generated economic tyranny which preempted government in its own bailiwick (making actual dislodgment unnecessary). It defined an area of unchecked freedom of operation, reflecting capricious decisions and total command. Davis completed the passage with this reference to banking and railroads: "In both cases it is a collection of officers drawing immense salaries under no oath or bond to the people, whose orders or decrees can make or break any town or citizen in the Union, and they can tax the citizen of the United States or issue bonds enslaving us and our children to build roads in Mexico, South America and Africa."[55]

When earlier Davis had contrasted an aristocracy of "industry, merit and honor" with one of "wealth, arrogance and idleness," he was describing two divergent forms of capitalism. He was speaking more of character traits than infrastructural differences, but he still isolated the import of arbitrary power. Invariably he was driven back to what was most elemental, but still pertinent: "The United States government was instituted to secure the rights of life, liberty and pursuit of happiness."[56] While the formulation lent itself to an activist state, the product of such effort had a more placid cast. There was a respect for what the Populists previously examined meant by the worthiness of labor (embodied in the first set of traits above), as opposed to a capitalistic assertiveness, unrestrained in the pursuit of ambition, and directed as much to control as to production. The latter (corresponding to the second set) endangered an integrated system of political imperatives and moral rewards.

Idleness was at one with arrogance in building from the appropriation of others' labors. This involved more than the wage relationship. For Populists, profit became increasingly a strategy of the unearned increment. It was unproductive, founded in legalized advantage, and above all socially intrusive. It was capable of rending the inner fabric of happiness, through denying to individuals basic expectations of comfort and security. The Populist economic vision, though capitalist, was quite modest. It stood for employment, opportunity, and well-being, but it did not encourage the individual to be an entrepreneurial motor which never shut off. Unemployment (and the widening arc of social misery), Populists reasoned, was hardly the staple of a family-centered universe, the ideological notation for that form of capitalism which was consistent with the happiness principle and which placed restraints on atavistic uses of wealth.

For Davis, the essence of arbitrary power was the concentration of wealth taking place on the land. The land became a symbol of democratic foundations ("all men's rights to the earth (the unborn as well as the present) should be protected and secured in every way consistent with the common rights of all"). It was also the basis for a producer-ethic ("as the earth is known to be the source of all wealth, we hold that there should be no monopoly of land"). But more, the land represented the locus of exactly the small propertyholders' livelihood which conduced to traditionalistic patterns of social organization and more equitable wealth-distribution. Davis viewed this democracy-producer-family nexus

as the rationale for instituting government in America. Not unexpectedly, he attached greater emotive significance to molestation
of landed rights than to violations in the remaining areas of concern, money and transportation.

This became a point of departure for the contrapuntal themes of
corporate power and the stable home. Homelessness in this period
was epitomized by the unemployed, who went out in search of
work:

That vast tracts of land held either by individuals or corporations,
without being occupied either as a home or used in the production of
wealth, is contrary to divine law, in violation of every principle of civil
liberty and justice known to Republican or Democratic government, and
retards the advancement of civilization, disinherits posterity and creates
an aristocracy of its holders and their offspring. A home and some portion of the earth from which to produce comforts, and upon which to
rest our weary limbs after a day's toil in production; a home around
which lingers a halo of endearment to every human being; a home, the
absence of which tends to make man an alien to his God, an alien to his
country, and to convert him into a vagabond, a wanderer and an outcast;
is so essential to human happiness that the decay of liberty, the downfall
of society and the wreck of happiness in every age and every country
have been measured by the homeless numbers within her borders.[57]

It is true that happiness was to be secured through a decent competence rather than through unbounded wealth. The noneconom-
ic concerns in which government was to safeguard the nation's
political as well as material patrimony were prominent. (Nation
and family became frequently linked in Populist discussion, imply-
ing that ideally the nation should exemplify a well-run family,
showing the same consideration for its members.) Yet in the
economic sphere, there was still a firm commitment to a capitalist
framework. This was perhaps so taken for granted that neutrally
worded descriptions sufficed to indicate and partially disguise
basic processes.

Government was at once the great equalizer (among capitalist
groups) and the medium for expediting transactions. Davis, in
drawing his discussion to a close, created the perfect amalgam of
producers' rights, anticorporate remedies, and vitality of the marketplace: "Our platform contemplates a civilization in which the
sacred rights of home in reasonable amount of acres, and the production and enjoyments of comforts are held inviolable, and when

you have produced more of any kind of wealth than you wish to consume, and you wish to send over some highway to consumers elsewhere, instead of chartering a soulless, heartless corporation to take your goods in transit and rob you and [the] consumer both for his own gain, the government will take your goods as it does your letters, and distribute them at actual cost." The passage suggests the penchant for self-deception in the movement whenever the property right was matter-of-factly assumed. Davis's socialism was grafted onto Locke's state of nature. The home, including its products, was the basic unit of property, and therefore it was held to be a sacred right. This conveyed the sense of idyllic functions in the middle economic range, as though production for the market was simple barter, that seriously understated the way in which the productive surplus assumed profitable outlets. If monopolies in land, transportation, and money were abolished, "all men would be equal in production and distribution of wealth. . . ." Here "equal" denoted not an equality of holdings, but the equal opportunity to gather wealth. Davis fittingly concluded with the creed of the small propertyholder: "Then the man who produced the most would be the most prosperous, and each individual would have to depend on his own industry or energy to make or secure his comforts and blessings."[58]

CHAPTER FOUR

The New Industrial Regimen:
Kansas Populists

Despite differing in the degree of capitalist modification they advocated, the preceding case studies all envisioned a propertied democracy which directly interacted with the contemporary structure of capitalism. This attempt to realize a capitalist formation in response to, yet significantly at variance with, the existing mode became a principal source of ideological ambiguity. The very rejection of emergent monopolism depended upon the acceptance of propertied elements that, through consolidation, were carried to their literal conclusion. The central issue was the necessity of severing powers of domination from ownership per se. From the standpoint of the prevailing configuration of structural development, social power, and class relations, Populists were American capitalists of the wrong sort. A new regimen, permeating every aspect of modern life, had been built on industrial concentration and the appropriation of law and public policy to corporate ends. The Populist economic vision of nonprivileged capitalism involved more than the reinstatement of the precorporate small producer. Rather, the collective features of economic organization were clearly acknowledged and were conceived of as being primarily within the public's jurisdiction. They also argued that equity and efficiency did not have to be inversely related. The target of their criticism was not modernity, but its particular expression: monopolization, corporate political influence, and the merger of business and government into what Populists regarded as a class state.

When we examine Populists' views, their socially fracturing doctrines continually emerge. These doctrines were based upon the belief in constitutionally derived premises of an overriding political authority, holding in trust for the entire polity the criterion of public duty that was identified with a sovereign people. To this basic position had been added certain themes already discussed: Peffer objected to the rapid coalescence of an industrial structure which had resulted in an actual loss of liberties, not only by concentrating wealth but also by expropriating the small producer, and rendering powerless the newly dependent laborers; Weaver condemned the normalization of private power through control of the legislative process, an imbalance of structural composition which, besides abridging public sovereignty, engendered systemic corrosion at the fount of justice (the corporate refraction of legal interpretation, judicial partiality, atrophied constitutional safeguards) and threatened social fragmentation in the resultant weakening of political-social bonds. Morgan pointed out the failure to recognize individual effort (the violation of ethics of fair entitlement rooted in the natural-law character of producer values), which revealed the exploitative purpose of the profit-orientation. This discounting of the individual marked the conflict between self-directed corporate organization and the larger public needs, and led, as in the insecurity of lesser propertied interests, to the widespread degradation of the community. Davis was concerned about the advent of private government, which was grandly solipsistic in its denial of moral-political obligations to society and which became the source of arbitrary economic power with dire consequences for the stable arrangements on which happiness was predicated. The common criticism here was directed against a state of usurpation. The corporation had assumed quasi-authoritative prerogatives, standing as it were above the Constitution. But Populists at the same time implied an affirmation of government as the locus of regenerative political and social relations; they suggested the positive notion, therefore, of a transformative antimonopolism seeking preeminently a democratization of power.

Transformative antimonopolism was centered on the workings of the industrial system. Specifically, Populists approached prevailing capitalism as integrally related to the degradation of the social community. Here, some evidence covered in an earlier book remains pertinent, though additional interpretation to take account of previously unnoticed themes is necessary: Not only was there a general political and structural reticence within Populism (earlier I failed to see that the Populist critique of capitalism encompassed alternative, yet propertied, ends), but also constitutionalism was itself a critical weapon in opposing monopolization. If "radicalism" carries assumptions of property, reform is nonetheless strengthened in meaning and conviction.

My starting point had been the basic condition of alienation of man from his own humanity, his product, and his fellow men, which was expressed in a mid-1891 commentary on modern capitalism in the Lincoln *Farmers' Alliance*. This editorial is relevant to the present work as well. In addition to making a statement about dehumanization, mankind "brutalized both morally and physically," it expressed the profound separation within the individual himself as a political relationship: "His contact with other people is only the relation of servant to master, of a machine to its director. How can you reach this man, how kindle the divine spark which is torpid in his soul, when he knows that it is greed that enforces the material labor that is crushing him down, when he feels it is the wage system that is stealing the fruits of his toil and abasing and enslaving him?" Though this was a penetrating psychological analysis of the human condition (the editorial also spoke of "the tendency of the competitive system . . . to antagonize and disassociate men"), startling and even modern, it equally reflected standard Populist concerns: dependence, loss of liberties, the violation of a producer ethic—having for Populists constitutional as well as psychological implications. Above all, there was dissatisfaction with the existing framework, because it did not allow social fulfillment: "Humanity must rise to its own needs, or the soul of man will flee, and the senses be left alone to reign." The editorial added: "The actual state of society to-day is a state of war, active irreconcilable war on every side, and in all things. Deny it if you can. Competition is only another name for war." This reference was not to impendent upheaval, but to corporate aggressiveness and antisocial values: "It means slavery to millions—it means the sale of virtue for bread—it means for thousands upon thousands starvation, misery and death."[1]

1. The Social Obligation of Property

Lorenzo D. Lewelling, the Kansas governor, in a speech delivered shortly after the collapse of the Pullman strike, provided a more inclusive view of the contemporary industrial structure. Lewelling had a rich and varied career before assuming the governorship. As a youth, he worked for the Freedmen's Aid Society as a teacher in the South, held several kinds of skilled and unskilled positions as a laborer, graduated from Eastman's Business College and then from Whittier College, before, at the age of twenty-two, building a career in Iowa as a farmer, editor, superintendent of Iowa's reform school for women, and president of the board of directors of the State Normal School. In Kansas, he continued his business activities and interest in penal reform. His address echoed the earlier use of the analogy between slavery and the modern capitalist system. If the speech was disjointed, his introductory points were as effective as hammer blows. Each idea could be extended, and together they touched on three central areas—property, government, and prevailing ethics—sharing in common an implicit denial of political and economic security:

The trouble has been, we have so much regard for the rights of property that we have forgotten the liberties of the individual. We have had some illustration of that in the great strike at Chicago and a number of other illustrations. I claim it is the business of the Government to make it possible for me to live and sustain the life of my family. If the government don't do that, what better is the Government to me than a state of barbarism and everywhere we slay, and the slayer in turn is slain and so on the great theatre of life is one vast conspiracy all creatures from the worm to man in turn rob their fellows. That my fellow citizens is the law of natural selection the survival of the fittest. Not the survival of the fittest; but the survival of the strongest. It is time that man should rise above it.

Going beyond Davis, Lewelling here invested government with a custodial function, the absence of which left society in dishevelment and the individual, because he was overshadowed in the property right, without basic safeguards. Through his negative phrasing Lewelling asserted the conception not only of the state's duty, but of its unique position within the polity for providing democratic anchorage to social relations. The Hobbesian shadow, appearing in the deprivation of liberties, could not otherwise be dispelled. After describing the destitution in Kansas, Lewelling continued: "I say now, it is the duty of government to protect the weak, because the strong are able to protect themselves." And he added, by way of emphasis: "I believe, and I say it freely, that the working men and women of this country, many of them, are simply today in the shackels of industrial slavery."

The patent rejection of social Darwinism is of lesser moment than the underlying contention that government must be a life-sustaining force, opposing both the integration of state power with the already strong economic groups and the rationale used by those groups to explain away the deprivation of the lower classes. This rationale included not only the putative self-debasement of the weak but also the policy of noninterference (which countenanced domination) in internal class arrangements. By contrast, the interventionist role Lewelling assigned the state was specifically protective and corrective; but correction would mean, one suspects, not so much equalizing opportunity as disposing the social framework to melioration. "All we want is a little relief, a little remedy."

The homeliness of his illustration, citing the armies of unemployed formed earlier in 1894, spoke eloquently to the rejection of economic orthodoxy and the support for a laboring underclass: "Why, I would take the Colorado contingent of the Industrial Army and set them out in Colorado to digging the silver from the native hills and making money out of it. Why, my Republican friends say, these men are idlers, and vagabonds, they don't want to work, yet the fact remains that out in Colorado they actually fought each other to obtain the picks and shovels with which to do work for the city in order that they might obtain a pittance to provide for themselves and families." After tracing the migration of the unemployed eastward to their vast assemblage on the Chicago lakeshore and describing the forcible dispersion in which men were "kicked out of the way by the heavy boots of the policeman," Lewelling continued with a plaintive question: "I ask you now, what can the poor man do today that comes to you and says, I have hands to work with, I have bodily strength, I am willing to give all those for a morsel of bread—but you say, 'I have no work to give you.' What is he to do then?"

This compassion, a response to the reality of mass unemployment, became inseparable from a wide-ranging critique that itself had class implications. After condemning the president for "throwing an armed force across the border into Illinois" to break the Pullman strike, Lewelling observed: "While I have talked to you about the condition of the laborer, the condition of the farmers is about the same all over Kansas, and I am specially glad to know the farmers to be in hearty sympathy with the cause of labor. Down in Arkansas City, they are bringing in supplies day by day to supply the men striking on the railroad. And I understand the same thing is done here [Kansas City]." Federal suppression of civil liberties (Lewelling said of a friend who publicly contributed to the strike fund: "Today he is arraigned by the United States Court and summoned to Topeka and placed on trial for aiding and abetting the strikers against the government of the United States.—Think of it!"); the decline in farm income ("His earnings are naught. Add several ciphers together and you will have the sum of his profits this year and last"); pervasive homelessness and even starvation ("We look at the city in a mass and we forget the individual sufferer"); theme followed theme to describe a general political-systemic deterioration.

For Lewelling, the only parallel was the decline of Rome. Pleas of patriotism could no longer disarm criticism: "And yet, the people down there in Rome said the same thing that the Republicans said to us last year. . . . 'Stand up for Rome.'" Appearances of wealth, in both contexts, were deceiving. Even in the original typescript, from which these passages are drawn, he seemed to find the analogy too distasteful to complete: "Yet, remember my friends, that underneath the City of Rome in that great day of prosperity were the grinning skulls and bleaching bones of more than six millions of paupers and laborers who had been driven to despondency and death by the same conditions which seem—." Again, there were searching questions which implied that decline followed the abridgement of rights: "I ask you in Honor, are we not tending in the same direction? And shall the future historian say of you and me that we as a nation of free men, have you submitted to this despotism of greed until the star of our liberty has sunk into night?"

Perhaps what is important is the presence of hope even within a dark portrayal of America. Lewelling spoke further of "30,000

tenants annually ejected in New York City" and of "10,000 farmers made homeless in Kansas every year," completing the thought
with a typically piercing aphorism: "The great throbbing centers
of civilization seem to me to be dead to the instincts of humanity." Yet he also asserted, because he thought the people's liberties
were at stake: "Relief will come, I believe this inspiration will be
found in every heart. I believe the effort will be made by the people. Already great labor organizations are uniting themselves for
battle, welded together in conduct and purpose and action." If
confidence was sometimes feigned, feelings of resistance were not:
"Our path will be conflict, but it will also be conquest. It must be
so! The demands of the people will be heard. They must be
heard."

One detects an ambiguous note at the close. Lewelling implicitly retained categories predicated on preserving the property right.
The formulation was so plainly stated (following the excoriation
of great wealth, personified by Rockefeller's fortune) as to suggest
that intrinsic limits upon Populist ideology did not check, but
were themselves a constituent of, the movement's affirmative
thrust: "The People's party has stepped into the breach between
the classes to demand justice for the poor as well as to the rich and
for every man." Stepping into the breach expressly disavowed the
intent to serve as the class-vehicle for lower economic groups.
Indeed, the very power of the conception of justice resided in its
nonclass character. The abolition of all classes stood outside the
purview of Populism. Instead, their continued existence was contingent on a framework of nonprivileged relations. The categories
of poor and rich were left intact here with the phrase "for every
man" signifying a justice that has been extended throughout the
structure.

Lewelling's was a quintessential statement of antimonopolist
capitalism, founded on the recognition that a systemic imbalance
discriminated against the laboring poor. To his credit, he focused
his concern on groups below the customary lower and middle
propertied strata, though that focus did not materially affect the
broader acceptance of capitalistic institutions. He said of the imbalance: "The machinery of government has been arrayed against
us. It seems to me that the Courts and Judges of this country have
become the mere tools and vassals and jumping-jacks of the great

corporations that pull the string while the courts and judges dance." And therefore he left no doubt as to its source: "So, these great corporations are forces against which we are to contend, but I am willing . . . to place truth against the world."[2] His phrase "instincts of humanity" became a tacit desideratum, the birthright of free growth posited in the face of monopolist-authored restraint, that refined further the Populist criticism of contemporary industrial structure.

Frank Doster, Lewelling's close political associate and after 1896 chief justice of the Kansas Supreme Court, expressed the same theoretical position more acutely in a Fourth of July (1893) oration in Marion, Kansas. He was widely read in political philosophy and economic theory, had a strong formal education, practiced law, went through a Greenback interlude, and was elected in 1887 as a district judge in Kansas on a nonpartisan ticket before coming into prominence in the state. Taciturn, withdrawn, ascetic, inaccessible, venturing forth only when in the comfortable realm of philosophic formulations, Doster was cast, perhaps despite himself, as the state party's ideologue during this period. He nevertheless remained closely in touch with dominant Populist currents. He was very like Thomas L. Nugent of Texas in mannerisms and inclination, and he too invested Populist ideas with an encompassing, almost pantheistic, religious quality. Doster made concrete the most hidden and elusive Populist aspirations by, paradoxically, enlarging the plane of discourse. Humanity was not for Populists a meaningless, or ahistorical, abstraction. It spoke to political and economic rights, derived from traditional principles, that had been denied in a specific context of deprivation.

Thus, if competition for Lewelling had degenerated into the chaotic activity present in the state of nature, Doster assigned to government a clearer remedial function. Government should be that ordered framework which took cognizance of inequalities in the state of nature, in order to ensure with civil society that differences did not produce harmful consequences. According to this reasoning, equality was not a natural condition, but an attainable political fact or stage. If equality meant unhampered activity in the natural state, then, Doster noted, it was "the equality of wild beasts, and the doctrine of the survival of the fittest is proved and exemplified in social as well as political life, and becomes established among the theories of constitutional government." Instead, that equality which alone merited preserving was grounded in the realization of social bonds, coterminous with the meaning of a democratic polity. Here government was decisive: "All government and all necessity for government grows out of the fact of inequalities and that government which does not provide for the leveling and equalizing of the conditions which grow out of the unrestricted exercise of the natural powers of its citizens has failed in the purpose of its creation."

The essence of government was in its antecedent powers; its function was primarily to curb selfishness, but it was also needed to prevent the clustering of private dominance in social affairs. What "we call equality," Doster continued, "must be realized through the process of human government, and it is the business of government to discover and enforce those laws of harmony which raise man above the barbarous antagonisms of the natural state into relationships of social unity and fraternity." Doster carried the notion of constitutional adaptiveness further than did the writers previously examined. He sought to integrate governmental power with overall social development. (For if, as he wrote in a Kansas literary magazine the preceding October, public sovereignty was an idea whose time had come, the goal of government must be "no other than the equality of human brotherhood.")

He added substance to Lewelling's "instincts of humanity," as part of the broader statement on public regulation: "I know that the world has set its face toward the humanities of life. I know that the equality of man means something more than equal privileges in money getting." He built heavenward, but his argument was solidly based on the shortcomings of current practice: "I know that personal liberty does not mean selling hell in 'original packages' to the heedless and weak. I know that the millionaire must go like the feudal lord has done. I know that the wail of the orphan is heard louder in the courts of heaven than the chuckling glee of the money changers." Finally, he stated the critical distinction: "I know that humanity is above property, and that profit making on the bread of poverty is an abomination in the sight of the Lord."

One other passage has unusual significance. There was a brief reference to his supposedly notorious maiden speech in Kansas politics (May 1891), in which he again attacked the nearly axiomatic view of a "mutuality between labor and capital." Rather, Doster insisted on the irreconcilable differences for the social order between principles founded on use and those founded on ownership. When he also observed in 1893 that "a wage earner does not sell his labor but sells himself," we come fittingly to the negation of humanity, the expropriation of individuals' lives.[3]

Much of the foregoing reached to, if it did not pass outside, the boundaries of capitalism. This was particularly the case in the 1891 speech in which, by denying capital-labor mutuality, Doster asserted (in a phrase that would later plague him) that "the rights of the user of a thing were paramount to the rights of its owner." Yet there is enough internal evidence, supplied by his biographer, Michael Brodhead, to suggest that he stayed within the context of antimonopolist capitalism. For example, though he strongly opposed usury and favored legislation to prevent forced sheriff's sales, Doster still made provision for interest per se. He made this important distinction, which became a bench mark of antimonopolism: "My judgment," he wrote the legislature in 1890, "is that capital which desires to come here and live *with us* instead of being frightened away, will prefer to come where people are protected and guaranteed against usurers and extortioners; and as to that capital which merely comes here to live *off of us*, we have had too much already" (italics, original). In asking that the legislature hold firm against "loan agents," he dwelt on the nonproductive role of the latter form: "It is that capital which locates nowhere, and identifies itself with no community but which comes to abide temporarily, while it advantages itself upon the necessities of the people, which is the curse of the industrial world."[4]

For Populists, this was a microcosm of capitalism in its prevailing make-up. The passage called attention to the prior distinction found in his differentiation of use from ownership, as antagonistic modes which, in Populist usage, roughly corresponded to producers' and monopolist capitalism. Doster implied as his criterion service to the community. Advantaging "itself upon the necessities of the people" was hardly the way to engender respect. Doster saw this as a sign of parasitism, as is apparent in his phrase "live off of us."

Despite his socialist pronouncements and his obvious delight in appearing provocative, his protest was directed against monopoly and not capitalism as such. The term *ownership,* even in 1891, had a specificity—the monopolistic appropriation of public necessities—that his detractors refused to concede: "For ownership the sordid avaricious clutcher after other men's homes absorbs the common heritage of us all, and withholds it except upon terms of abject and remorseless tenancy. For ownership the great railways and navigation lines seize upon the public franchises, and dole out their use to the necessitous traveler and shipper at profits, which in half a century have made the transportation business the greatest capitalistic institution of any age." Undoubtedly, this was left-capitalism (if the term is meaningful), and it cannot be allowed to subtract from the position's critical vitality. However, the point is precisely that, a *vitality* which was the more self-deceiving the more far-reaching it became and which had not broken incisively from the existing system.

The term *use* had specific meaning. It was not part of a simple dichotomy in which production had been divorced from profit. Rather, it conveyed a more direct sense of effort and reward, best adapted to a producer ethic, nonrestrictive business activity, and greater allowance for labor's economic contribution. All of this implied that the property right was still valued. In perhaps the most fiery portion of the 1891 speech, Doster stated: "Stripped to its nakedness the proposition is that the owner of property does not possess with respect to such property an equality of right with the user of it, and upon the truth of that proposition, let me say to you, members of the Farmer's and Citizen's Alliance, and you People's party men, rests the entire fabric of your political platforms and your demand for industrial reform." Property itself was less at issue than the alternative modes of utilizing it. There could not be absolute control of property if the result was to stifle further enterprise. The crux of Doster's supposed radicalism lay in the tacit equation of ownership and monopoly, an investiture of rights which heightened the dependence of all others within the same propertied community who were denied access for their own purposes to property's benefits. Hence the absence of mutuality pertained not to class warfare, but to conflicting forms of ownership and the residual economic and social rights to be inferred from each form. He elaborated further: "You demand that the lenders of money, the owners of that species of capital, scale down their interest rates to accommodate you as the users of the same. Do you not? You demand that pools and trusts be prohibited, because you as the users of the property they sell, have greater interests in the same than they as owners have. Do you not?" The same could be said of "patent and copyright laws," prompting Doster to conclude: "And you are right in all these things."[5]

It is possible that we have traced what was more than an intra-capitalist contest, a matter which also has bearing on the larger argument. In describing conflicting modes within the same formation I have not intended to make light of the Populist challenge but to understand it with greater precision. If it can be shown that Doster did not break cleanly with a capitalistic order, then what might be said about the inner boundaries of the possibly dominant expression of Populism? For it did not pretend to a socialist identity or systemic diagnosis, nor did it possess the evident acuity to press for distinctions at the heart of ownership's prerogatives, rather than in the areas of power, size, and conduct alone. Doster's criticism moved beyond the attributes of power to the plane of integral repressiveness. Even when he confused ownership with monopolization, he identified and questioned a primal category of capitalism and therefore was more vulnerable to attack than others. This gave to the analysis a potential for overcoming propertied restraints; but he nonetheless did not fulfill this potential.

A final clue to the limits he observed is in his attempts at clarification during and after the 1896 campaign. Doster seems entirely consistent here. He did not qualify the substance of the earlier analysis of ownership and use. The 1893 speech referred to *Munn v. Illinois*, wherein Chief Justice Waite, speaking for the Court, affirmed as compatible with due process that custom sanctions regulation of property devoted to uses in which the public has an interest. The decision, notwithstanding Justice Field's dissenting opinion (which in spirit embodied all that Doster contested against), made complete sense of the 1891 statement and was itself within a capitalist, though not monopolistic, framework. Thus, when charges of subversion again surfaced in 1896, Doster, as the party's candidate for chief justice in Kansas, declared in late

August: "What I referred to was where a person or corporation had dedicated property to the use of the people. In that I said just what Justice Waite of the supreme court decided many years ago. Telegraph, telephone, railroad, and like companies dedicate their property to the public, and in such cases I am willing to stand by my assertion." With what may have been a sigh of exasperation (so far had the Fieldian transmogrification of the Fourteenth Amendment proceeded in contemporary social thought), he added: "I still maintain my position as before, and at the same time I declare that I am not an anarchist."[6]

In view of Doster's reliance on common-law principles in his treatment of issues concerning the public interest, his remark to the Populist state nominating convention in July deserves mention: "If elected, though hampered by technical decisions in the interests of wealth, I will diligently search the books to find some law through which the interests of the common people may be subserved." This statement as well gave Kansans pause, because it marked a judicial revolutionism which was at one with the concept of use. And yet, when questioned directly, in postelection interviews, Doster again revealed an antimonopolist perspective which depended on a return to and respect for fundamental law. Speaking to a reporter on the presumed difference of his position from that of his colleagues, he said: "No sir, I know only one code of law and that is the same one studied by the other lawyers and I shall try to follow it as best I can." His traditionalistic roots can be seen in his reply to another reporter: "[M]any of the recent decisions have been along lines of new legal departure, extorted from the courts by the capitalistic institutions of the country. If I have any views at all different from that of everybody else it is that we need a return to the old ways and the old common law precedents." Imperfectly realized as was Doster's separation from existing society, intracapitalist differences like those his ideas exemplified merit serious elaboration. These differences indicated alternative developmental patterns laden with meaning for the political and structural concreteness of a humane social order. Referring to the "common law precedents," Doster closed in dignified understatement: "They will be found more consonant with theories of popular right at least."[7]

In a Labor Day address in 1894, Doster raised the distinction between technology and the social context in which it operates. I once discussed the speech, as part of Populism's rational acceptance of industrial growth, and I still find the distinction useful. It enables us to make two points about modernity (in the Populists' own time, as well as later) which might otherwise escape our notice. First, to criticize existing capitalist practices, as Populists did, was not necessarily to attack the industrial process. Rendering capitalism synonymous with industrialism merely fended off discussion of the former. This usage attached the stigma of irrationality (the putative rejection of modernity) to the analysis of capitalism and protest against specific abuses. It precluded the expression of alternative patterns of development, because they were presumed to be anachronistic and/or socially destructive. Second, distinguishing industrialism from capitalism conversely permitted the more direct assessment of responsibility for the features of degradation which converted potential abundance into widespread economic privation. Simply, the machine did not inherently dehumanize man. To understand the consequences of production, Populists maintained, one had to look to the framework in which it was organized. In this case, they saw a profit orientation which had become associated with political dominance and which had proven extraneous to productive efficiency and to humane performance. Feelings of exploitation were heightened by the seemingly nonsensical disparity between the forces available to overcome want and the continued existence of social misery. This incongruity was perceived variously as a gap between material possibility and political reality, the malappropriation of technology, and, above all, a systemic disposition to the creation of impoverishment (as necessary to capitalistic industrial success).

According to Doster, industrialism had to be set free. It had to be loosened from its restrictive moorings, and the essential neutrality of the forces of technology recaptured. In this passage on alienation, expressed as social dependence, he said of the laborer: "Everything which goes to sustain his physical life, which enables him to conduct his daily toil, which makes existence possible in this fierce competitive strife have become the monopoly of others—others to whom he sustains only the harshest and most exacting kind of contract relations." This unwanted supervention, ownership/monopoly, deflected technological advancement from humanly fulfilling ends, and to the (highly unneutral) enhancement of class dominance. In preindustrial times, productive elements were within the producer's reach; since then, they had taken on a more complex and social aspect. The new forces (Doster had particularly in mind primal sources of energy: "steam, electricity, compressed air") were still theoretically susceptible to the community's direction, but they had instead become privately appropriated. They were more distanced from the needs of the producer. "But these, the common property of all, have been made the monopoly of the few, have been turned aside from the beneficent ends for which designed, to serve the selfish purposes of avarice and greed."

The preceding passage reflected an irreducible plateau of rationality concerning the industrial question proper. Far from adopting a retrogressive standard, Populists would liberate productive forces, especially from political constraints associated with monopolism. Indeed, one of their principal charges was that the opposition parties had proven incapable of meeting the challenge posed by altered circumstances: "In the face of the power exerted by the monopolists of these tremendous engines of industry and commerce the republican and democratic parties stand paralyzed—hypnotized as it were, unable to control it or give it direction and shape for common good." It is not difficult to see the political and psychological advantages of the foregoing distinction. For if the major parties retreated before the combined impact of monopolism and industrialism with the monopolist element probably decisive, Populists, on the other hand, by separating the components, could more clearly view the industrial process. Not only was it not menacing; it was itself menaced by patterns of ownership that were extrinsic to it. And they could therefore isolate specifically the factor of concentrated wealth as requiring attention. As Doster further noted, "against the tyrannical exercise of this power the People's party in behalf of the laborers of the land protests." Significantly, he added: "The failure to adapt the legislation of the country to the strange conditions which this new life has forced upon us is the cause in greater part of our industrial ills."

In recognizing that a qualitative change had occurred with the advent of modern industry, Doster introduced a more explicitly political or constitutional argument. In keeping with other statements, it complemented and extended the structural discussion, because beyond the analysis of technology lay the more enduring insight into the flawed nature of the general framework. The use of "tyrannical" itself denoted the political cast to any intended solution, for the restoration of rights was necessarily contemplated. Also the reference to legislation affirmed men's controlling powers. Far from being a runaway process, industrialism, removed from a monopolist-defined social context (this is the full import of "strange conditions"), could be placed within the jurisdiction of democratic principles.

Doster broke the encrusted surface of modernization to delineate the social determinants of an effective solution: "The Populist Party proposes as the only means to the desired end to utilize the power of the combined whole, to bring the power of the social mass to bear upon the rebellious individuals who thus menace the peace and safety of the state." If it was intended to justify political activity, the more basic purpose of the statement was to posit government's protective function. The phrase "peace and safety" was reminiscent of the common law from which Doster drew inspiration. Hence here as well he mentioned the governing dictum of 1891 and 1893: "It says that the subjects of those monopolies and trusts are public in their nature, and that the powers exercised through them are in reality the functions and agencies of government itself." Why not then transfer power to its correct, because more just, locus? This was the implicit constitutional question that had been raised by monopolism's quasi-public role in, and control over, the industrial system. We find a social paradigm of public ownership, marking the progression from Davis to Lewelling, and finally to Doster. The obligation of the state extended beyond ensuring survival, to countering directly the monopolistic pressures which created the problem: "It would have the government, that is, the people, assert their rightful dominion over the same, and as the philosophic basis of its claim it prescribes at least two political formulae: One that it is the business of the government to do that for the individual which he can not successfully do for himself, and which other individuals will not do for him upon just and equitable terms; the other, that the industrial system of a nation, like its political system, should be a government of and for and by the people alone."[8]

2. Economic Foundations of Repression

The Topeka *Advocate*, edited by Stephen McLallin, offered still more trenchant commentary on the industrial system. This commentary constituted a remarkable and sustained recording of national labor disturbance, which was the groundwork for inquiring into the coercive aspects of modern capitalism. Lewelling fairly soared in the antipoverty clouds. He was an eloquent political visionary, as will be seen from his inaugural address. Doster verged on a peculiarly American philosophic socialism: intellectualy tempered, genteel, in Bellamy-fashion above the uproar. But McLallin emerged as that subtle blend, the pragmatic theorist, matter-of-factly open to socialist ideas and capable of turning the constitutional discussion from the emphasis on individual opportunity to the more basic guarantees to the person, his right to organize, to speak, to protect himself. A recurrent theme was that of freedom from intimidation. McLallin was a physician, trained at Albany Medical College, who practiced for nearly two decades before founding a newspaper in Meriden, Kansas in the mid-1880s. His newspaper was relocated in Topeka in 1890 and became the state's major Populist weekly. He was the "compound of a Greek philosopher, of the austere, undemonstrative Scotchman, and the modern socialist," according to Annie Diggs, herself more astute ideologically than the better known Mary Elizabeth Lease.[9] For McLallin, systemic irrationality defined the nature of the contemporary framework. This irrationality was manifested in the callous treatment of working people (who were made victims of structurally induced poverty to enhance the profitability of operations) and in the disparity between industrial potential and actual performance. Together, these factors made up a statement of surplus hardship and misdirected economic policies and goals.

Improved technology symbolized the practicability of more equitable relations of production and distribution. But in a context of monopolist appropriation, the result had been otherwise. Machinery had cheapened the working populace by displacing numerous laborers. In turn, this led to the formation of a huge reserve of unemployed, who were forced to compete among themselves, further depressing the wage-level for all. Security was nonexistent. With this summary of much that appeared in the *Advocate*, one turns to an April 1894 editorial, published at the time of horrendous unemployment and marching victims:

> Let us admit, for our present purpose, that there is more of everything produced than the necessities of the people require. The fact that all are not supplied, then, shows that there is something wrong in our system. . . . Look at the multitudes who have been but recently thrown out of employment, and whose families have been destitute in consequence. . . . It is cruel, it is inhuman, to attribute these conditions to laziness, drunkenness and incompetency. They are the natural product of a false and vicious system by which the few grow rich beyond all human need, and the many are doomed to eternal poverty and want.

The alacrity with which such a judgment, in effect an outright and total condemnation, was reached bespoke more than an evident sense of injustice. "False" and "vicious" were terms designed to probe to the infrastructure of capitalism, to a modal pattern of social dominance, resting on absolutist controls over, and claims made on behalf of, property. The result not only defined a new *Zeitgeist* (analogous to Doster's "strange conditions"), but inexcusably degraded—a planned misdirection—human beings for the sake of profit maximization.

The *Advocate* was clearer on the qualitative change: "One of the causes of this 'modern condition' is the monopoly of machinery and other means of production and distribution by which the few are benefited and the many are deprived of fair opportunities in life." The shibboleth for an age now became a term of reproach, modernity devouring its own commitment to a progressive future: "Contrast this 'modern condition' with what might be attained by a proper use of the instrumentalities of modern production and distribution." The implicit standard (it spoke as well of "a proper distribution of labor") was that of socially determined needs. These took precedence over narrowly capitalistic operating principles. The disposition was toward measured growth—Populists would not destroy the current generation in the name of economic progress—and a more balanced sharing of material benefits.

Work, and its denial, was of central concern: "Suppose, as we propose, that machinery, instead of being used to displace labor, were used to diminish the hours that each should be employed. . . . Under such a system, no one who has the disposition to work would need to be idle." The statement proposed more than a spread-the-work expedient. It advocated access to the means of securing a livelihood ("thereby continuing," the editorial noted earlier, "the opportunities of all to provide the comforts and luxuries of life for every member of society"). And beyond that, it referred to work as the political-ethical criterion of reward: "Work should be so distributed that each should do his share and receive the reward of his labor." If unconsciously this was a Kansas paraphrasing of the Marxian adage, explicitly the argument was that monopolistic capitalism reflected an epochal change. Through control of the productive instruments, the distribution of work was shaped by the powers and requirements of ownership.

At issue was the fundamental ordering of priorities: equitableness; an inclusive entitlement to labor (and, to be inferred, a political economy organized to provide work for all who were willing); and, with pressures eased, the goal of a multifaceted individual. None of the foregoing was thought realizable in the prevailing circumstances. The last, particularly, dramatized the conflict between untrammeled development and a conception of *pace* that did not violate human growth. The conclusion, which merged abundance and fulfillment, was seemingly visionary. Yet it supposed the rational direction of productive forces and not their dismantlement to be effective: "Work enough should be done to supply the demand of the whole people for every comfort and luxury of life; and the time not required for such production should be devoted to rest, to mental culture, to social intercourse and recreation."[10]

Several months before, McLallin had already crisply stated the socialist potential in his analysis: "The best features of our government to-day, national, state and municipal, are those which are purely socialistic. We would refer especially to our public school system and our postal system." What redeems McLallin from the innocuousness of a Davis is at first glance his added concreteness: "Municipal ownership of waterworks, gas works, electric light plants, and other public utilities by which the people receive the maximum of service for a minimum of cost afford other examples of pure socialism, by which serious abuses are corrected and great benefits secured to the public." It is not so much his agenda for action, however, as his reasoning about the corrective function, which proves instructive. One identifies here an internal resilience. There is a capacity for extending the argument, because it is not blocked by doctrinal antisocialism. This set the *Advocate* apart, to a certain degree, from much of Populism, especially in viewing the municipal plane as a precedent rather than an acceptable upper limit.

"It is undoubtedly true," the *Advocate* continued, "that observing and studious Populists with such examples before them, have come to believe that a still wider extension of socialistic doctrines and practices would be beneficial to mankind. Looking about them they see nearly every industry monopolized by a corporation; and they are conscious of the robbery practiced upon them for private gain." McLallin addressed not merely the service aspect of public ownership, but the specifically political question of corporate power. This removed the discussion from an abstract context of social efficiency to a specific one of a necessary response. Attention had been fixed on the state's protective role in achieving economic balance: "They have come to believe that many of the abuses to which they are subject might be remedied, and their condition be bettered by a proper exercise of the power of the government."[11]

The case for public ownership of railroads was put more bluntly (it "is basic and fundamental, and can never be surrendered") still earlier in 1893, primarily because regulation alone had been entirely ineffective: "Every effort at control either by state or national authority has been a dismal failure, and will continue to be, so long as these great highways are owned by corporations. The transportation question is one of transcendent importance to the people, and experience has demonstrated that the government must either own the railroads or the railroad corporations will own the government."[12] There was no illusion in the treatment of public ownership that the government as then constituted was an unwitting accomplice to the growing political-economic copartnership. The argument, particularly in its constitutional form, was presented in exhortative terms. Ownership became the government's positive responsibility, were it faithfully to perform its custodial function.

The practical extension of the collective factor was carried forward shortly after, in early 1894, when labels such as socialism were not present to induce caution: "We hold that public ownership of railroads, telegraphs, telephones, and all other utilities now monopolized or susceptible of being monopolized for private gain at the expense of the people, would inure to the benefit of the people, and that it is therefore the *duty* of the government in execution of the constitutional obligation to provide for the public welfare to *assume* the ownership and management of all such utilities and monopolies in the interest of the public" (italics, original). The preceding is noteworthy in two respects. The editorial broadly defined utilities, taking in enterprises having a public character, and public ownership in such areas was to be applied to incipient monopolization. Whatever tended in the direction of monopoly, whether or not structurally consummated, was included. Yet despite the vast stretch of antimonopolism covered, one is struck by the way socialism and public ownership were treated as separable questions. The *Advocate* showed greater boldness on the latter.

Partly, this was a politic shuffling of the ideological deck. The *Advocate* had transferred the same activity from one category to another to fend off opposition. Still, the tentativeness in approaching socialism, which was even more apparent in the movement at large, recalled the essentially capitalistic framework—once below the sectors of principal concentration—to be conserved. The dissociation of topics reflected the unwillingness to fuse theoretical and pragmatic elements beyond that line where intra-capitalist distinctions had been left behind. Public ownership was the systemic wedge; and socialism, the more pious/visionary, though equally believed and consciously retained, outer cover. The *Advocate* may have conceded too much (and to little avail). In truth, the movement's enemies did not bother about ideological gradations of anticorporate practice. To favor public ownership was sufficiently opprobrious, as the editorial noted in commenting on press attacks on the position: "The *real* reason for all this opposition is found in the *profits* of monopolies" (italics, original).[13]

Further statements reflected the protosocialist disposition (within the mental frame of programmatic antimonopolism). The analysis centered on and sought to reverse what appeared as indefinitely expandable lines of capitalist influence. There was a reluctance to spell out matters of doctrine, but the view of the conflict as assuming total proportions gave specific remedies and criticisms the sense of constituting a structural alternative. One sees a logic of intentional replacement, as in the statement, "we propose to so revolutionize our economic and social systems that labor shall enjoy what it produces," taken from an editorial in August 1894. The position was not predicated on attaining socialism, but, self-evidently, neither did it accept the prevailing mode of capitalist organization. By "logic" I mean the reasons set forth, as in the remainder of the editorial, for a basic alteration. Systemic problems dictated the necessity for implementing far-reaching measures of social change. One example suffices: "We propose that the people shall own and operate the railways, telegraphs and telephones for their own interest and benefit; and that private corporations shall cease to monopolize these public functions for purposes of public plunder." A new or contrasting mode was contemplated: "We propose that every monopoly, as soon as established, shall be seized by the people and used for the public good, instead of, as now, for private gain."[14]

This logic, which led from concrete practice to a generalized indictment, could be applied to precisely such an issue as the capitalist appropriation of technology and the resultant deformation of the labor force. Later in 1894, the *Advocate* stated the problem: "Machinery has made it possible for women and children to do the work of men, and . . . they are employed in the place of men at from one-half to one-fourth of men's wages. It is thus that things which should afford the richest blessings to humanity, are converted, by a false and malicious industrial system, into instruments of the greatest evil." It was not that *the* solution automatically followed from this statement. Rather, as the terms of systemic probing would appear to suggest, a line of reasoning had been initiated. It would eventuate in some such question as "Whither?" "To what purpose?" or, as occurred here: "What is the remedy?" An answer had to be and was forthcoming. "Ours is public control of these means of production and a sufficient reduction of the hours of labor to afford every willing hand an opportunity to work, thereby giving the benefits of improved methods to labor rather than permit capital to absorb vast profits and turn labor out to starve."[15]

The issue of labor displacement elicited further commentary the next year: "Under the existing monopoly system of industry capital owns and controls all this labor-saving machinery, and derives all the benefits resulting from its use, while labor is forced into idleness and compelled to beg, steal or starve." The reference was to the so-called tramp problem. Large numbers of the unemployed, seen as a direct product of this capitalist formation, had been turned out to scratch for a bare existence. Meanwhile, any sense of public obligation to the welfare of the poor was nonexistent: "At the same time we are told that state and national governments are powerless to provide employment to these enforced idlers or assist them in any way to supply the necessities of themselves and families, because to do so would be paternalism." Only as criminals are they brought under governmental jurisdiction; then "places are provided for them," and "the products of their labor" made to compete "with those of free labor."

The bitterness of the denunciation was expressed not only in the term "enforced idlers," to designate the systemic roots of widespread impoverishment, but also in "paternalism," the epithet used by Populism's opponents to dismiss all humane and publicly sponsored alternatives. (For the *Advocate* especially, "paternalism" became a coded word with highly positive connotations. It covered the vague ground including and/or between public ownership and socialism, when the latter term proved too strong or inconvenient.) The *Advocate* had pointed to the contradiction of technological potential and concrete social misery, compounded by the conversion of unemployed into criminals (usually for purposes of legal identification, in that unemployment had itself been deemed criminal behavior) before work was given. The inevitable question followed: "Isn't it a system to be proud of?" Here, the interrogative thrust led to a warranted lament: "While such a state of things exists, the evils and disadvantages of which are generally acknowledged, every person who has the temerity to suggest that changes are possible by which a better state of society might be secured, is denounced as an impractical visionary and a crank."[16]

This was only one strand feeding into the diagnosis of what had been politely termed the "modern condition." In addition to structural criticism, evidences of human sympathy were important. In early December 1893, Governor Lewelling had issued his "Tramp Circular," urging compassionate regard for the poor on the part of local authorities, instead of the chilling enforcement of vagrancy statutes against those whose only "crime" was poverty. Immediately, the *Advocate* came to his defense. This was a penetrating statement of the reasons for structural change:

We are confronted to-day with very peculiar conditions, peculiar, not because they are new, but because they are so entirely unnecessary. In a land of unlimited resources, and of most marvelous plenty, millions of honest and willing hands are idle and in consequence thereof, they and those dependent upon them, are suffering from hunger and cold. These unnecessary conditions are the result of our vicious social and economic system. Idleness is enforced in consequence of vicious and discriminating laws, and to treat the helpless victims of these unnatural conditions as criminals is itself a crime against which every instinct of humanity revolts.

The discussion stripped America bare in its contemporary state. It offered no ideological solace from balmier days of the Republic. There was only the immediacy and pervasive hold of capitalist structure. It was as though the country were a current exemplification of centuries-old degradation. Borrowing Lewelling's own analogies, the editorial concluded: "Is poverty more tolerable in one age than in another? Are the poor of America poor from choice any more than were those in the reign of Queen Elizabeth, or in France under a 'dissolute monarchy?' Is a dissolute monarchy any worse than a dissolute republic?"[17]

Shortly after, the *Advocate*, in noting that the hungry were becoming dangerous, wondered, "and who can blame them, when surrounded by an abundance of everything they need, and which a false and vicious social and economic system had made it impossible for them to obtain by honest toil?" Behind the evident perception of structural breakdown, the sense was that the framework of rewards, founded on the value of industriousness, had also received a beating. There had been an arbitrary denial of work and the increased disparity in living conditions. When men were cheapened in the midst of plenty that yet remained outside their reach, where was the stimulus for accepting the work-discipline?

The *Advocate* may or may not have been concerned about upheaval; it *was* concerned about the traditional values, which were placed under continuing and tremendous stress by a social order tending toward the destruction of salutary and harmful elements alike. This was the fuller meaning of "dissolute," a coming-apart even of the propertied world per se and the impendent rupturing of the existing order: "The system under which wealth is concentrating, and poverty extending, is creating a wide gulf between the rich and the poor not only in condition but in feeling." This time, the inevitable question had an activist ring; the situation did not seem hopeless: "Shall the fear of 'paternalism' prevent interference with the system which has caused these conditions?"[18] In a separate editorial, the conventional social wisdom was turned upside down. Legal authority, not the supposed anarchist, presently endangered society: "Whither are we tending, anyway? We hear a great deal in these latter days about anarchy, but we hear very little about the unwarranted and lawless invasion of human liberty which is every day practiced under the garb of respectability by national, state and municipal governments."[19] Chiefly, the paper had in mind the denial of basic rights to the indigent under the vagrancy statutes, a legal order which made a mockery of equal protection by subjecting only the penniless to punishment, while encouraging summary arrests and flatly curtailing freedom of movement.

The further theme of intimidation emphasized a purposive disdaining of human worth. The resort to force made worker dependence the ratifying condition for the capitalist appropriation of technology. Here, the "tramp" was a punitive residue, both of avaricious values and systemic trends. Subsistence was the industrial norm wherever it could be accomplished. For the *Advocate*, the Homestead lockout of 1892 represented "the general unrest that everywhere pervades society throughout the world." It was the local expression of the drift of world capitalism: "In nearly every country upon the globe the rapid concentration of wealth in few hands is constantly widening the gulf between the patrician and the plebeian classes. . . . The tendency of the times is to constantly lower the standard of wages paid to labor in order to constantly add to the accumulations of the nonproducing classes." The already unemployed composed, with laborers imported from overseas, a surplus that could be used "to displace organized labor, always at lower wages than have been formerly paid." If capital accumulation was perceived to state a class relationship, repression, as the mechanism sustaining the "general policy," was seen as more basic: "The Pinkerton army, or if need be the state militia or the army of the United States, under the pretense of protection to vested rights, can always be relied upon to assist in the displacement and to see that it is accomplished to the satisfaction of the employers of labor."[20]

Later, following the success of management's lockout, the paper observed: "The fight at Homestead is only the beginning of the battle against organized labor. What has been done there will be repeated in detail in every great plutocratic establishment now employing union labor in the United States."[21]

Beyond an evident sympathy, one finds a penetrating critique of the role of organized violence, public as well as private, in disciplining the labor force. Unions had to be smashed, and workers' effectiveness in bargaining had to be prevented. Yet the analysis ran deeper, to the social characteristics of a polity in which laboring people knew little protection. Referring to vagrancy laws in 1893, before the Lewelling circular, the *Advocate* extended the discussion to what it had termed "the proper exercise of government power." Now it asserted the element of public responsibility: "Here is where our whole governmental and social system is fundamentally wrong; and right here, also, is where a perfect misconception of the objects and the proper functions of government prevails. Government is regarded as a big policeman with a club, whose sole business is to coerce its subjects into obedience to arbitrary authority." One can infer that the conception of government as a noncoercive instrument, registering the people's will, was more to its liking. It added: "The declaration that governments are established 'to provide for the general welfare' seems to be forgotten, and the horror of 'paternalism' hangs like a black pall over the burried [*sic*] hopes of the helpless poor—the vagrants—the criminals, under our Christian system of organized society."[22]

In remarking on Pennsylvania mining riots at the start of 1894, the *Advocate* contrasted putative anarchism with the systemic provocation of labor disturbance: "We have noticed that these same daily papers, so loud in their denunciations of the 'anarchistic' demonstrations of laboring men, are as silent as the tomb concerning the avarice and greed and systematic plunder which have driven these men to desperation, and thereby provoked the violent acts which are so severely condemned." And it queried: "Are these men demanding the overthrow of civil government or are they simply demanding justice for themselves and families?" Clearly, not civil government, but its prevailing organization and purposes, had to be replaced. The so-called anarchist sought to achieve a "condition of society" that would "equalize social conditions, remove incentive to crime, and establish an era of universal peace and brotherhood."[23]

The Coxey industrial army was among the most compelling symbols of human misery in this period. During the late winter and spring of 1894, the unemployed wended their way on foot to Washington from various distant points to make representations to Congress on behalf of financial legislation and public works. They were disbanded or arrested on arrival. Taking note of the sad procession, like so many brigades of the impoverished, the paper was not persuaded by the antiradical climate. It demanded that any inquiry be centered on the causes of impoverishment. The major-party press, it stated in mid-April, had avoided "all reference to the causes which have produced" the movement, "contemptuously" speaking of the men as tramps "who deserve to be arrested and treated as criminals upon general principles." The foundations of privation were the greater menace to society. Left unchecked, these conditions would indeed tend to criminalize the hardworking producer: "The causes which produce tramps and vagabonds are never alluded to. It is in this fact that the danger to the peace of the country really exists. Men do not become tramps and vagabonds from choice. When forced into idleness and compelled to take to the road in the fruitless effort to find employment it requires but a short time to make a vagabond of the man who under other and more favorable circumstances would be numbered among our best citizens." Similar to Morgan's concern for the imperiled estate of those "fortunate enough to accumulate anything," the paper tacitly equated independence with a less-propertied state. But it moved beyond expropriation to the roots of social criminality, lodged in the control over employment and the labor force: "The causes which force people into idleness are therefore responsible, not only for this Coxey movement, but for nearly all the lawlessness and crime of the country, as well."[24]

The Coxey experience raised a further issue. If calling attention to the plight of an underclass was its historic and symbolic function, the more immediate question posed was that of the inclusiveness of representative government. Did the poor enjoy the right to be heard? Were they even members of the political community? "These men have as much right to go to Washington and demand justice at the hands of congress as bankers, railroad magnates and corporation attorneys have to go and lobby for measures by which to plunder the public; and if their rights are not respected there will be trouble; rest assured of that."[25] The warning, if part bravado, pointed up the basic problem, which was explicitly treated the next week: "Who is it that is threatening violence to-day?" The socially dissident, "American citizens" who are "marching to Washington peaceably" to petition the government, encounter the resistance of authority: "The commissioners of the District of Columbia have issued a manifesto warning these men to abandon the idea of invading the territory. In the meantime the Washington police and the national guard are drilling for service against them; and all the threats of violence that have been made, and all the demonstrations indicating that violence is intended by anyone have been on the part of the national and district authorities."[26]

For the *Advocate*, the Pullman strike (July 1894) further exemplified the repressive consolidation of business power. A "military despotism," it noted in the strike's aftermath, appeared likely. The paper's initial commentary was reserved for the intervention, the unwarranted use of federal troops for strikebreaking purposes. It also objected to violence "deliberately created" by capital "in order to manufacture sentiment against the strikers."[27] In light of later historical accounts, the paper's contemporaneous observations, particularly those of late July, are not without merit. Here it described the underlying events and the concerted strategy of management:

The managers of the several railroads established headquarters at Chicago and were in constant consultation. They enlisted the press . . . in their support; and one of the methods adopted to the injury of the cause of labor was the constant and persistent misrepresentation of their claims and of their acts. Bums and hoodlums were employed by the railroad managers to incite riots and commit lawless acts, which the press at once attributed to the strikers in order to create prejudice against them in the minds of the people. These lawless acts were also designed to afford a pretext for police and military interference, and the promptness with which this was secured on demand of the corporations has been observed by everyone.

The *Advocate* had discerned a pattern: A core of opposition to labor enjoyed complex kinds of institutional support. Moreover, this led the writer to broader conclusions: "It has become apparent in this contest that in any difference between capital and labor the courts and all the civil and military authorities are at the service of organized capital. Labor has no right that capital or its allies are bound to respect." This had been stated numerous times before; however, the difference now was in the shock of direct military involvement. It was the final element of a unified antilabor posture, requiring that fresh thought be given to other manifestations of social reaction. Partly, the *Advocate* was drawing on its previous experience with vagrancy statutes: "As the men affected in this case are poor men, there is no likelihood of there being any constitutional bar to their punishment discovered." But it also scrutinized what then, and later, was taken to be reform legislation; presumably, given insight into the nature of the framework, little that was commendable could be expected: "Laws are made now-a-days to shield men of wealth—not poor men; and the interstate commerce law is no exception to the rule. Neither that or the so-called Sherman anti-trust law were ever designed to operate against the interests of organized capital." It is singular that these were mentioned in the context of the Pullman discussion, further illustrating the attempt to generalize from specific events. The imagery of aggression is also noteworthy: "They were designed solely as covers for legislation by which organized capital should be enabled to make further conquests over labor."[28]

In September, the paper said of the trial of Eugene V. Debs that "the case is prejudged, and no matter what the testimony may be, no American Railway union man can hope for justice in a Chicago court." It had not abandoned the view that there was a continuing onslaught against labor. Judicial partiality was one aspect. In the Debs case, "it has been the policy of the government to simply establish the fact of the commission of violence during the continuance of the late strike, and without offering an iota of testimony to connect the officers or members of the American Railway union with this violence, to infer their responsibility and punish them accordingly."[29] But even if due forms were observed, the larger purposes and design, as typified by the intervention, would remain unmodified. Hence, even into 1895, the *Advocate* continued its exploration of the subject: "So long as the authority to send troops into any part of the country under the pretense of enforcing some law, is exercised, we do not see that it is as much a question whether that authority is exercised in accordance with law or in defiance of law, as it is what the consequences will be to the liberties of the American people." It added in summary: "The main question is, are we ready for the recognition of an imperial government?"[30]

In October 1894, the paper's reference to military despotism was intended not to alarm, but to indicate the widespread character of repression. More was involved than a brutal social process associated with labor-displacing technology. For dominance per se in which armed strikebreakers gave concrete meaning to intimidation in class terms had to be demonstrated and secured over time. In commenting on the deployment of military posts at railroad and commercial centers, the *Advocate* fused the practical and the symbolic in stating the quasi-authoritative force of corporate power: "The companies and regiments organized to occupy these city bastiles and equipped with the latest improved instruments of death constitute a private army directly under the command of the capitalists of these cities, and ready, at their instance, to suppress any uprising of the common herd." This captured the negativism of the existing state; in addition to its suppressive activities (as in the Pullman strike) and in further contrast to the vision of political democracy, it approved the maintenance of private armies, chief among them the much hated Pinkertons. Here the emphasis on basic guarantees to the person assumed more definite form. Not only had the rights to organization, speech, and protection been denied, but this abrogation had been permitted to occur under private auspices. "In addition to these forces we must not forget the 30,000 Pinkertons, who constitute another private army, larger even than the present army of the United States, and also under the direct and immediate command of corporations and capitalists. These forces have for years stood ready at the call of the railroads and other large employers of labor to suppress strikes and carry terror into the ranks of the oppressed and discontented."

The enumeration continued, suggesting a society having multiple points of localized coercion: "But this is not all. The railroad companies themselves are organizing forces of their own, and equipping them with arms of the most approved patterns, thus constituting still another private army." The public sector also functioned to satisfy private requirements: "The excuse for the maintenance of a standing army in the United States has been the necessity of protection to the frontiers and the harbors and cities of our seaboards; but the policy now is to withdraw the troops from the frontiers and concentrate them near the large inland cities." The sentence which followed conveyed with a certain exactitude the militarized framework and strategy of capitalist development, which divested the state of its popular foundations, character, and goals: "It would seem sufficiently clear to the unbiased mind from these facts that we are even now far on the road to the establishment of a military despotism in this country."[31]

The phrase "military despotism" reappeared several months later. When *The American Banker* in late March of 1895 indicated a willingness to support the constitutionality of the income tax (at the time arguments were being heard before the Supreme Court), as a concession to forestall social revolution, the *Advocate* quickly rejoined that, "it is a hopeful sign" when upper groups, previously blind to "impending disaster," now "begin to permit themselves to see." The response, of course, was too limited: "If they would avert the revolution, however, they have something to do more than to pay an income tax. That is a very small matter." Precisely here it offered a counterstatement of the outstanding problems facing America, and, by implication, the substance of Populism's contrasting economic vision: "Monopoly of the resources of nature and of the means of production and distribution will have to come to an end. Robbery under sanction of law will have to stop. Equal rights and equal opportunities will have to become a reality. Military despotism will have to be done away with and courts will have to cease their usurpations. Conditions that will permit the producer of wealth to retain and enjoy that which he produces, will have to be established and maintained."

This alternative mode was, in one respect, moderate. It represented a literal insistence on the safeguards of fundamental law, to be seen as the mark of, and to be incorporated within, antimonopolist capitalism. Monopolistic restrictions on enterprise and the consequent legalization of privilege had to be halted. Robbery was the antithesis of fair entitlement, rejecting the social welfare and producer values through the alliance of business and government against the laboring classes. While its militarized features energized the coalition and multiplied the possibilities of repression, they were neither exceptional nor adventitious. The paper's distinctive contribution was to suggest that these features fit in logically (if not also inherently) with monopoly-capitalism's preferential situation in the existing polity and its command over the work force. By this account, Populism called for the wholesale deflation of all historical, structural, and class practices that formed a superfluous constraint on traditional rights, autonomous public functions, and, not least, political and economic self-expression. To be moderate was not to be quiescent: "There will be no security against revolution until these things are accomplished. It is in the air."[32]

3. The Human Purposes of Civilization

Governor Lewelling's inaugural address (January 9, 1893) provides a fitting close to the discussion of these Kansas materials. It suggested the philosophic and systemic differences still possible within the confines of capitalism. As state papers go, this has few parallels as an unabashed pleading for human welfare. Lewelling's was a temporary voice of authority, which denied the majesty and hold of authority itself when it failed in its mission to protect the people's liberties. (This was his informal compact theory.) And like Martin Luther King, Jr. in his famous statement of 1963, Lewelling too had a dream of the future which called for the abolition of poverty as the precondition for justice.

The opening lines already charted government's direction: "The survival of the fittest is the government of brutes and reptiles, and such philosophy must give place to a government which recognizes human brotherhood." Yet one finds this in the context of ideological ambiguity. Modifications to capitalism were in tension with capitalistic premises: "It is the province of government to protect the weak, but the government to-day is resolved into a struggle of the masses with the classes for supremacy and bread, until business, home and personal integrity are trembling in the face of possible want in the family. Feed a tiger regularly and you tame and make him harmless, but hunger makes tigers of men. If it be true that the poor have no right to the property of the rich let it also be declared that the rich have no right to the property of the poor." Given the unjust distribution of forces, culminating in the danger of "possible want in the family," Lewelling offered a clear indictment of the state for its inability to preserve an equilibrium of social rights. Still, yearnings were expressed that supposed a propertied framework for their realization. I refer not to business, home, or personal integrity, but to hunger as a coefficient of protest in which an implicit harmony would follow with the restoration of class balance. No one desires people turned into tigers in the upper or lower strata.

The last sentence in the passage was nearly axiomatic and revealed the notion of balance in its wider dimensions. It went beyond the proper relationship of government and business to stress the security of ownership, place, and liberties at all levels. Enjoyment was universalized on the condition that it would be neither privileged nor restrictive to others. The disavowal of expropriation applied to both rich and poor; and the shielding of lower groups from political and economic depredations was viewed as itself a sufficient structural reform. The formula did not leave the prevailing formation intact. It did, however, retain the categories of rich and poor, with property as much a cementing as a divisive force. What redeemed the passage (particularly the last sentence) from being a mere affirmation of the existing political and structural condition of society and instead strengthened the Populist challenge was the recognition that a balance had not been achieved and could not be achieved without somewhat drastic remedies. Thus, to reach the desired equilibrium required an active process of systemic reconstruction. Balance, in turn, supposed the directing of governmental pressures toward upper economic groups, avowedly for the laborer's welfare. Only then would enjoyment begin to have meaning.

Property was respected; however, its structural matrix had to be democratized, to the extent, at least, that internal conflict and attendant hardship would cease. Ideally, all would receive protection. Practically, the cause of the poor was to be the first priority: "It is the mission of Kansas to protect and advance the moral and material interests of all its citizens. It is its especial duty at the present time to protect the producer from the ravages of combined wealth. National legislation has for twenty years fostered and protected the interests of the few, while it has left the South and West to supply the products with which to feed and clothe the world, and thus to become the servants of wealth." After discussing key discriminatory policies, Lewelling added: "The instincts of patriotism have naturally rebelled against these unwarranted encroachments of the power of money."

He turned to political philosophy. For Populists, the state had to be strengthened as it was subordinated. The contradiction is resolved the moment one poses the traditional question, sovereignty to what purpose? Populists did not indulge in state-worship. Sovereign power exercised for its own sake denied the construction they placed on the nation's founding principles. Still, not to consider them statist of a special kind falsifies, even among those who had never thought about such matters, the deepest level of their social perspective. Populism, as a fairly cohesive ideological stance, necessitated a reliance on the state to effect its measures and, more important, to focus its sense of wrong and to define what was practicable in America. Abstract the state from Populism and antimonopolism ceases to function as the propelling force. One is left with Smithian economics, inchoate humanism, and added reinforcement to an agrarianism which, when integrated within a more specifically industrial mental frame, is in fact partially muted.

Strengthening the state was the prerequisite for a concrete social transformation. The state's augmented power would define the process and direction of change. But subordination, on the other hand, supplied the substance of the intended framework for social change. Populism did not lose sight of the individual (even if, at the highest level of abstraction, this set up an antagonism to the notion of class). From this baseline, it had generalized to a conception of the public, not as a mystical entity or the sum of individuals merely aggregated, but as a collective populace which had been endowed with basic rights. The public became an individualism en masse. It reflected a separable and overriding interest, the public interest, which took precedence over, and was subserved by, the state.

Sovereignty was coextensive with the endeavor to secure and preserve individual liberties. This principle was not to be applied in Lockean fashion, wherein property (hypostatized as the community of propertyholders) possessed antecedent claims. Instead, it was consciously democratic in scope with such claims resting on human requirements. Property was thought to be an important, though not the exclusive, component. Populism, contrary alike to classic liberalism and late nineteenth-century American social ideology, contended that nonpropertyholders were inherently endowed with the attributes of humanity. These were to be respected and nourished by government as its primal task.

In a memorable passage, Lewelling expounded the foregoing relationship of the individual and the state. One finds here not only a Populist compact-theory, but also the derivative argument sanctioning governmental activism. It was one which treated constitutional guarantees with seriousness. These guarantees comprised a fully realized mandate of political democracy: "The problem of to-day is how to make the State subservient to the individual, rather than to become his master. Government is a voluntary union for the common good. It guarantees to the individual life, liberty, and the pursuit of happiness. The government then must make it possible for the citizen to enjoy liberty and pursue happiness. If the government fails of these things, it fails in its mission, it ceases to be of advantage to the citizen; he is absolved from his allegiance and is no longer held to the civil compact."

Consent rested on the belief that sovereignty had to be directed to the common good. This was the expectation. It was also the grounds for subordination, the explanation of the genesis of civil society, and the measure of performance. While abrogation, like revolution, was more symbolic defiance, its mention, besides registering extreme displeasure, called attention to the meaning of the compact. Government was the people's servant. It was a mere instrument, a structural convenience to ensure equitableness. It was not an entity set apart. It was not controlled by, or beholden to, social interests which demonstrably worked to infringe the safety, rights, and opportunities of the generality. Government was chargeable with whatever occurred for good or ill within the polity. It had to be judged accordingly. Lewelling added (indicating that abrogation was not a matter of whim, but concerned basic defects): "If old men go to the poor-house and young men go to prison, something is wrong with the economic system of the government."

State-responsibility was a grave matter. The Populist emphasis on government served frequently to deflect criticism from capitalism's internal, systemic features. Dichotomizing the sources of abuse resulted in misplaced confidence that political change in the narrow sense would suffice to contain monopolistic power. In the present case, however, concentrating on one predominating factor, the state, enabled Lewelling to fashion an indictment which called into question the prevailing industrial structure. The analysis struck deeply, so that whether or not it bypassed capitalism, it underscored the presence of needless suffering. It also suggested, through the interrogatory approach, the logic of an alternative vision:

What is the State to him who toils, if labor is denied him and his children cry for bread? What is the State to the farmer who wearily drags himself from dawn till dark to meet the stern necessities of the mortgage on the farm? What is the State to him if it sanctions usury and other legal forms by which his home is destroyed and his innocent ones become a prey to the fiends who lurk in the shadow of civilization? What is the State to the business man, early grown grey, broken in health and spirit by successive failures; anxiety like a boding owl his constant companion by day and the disturber of his dreams by night? How is life to be sustained, how is liberty to be enjoyed, how is happiness to be pursued under such adverse conditions as the State permits if it does not sanction?

One senses in Populism that a social transformation was being advocated primarily by implication. For more than the remedies (however structural), the searching question carried the force and conviction of a basic change. Lewelling's queries were unanswerable under the existing circumstances of society. Not even his inclusion of the businessman blunted the call for social change, which in any case was not thought incompatible with antimonopolist capitalism. This example accented the theme of pervasive failure and systemic breakdown. Lewelling, unlike William Jennings Bryan in 1896, did not make the businessman a symbol for all working people. Laborer and farmer were still distinct; their deprivation originated in a common framework. But the final question above, on the practical realization of life, liberty, and happiness, best suggested advanced criticism. One sees here an illustration of Populist literalism, the insistence that first principles had to be implemented. The state not only had defaulted in its public responsibilities, but it in fact performed an inescapable role in the functioning of capitalism. This set the stage for the most fundamental question a Populist might ask. It was one which expressed the uncommon trust he placed in government: "Is the State powerless against these conditions?"

The question drew together Populism's affirmative elements, which rested on the belief in the efficacy of human activity. It was this conviction which fueled their confidence in democratic prospects. Political consciousness, faith in the restoration of a reform-matrix identified with constitutional rights, and unrelieved social discontent, all merged in the Populist assertion of mission. The movement's burden, assumed willingly, was to organize in defense of social liberties and popular governance. Lewelling responded to his own question: "This is the generation which has come to the rescue. Those in distress who cry out from the darkness shall not be heard in vain. Conscience is in the saddle." The propertied idiom reappeared, but it became practically engulfed in the more consequential needs facing an impoverished people: "We have leaped the bloody chasm and entered a contest for the protection of home, humanity, and the dignity of labor." The listing superbly distilled the movement's aims.

Borrowing a phrase from Ignatius Donnelly, Lewelling blended awakened feelings and the dream of a perfectible society, to be attained through extending the reach of government: "The grandeur of civilization shall be emphasized by the dawn of a new era in which the people shall reign, and if found necessary they will 'expand the powers of government to solve the enigmas of the times.'" To return to our question on the purpose of sovereignty, a conception of people's government logically would, and did, follow. This became a transcendent public standard to satisfy individual needs, taking precedence over conventional, because they had become oppressive, arrangements: "The people are greater than the law or the statutes, and when a nation sets its heart on doing a great and good thing it can find a legal way to do it." The people were not above, but the source of, law. Finally, sovereignty *was* the people, and government, a projection of its collective authority, existing to do its will.

Lewelling affirmed, then, the capacity of the governed to govern themselves. He closed with an open-ended, natural-rights position. It was fixed not on property, but on popular rationality. This vantage ground helps to account for an unashamed expansiveness of vision, though the eloquence remains peculiarly his own: "I have a dream of the future. I have the evolution of an abiding faith in human government, and in the beautiful vision of a coming time I behold the abolition of poverty. A time is foreshadowed when the withered hand of want shall not be outstretched for charity; when liberty, equality and justice shall have permanent abiding places in the republic."[33]

4. Postscript: Industry and Unbridled Wealth

To extend these findings and suggest a congruence of ideas, I turn very briefly to a different quarter, several statements of Henry Demarest Lloyd that apply to a coercive industrial structure. (I will also return to Lloyd in chapter 8 in a discussion of the moral dimensions of political sovereignty.) The public welfare doctrine, to which the Kansas Populists gave statist features, became more staunchly anti-laissez-faire in the original thought of Lloyd. Lloyd, a brilliant social critic, economic analyst, and investigative writer, was deeply involved in Populist intellectual and political activities as part of a distinguished reform career that spanned more than two decades. He preeminently represented the small, yet influential, urban expression of Populism. Lloyd sought to infuse the political structure with ethical content in order to ensure a democratic reorganization of industry, making explicit provision for "a people's government" to make certain that economic arrangements were subsumed under the social needs of the larger community. The reorganization, he explained in a speech that climaxed the 1894 Populist campaign in Chicago, would be based on the following principles: "1) No use of public powers or public property for private profit. 2) The public have the right to use public powers for the public welfare to any extent the public demands." In urging a separation of the private and public realms, Lloyd did not renounce the market mechanism where it still could be applied (to a nonmonopolistic scale of private activities), but he altered the relationship of forces on behalf of an independent state and, even more important, he identified the public as the moral underpinning of state authority. If the prevailing order had led to "the workingmen tramping about, to find no doors open for them in the palaces of industry they built," this fundamental dissociation from economic and social processes would be remedied through more responsive institutions that fulfilled "the hope of realizing and incarnating in the lives of the common people the fullness of the divinity of humanity."[34]

In his correspondence, Lloyd frequently voiced skepticism about classical liberalism, particularly in its contemporary operations. Free trade would not be free, he wrote, until the articles "were freely made as well as freely traded, and 'freely' means in obedience to true laws of honor, health, and beauty. Trade that exchanges the products of slave labor, whether of plantation or slum, cannot be free." He implied the rational standard of an economy predicated on service when he declared that Andrew Carnegie was "one of the worst representatives of our merely mercenary system of ordering industry which is perverting it from the supply of demand and the production and distribution of the wealth in nature for the use of all men, and making it an instrument of personal aggrandisement and cannibalistic selfishness." He further decried the centralization of power attendant on "controlling the markets, with all that that implies of other control, social, ec[c]lesia[s]tical, political and educational," a permeation of corporate influence that posed "a question as great as any of those which have made the previous crises in history."[35]

Lloyd endorsed the idea of "social intervention," and in response to a critic's charge that the result would be mediocrity in society, he contended that the action of the state was necessary to enhancing the progressive dimensions of civilization. In the process, he turned the existing value system upside down: "The whole idea of the State and of society does not seem to be the preservation of the weak but the preservation of the strong. Those who rely upon the grosser motives and powers seem to me to be really the weaker. Those whose inspiration is of a higher sort seem to me to be the stronger; and the net result of civilization has been to preserve the stronger from the insanities of the weaker and lower. Men like our great monopolizing capitalists of today are not the stronger unless lunatics are the stronger." On the ethical plane, the analogue of social intervention was the redefinition of the self-interest that was at the core of laissez-faire ideology: "The whole problem can be argued out from the point of view of self-interest, putting the self-interest of the community against the self-interest of the individual; the self-interest of the better against the self-interest of the worse; and reading the survival of the strongest to mean the survival of the stronger virtues, not the stronger greed." A structural change, however far reaching, would not have lasting effect unless it was accompanied by a transformation of individualistic values: "A revolution that should break up all these properties and re-distribute them among the people [his reference was to concentrated wealth], and leave our present motives in operation, would only end, ultimately, in reestablishing all the monopolies again."[36]

Lloyd viewed large-scale enterprise as predaceous; it aggressively pursued a labor strategy designed to discipline and break the will of the work force, if necessary by means of starvation. His ironically titled *A Strike of Millionaires Against Miners* (1890), a case study of how the lockout was used to institute a drastic cut in wages and to destroy the union, described a context of virtually unrestrained private power in "flagrant nullification of law." Lloyd cherished few hopes of a return to unmodified laissez-faire: "The corporation, which the great political economist Adam Smith predicted would never come into general use, has grown to be the almost universal instrument of modern business." Its "cloak of invisibility," "secrecy," and "anonymity" made possible "a concert of action," but rejected any principle of obligation or accountability to the workers or to the general public. Corporate policy in this instance was centered on the creation of a company town to be peopled by a large surplus of workers who had been attracted by promises of high wages and steady work. In explaining the policy, Lloyd was openly scornful of classical theory: "The 'supply' of labor is in this way made to overrun the 'demand,' and the sacred character of the 'immutable law of supply and demand' is given an illustration which workingmen understand, even if political economists do not." The result was to make "wages low by the underbidding of the unemployed against the employed," in turn keeping "the men poor, humble, and submissive" to the corporation's "regulations and exactions." Even when they were employed, the miners "got for their lives and labor a scanty allowance of food, clothing, roofing, but not enough," and "practically nothing" to maintain "their health and strength," or to provide for "their old age" and "their duties as fathers and citizens."[37]

With a protracted lockout, issued without warning, the situation created destitution, sickness, and fear, prompting on Lloyd's part a revealing distinction between human perishability and the inanimate nature of capital: "It was a strike of dollars against men; of dollars which could lie idle one year, two years, longer if necessary, and be dollars still, against men who began to fade into nothingness the next day." The utter depersonalization of working people, sanctioned because "our market morality has overgrown all other morality," had reached a culmination in the conditions that were imposed on the men when they were rehired. They "were to be made helpless, then asked to make a *free* contract," at one-third the previous scale, in which all matters "which lay at the very foundations of livelihood and rights" were surrendered; work could be had "only at the price of dumb submission and disunited helplessness." In this "open letter to the millionaires," Lloyd focused on the coercive nature of the labor contract; it was based on a class relationship that denied humane principles, legal rights, and any possibility of self-protection for the poor: "You have in the mines a class of useful and docile animals in the mules which stay in the depths for years, and sometimes never come back to the surface. You always treat with them 'individually.' If your plans succeed, it will not be long before you will have the power to keep your miners like your mules—down below from year's end to year's end. There will be nothing left them worth coming to the surface for, because, if you can make them give up their unions, you can make them give up everything." Freedom was perishing as well: "No wonder the workingman has to be locked out and starved before he feels 'free' enough (of food and manhood) to make such a bargain. . . . The miners, in submitting to it, and we, in allowing them to submit to it, degrade their manhood, and that of the republic."[38]

CHAPTER FIVE

Alternative Views of Government:
Nebraskans and Watson

The preceding Kansas materials suggest that antimonopolist capitalism was not a paper tiger. Lewelling, Doster, and McLallin provided a specific industrial analysis that indicated a protosocialist dimension of Populist thought which seriously qualified the ethical standards and economic operations of the prevailing framework. The displacement of labor was only one aspect of the capitalist appropriation of technology, which created wider systemic conditions of underconsumption and the pervasive degradation of working people. From the critique these Populists offered, they appear to have believed that structural remedies alone would furnish an adequate corrective. Further, such remedies required the activation of the state, most visibly in the form of public ownership, but also politically and ideologically as the representative of a broader definition of human welfare. This collective direction, however, did not necessarily predominate in the movement. Nor did it stand itself in isolation; rather, it built upon, more than departed from, Populism's basic ideological statement. Constitutionalism remained a foremost concern, which looked to enhanced governmental powers in order to address modernity and realize traditional liberties. In this chapter, I will examine further strands, affecting the role of government, of the Populist view of antimonopolist capitalism.

The presence of an independent state, as the mechanism for arresting monopolistic trends, effectively distinguished Populism from a Smithian framework of laissez-faire capitalism. For the latter, the system of exchange and its corollary of the trust in automatic processes took on the interrelated responsibilities of economic regulation and social welfare. Populists accepted basic features of capitalism and, with Adam Smith, expressed the more specific desire to actuate development through the system's internal competitive energies. They nevertheless rejected—sometimes explicitly, as in Morgan's analysis—the classical model of capitalism, because they were fearful that laissez-faire in practice had an organic and historical connection to emergent monopolism. When it was left unregulated, laissez-faire generated aggregations of wealth which could no longer be contained by a market economy. It also destroyed any meaning for the concept of individualism, the principle on which this economic stage had presumably been founded.

According to this reasoning, government would supply the safeguards that Smith thought unnecessary, if not also infeasible. Populists proposed such safeguards to open opportunity in opposition to monopolist restrictions and simultaneously to democratize opportunity through the broader participation of lower groups in the economic process. Further, a conception of social property, corresponding to the notion of public sovereignty and applicable where competition did not or could not obtain, would be established. Populists freely entertained quasi-socialist forms, manifested in public ownership, to heighten capitalistic activity in the remainder of the structure. This became a political economy of competitive capitalism, which, in placing antimonopolism on augmented state foundations, would significantly modify puristic laissez-faire. (Though the labels may appear similar, I here point up and will explore elsewhere the distinction between the classical Smithian framework and competitive capitalism, as understood by Populists.) Directly questioning the property right in a selective area, the corporate sphere, it sanctioned property itself when it was compatible with individual and community rights. Property must not be organized into a locus of private dominion, a rival sovereignty.

To the degree to which Populists valued a self-adjusting economic framework, they insisted that it should be predicated on government powers of supervision to be workable. For Populists, competition applied to the vast range of indeterminate transactions below the public level, which were synonymous with a decentralization of market-power, because they could not exist in the presence of economic clusters exercising private control over the state. Competition was not intended as the organizing formula for the totality of economic relations, but rather, only those consistent with, and made possible by, political democracy. Nor can the Smithian value system, grounded in self-reinforced material norms and associated with fragmented social bonds, be said to carry forward. The emphasis on antecedent moral and political rights, voiced through a cooperative ethic, had furnished Populism with an independent standard of human and structural valuation.

The existence of the public welfare could not be assumed, left to impersonal forces, or entrusted to the workings of prevailing corporate capitalism. The state was to be a guardian as well as a regulator. If competition could be confined to enforceable bounds, this condition not only would shift the burden for achieving beneficence from automatic self-regulation to governmental activism but also would provide for economic fluidity and nondominating political relations. Productivity would become a measure of the decline of monopolist restrictions and stagnation. Moreover, when liberated in its own right, it would become the path to widened opportunity. Economic growth therefore assumed for Populists a crucial democratic import. It represented both the reversal of underconsumption and the stimulation, under principles of equitable distribution, of economic participation in the bottom layers of society.

1. The Implications of Corporate Power

In tracing the views of the Lincoln *Farmers' Alliance,* one appreciates more the complexity of antimonopolist capitalism. Public ownership existed alongside the basic acceptance of property, and both existed in tension with a socialist potential which had to be rejected. Throughout its discussion, however, the attack on the corporation remained unrelenting. Criticizing eonomic trends, the *Farmers' Alliance* in 1890 tied productivity and an equitable distribution to the arrestment of business consolidation. The duty before us "is to firmly and persistently demand a just and adequate solution to the problems of money, land, and transportation, that industry may be fostered and all labor fully rewarded. It is to check by every lawful means the future concentration of wealth, and to destroy forever the iniquitous domination of railroad and other corporate power in the politics of our state and nation."[1]

The next year, Smithian principles came under direct scrutiny: "The plutocracy of to-day is the logical result of the individual freedom which we have always considered the pride of our system." When "allowed unlimited scope," individual enterprise evolved into the corporate structure. This became a new mode for organizing society in a framework of political domination: "An artificial individual was created . . . and was named the corporation. This individual, the creation of the law, soon began to bend to its uses the forms and powers of the law. While in its nature and development it is only the original and cherished principle of individual liberty, it has absorbed the liberties of the community and usurped the power of the agency that created it. . . . The blind selfishness that led the slaveholder to demand a larger dominion for the safety of his peculiar institution, leads the plutocratic millionaire to demand larger expansion for his already overgrown privileges." The passage revealed the heart of the Populists' ambivalence about how far the challenge should proceed; they were partially trapped by their own assumptions of property. Restrained by what they cherished, the principle of individual liberty, they were still maddened by its falsification, and hence, they were prompted to press forward, even on behalf of a restoration of principle. This ambivalence was captured by a categorical statement that could serve as the Populist epitaph for Adam Smith in America: "Individualism incorporated has gone wild." It was not the principle of individual rights which was in dispute, but the corporate transmogrification of liberty: "The welfare of the individual must be the object and end of all effort."[2]

As the paper stated later in 1891, what rankled, concerning such a "pauper-manufacturing system," was the way modern capitalism had appropriated laissez-faire for purposes of business aggrandizement. Inferentially, this had occurred because economic processes had not been subjected to public controls: "The beautiful economic law of the competitive system reduces wages by an iron rule to the lowest level (at last) on which the workers can live and rear children to recruit their ranks. Observe, by this law the profit to the idle capitalist is made to increase with the increase of the number unemployed. His wealth depends upon their destitution; his fortune grows relatively as the poverty of the poor makes them powerless." The issue of modernity was not in dispute. Unimpeded profit-maximization, as a function of differential power, had been added to the indictment: "To make him a millionaire thousands must be over burdened, filled with anxiety, deprived of a share that they produce, and suffer from constant deprivation." In regard to modernity itself, positive intervention was clearly implied: "Why is all this necessary? It is not necessary. By the aid of invention, machinery and free motive power the work of the world can be performed in about half the time, with less than half the labor that was formerly necessary." To "make of this nation an industrial democracy," the editor noted elsewhere in the issue, Populism was brought into being.[3]

The *Farmers' Alliance* also deplored the closing of opportunity. This was seen as the expropriation of the less-propertied stratum and the destruction of independence. In early 1892, the paper commented: "The army begging work is every year increasing, the small capitalist is being crowded down into the ranks of the wage earners by bigger, richer business rivals, and capital is concentrating and drawing to itself all power."[4]

The defense of property became integral to the rejection of aggregated capital on grounds of democratic opportunity. In 1889, the paper fell back on nonsocialist solutions precisely when the issue of state power was raised. Though the early date may partly account for the paper's reticence, it furnished a classic instance within Populism of propertied attachments coexisting with anticorporate protest. Criticism was directed less to wealth per se than its politically derived advantages and methods of accumulation.

The editorial apprehended the danger in large individual fortunes and identified the shift to private sovereignty as the leverage for increased business power: "The enormous accumulation of wealth in single families which modern agencies have made possible is cause for serious alarm. Given a thousand millions under the control of one man of great ability and an ambition directed toward empire, and the subjugation of the government to his domination would seem to be inevitable. The appearance of such a man at any time is quite possible. . . . These accumulations are only made possible by the exercise of quasi public powers—by the application over large areas and to great populations of the principles of taxation and of the accumulative power of interest." Functions of government were taken into private hands. (The Populist definition of taxation included those charges, such as freight rates, that pertained to necessary functions, were set arbitrarily, and were levied on a dependent populace.) This was evidence of the general abdication by government of its regulative powers.

In regard to corporate wealth, the same attack upon the private extension to state authority was relevant: "Limitations of wealth should be applied in the direction of limiting special privileges conferred by law. The incentive to issue watered stocks is derived from the power to fix rates. The exercise of these two powers involve [*sic*] all the corruption and fraud and deviltry connected with our railroads." The focus was on special privilege. Yet the basic matter of limitation was also applied to privilege and not to wealth as such; this was the germ of a distinction later explicitly developed. There was a clear recognition of the abuses which arose from this extension of private power (a grasp of essentials that renders the conclusion the more surprisingly moderate): "The right to issue money is an inherent government power. . . . In all cases where governments have delegated this right, the recipients have become government agents, as are today our national banks. . . . They have never long exercised the right without acquiring a power which threatened that of their principal. This is the case today with our national banks and their national associations."

Presenting the situation so lucidly, the *Alliance* did not capitulate, so much as recur to a circumscribed definition of wealth-limitation. Accumulation proved of less moment than safeguards against its politicized consequences. Property was not questioned and, when dissociated from privilege, would appear to be protected from specific institutional challenge: "In the direction then of limiting the quasi public powers which have been granted to artificial persons will be found the only just as well as the only necessary limitation of wealth. This is in the direction of equality of privilege and equality of opportunity." The tendency among Populists (the present source was among the more radically disposed) was to refrain from the direct examination of capitalist internal processes. The genesis of monopolization was found to lie essentially in special political circumstances. These were correctible through impartial administration and the precedent separation of governmental and private spheres. However, the central ambivalence remained. Populists simultaneously affirmed individualistic propertied beliefs and an independent state formation. In the case at hand, the result was definitely antisocialist: "We have no sympathy with socialistic levelers, and are no believers in equality of intellect or equality of powers. But the government which by special grants or special laws destroys equality of privilege and opportunity is on the certain road to decay."[5]

In 1889, the paper also furnished a glimpse of representative conditions in which hardship was filtered through a small holder's lens. The discussion was not meant to praise the expectant capitalist, but to indicate the threat to property by corporate wealth:

With corn at from 10 to 15c.; with oats at 8 to 12c.; with the cattle market in the hands of a combine making the feeding of steers a mere lottery, with the chances in favor of selling at a loss after they are fattened; with the prices of horses, which comparatively few farmers raise for sale, demoralized by the general depression, the outlook for farmers is unusually gloomy. If a farmer is out of debt, and can remain so, he is master of the situation. But very few indeed are in that fortunate condition. Our financial system, based on debt, and furnishing an entirely inadequate volume of money, forces the business of the country upon a debt basis.

If real and justifiable, the complaint was not that of the landless. Fears of expropriation had shaped the frame of reference for protest: "There is a very large class of farmers who are absolutely compelled to either borrow money or make store bills or give notes for machinery, etc., or quit the business. The rates of interest in one case, and the added prices in the other, are simply ruinous. As a result of this, chattel mortgage sales are almost of daily occurrence in all our considerable towns." The point was not the intensity or breadth of deprivation, the absence of which would have made Populism's rise unintelligible. Rather, it was that less-propertied goals served to energize resistance to existing capitalism: "Property is ruthlessly sacrificed, and men left with families on their hands—just their bare hands."[6]

One correspondent, who had been prominent in local Alliance activities, suggested the Populist middle ground between the individualism-monopoly position and socialism. The partial resolution of the ambivalence became synonymous with competitive capitalism. He started with a basic insight of the movement: "The agricultural classes are suffering from a variety of evils, the leading cause of which is 'Wealth as a Political Power.'" He added: "The present system of transportation, tariff and finance are all the creations of this power." But then he spoke of equally unacceptable alternatives: "Believing as I do that when any system usurps the place of man in government it becomes man's oppressor, I am opposed to a socialistic system wherein the powers of government are invoked for the sole benefit of the few. I am also opposed to a system of individualism that leaves the individual at the mercy of corporate creatures that the power of government can alone either create or control." We shall return to W. A. McKeighan, of Red Cloud, Nebraska, for subsequent elaboration. Yet it is significant that this anticollective animus was part of an attack on corporate privilege: "The relief we seek can never be obtained until corporations are brought under the control of the people from whom they hold their charters, and we abandon a tariff policy based on the idea that taxing all for the benefit of the few will in some way (which has never been explained) make all prosper."[7]

An editorial in April 1890 depicted the anxiety of farmers who constantly faced possible dispossession. Under such circumstances, there was little solace in being propertied. One's condition remained precarious, collapsing all distinctions of wealth among the lower strata. Property, as is evident, was not per se a barrier to protest (nor protection against hardship):

When we consider the *kind* of distress which may be found among Nebraska farmers, a glimpse of the nature of the remedy needed may be obtained. These farmers are not distressed for food. . . . They are not distressed for fuel. . . . But when the interest on their mortgages, or the mortgages themselves, or their taxes, are due, then the pressure is felt. Or when they need something which calls for money—something which they must have and must pay money for—then there is a pinch. Old debts call for money, or a new note with interest compounded, which soon again becomes an old debt. These debts are taking the best colt, and the best calf, and the best bushel of potatoes—are eating remorselessly day and night, week-days and Sundays, three hundred and sixty-five days in the year, and are rapidly whitening the hairs of four out of five of the farmers of Nebraska to-day. . . . A man . . . may see a shadow growing over his home—he may see the day surely approaching when his wife and children will be homeless and houseless, and may feel a torment of consuming dread daily and hourly without being either hungry or cold.

This was not the psychological ground for illusions about the past (perhaps befitting a crisis-oriented lower nobility). Nor did it mark the path to aggressive social mobility or capitalist speculation. Being "homeless" and "houseless" would nullify the elemental quest for material security and well-being, for conditions of fair entitlement, and not least, for a vision of propertied democracy. Yet property, if not a barrier, ultimately checked the clear perception of the situation (here, an emphasis on monetary and banking practices) and its remedy: "Money which would raise prices, lower interest, and open the channels of trade—money to the farmer on the same terms it has long been furnished to the banker—would relieve this kind of distress." That the outlook of the expectant capitalist did not prevail can be gathered from a further remark. Mortgage indebtedness had been incurred out of necessity and not for ambitious designs: "Senator Paddock's lame denials about the mortgage indebtedness of Nebraska and his efforts to convince people that it was all made for improvements, go for nothing, and are not borne out by the facts. We refer him and his Wall street friends to the official figures recently published in Saline county. We venture to say that four out of five of all the farm mortgages now in force in Nebraska were originally made for purchase money, and that an investigation will so prove."[8]

In an article entitled "Wealth as a Political Power," McKeighan, the same month, blended the critique of a unified power-structure (based on railroads, banking, and protected manufactures) and the affirmation of laissez-faire principles. Even the corrective to Adam Smith betrayed partial allegiance to him. McKeighan offered a rough diagram of existing power: "The present political power of wealth in our government is rendered possible by its accumulation in the hands of a few men. First. Through the railway corporations controlling the transportation of the country. Second. Through the banks and money loaners controlling the currency of the country and exercising the power of contracting or expanding its volume whenever it is their interest to do so. Third. By a vicious system of national taxation, which enables the protected manufacturing class to levy and collect tribute from the wealth producing classes." He found concentration to be unprecedented ("reference to the history of other nations fails to afford a single instance of the accumulation of so great wealth in the hands of a few individuals") and of recent origin in the past quarter-century. Yet, partly at the expense of capitalistic internal processes, he placed responsibility for the problem on government and its favoritism toward corporate wealth: "Extraordinary causes must exist to produce such abnormal results. They are found in the special legislation of the country, extending aid and protection to capital."

While such terms as "extraordinary" and "abnormal" suggest the efficacy of solutions designed to withdraw this aid and protection, and hence, restore principles of balance and impartial public conduct, McKeighan could not wholly exonerate capitalism. The state had been receptive to blandishments, had falsified its ostensive mission to secure equal justice and opportunity, and had even lost control to dominant private forces. But neither the state nor capitalism existed in a self-contained realm, Populists realized, and the mutual penetration they described reflected as poorly on the corrupter as on the corrupted. To rectify state practice inevitably undermined the basic pattern of existing capitalist development, whether or not capitalism as a system was called into question. He pointed to the collusive relationship between government and railroads: "What are the facts in support of this proposition? In the first place the railways have been aided by the government in the grants of land to the extent of over two hundred million acres. They have also received the credit of the government to the extent of more than sixty millions of dollars. In addition the people in their corporate capacity have bonded their municipalities to an incredible extent to aid in their construction. So general has this become that there is scarcely a county, city, town or village in the west that is not mortgaged to the railway corporations." In speaking of the tariff, McKeighan summarized the thrust of prevailing state-intervention: "The present condition of the laboring classes of the country shows clearly the effects of this policy, wherein the powers of government are invoked for the sole benefit of capital."

That corrective action had positive implications (it was more than the withdrawal of business privileges) emerged from the agenda he proposed. Of "three things" to be "done quickly," he noted, "the first is for the people to rise above party . . . and place the private corporations in their proper place as servants and not *masters* of the people." The second was to oppose banking monopoly through free coinage, the retirement of the "present bank currency," and full governmental powers to issue a "legal tender currency . . . in its stead to an amount equal to the wants of the legitimate business of the country." This last phrase, a reminder of capitalistic intent, served to introduce his third point regarding laissez-faire. Taken alone, it appears definitely Smithian. But in the total context, hostility to wealth-concentration stands out, and significant government activity has already been established; therefore the sentiment was more that of competitive capitalism: "The third thing is for the people to demand that the government undo its mischievous legislation protecting capital employed in manufacturing, and leave the distribution of wealth to follow natural laws free from government *meddling* and interference. Protection disturbs trade, establishes monopolies, creates trusts and interferes with the operation of the national [natural?] laws that otherwise would govern the creation and distribution of wealth."[9]

Especially in 1889–1891, preceding the national formation of the People's party, there were statements reflecting capitalist sentiments, though references to property were studded with anger and concern about the difficulties of survival under the prevailing system. In June 1890, the president of the Nebraska Alliance reiterated earlier points on mortgage indebtedness and freight charges. He then turned to the larger terms of trade under protected industries, which he related to the theme of the security of the home and feelings of inadequacy and anguish caused by being unable to realize propertied dreams: "You raise wheat, the wheat is yours, but it is the miller's flour. All of your flour comes through a trust. Your flour costs too much. A binder that costs $50 you pay three times as much for. Your coffee, sugar and everything you buy comes through a trust. More than that the homes are in danger. You sympathize with Ireland when you hear of the evictions; there were more evicted in Nebraska last year than were evicted in Ireland. But few resisted the foreclosure of their farms, as they were ashamed to think they had lost their farms and, they just quietly moved off to the sand hills." Almost gloomily, John Powers added: "And what is true to Nebraska is true back east."[10]

In September, referring to railroads, the *Farmers' Alliance* developed a far-ranging analysis from explicitly capitalist premises, which linked the transportation issue with imposed economic backwardness for the western region. A main source of abuse, it began, lay in the manipulation of long- and short-hauls: "While claiming that local business is only a trifling per cent of the total business, they still insist on charging for it an extortionate rate, and making all concessions on the long haul. This is a vicious principle, and its practical application is keeping the farmers of the west poor, retaining manufacturing and wholesaling in the east, and building up eastern centers and eastern capital at the expense of the west." Even though this was clearly a statement for auton-omous regional growth (similar to the argument against colonial dependence used by more perceptive Populists in the South), the charge that capitalism had created a national division of labor was close to the surface: "In other words, the true interests of the farmers of Nebraska demand a low local rate, instead of a low through rate. While we have raw products to export it is certainly desirable that we should have low rates of carriage. But no people ever became wealthy or fairly prosperous exporting raw products. The people who export such products are tributary to those who apply labor to them. To claim wisdom for a system of rates that compels a people to continue to be exporters of raw products and drives labor away from its country, is very absurd indeed."

Confinement to a primary stage of production meant economic retardation and inequity, but the paper also posited the converse situation of vibrant activity: "To build up a prosperous state in Nebraska we want diversified industry—we want classes of work-ers who co-operate but do not compete with each other. Under the mistaken system adopted by the roads this is impossible." A more ordinary, and avowedly capitalist, matter, not at all incon-sistent with Populism, was raised as well: "For a wholesale dry goods house Lincoln is to-day one of the best points between the Atlantic and Pacific oceans. But there is no such house here. Why? Because these goods can be distributed to interior points tributary to Lincoln from Chicago, New York and Boston cheaper than they could from Lincoln."[11] Even if it was not seeking to depress the condition of labor, competitive capitalism had an eminently practical side.

Resuming its discussion of long and short hauls the following week, the *Farmers' Alliance* equated restrictions on economic growth with the fostering of antidemocratic and irrational economic practices. The concentration of wealth worked against the interests of capitalism. This was the salience of Populist economics, albeit presented here on the strict ground of systemic activation and productivity. The rate-structure, the paper noted, "prevents the establishment of manufacturing and wholesale houses at rural centres, and thereby prevents the diversification of farming industry, confining our agricultural productions to a few staple products which will bear long transportation. It concentrates wealth into the hands of comparatively few people." But more important were the political and economic implications of this condition: "It is thus building up a monied aristocracy, fostering a government of class, and endangering our republican institutions, and it finally re-acts against the best interests of the railroads, which would be largely promoted by the greatest diffusion of wealth among the whole people." The fear that underdevelopment (the editorial referred to an "enforced system" of agricultural production) presaged a monied aristocracy was more than self-serving. The absence of development was a symptom of the wider expropriation and permanent subordination of a whole class, particularly since agriculture no longer enjoyed the advantages of an earlier period of growth: "Deprived of home markets he is prevented from diversifying his industry; and without this power he is doomed to perpetual poverty. The only real reward which has been found in western farming for many years, has been in the advance of farming lands. Deprived as he now is of the resource of cheap lands and at the same time continue the present system of concentrating capital, manufacturing and population at the great centres, and farming must inevitably drop to an occupation which will afford a mere subsistence, and farmers themselves become mere serfs. This is undoubtedly the tendency of the times."[12] This last concern inspired in great measure the drive for an alternative framework of modernization.

The statement, "individualism incorporated has gone wild,"

coming only five months later, marked a dramatic shift in emphasis. As conditions worsened, they provided an impetus for organization; the movement had passed through its ideological puberty, and capitalism, though hardly forgotten, was fixed in the background. Two months after that, still before the national formation of the People's party, one finds an encompassing view of public supremacy over the corporation:

> There is only one way to destroy them. They must be absorbed by the government. The public functions which have been delegated to them must be resumed by the people. Gas, electricity, water, must be furnished by the municipalities; the railroads and telegraphs must be operated by the general government as the post-office now is, the control of the money of the nation, in all its branches, must be taken from the hands of corporations and placed where it belongs, in the hands of the government. All these things could be soon and safely done at a great saving to the nation were it not for one thing, the opposition of the corporations themselves.[13]

Yet these collective measures were detached from all reference to class and placed on a formal political plane. The words, "at a great saving to the nation," imply capitalism's growth and efficiency, more than a fundamental alteration of structure.

In June 1891, a Cuming county farmer expressed the sense of basic differences within capitalism, that capitalism would be ripe for modification because of the evident injustices in the prevailing framework. He made public his response to an item in the census questionnaire on mortgage indebtedness: "I have worked like a dog on this farm for the past twenty-four years. I have been sober, industrious, and severely economical, and yet have not been able to make necessary improvements without incurring the above indebtedness."[14] When traits of character, virtues prescribed in the first instance by capitalism, seemed to little avail, the makings of a revolt in thought appear obvious.

Exploring the low returns from farming, the *Farmers' Alliance* in November presented an extensive critique of economic concentration, underconsumption, and the ethics of self-aggrandizement, all of which were thought to contradict the Populist labor theory of value. It began: "The farmers have sent to market a considerable portion of their crops. What did they do with the money? It was in large part used to pay interest on mortgages, deferred payments, chattel mortgage loans and machinery notes." The result was to weaken or impede the circulation process. Wealth had been consolidated and diverted from productive reinvestment: "Only a little of this money after leaving their hands was exchanged for goods. The most of it was locked up in safes to re-loan or was sent east to swell the bank accounts of rich men who would keep it for speculation. The railroad freights absorbed also much too large a portion of the money value of the crops carried to market and of this money most of it went east to those who could not therewith increase their power of consumption." If the point was relevant to the velocity of circulation, the paper also maintained that the draining off of wealth increased fluctuations of the business cycle and created harmful tendencies toward stagnation of the economy: "These facts show the chief causes of full glutted markets and workers in want." Notwithstanding the internal focus, which itself gave meaning to intracapitalist differences, this analysis verged, as a response to prevailing malfunctions, on a critique of profit-maximization as a standard of operations: "But there is one evil in our present commercial system which is the fruitful source of all evils that afflict society. It is the tacit understanding that each may get all he can, the belief that the interest of buyer and seller are not the same." Capitalist relations were preserved, as the words reveal, but on the basis of a cooperative vision: "If equal values were always exchanged, whether the exchanges were of labor for labor, labor for money, labor for goods, money for goods or money for money, we should have a circulation balanced, just, complete, continuous."[15]

By March 1892, the *Farmers' Alliance* had quoted Karl Marx in its discussion of inequitable circulation and distribution. The departure point was Marx's commentary on the reserve army of labor, which included this sentence: "The condemnation of one part of the working class to enforced idleness by the overwork of the other part, and the converse, becomes a means of enriching the individual capitalist and accelerates at the same time the production of the industrial reserve army on a scale corresponding with the advance of social accumulation." The citation of Marx commands notice, but more significant was the accuracy of the paper's paraphrase and adaption of the thought: "Capital is glad to see half a million poor emigrants land here yearly, because with more seeking work it can force down the price of labor and absorb a larger percentage of labor's product. The army of destitute unemployed is the source of its power, the misery of the unemployed is the club with which it enslaves all workers."

Beyond the creation of surplus value was underconsumption, and beyond both, for this Nebraska source, was private concentration, which prevented widely participatory and balanced exchanges: "The legalization of land monopoly, and interest, are the sources of its strength, the canals by which it turns wealth from the channels of natural and just distribution." Invoking Marx in the service of competitive capitalism is not entirely surprising, because of a common appreciation for the vitality of premonopolist formations and a common identification of social impoverishment as the inner mechanism of capitalist power. Thus, concerning the expropriation of wealth, the editorial added: "Again capital enslaves otherwise independent labor, that which is in possession of land, by monopolizing the means of transportation, so controlling commerce. Standing between producers and consumers and exacting an unjust price for its labor it makes itself a king, levying tribute upon all classes."

This last point, that monopolism was the epicenter of the entire structure, stated succinctly the burden of Populism's economic case. Namely, when corporations could successfully assert their prerogatives of intermediating in, blocking, disrupting, and profiting from normalized activities, the potential harmonization of interests in society could not take place. Monopolism obstructed all meaningful relations. It did so, partly, through the state's abdication of responsibility for safeguarding the public interest: "Capital with its present legally conferred and popularly permitted kingly power, will rule despotically as long as it can make labor work for it upon its own terms, or collect tribute from those who need credit."[16]

One year later, the paper more directly addressed the question of public ownership. If capitalism per se remained intact, the notion of social property came to the foreground as a public right and not merely as an attribute of efficiency or even economic activation: "The Populists will not be satisfied until the people collectively get all the benefit there is in the telephone by the government owning all the telephones and running them in connection with the postoffice. The telephone is not only a luxury any more;

it has become a business and social necessity and must be run as a social institution. Its accommodations and profits must be socialized; it must not continue to be the property of private parties." The *Farmers' Alliance* made no concession to the sensibilities of property when areas of necessity were considered social institutions: "Its functions are public; it therefore must be owned and operated by the public in the interests of the public."[17]

Later in 1893, the argument was again made for distinguishing between the public and private spheres of the economy. The sovereign obligations of government could not be entrusted to private control or otherwise become a source of profits: "To use the power of government in doing something which it is dangerous to permit a few individuals to do is wise statesmanship. In fact that is the only final protection the people have against the oppressions and extortions of monopoly." The source was neither Adam Smith nor Marx; it was Mill. Natural monopolies, economic sectors in which competition had been eliminated, or appeared unworkable, came under public jurisdiction. Here the concept of social property turned less on its specific economic function than on the sheer fact of monopolization: "John Stuart Mill lays down the true principle when he says that when any branch of human industry tends naturally to become a monopoly the government (the whole people) must assume its ownership and control."

The assertion of a people's realm, through nationalization, had itself a participatory character. The citizenry by means of its direct tax contributions could reclaim social advantages to the community. Taxation in its strictly public form rather than in private exactions legitimated the collective appropriation of property: "Under nationalism the people may be taxed to enable the government to assume control of an industry, but the money they pay out of their individual pockets is paid into their collective pocket, (the treasury); it is spent in securing or establishing property that belongs to them collectively; and all increase, revenue and benefit resulting from the operation accrue to the whole people."[18] The individual's right of entitlement to the product of his labor had been extended to the sharing in what properly fell to the nation's social product.

In fact, the right to labor peacefully, brought dramatically to the forefront in conditions of widespread unemployment and agricultural poverty, became a special case of entitlement. Even when it was directed to survival, the concept of opportunity retained a capitalistic meaning. But now, as was clear from some Populist verse that appeared in the *Farmers' Alliance* in 1894, the demand for work partook of the same elemental moral right to earn a livelihood and avoid degradation. Society's potential wealth could provide conditions of economic independence. The poem was entitled "Tramp, Tramp, Tramp," in honor of the marching armies of the poor. Its chorus related jobs to the productive contribution which the lower classes would make to America:

> In the sainted Lincoln's chair
> Beats a heart which knows no care
> For the lot of those who toil in his domain,
> For the many millions poor,
> Seeking work from door to door
> That they may the honest needs of life obtain.
>   CHORUS
> Tramp, tramp, tramp, the tramps are tramping,
> Seeking an opportunity
> By their labor to create
> Wealth for all within the state,
> And retain enough to keep themselves alive.

The nation's decline from Lincolnian compassion to the indifference of the Cleveland administration had an economic as well as political character. It was the more to be deplored because the poor were simply asking for life's necessities.

In the final stanzas, the poet bitterly assailed overproduction, and she restated, in the context of the theme of lost liberties, the right of Americans to labor:

> Is there then no work to do,
> None who need a garment new?
> Is the work of all the nation wholly done?
> Are there no more homes to build,
> no more granaries to be filled,
> Not a want to be supplied for any one.
>   CHORUS
> Tramp, tramp, tramp, etc.
>
> May the weary blistered feet,
> Tramping up and down the street,
> Like a curse within the ears forever sound

Of the robbers who have planned
Death and ruin for our land,
Where the right to live and labor once was found.[19]

This poem, written by the secretary of the Nebraska Alliance, anticipated by two months the national attention received by Jacob Coxey's earnest battalions. It mirrored in spirit the same larger dynamics of controlled outrage. There was a sense of respectful desperation. Social revolution was manifestly rejected on behalf of gainful employment within a more rational and equitable system of production than currently existed.

2. An Organic Structure of Capitalism

Tom Watson, the Populist leader of Georgia, offered a more complex example of Populism's affinity with, and yet departure from, a Smithian framework of capitalism. Watson had been elected to Congress as a Democrat in 1890, but he quickly asserted his independence in order to stand for Alliance principles by joining the Populist caucus. He was fraudulently denied election in three succeeding contests and became the People's party vice-presidential candidate in the 1896 campaign. Watson is reputed to have been among the most radical of Populists, who stood for advanced economic demands, including a comprehensive attack on the prevailing structure of capitalism, and who attempted to formulate the grounds of and organize a biracial coalition along class lines to achieve the purpose of political equality in the South. For the present, the conventional wisdom about Watson's political orthodoxy, economic radicalism, and social enlightenment might best be held in suspension. It should be stated, however, that the seeming change in Watson, following his disillusionment and frustration in the years after 1896, when he expressed violent antipathy to Negroes, Catholics, and Jews, as well as radicals and socialists, had left its clear traces in his presumed more emancipating days as a Populist. There were not two stages in Watson's attitudes and behavior, but rather a fairly coherent process of development. Its underlying fount, at least as describable in ideological rather than psychological terms, was a deep and abiding devotion to the South, its cultural and institutional life, and what he perceived to be its organic historical, structural, and social character. He would not revitalize plantation slavery, but neither would he abandon the patterns of order, deference, and hierarchy on which it rested. I would designate his framework of society as a "paternalistic modernity," which shaped his thinking on political, economic, and racial matters coming before him.

In this chapter I have selected two basic and well-known statements that Watson presented on economics and labor. It is merely a first installment, to establish the fact of his somewhat moderate or conservative views in an area pertinent to the doctrine of government power and public welfare, which I will elaborate using more abundant evidence in a subsequent book about his intellectual framework. In the discussion here, one notes Watson's acceptance of public ownership, but he appears ambivalent because he was also strongly attracted to capitalism's traditional or premonopolist order. Watson was a brilliant writer; he was not an equally gifted theorist or even a disciplined thinker. Frequently there was the dramatic juxtaposition of apparently contradictory elements, which became rather too facilely reconciled when his oscillating thought could not sustain the tension of his potentially critical insights. Watson stated a peculiarly savage indictment of existing capitalism, as will be seen, but it was based on paternalistic and idiosyncratic grounds; his framework engendered feelings of persecution and martyrdom on the individual level, and a disposition toward an organic society, combined uneasily with laissez-faire, on the structural level. In neither case, however, was capitalism per se subject to question.

Watson's first statement was a Labor Day address which he delivered to the Locomotive Firemen in Augusta in 1891. He later reprinted it as a main item in his continuing efforts at fostering a campaign of political education. Watson began from the premise that there was an unequal sharing between labor and capital, which he discussed within the frame of reference of a labor theory of value. He possibly confused value and product, but he was emphatic on the source of wealth-creation and the legal favoritism shown to capital:

What is the labor question? In a nutshell it is this: Labor asks of capital, "Why is it you have so much and do so little work, while I have so little and do so much?" That is about the size of it. . . . What is capital and what is labor? Originally they were the same, to the extent that cause and effect are the same. There was a time when there was no capital. There never was a time when there was no labor. . . . The process of production is labor. The thing produced is capital. Labor creates wealth, but the very moment it is created it becomes capital. . . . [From Jamestown, our national wealth] lay in the muscles of the laborers yet unborn, in the brains of the thinkers yet to be. This is literally true. No man denies it. Yet there is this queer thing. Everybody wants labor protected when it becomes capital, while most people laugh you to scorn if you propose to protect it while it is still labor.

Halfway through the preceding passage, Watson made this pithy summary: "Capital is the child of labor."

Yet what seemed an ordered sequence—capital as a derivative of, and secondary in importance to, man's labor-power—permitted the assignment of an independent and coequal role to capital. At the outset, the question became the impartial protection of both labor and capital, which credited the existence and integrity of each one. Thus far, labor had been underprotected: "Let me illustrate: Capital consists of money, lands, stock, provisions, goods, chattels, etc. Protective legislation provides for their welfare. What produces them? The labor of yesterday. But when you propose to throw protective legislation around the labor of today (which has not yet become capital), clamor at once arises and you are denounced as a fanatic and a demagogue." On close reading, it is clear that Watson did not set priorities. The initial qualification followed at once. While "the natural reward of labor is that which it produces," (the example given was gathering rushes and making a basket), this illustrated "labor in its simple state, where it supplies itself with material and furnishes all the work." Watson here proceeded as carefully as did Locke in discussing the state of nature, and to the same effect of warranting capital's separable contribution: "It is only when we advance and get to a stage where material may be furnished by one while labor is supplied by another that trouble begins."

There was, he noted, no certain formula of reward, although the explanation he now introduced legitimated the salient categories of capitalism: "How much ought labor to get? No man can be more definite than this: 'It should get all that it makes after due allowance for material and the use of the capital.'" This was the anatomy of a Populist labor theory of value, but it lacked the more incisive ethical postulate of entitlement found, for example, in Peffer's treatment of the subject. What concealed the remaining capitalist ground (this applied to other Populists as well as Watson) was the objection to the manifest inequity of distribution. This gave to the position a semblance of radicalism: "But we can be perfectly definite on this point. It does not get a fair share now." The matter was hastily dropped in favor of a more diffuse critique of overproduction: "Eight million bales of cotton flood the markets of the world, and have hammered the price down to zero. Yet millions of laborers haven't decent clothes to wear!"

Watson viewed overproduction as a major area of contention which had to be challenged. But if his implicit message was one favoring a just apportionment of claims, and presumably affording the worker higher wages to stimulate consumption, he still rested the capital-labor relationship on narrowly quantitative factors. It was not confronted directly. Thus, even overproduction, unless it had been put into the more vital context of governmental activism, left intact the structural features of capitalism. The passage was deceptively militant: "Overproduction? I will tell you where the overproduction is. It is in the cold-hearted and hard-hearted men who will not see any thing which does not belong to their class!" These are men "who have grown proud and cruel because they possess capital (the thing which was labor yesterday), but utterly despise the labor of today." Then, despite the further reminders that "all capital was produced by labor" and that "all the necessaries of daily life are being created by labor," he immediately specified what "labor is entitled to," without regard to the labor-creation principle, or the evident class relation which framed the interplay of labor and capital.

As a result, the laborer himself was fit into the discussion as something of a lesser capitalist:

A sufficiency of food, clothing and lodging for the needs of today; a sufficiency of leisure from daily toil to preserve the strength of the body and to cultivate the capacity of the mind; the shortening of the hours of labor so that a man or a woman may not become a mere beast of burden, but will be a citizen, who, like other citizens, has a portion of the day for recreation, for social intercourse, and for self-improvement. But further still, I believe that he should have his fair proportion of the profits made by his labor to constitute a surplus for his time of sickness or old age and to transmit to his children, so that the condition of the producer may prosper in just proportion to the amount of his production.

One cannot deny that Watson had a vision of social betterment. But his notion of "sufficiency" was an extremely modest criterion of well-being in light of the promises he had tendered already on labor's behalf. Labor was the source of capital; its rights and place in society should be secure beyond all doubt, and not, as here, elevated through mere improvement. And even this enumeration of rights was partly based on negative reasoning: "This is a puzzling job for the legislator, but I firmly believe the law can be so framed if the government is to escape revolution."

The most original portion of Watson's address dealt with the social-control functions of law. His historical description of repression, drawn from India's caste practices and early modern Britain's statutes on vagabondage and impressment, was designed to show the consistency in legal deprivation of labor's rights. He stated, for example, that "the old caste system of India was but the law which capital made to keep the rich forever rich, and the poor forever poor," and then he related the kinds of punishment which were inflicted for breaching the social code. Curiously, Watson did not draw parallels with the racial system of the South, which would be apparent in this passage if one substitutes "Negro" for "laborer," nor did he bring his findings to bear on the contemporary American legal system: "Marriage between the upper and lower classes was prohibited under the awfulest penalties, and a law of the realm declared in plain terms that the laborer should not acquire wealth and that his name, laborer, should be an expression of contempt." To be sure, Watson explained that he dwelled on India "because I wish to emphasize this fact: the code of every other nation has had substantially the same inhuman laws against labor," and he asked of scholars, "let them look deeply and soberly into every social system and the same features will be seen again and again." However, when he attempted to derive meaning from the survey of conditions, the analysis began to fall apart.

Watson speculated that there was a recurrent pattern of "protest and petition" in which rights were gained only in the wake of suppression; this led him to see the role of martyrs as critical to popular liberty: "Thus it is that the cause of the common people progresses. Every step has been a struggle, every concession has been stained with blood. No chain has been struck from the limbs of fettered labor save at the cost of some brave man's life." While his imagery was plausibly based in the suppressive response to political demonstrations (Watson seems to have had Peterloo in mind), he avoided any reference to class conflict. History itself was a recurrent ceremonial; sacrificial rites, focused on the individual, became the means to social advancement: "In ancient times no great thing was undertaken, till sacrifice was made. The altar must be erected, the victim chosen and garlanded, the sacrificial fire lit." And he added: "How strangely these old customs reappear, the ceremonial altered, but the substance preserved." Whether or not his references this early were personal (as they were in the 1896 campaign), the elegiac rhythm is striking, as though brutality and redemption have been regularized: "No vessel ever lifted anchor to bear the liberties of the people through the stormy seas to sunlit heavens, no army marshaled to redeem the lost provinces of freedom, ever yet made successful venture without the altar and the victims—without the splendid heroism which offers the one, and inexorable custom which exacts the other."

Watson's vivid imagination provided a balance of historical forces which was not often found in Populism. There was no clean victory to be won. Protest and response were in equilibrium, ensuring that capital would exist as the complement to labor and suggesting for Watson the desirability of retaining and blending the two. He did not ignore labor's deprivations. He spoke of conspiracy laws applied to labor and not capital; of the bloody New York Central strike in which Pinkertons were freely employed; and the outright social misery, epitomized in the "bent and feeble sewing women of New York City, crouched in dreary garrets and plying their needles," then prevalent. Yet precisely at this point, a massive shift occurred in his argument. His criticism had been turned back upon itself: "Don't understand me to be making war upon capital as such. I am but denouncing that capital which is used tyrannically. I recognize the fact that without capital there can be no progress. If labor consumed its products day by day, and there was no surplus collected anywhere, advance would be an impossibility." While Watson's condemnation of the tyrannical use of capital closely followed Populists' distinctions on that issue, he went on to make a shambles of the labor theory of value, introducing substantive concessions which tended to cancel his previous insights.

In conformity with his larger view of paternalism, Watson accepted the ideological rationale for upper groups: "There must first be a surplus somewhere (capital) before there can be a leisure class to devote themselves to science, to music, painting, bookmaking, law-making, school-teaching." Society was held hostage to a leisure class; but more, his notion of society's progress had been made contingent upon a specifically capitalist surplus. This assertion undermined the very conception of social wealth. In his next sentence, he advanced the more fundamental rationale. Individual accumulation was alone responsible for the elaboration of a productive system (here Watson reproduced much of capitalism whole): "Without capital accumulated in the hands of some citizen, there could be nothing but the simplest manual labor—there could be no manufactories, no railroads, no steam boats, no foundries, no merchants and no bankers." And in his *next* two sentences, logically enough, he endorsed capitalism's ultimate rationale: In a harmonious society, each class required the presence of the other class. In this organic model of society, the permanence of capital was guaranteed and Watson's dictum that capital was the child of labor was practically obliterated: "The healthy, happy prosperous community is not that which consists either of capitalists alone, or of laborers alone. Neither can do without the other."

We come, then, to Watson's thesis of a just harmony (its middle-class implications are discussed in the next document). Although the Populist emphasis on a political and structural balance remained present, the elements have been so rearranged that now working people specifically have been made hostage to the well-being of upper groups. (Like his racial framework, Watson did not provide for the autonomy of the lower classes; indeed, the purpose of both frameworks, racial *and* economic, was to discourage this autonomy.) The theme of class reconciliation, appropriate to an organic society, tended to preserve the system and its existing social relationships. At the same time, the principle of equity had been defined as strictly a quantitative matter: "The truly prosperous community is that in which a just harmony is preserved between the two, and they become allies instead of enemies. Every class has its legitimate work and cannot be dispensed with. The banker is as natural a part of the business system as the borrower. In fighting an abuse in the banking system I do not wage war on banking itself—for some poor man will always want to use the surplus of the rich one, and if he can do so on equitable terms, both are benefited." Clearly, in this speech to laboring men, he did not contemplate basic structural alterations.

Watson directed an analogous pronouncement to industry. He not only credited capital with the performance of actual labor but also blurred the lines of objective class differences: "The manufacturer is a necessity to his countrymen—working up into finished fabric the cruder material of a simple laborer. In making war upon an advantage which he unjustly holds as against others, I do not for a moment forget that his prosperity is absolutely essential to national welfare." Once the "advantage" had been disconnected from prosperity, the result would be perfectly acceptable, even though it meant the normalization of wealth would be regarded as a just condition, unless it was demonstrated to be otherwise. The willingness to normalize the conception and existence of wealth was a common failing among Populists because their acceptance of the property right at the outset made it difficult to set specific limits on the accumulation of capital. Yet rarely does one find among other Populists this unstinting praise of the entrepreneur and his putative contribution to society. When Watson termed the prosperity in upper groups "absolutely essential to national welfare," not only did he step back from his labor theory of value, but he practically supplanted it with a trickle-down theory of the formation of wealth. In other words, he came very close to defending corporate capitalism in the precise terms of Rooseveltian Progressivism (which the president stated almost exactly one decade later in his first annual message). Watson's admiration for the productive function of capital appeared so great that, even when he criticized the operations of railroads and afterward endorsed public ownership in this area, his support for the measure had a grudging quality about it. It was less than a forthright endorsement of the people's appropriation of social property.

Understandably, Watson, in common with his generation, valued the technological achievements of railroads. Even Populists, consistent with their praise of technology when it was free to operate as a neutral force, saw the potential for good which railroads might render to society. Thus, Watson has occupied standard Populist ground in the following passage, except that his ambivalence about major holdings meant that he would not initiate departures from reigning capitalism on other than pragmatic, nonideological lines:

In this age of speed and progress, who can undervalue our railroads? I never in my life watched a train of cars without some thrill of pleasure— so instinctive and typical is it of man's power and skill and success! Yet when I see the railroads so frequently used for illegitimate purposes; when I see them become the mere "chips" in the great game of colossal gamblers; when I see them used to crush out this city and build up that; to bottle up this great harbor and develop that; to help the monopoly (like the Standard Oil Company) to beat down its competitor; when I see them bribing newspapers, and Senators, and Representatives to aid them in perpetrating wrongs upon the balance of the community, then it is that I find it impossible to refrain from denouncing the manner in which the magnificent blessing of the railroads is sometimes turned into a blasting curse!

Although his criticism was partially muted in the closing words of the passage, Watson was representative in identifying specific abuses which Populists universally condemned. He stood apart, however, in subtleties of political intonation, shifting the perspective from possible systemic wrongs to the conduct of upper groups. He could not forgive them their lapse in responsibility. Like many other Populists, his quarrel was not with capitalism, but with its privileged character and its untoward practices. But, because of his generally favorable attitudes toward wealth and upper social groups and because of his reluctance to concede the desirability of enlarged governmental powers, Watson, unlike other Populists, did not specifically invest the railroad question with a broader, structural significance. He did not sufficiently distinguish between railroads in their organized and their purely technological capacities, and he did not view public ownership as a potential extensible power which might be applied to other areas of the economy as well. There was no propulsion for projecting the analysis further. Capitalism was an uncontested good. The specifics of abuse were not intended to produce cumulative generalizations, and instead, in this case, labor had been subsumed within the imperatives of capitalism. Watson reserved the savagery of his indictment for irresponsible elites who, by their actions, had jeopardized the possibility for harmonious relations in society.

Watson's discussion of the various economic sectors had the effect of strengthening the legitimacy of capital. Further, in a speech to workers which had raised their expectations of labor's commanding position, he called on labor to adopt a nonhostile course toward capital. (He did the same thing with respect to blacks when he said that the color line had to be erased from politics.) His recommended course was passive, even Algeresque. Its effect was to deny the need of opposition: "I long to see public sentiment change on this labor question. I hope to see the problem studied and discussed more frequently among us. I hope to see all ranks meet the difficulty in a spirit of fairness and conciliation. You are a laborer. Remember that it is possible you may be a capitalist tomorrow." Populists highly valued opportunity, but not as a drug to promote social absorption or instill quiescence. In this case, Watson's promise made light of past suffering and contemporaneous prospects; his political tone became quite unsubtle: "You are a capitalist. Remember you may be a laborer tomorrow. This is the spirit in which serious issues should be adjusted. The man who despises the poor simply because they are poor, is too contemptible to be blamed for it. The man who hates the rich, simply because they are rich, has sinned just as much. It is the injustice and wrong which ought to be combated, whether among rich or poor."

Watson had denied the basis for any conception of institutionalized wrong. He further diminished the systemic perspective through his impartial repudiation (and contrariwise, exoneration) of both the rich and the poor, which served to endow them with a fictive equality. The categories of class were preserved, and perhaps even reinforced, by his insistence that individuals had to be treated exclusively as individuals. Each individual was to be judged by the same standard of behavior, as though the factors of wealth and power were extraneous considerations and bore no relation to the issues of wrong and injustice. Watson's desideratum of mutual respect, above all, kept rich and poor structurally in place; in the circumstances, the burden weighed differentially on the poor to maintain the social peace. Not surprisingly, his message, when he looked finally to the question of remedies, was one of forbearance. Nowhere did he recommend here that laborers could resort to the strike.

Everything was pressed toward the winning of public opinion. "I believe the evils of our present system can be remedied. How?" The initial groundwork was unexceptionable, except that, for Watson, the grievances of working people had to be explained and even demonstrated to in fact exist: "1. By co-operation among the laborers. You must organize, agitate and educate. Organize yourselves to get the strength of unity; agitate the evils and the causes thereof to arrest public opinion; educate yourselves and the public upon the principles underlying the issue in order that there be a proper understanding of the abuses complained of and the remedies proposed." Watson had taken the familiar Populist slogan, "organize, agitate and educate," which derived from the Alliance experience, and had now tilted it slightly away from its commonplace meaning. While its purpose was to emphasize the phase of consciousness building, based on the recognition that internal solidarity was essential to effective political action, Watson rejected its logical corollary, an adversary relation, in favor of converting the more inclusive constituency, or really, melding labor within the model of an organic society.

His second remedy, seemingly in the name of a social confrontation, did not alter labor-capital relations and did not move specifically against capital. Instead, he created a framework of countervailing powers, which, at best, would lead to a realignment that confirmed the existence of capitalism. Watson incorporated labor into the result, but on such nonspecific terms as to suggest the organic model rather than a mandate for labor's ascendance or even equality: "2. By a radical change in our laws. I firmly believe that before co-operation among laborers can secure complete success, we must have legislation which either takes from the tyrannical power of capital, or adds to the defensive strength of labor. We must make capital lay down its pistol, or we must give labor a pistol, too. When each man knows that the other has a 'gun' and will use it, they get exceedingly careful about fingering the trigger." To embroider a figurative pattern of mutual deterrence neither provided concrete safeguards for labor nor raised the concept of class to an organizing principle of social protest. Watson constructed a standoff between capital and labor, which forced labor to adopt pressure-group tactics, as meanwhile public opinion became the paramount object of attention.

The question of a conversion of sentiment ran deeper. Labor had to sue for entrance into the wider community. It started from a position outside the established contours of thought. To gain legitimation in the eyes of society was not a matter of the instrinsic rightness of labor's case, but of making a satisfactory presentation of it:

3. By a change of public opinion, which will bring the irresistible power of moral support to the side of labor as against the unreasonable exactions of capital. Every pulpit, every newspaper, every leader of thought in every profession, should give to this question earnest attention and then speak out. I dwell on this because I regard public opinion as omnipotent. It cannot be seen, but its pressure is despotic. The bravest man quails before the silent aversion of hostile public opinion. The stoutest leader weakens before the frowning face. It changes policies, customs, manners. It enforces an unwritten law, and the criminal who violated it swings from a limb! It nullifies a written law and bears home in triumph the man who broke it.

Clearly, Watson ascribed tremendous force to the influence of public opinion. Even his prototypic martyr would have been powerless in its grasp. Nor was such a situation to be deplored. Watson viewed public opinion as the embodiment of society's institutional and cultural foundations. Although he was trained as a lawyer, he plainly gave it precedence in the final sentences of the passage of the law itself. (On a more visceral level, his veiled reference to lynching also magnified community sentiment for the purpose of racial stabilization.) He did not deplore public opinion because, despite his emphasis on law and order in other contexts, it had the effect of controlling and moderating the pace of social change. In the present case, it had an equally important effect: It denied to labor specific, ascertainable standards of social welfare, which might hold true regardless of the prevailing state of opinion. Although many Populists viewed primordial human rights as antecedent to the law, Watson, strikingly like William Graham Sumner, rejected the emphasis on both human rights and the law for what was presumably their functional antecedent: public opinion. The result was simultaneously to narrow the grounds of protest, enshrine the place of custom, and invert the Populists' insistence that democracy possessed not mere numbers but objective ethical content: "You think you hold your life at the mercy of the law! You do nothing of the kind. You hold it at the mercy of public opinion. In a democracy or a republic it is at once the strength and the weakness of the system. Hence I say you must get this enormous power on your side. Once you get it—the way broadens and the light shines upon it."

"How can you get it?" Watson asked. Whether public opinion was a barrier to overcome, or, when it operated to his satisfaction, a mechanism which supported existing arrangements, he recommended precisely the same attitude of awe. The omnipotence of public opinion became intimidating. Even when the laborer had justice on his side, he was expected to show deferential behavior. The point followed not only because it was part of Watson's intellectual baggage of paternalism but also because he had implicitly proscribed a position of social militance, and beyond requiring deference, Watson perhaps unconsciously sought to humiliate the victim. In the final analysis, and perhaps as part of the art of persuasion, the laborer had to debase himself. He had to pull out the emotional stops in parading his misery. Although he had first assured labor that it was the salt of the earth, it still remained for the community to bestow rights in a downward direction. After posing his question, Watson concluded the thought: "By showing the public that you are right. Spread before the people facts which call aloud for attention; arguments which challenge reply; principles which defy criticism. Let the mistreated laborer show his wounds and ask sympathy; lift up his chains and ask freedom; hold on high, yes on high, the white face of his little child, hungry and sick, wasted and wan, and strike a thrill of pity through the great heart of the world!"

Watson deeply regretted the existence of poverty. "How can men love their homes when these homes are leaky hovels lit up by no comforts, but filled with wretchedness, sickness and want?" Nor did he lack a certain empathy with working people. In the speech, he invoked memories of the reversal in his own family's fortunes after the Civil War: "Fellow-citizens, my heart goes out to you in sympathy at your effort to better your condition. It has not been so long since I was as poor as the poorest man here. It has not been so long since I went weary up and down your streets asking for work and finding none. It has not been long since I knew what it was to have no place to lay my head when the night came upon me, and when today lost some of its gloom in the great fear that tomorrow might be darker." He sometimes slid too readily into a mood of blackest despair or appeared poised, as in the preceding sentence, on the threshold of inauthenticity. Yet one aspect of his statement deserves notice. Watson, who had aristocratic predilections, nevertheless insisted that his credentials as a self-made man be acknowledged. The powers of darkness and the personal quest for eminence met in turbulent confluence: "The horror of that dreadful time I shall never forget. It has left its mark on my mind and on my heart. It has shaped my convictions and controlled my feelings. When the easy owner of inherited wealth or position sneers at the warmth of my utterances upon this subject, I beg to remind him that it is the man who has been burned who can best describe the pain of the fire."

At moments of great emotion in his speeches, Watson would frequently bare his feelings in public. But the more important point was the context of his remarks: an exhortation to individualistic striving. *He* had surmounted hardship. Presumably others could do so as well. This was really an implicit factor operating in his mind, for he did in fact provide an explicit paradigm of social improvement which looked to the elevation of labor. Yet precisely here Watson appears most limited. Labor's elevation would come from upper groups and from within its own ranks, and it emphatically would not come from class agitation expressed as political or social disturbances. "Press on, workmen, in your worthy efforts. Whenever I can help you, call me. Preach the sublime doctrine of right. Demand it of others and practice it yourself." He had now created a wedge between himself and working people. He had also created a fixed structure, prefigured in his limited conception of public opinion and the labor theory of value, rather than the more open-ended democracy favored by such Populists as Morgan, Weaver, and Lewelling. Watson's seemingly beatific conclusion actually was a hymn to gradual, nonfundamental social change. The distribution of wealth would suppose the existence of major enterprise, and the summit of expectations would be reached through a partial diversion to the poor—in fine, a trickle-down theory: "The time will surely come when the producers of wealth must share equally its benefits, when the bounteous results of your toil will not all turn in at the gates of the palace, but a portion thereof will pass on down to the cottage and lift that humble tenement into dignity, comfort and happiness of a home."[20]

Our second document is Watson's famous political manual, *The People's Party Campaign Book*, which he published in 1892 for the wider party electorate as well as political lecturers and candidates. It was a storehouse of statistics, roll-call votes, and other information pertinent to the main issues of the campaign. He concisely stated the supporting arguments for basic Populist demands, and yet standard doctrine inevitably was filtered through his own unique prism of social order. The resulting synthesis had sufficient clarity to determine where his personal imprint was decisive. From the range of issues he took up—income tax, Pinkertons, financial legislation, public ownership—it is clear that one can speak of modal discriminations within capitalism. Yet, especially in Watson's case, collective economic features tended to complement rather than alter the propertied basis of society.

If Populism and capitalism were reconcilable, Watson tended rather more in a Smithian direction. He narrowed the scope of modernizing options through a concern for law and order (which he had only partially transvalued in meaning from their customary rigid definition), and through a social equilibrium which rested securely on middle-class foundations. He negated the general resilience of a collective orientation by often citing the needs of the less-propertied in his defense of basic demands. He similarly failed to identify an objective social potential which was latent in such issues. One detects an ideological shortfall in Watson's position, which derived not from Populism's reluctance to depart from capitalistic institutions, so much as from his own view that social change was primarily and avowedly restorative. He placed social change in the service of harmonious and stable relations of production.

Watson's discussion of the wartime income tax, its repeal, and the failure of its reenactment showed concern with tax relief for the enterprising poor, and secondarily with taxation as a means of basic redistribution of wealth. For one who "has to pay upon a tract of land at a time when he is actually losing money, farming on that land—such payment is a burden which he most keenly feels to be unjust," particularly when men of wealth, such as bond-holders, national bankers and railroad leaders "are exempted from tax." Though Watson stated that an income tax "would put the burden on the class most able to bear it," and that it would check "the growth of concentrated wealth," his rationale for equity pivoted on the notion, not unlike Hamilton's case for funding, of linking this burden to the benefits conferred: "It would put the support of the Administration upon those who derive the greatest benefits under the Laws." This was to stimulate closer interest in government, not remove the structure of privilege itself: "It would interest the most powerful class in the cause of Economy. Rich men get particular when they know they must foot the bills." In further defense of the income tax, he underscored the reliance of small propertyholders on the reallocation of the internal flow of gathering revenue. There would be a shifting in the sources of tax-ation, which nevertheless failed to question the existence of dispar-ities of power. Consistent with his advocacy of free trade, Watson supported an income tax because "it would abolish the Tariff, which, as a system of collecting taxes is the most costly, one-sided and monstrous the world ever saw." In addition, the income tax would provide relief for the lower strata (and perhaps check the centralizing tendencies of government) because "it would supplant Internal Revenue Taxes upon Whiskey and Tobacco—which sub-jects of taxation should be relegated to the States." In summary, the income tax "would give to tax-oppressed people all over the land a relief from the crushing burden of indirect, cowardly and illegal taxes which are wrung from them in the name of the Law for the benefit of privileged classes."[21] At most, one finds here a fiscal activism which was based on the rejection of regressive prin-ciples, but it was radical, if at all, only as a corrective within an al-ready limited framework.

Watson's attack on the Pinkerton system revealed the same limi-tation. The Pinkertons were a private army which was engaged in the suppression of labor. He fully understood the import of this activity. Yet he placed his opposition to Pinkertons within a broader context of public order which pronounced equally unac-ceptable the supposed excesses of working people. The Pinkerton strikebreaker and the militant striker alike were undesirable threats to society. While Watson introduced an anti-Pinkerton resolution in Congress (symbolically this was one of his most advanced public acts), his statement on its behalf, contained in the handbook, was not different in kind from his earlier emphasis on a just harmony.

First, he asserted an overriding tenet of order—somewhat gratuitously, in the circumstances, since he had mentioned, only moments before, what had occurred in the New York Central strike. Pinkertons, "paid by the railroad authorities," had "shot down in the streets of Albany men, women and children, who were noncombatants, who were violating no law, and not disturbing the peace." Yet, notwithstanding this sufficient ground for his resolution, he was anxious lest any side destroy the social balance: "Now, Mr. Speaker, we say that this is a country with law and order or it is a country of anarchy. If the regularly constituted authorities can administer the law and preserve the peace, we want to know it; if they cannot, we want to know it, that we may strengthen their hands."[22]

At first glance it appears that Watson was merely bidding for support against a challenge to political authority from the right, but he went on to provide an inclusive definition of anarchy: "I am as much opposed to laborers having a standing army as I am to capitalists having it. I believe in law; I believe in order; I believe that when there is civil disturbance the peace should be preserved by an impartial magistracy, not by the armed belligerents on either side." The actual and the purely hypothetical stood on the same plane (as though a largely unorganized labor force had such an offensive capability, or, what was even less likely, the wish to so engage authority). Watson described a condition of fictive equality which recalls his ascription of the powers to rich and poor to abuse their respective property shares. His concluding remark on this potentially volatile issue made clear that placing limits on corporate practices was not viewed as antithetical to the propertied balance of an organic capitalist structure: "Let us see whether there is not an evil which deserves to be restrained or corrected in the interest, not of the laborer, merely as a laborer, not of the striker, merely as a striker, but in the interest of the citizen, whether he is a laborer or a capitalist—in the interest of the good order, the peace, and the dignity of society."[23]

Watson's treatment of railroads was not an ebullient call for the people's appropriation of social property, although it managed well the standard arguments for government ownership. He fragmented the discussion, however, by dividing his analysis into objections and advantages without supplying positive connections to signal an affirmation of the public realm. His view of the advantages was predicated on the liberation of an interdependent, freely moving system of trade, which was designed to foster a more even pattern of capitalist development between industry and agriculture. In this respect, Smithian antimonopolism would not be an unwarranted designation of his position. He regarded corporate power as emblematic of the retardation of agricultural regions; public ownership, conversely, stood for the entrepreneurial functions to be encouraged.

Watson countered the first objection to public ownership, "That there is no law for it," by presenting a weak statement of sovereignty (eminent domain merely restored lands and did not create something entirely new). To lessen the blow, he emphasized the fact of compensation to private owners: "The answer to this is that Railroads are Public Highways and necessarily under the control of the Government. The law of eminent domain condemned the land when the Roads were built. Surely what the law took from the people it can restore. We propose to pay a fair price for the property, to be assessed according to law." He met the second objection, "That they would cost too much," on the firmer ground that savings would be effected and that the government had the right to determine a method of payment. A general propertied idiom was still present: "No man loses anything by purchasing good property; especially if that property is injuring him. No tax would have to be laid on the people to pay for the Roads. Legal Tender Treasury Notes can be issued direct from the Treasury to pay for them; thus adding to our circulation without taxing anybody. By operating the Roads upon a basis which would yield 4 per cent upon their actual value, we would save $250,000,000 per year in freights and yet accumulate a fund in the Treasury which would soon pay the price of the property." Watson's scrupulous regard to detail conveyed the sense of the normality of these operations, so that when he turned to the third objection, "That it is Paternalism," he settled (exactly where decisiveness was needed) for a less than resounding summons to structural change: "No more so than the Post Office. No more so than coining money is. When a power becomes dangerous to the life of the Republic, the Republic must subordinate that power or die. That is the situation to-day." Similarly, his response to the fourth objection, "That persons injured by the trains will have no redress," easily adjusted public ownership to existing mechanisms: "The jurisdiction of the Court of Claims can be extended to embrace such issues."[24]

Watson flawlessly (from a Populist standpoint) answered the last objection, "That it will put the Roads 'in Politics,' " by turning the tables on the critics and placing public enterprise itself under civil-service norms. "Would to God we could say they are not in politics:—controlling, corrupting and enslaving. By substituting Government ownership, we take away the motive for plundering the people and the crime will die with the motive." Yet only in one sentence did Watson go beyond commonplace statements of moderation: "If the people are capable of Self Government, they can be trusted with the Railroads." Then he continued: "Civil Service Reform is an assured fact of the near future and this will prevent indiscriminate use of Railway appointments for Political purposes." He had not invoked the higher standard of an independent state, but, on the practical level, he effectively dramatized the existence of private abuses: "Certainly the isolated, moderately paid, closely watched Railway official, whether Republican or Democrat cannot do anything like the harm that is now done by closely organized, lavishly paid Railroad Kings who defy watching and control elections, and legislative issues, by shameless use of the Corporate funds."[25]

In framing the objections, Watson perhaps never intended to raise fundamental questions of structure (he studiously avoided a qualitative assessment of capitalism). But neither, when he presented the advantages of public ownership, did he seek to build a case for enlarged governmental powers. The principle of extensible powers, an integral feature of advanced Populist thought, was absent. Instead, Watson remained near the surface: "It would give a death blow to the 'Reign of the Corporation.' The people would be boss again." The second advantage of public ownership was that it "would stop corrupt Legislation" on behalf of corporations, and the third advantage conveyed a sense of competitive capitalism: "It would unshackle Trade and Commerce from 'the Trust' and 'the Ring.' They cannot operate without the aid of the Railroad." The fourth advantage more specifically advanced a belief in opportunity: "It would stop discriminations against certain persons and certain places. The motive would be gone. The Post Office treats all alike. So would the Government Railway." The fifth and sixth advantages held that speculative railroad building and antilabor policies would cease under public ownership, while the seventh reiterated the dimension of capitalism: "It would enable the Cotton Planter to exchange products with the Corn Planter on fair terms which would leave a profit to both. At present the Railroads impoverish them both." The eighth advantage spoke of the reconciliation of classes: "It would remove the causes of the hatred of the people to the roads and harmonize all interests." And the ninth advantage extended the harmonization of social interests into the economic realm, because all could enjoy a fair starting place, and not be subject to discriminations affecting commerce: "It would equalize all avocations and shippers; and would take away the power the Roads now have to destroy a business, a section or an individual."[26]

It should now be apparent that Watson conceived of public railroads as a self-contained measure which did not promise further collective activities. As the tenth advantage suggested, he made government ownership synonymous with breaking down economic restrictions: "It would put into the hands of the people a weapon with which they could destroy any Combine among Capitalists in any Article of Commerce." The eleventh advantage was the saving of "enormous sums now paid in fancy salaries," and the twelfth, the saving of human lives "lost every year for lack of safety appliances."[27]

Many of these advantages, including the last two, were not trivial and figured prominently in Populist discussions of the railroad. Watson differed from other accounts in his reiteration of the liberalization of trade. His final point was a catch-all declaration which had set grievances entirely within a capitalist context. A disequilibrium had to be righted. Even his remark on class structure pertained less to the inequitable distribution of wealth than to arrogance and underhanded gain:

It would bring about absolute Free Trade and cheap traffic between all sections of this great Country; destroy "the pool:" knock the pins from under the Stock broker: put an end to the insolence with which so many officials treat the Public: remove the leverage which English Capital has on our Labor and its Products: give a death-blow to this infernal "booming" of towns and cities at the expense of the country and for the benefit of a few Capitalists over many Laborers. It would be a giant strike in the direction of equality and manhood rights and to the destruction of our Class System of Special Privilege, Shoddy Aristocracy based on Commercial Spoils and advancing through the dirty lanes and perils of bribery and corruption.[28]

Public ownership, rather than serving as a goal, had an instrumental quality (as if to settle existing scores). But the more serious negativism concerned the limited meaning of equality, more commercial than political, and addressed to the shoddiness rather than to the substance of power.

Still, Watson's thought, at least in 1892, was more complex than I have made out; or rather, it was the very Smithian traces I have discussed that, in conjunction with his call for revolt, helped to define its complexity. Means of seemingly frightening import were harnessed to ordinary, if still Populist, ends. This disproportion rendered the movement's purposes intelligible in its broader attack on privileged wealth and power, while at the same time keeping intact Watson's own conservative potential for a middle-class framework. In the closing chapter, he entered on the ground swell of discontent, where the intransigent leadership in America was likened to the "profligate nobles" of prerevolutionary France: "Carlyle is quoted as saying that they sneered contemptuously at Rousseau's Book on the social contract wherein was taught the doctrine of Liberty, Equality and Fraternity, but that the second edition of the work was bound in their skins." There was an implication of irreconcilable conflict and a commensurate militancy: "In this country we have appealed to reason. We have stated the grievances, their causes and their remedies. We have been met by both the Old Parties with ridicule, with slanders, with abuse, with mere mule-headed opposition. We have never owed an advance to the generosity of our adversaries." Only "when their fears were aroused," whether in England, France, or America, had concessions followed.[29]

Watson's depiction of repression was uncommonly acute: "It is always the same. Petitions are rejected: remonstrances spurned: complaints laughed aside: protests silenced: resistance stamped out with iron heel. All these things are done as long as it is supposed they can be safely done. It is only when Tyranny sees danger that it hears reason." But he introduced, along with repression, the less consequential theme of sybaritic life: "Belshazzar is repeated at every epoch and wherever the mad King reaches his last evening on earth his feast is certain to be had. . . . The pampered Aristocrats will listen to no warning, until Daniel strides into the Hall and the laugh of the voluptuary freezes on the lips of the quaking coward."[30] If Watson's focus was useful in highlighting conditions of deprivation, it nonetheless too readily personalized the ruling structure, leading him to substitute bad conduct for capitalism as the principal consideration.

At this point there occurred his well-known indictment of Congress, which included not only the charge of drunkenness that received contemporary attention, but an accusation of deeper irresponsibility and lack of purpose that went largely unanswered. This passage, too, with its puritanical cast, gives the impression of unmitigated opposition, even though essentials were only partly touched:

The Congress now sitting is one illustration. Pledged to Reform, they have not reformed. Pledged to Economy, they have not economized. Pledged to Legislate, they have not legislated. Extravagance has been the order of the day. Absenteeism was never so pronounced. Lack of purpose was never so clear. Lack of common business prudence never more glaring. Drunken members have reeled about the aisles—a disgrace to the Republic. Drunken speakers have debated grave issues on the Floor and in the midst of maudlin ramblings have been heard to ask *"Mr. Speaker, where was I at?"* Useless employes crowd every corridor. Useless expenditures pervade every Department.

Watson continued to bear down on Congress: "Honorable members made strenuous efforts for a Relief Expedition to the starving Russians. They hooted at the idea of relieving the starving Americans." And in the "business world," this narrow vision was also manifest: "The Capitalists will not see; will not hear. They offer no conciliation. They not only claim all the advantages they illegally hold, but demand more." Further, he wrote: "The Corporations do not lessen their exactions. The actual Railroad returns show fat profits all around. . . . The Money Kings were never in higher feather. They feel good. The money is on their side; the Law is on their side: the Government is on their side." Watson pictured a condition of widespread deterioration, which he summarized eloquently in a single sentence (referring to Vanderbilt's ostentatious displays): "Millions were wasted on feasts while gaunt starvation walked the streets."[31]

Much of this phase of the discussion blended Lewelling's concern over uncaring ruling groups, Weaver's analysis of governmental inertia, and Peffer's treatment of the partiality of the law, making it authentically Populist in flavor and content. It thus provides the reader with further illustration of a critical aspect which, by definition, worked against the facile acceptance of property. Like Donnelly, Watson scrutinized economic development and passed judgment on the false worship of wealth as well as the practice of philanthropy: "Carnegie cuts his wages and robs his workmen of a million dollars. He gives ten per cent. of it to Charity; and the Pharisees all cry out, 'blessed be Carnegie.' Rockefeller plunders the people to the neat extent of Ten Millions per year on the Oil Monopoly. He puts little dabs of the booty here and there among Colleges and Schools and they all flap their wings and crow; while the press says, 'blessed be Rockefeller.' The pity of it is that humbuggery is so victorious. Nearly every scheme of the Corporations obtains popular favor under the specious pretext of 'developing the country.' " Misery was to be seen on every side; at one point, he plaintively observed: "The red flag of the auctioneer is in every street. The Sheriff's hammer is never idle, and with every minute which passes the light of some home goes out forever." With this cumulative outpouring, it was only natural that he should exclaim: "Where will it stop? How can human nature stand it always! Let no man dream that it can last. The sword of Damocles never hung by a slenderer thread than does the false system of to-day."[32]

For Watson there was a compounding of hardship, to be measured ultimately by the debauched misappropriation of just wealth on the part of dominant groups. This became a two-stage configuration from revolt to revolution:

When men suffer for food it is hard. When their wives and children so suffer it is harder. But when that suffering is felt to be undeserved, then it is hardest. And when to this undeserved distress is added the belief that some other man is withholding just dues, honest wages, fair reward of toil, then revolt is at hand. And when, to this condition, is added the fact that the man who withholds those just dues is feasting on them, reveling on them in riotous excess of gathered spoils, while, in the wretched hut of the man to whom they rightfully belong lies the worn and faded wife, dying of hunger,—lies the frail and withered child, gasping for God's pure air, then revolution is as inevitable as the laws of the universe.

Clearly, in the handbook's closing paragraphs, Watson carries us to the verge of the politically unthinkable, to the idea of revolution. No matter his concern with bad conduct rather than structure, as when he stated, "Woe unto the system which robs the people and then mocks them in their agony," for he now proclaimed—in words that gave to the work its popular title: "As the Nobleman said to the King, the night the Bastille fell, 'No sire, it is not a Revolt, it is a Revolution.' "[33]

Not a Revolt; It is a Revolution never became the Populist landmark Watson perhaps hoped it would. Yet the phrase has come down as an unexamined stereotype of Watson's role especially, suggesting a superseding radicalism which eschewed not simply political compromise but all forms of equivocation, whether on structure, class, or government. Indeed, Populists may have deceived themselves by not carefully weighing Watson's words. The crux of the complexity lay in the meaning he assigned to revolution. In essence, it represented a reimposition of law and order for the purpose of removing extremes in society and strengthening its middle-class foundations and perspective. The Watsonian revolution became the preventative to revolution.

While separate parts of this complex attitude occurred throughout Populism, the combination as Watson developed it stood for something different. It was more conservative in genesis, because it refused to consider any autonomous role for the lower classes and hence any realistic call for the democratization of power. Watson was remarkably contented with society emptied of its monopolistic wastes and purified on capitalist lines. The

purification of society, as he expressly maintained, held no promise of subduing the effects of class or realizing some new or transcendent goals. Watson had no lively evolutionary sense. History
ceased, or as he stated, the revolution was completed, when the
propertied equilibrium was restored. In the last analysis, his indignation was not feigned. He shared the description of contemporary privation with other Populists and even vivified it. He took
this, however, as evidence of the breakdown of authority, the ascendance of unsavory ruling elements, and the consequent need
for a return to order.

Upon calling the movement, "not a revolt, but a revolution,"
Watson began this final portion: "So it is. Peaceful, bloodless, un-
stained by crime, but as resistless as destiny." Such colorful imagery of the purported revolution as "the roar of the rushing
tide," and "the burst of flame all along the advancing front of battle," could not disguise its sober-minded, restorative character.
"To restore the liberties of the people, the rule of the people, the
equal rights of the people is our purpose; and to do it, the revolution in the old systems must be complete." Even this last point
signified that change would be gradual, piecemeal, nonconfronta-
tional, above all, geared to the improvement of what already existed: "We do not blindly seek to tear down. We offer the good Law
for each bad Law; the sound rail for every rotten rail. We work in
no spirit of hate to individuals. We hate only the wrongs and the
abuses, and the special privileges which oppress us. We call on
good men and good women everywhere to aid us. We call on God
above to aid us. For in the revolution we seek to accomplish, there
shall be Law and order preserved in-violate."[34] This passage appears to concern only the process of social change, with the substance of revolution to follow. But law and order defined the revolution. Watson was on firm Populist ground when he emphasized
a rational, constructive approach, rejected nihilism, and singled
out special privileges for mention. Yet these positive factors quickly turned to the partial arrestment of change in which a brittle
reading left disparities of wealth and power not directly traceable
to special privileges solidly intact.

First, Watson recognized that he had to qualify his statement
about the preservation of law and order, because it was hardly dis-
tinguishable from the existing system: "But the Law shall be

founded on right and the order shall silence no man's cry of distress." However, he immediately continued in a manner less oblivious to this injunction than unwittingly revelatory of its limited application through which "right" by removing privilege still countenanced normalized inequalities. Simply, there must be an end to law-sanctioned oppression. Cries of distress might and *would* continue, though they would no longer be silenced by "order," as Watson placed poverty, crime, suffering, and the presence of the strong over the weak within legitimate bounds:

We do not assert that poverty will disappear. We do not assert that the Law itself shall make no more of it. We do not assert that there will be no more crime; we do say that vicious Legislation shall cease to produce it. We do not say that there will be no more suffering; but we do aver that hereafter and forever the statutes shall not empty the homes of the people, turn their children into the streets and fill the hospitals and the alleys and the gutters with the distracted victims of the Law. We do not say that the strong man will cease to have the advantage of the weak one. But we do say that the infernal shame of the Law in aiding the strong man to pilfer the weak one can be stopped and must be![35]

Watson had somehow sanitized the law. He elevated it above—rather than made it the active instrument in the rearrangement of—the workings of society. If this were a question of modesty, of properly qualifying the hopes of what might be accomplished, his tone would appear justified. But the modesty here reflected what was thought desirable in the coming social order. Watson's formation would encompass specifically capitalist traits, and hence consciously avoid the promise of any thoroughgoing alteration. On this plateau, he turned to a centrist vision of society originating partly in the fear of revolution and partly in unstinting admiration for productive capitalism.

The key feature of his vision was a social equipoise, permitting a return to the ways of enterprise. Therefore, the utter destitution of the poor and the debauchery of the wealthy posed like threats to social and political stability: "The hot-beds of crime and vice today are at the two extremes of Society. One is among the class who will have all the work and no money; the other is with the class who have all the money and no work. The one class is driven to crime and vice by hardships, despair, desperation. The other class chooses crime and vice because of their surplus of money, their lack of purpose, their capacity to live in idleness and gratify sensual pleasures." The extremes become a convenient foil by which Watson could certify the fundamental soundness of what remained—much of the social structure, with the sting of legalized favoritism removed: "The great Middle Class is the mainstay of life. It is the judicious mixture of work and leisure which makes the complete man; the useful man; the happy man; the God-fearing, law-abiding man."[36]

This "mixture" symbolized not merely a balanced existence within the individual (producing if not Cromwellian man then one likely to adhere to principles of order), but the more crucial balance, to be located at society's institutional core, between enterprise and remuneration. When Watson rejected both extremes, it is difficult to tell whether he was equally out of sympathy with each one. Yet what is apparent is their common threat to a stable society. The idle rich offered no guidance and deflected the economic process into unproductive channels (they meanwhile undermined the system of incentives). The demoralized poor, in addition to raising the prospect of rebellion, were excluded from the economic process through their impoverishment, even though, of course, they supplied the bulk of society's labor-power. Watson presented the middle-class framework of society as alone sufficient for harmonious, productive economic contributions, and he saw this as exhausting the remedies and purposes of Populism: "Any system which increases the Moneyed Class where there is all money and no work, debauches Society. Any System which increases the class where there is all work and no money debauches and endangers Society. Any system which will add to the great Middle Class where there is reasonable work and fair reward, secures to Society the best results of which humanity is capable. Every principle advocated by the People's Party seeks that end and logically leads to it."[37]

The vision had been achieved in its propertied realization. "When this System comes, (and it is bound to come) the Revolution will be complete." From there one finds what I termed "the emptying of wastes," allowing a resumption of middle-class purity: "The dens of vice will loose their feeders. The supply-trains of crime will be cut off. The Bar-room will disappear and the gambling hell sink to its larger namesake. The attendant train of evils which the present system carries with it will vanish with the system itself." If Watson had included an affirmative discussion of structure and class, the remainder of the passage would not seem to be an anticlimax, a pale imitation of Donnelly and Lewelling: "Manhood will count for more than money. Character will outweigh the dollar. The Laborer whether he work with brawn or brain, with thought or speech, will be the monarch of the new order of things."[38]

Finally, after remarking that Watson did not possess a "lively evolutional sense," chiefly because his conception of revolution was both antirevolutionary and finite, I should add that on the closing page he displayed an overarching vision of happiness. Yet his statement was more brittle and rhetorical than can be found in Lewelling and Donnelly. It did not give promise of going beyond the propertied equilibrium he had already constructed. Watson wrote:

I see no reason under the sun why the Laws should not be so framed and humanity so directed that happiness could be possible. Believing as I do in the upward tendency of the human race, profoundly impressed with its wonderful capacities and achievements, I cannot believe that the splendid vigor of the Race which has conquered the land, the sea, the air, will allow itself to be sapped and destroyed by the artificial checks and hindrances and oppressions of the Law, as we now have it. The Race will throw them off as the old bark is cast off from the tree; and towering upward toward the sky, humanity will take its imperial growth, fragrant with buds and blossoms.[39]

The only tangible reference was to the contemporary abuses of the law, which, once rejected, would permit fruition and growth. Completion was at one with restoration. The abuses were themselves of entirely recent origin: "Over all the grand institutions of our past; over all the glorious principles our fathers bled for, the flood of corruption, consequent largely upon the Civil War, has passed in ruinous strength; burying the landmarks of popular rights; engulphing the boundary lines between might and right, between justice and wrong." Watson underscored restoration: "Blessed be God for the faith that the waters will ebb away; that the turrets and steeples of our buried institutions will reappear above the turbid tide; that the fruitful land shall once be the home of a chastened and contented and fraternal Human Family."[40]

This chapter has presented contrasting emphases on the meaning and structural possibilities of antimonopolism. If the Nebraska

Populists shared with Watson a common discourse, they neverthe-less achieved a greater specificity of economic and social criticism. In the Lincoln paper, the distinction between competitive capital-ism and puristic laissez-faire was forcefully stated. The corporate structure was identified as a source of antidemocratic political rela-tionships and social trends. Despite propertied acceptances, there was a vitality in their concept of public ownership which carried beyond the limited purposes of a more effective market economy.

This contrasted with Watson's comparatively nonstructural analysis and attenuated sense of public sovereignty. Whether or not one wishes to consider him a conservative offshoot of the main stem, it is evident that he at least passively legitimated basic elements of capitalist society—as in his theory of middle-class foundations—that many Populists either questioned, or sought to modify in light of prior ethical concepts. Historians have begun the reevaluation of Watson's supposed radicalism. I will attempt to extend such discussions in *all* areas and will center them in the framework of paternalist modernity. For present purposes, what emerges is a context of ambiguity concerning property which is partially clarified in the Populists to be discussed next. Particularly in the case of Ignatius Donnelly, one grasps the importance of government so incompletely developed by Watson. From that point, it is a short step to the Populist treatment of political sovereignty.

CHAPTER SIX

Government and Human Welfare: Donnelly

Despite numerous and significant variations, largely originating in interregional historical, political, and cultural differences, Populists ascribed to government the constitutional mandate and the structural potential for providing a democratic context of legal and socioeconomic rights. They further maintained that, in achieving this framework, the state would necessarily have to direct its activities against the contemporary operations of capitalism. Monopolism was the source for existing patterns of economic and social deprivations, and its powers had to be challenged and eliminated. Populists meant by a "people's government" the creation of an independent state formation which was no longer in a symbiotic relationship with the business community. An independent state would halt the preferential treatment of business as well as extend the scope of the public's jurisdiction. It would establish the basis for a nonprivileged capitalism, which would place emphasis on internally generated economic forces, rather than political solutions, for its expansion and development. In contrast, a business-government partnership indicated the private control of the state. It represented the political stabilization of monopolistic power. The corporate structure would supplant the basic law; favoritism would become, if it were not already, endemic. The result would be an economic framework of restrictive practices wholly inimical to standards of fair entitlement and free productive energies.

Even where Populists might differ on the purposes, scope, and ultimate boundaries of state power, they were clearly prepared to agree on the principle of government intervention in the economy and on the specific objective of curbing monopolistic dominance over private activities. In the South and West alike, Populists explicitly identified economic stagnation and the closing of opportunity as major issues which derived from the functioning of corporate capitalism. They were of like mind, but not always of like intensity, in raising antecedent issues which affected the Populist conception of the democratic state itself. Westerners were frequently more explicit, and southerners more implicit in articulating their concerns about the determination of where power resided in society, of whether economic processes could be subject to public governance, and of what underlying principles would define the nation's forward course.

In spite of a tradition of constitutional explorations, southern Populists tended to adopt a narrowly economic focus, which was directed to raising farm income through monetarist solutions. The internal stimulation of the economy, which followed from a reliance on the remedies of monetarism, had the effect of encouraging a belief in the natural processes of recovery and growth, specifically at the expense of a comprehensive role for government intervention across the range of corporate and monopolistic political-economic influences. Whether southern Populists were inclined toward strict greenbackism, including inconvertible paper, or free coinage, lower tariffs, and an equitable program of taxation, they centered their agitation and discussion on the financial sector of the economy. They narrowed their diagnosis of the problem of monopolism to the interrelated areas of fiscal policy, the national banking system, and the money supply. And, perhaps most important, they conceptualized the total framework of exploitation as limited primarily to the situation affecting agriculture. Few southern Populists, including the predominant greenback sentiment of the Southwest, had diagramed a national structure of power. Finance capital, not the corporate system, became the devil, if there was one.

Of course, Populist measures which called for the control of the banking system required the presence of extensive government powers. This was particularly evident in the exercise of sovereign authority over such functions as the issuance of legal-tender notes, the management of the currency, and the mobilization of credit, to be made widely available at low rates of interest. The subtreasury plan, which some recent historians consider the most radical manifestation of Populism, or at the very least, a test of Pop-

ulist economic and political orthodoxy (and presumably imbricat-
ed with greenbackism and the cooperative movement), fell principally under the third category of these functions. The national
government would construct storage facilities for the receipt of
nonperishable staple farm commodities and issue certificates of
deposit equivalent to the value of 80 percent of the stored commodity, to be used as legal tender in the payment of debts. The
farmer would thereby have been able to withhold his crop from
the market until there was a favorable rise in price; the money
supply itself would have been enlarged through this subvention,
precisely at the moment of greatest pressure on currency and
credit because of the need to finance the movement of crops; the
government's sovereignty would have been confirmed and
strengthened in the specific area of agricultural credits by issuing
directly these loans in the form of payments to farmers without
the intermediary role of private banks; and the farmer would have
received not only low cost loans (depending on which version of
the plan is consulted, the charge was 1 percent or 2 percent) but
also an informal price support for his crop, four-fifths of its value
at the time of deposit, since he would have been free to allow it to
remain unredeemed in government storage. Certainly, we are
speaking here of massive intervention into the economy. But I believe the subtreasury plan illustrates the larger point about possible ideological differences between southern and western Populism, the emphases found in the respective regions concerning the
attitude toward the powers of government, and, assuming the issue really mattered, the degrees of radicalism in each one.

For some reason, historians of western Populism have never
made extravagant claims about the comparative radicalism of the
region in relation to southern Populism; historians of southern
Populism have always done so implicitly or explicitly with respect
to the West. Ever since the distinguished southern historian
C. Vann Woodward presented this view in 1951, it has become
an article of faith, which every scholar writing on the subject uncritically accepted. The issue is a false one. No one should really
care about the comparative radicalism of the different regional expressions of Populism, unless it furthers some analytical purpose,
because it is self-evident that both regions were important to the
movement and that each region faced its own peculiar problems,

drew upon its own historical and cultural experiences, and confronted its own specific obstacles in advancing a position of political and economic dissent. Populism was not an interregional beauty contest to determine who was most radical, although southern Populists (and here historians merely reflected their sources faithfully) often thought so. In this regard, their inflated self-image is not beside the point in understanding them better.

The subtreasury plan, although it covered wheat and corn, as well as cotton, was primarily southern in origin and popularity. From what I have said, it is clear that the program was ambitious, involved active government participation, and, most notable, demonstrated careful planning and a mastery of technical details. I have no quarrel with the plan or its separate provisions, nor do I have any doubt that it represented a basic modification of the marketing framework in agriculture, possibly having ramifications as well for the composition and velocity of circulation of the money supply, the behavior of the business cycle, and the credit structure. The funding of the plan also had a bearing on the methods for deriving the necessary government revenues, and hence a bearing on taxation policies, the tariff, and Treasury decisions affecting a gold outflow, trade deficits, and the servicing of the national debt. Not surprising, the business and banking communities both in the region and the nation universally opposed the subtreasury (when they would even dignify its presence by noticing it). It was worthy of consideration.

Yet when one studies the arguments which were presented on its behalf, the specific provisions, and the objectives to be served, the overriding impression one has of the subtreasury plan is of a framework of relief which fit in well with interest-group politics rather than class-conscious protest and which, for southern Populists, did not provide the economic or ideological basis for generalizing to the larger social welfare. It was a plan for agriculture, not for the lower classes on the land. It would confer a direct benefit on the substantial farmer, who was wholly free from, or only partially trapped by, the strict enforcement of the crop-lien system, and who was therefore still able in the late 1880s to dispose of his crop; at most, it would confer only an indirect benefit on the marginal landowner, who could not freely dispose of his crop, but merely strengthen his bargaining position as against the supply merchant by a hoped-for rise of price; and it would confer absolutely no benefit on the tenant and share-cropper, who were the most hard-pressed and in need of direct federal help, and yet had no crop even to call their own. (I am reminded here of the implementation of the domestic-allotment plans and the marketing agreements under the Agricultural Adjustment Administration (AAA) to which the subtreasury plan on the critical question of the structure of benefits payments bears a strong resemblance. There were no Rex Tugwells or Jerome Franks in southern Populism, however, to fight for the alteration of the plan so that it would positively affect the bottom rungs of southern agriculture. Needless to say, the Negro in the South might as well have cultivated tundra in the Arctic Circle insofar as the subtreasury plan reflected his welfare.) It should not be forgotten that the subtreasury was a demand which was primarily confined to only one phase of southern Populism, that of the Farmers' Alliance proper, and it barely outlasted the Alliance when the organization itself began its decline. To some recent historians, this is important because, if the plan was the touchstone of Populist orthodoxy, the proof was at hand that the second phase of Populism, its political organization in the People's party, was a sham, the inauthentic article, the Great Betrayal of the movement culture. Curiously, once into the 1890s, Tom Watson, a hero of this school of interpretation, turned vehemently against the subtreasury plan, and Charles Macune, reputedly its originator, turned against Populism. But that is merely in the nature of tweaking noses, for the significance of the Alliance sponsorship is that the subtreasury plan would reflect many of the organization's own underlying characteristics—of vital concern here, its essentially propertied economic and social base, nonclass appeals, and agricultural scope of interest. The subtreasury plan served to disguise internal class differences within agriculture and within southern Populism. It also reinforced the monetarist perspective.

In the case of the subtreasury plan, the world of technical solutions spoke to the normalization of capitalist relations. Government storage was the functional equivalent of domestic allotment and the reduction of acreage: a framework of publicly administered scarcity in order to ensure higher returns for participating farmers. (And in practical terms, the condition of participation was landownership, a marketable surplus, and a preexistent solvency.) In the same way, certificates of deposit were the functional equivalent of land bank currency or farm-secured mortgages. Qualified farmers had proposed an alternative method for gaining access to the credit markets. Proponents of the subtreasury plan would not have blanched at the statement of these and related objectives. Charles Macune, Harry Skinner, and, slightly less so, Harry Tracy were eminently practical men, proud of their achievement. And well they might be, for, despite the hostile reception given the plan in Congress, the national press, and interested business associations, what most characterized it (in addition to its interest-group complexion) was its sensible quality. They did not conceive the demand for the subtreasury, contrary to the hopes and expectations of recent historians, as the means of destroying the crop-lien system, but only of bypassing it, and perhaps, just perhaps, in the long run encircling it, so that it might collapse, or be contained, under its own dead weight in the ultimate liberalization of credit facilities. The subtreasury plan was not radical. It was thoroughly capitalistic, and these two elements, even more than oil and water, do not mix. Its application, like that of AAA, would have widened class relations on the land, not only by favoring those who were already in a position of advantage (and also possibly leading to the further engrossment of lands of marginal owners) but also, in the very terms of its operation, by circumventing direct aid to tenants and sharecroppers. One searches in vain here for a program of land reform. Holdings, to state the obvious, would not become more equitably distributed. Economic categories, just as racial categories, would remain the same: There would be owners, and there would be tenants. The search for credit was not the road to the democratization of class relations, still less was it the road to confiscation and the redivision of the land, on which such democratization realistically depended.

Have I posed an impossible standard? No, I merely wish to return the discussion to the salience of the matter: the quality of sensibleness inhering in every feature of the subtreasury plan. Southern Populists were not ashamed of this characteristic; why should we be? They frequently defended the plan in terms of the Jeffersonian formula, "equal rights to all, special privileges to none." This meant, in the present context, that the federal government had constructed storage facilities for whiskey distillers, their product serving as the basis for secured loans at low interest rates. Therefore, why not us? Even more pertinent, the national banking system had been founded on the requirement that banking capital be invested in government bonds. These bonds became the basis for the issuance of currency. The banks were charged 1 percent for the use of the fund, and yet were free to charge whatever the traffic would bear, perhaps 8 or 10 percent, for the use of their bank notes. Therefore, why not us? The reasoning was almost embarrassingly direct: Privileges would be universalized rather than restricted, but the concept of privilege—because the application of public policy was successively confined by considerations of economic sector, class relations, and the very premise of self-interest—would be only partially rejected. The reason, then, that the air of practicality, the world of technical solutions, spoke in this case to the normalization of capitalist relations, and capitalism as the fundamental system, was that the subtreasury plan did not have to raise definitive principles of governance for its successful implementation. It was not only sensible, it was perhaps too sensible. It could be fit into the existing structure because its advocates had conceived its purposes in finite terms—the solution to the problem of agricultural credits, the consolidation of middling propertied groups on the land, the creation of a flexible, open marketing system.

The fact of massive government intervention in the economy in reality tells us very little. The more compelling matter is the animating spirit behind this intervention—not only whom does it benefit, how does it affect the democratization of power, what are its structural potentialities for creating changes at the economic and social foundations of capitalism but also what does it say about the political obligations of government, the nature of sovereignty, and the conception of human nature in a democratic society? Populism, whether western or southern, was not a movement of philosphers, at least not in the common acceptation of the term. But neither was it a movement of mindless actors. The questions I have just raised were formally and informally addressed, even if at times negatively, by the very act of calling for the powers of government. What was not said is as instructive as what was said. Few southern Populists developed a rationale for the use of government, and fewer still stated the moral and ethical postulates which located government in the overall workings of society. This was not for want of a hospitable intellectual climate, at least through the pre–Civil War era; from Jefferson through Calhoun and Fitzhugh, political speculation was a recognizable regional trait. But after the Civil War, social control was no longer an uncontested given of southern society, and unless one was prepared to conceptualize the desirability and efficacy of a repressive state, it was best to leave the matter altogether alone. The "matter," naturally enough, was the place of the Negro in the South, or since there was little substantial disagreement among southern whites about confining blacks to a subordinate position, the frame of reference for discussion shifted from the state to the retainment of southern culture and institutions as the coded terms of racial stabilization. Massive government intervention, even when it was specifically limited to the economy, was a sensitive, possibly a volatile, topic. It is relatively easy to suggest that white southerners in the late nineteenth century, Populists and non-Populists alike, had been disposed, because of long tradition, to an acceptance of laissez-faire, state rights, and individualism. But I think it is more plausible to suggest that this generation of the white South intuitively shrank from a focus on government because national power raised the prospect of a supervening force on behalf of human rights. Government was inimical to contemporary racial arrangements. In any case, southern Populists could not borrow anything of substance from Calhoun or Fitzhugh, but neither could they adopt a form of inquiry which might legitimate the state as an autonomous factor in determining the social welfare.

Thus, to reapproach the subtreasury plan is to see the benefits conferred by the state, but not the state itself. Southern Populists, like their western cohort, envisioned a neutral state, but they also, unlike their western cohort, confused a neutral state with a passive state. The state might establish an equilibrium of social forces, based on the equitable settlement of immediately pressing grievances, but it would not enlarge the conception of equity as a dynamic principle. The program was everything; southern Populists were not encouraged, and did not encourage themselves, to look underneath the specific provisions to antecedent standards of the social welfare. The subtreasury plan lacked philosophic dignity. One might argue correctly that hungry men cannot eat philosophy, but hungry men also cannot get beyond an interest-group perspective and approach, even to their own hunger (which may or may not be remediable through the program they support), unless they are prepared to eat, sleep, and dream a "philosophy" of moral, legal, and structural advancement. The interest-group perspective not only denies out of hand the organizing principle of class (which, like government, contains the potential for upsetting canons of race) but also strips away all pretensions to any but a reformist orientation. It fails to provide a more inclusive sense of, and achievement of, welfare, and it fails to seek a transformation of structure. Southern Populists, deriving from a political and social culture of purported romanticism, produced little transcendent thought in their own right.

What I have said about the subtreasury plan applies with equal force to the broader expression of grievances and demands. My initial point was that southern Populists tended to adopt a narrowly economic focus. Specifically, they were conspicuous in their failure to articulate the basic principles of a justly governed political order. They were not indifferent to questions of public rights, constitutionalism, and law, as our examination of Morgan, Davis, and Watson has shown, but with the possible exception of Morgan from among this group, they—and the predominant sentiment of Populism in the South—were extremely reluctant to grant extensive powers to the state, or to see the antecedent source of power in the people themselves, or finally to affirm a conception of welfare which might result in the transformation of economic and social relations. Programmatic remedies, although they were a salutary influence in breaking down the cultural barriers to a disciplined investigation of southern life and politics, almost consciously served to deflect critical attention away from the fruitful possibilities of a people's government; such remedies were a surrogate for the direct clash with capitalism as a system of power. There would be a concentration on the financial question (the subtreasury plan was merely a tactical variant of this emphasis), which, through placing the burden for rectifying grievances on monetarist solutions, looked emphatically to internal processes of growth—and therefore predicated the essential soundness of the social system—rather than extrinsic pressures aimed directly at the integrated structure of corporate power.

If western and southern Populists shared in common a restorative conception of American society, they meant by this that America provided the legal, moral, and philosophical context for a statement of democratic rights. This also implied a common faith in the redemptive powers of the nation's democratic heritage. In the case of neither regional expression of Populism was the intention literally to revert to a prior stage of political and economic development. But precisely here a subtle disjunction in thought occurs. For western Populists, the restorative conception of America stimulated a propulsion of society forward; the formative context of rights, which they rooted in the individual's own rational capacities and (especially as stated by Ignatius Donnelly) his human attributes of divinity, led to a trust in government as the exponent of man's reason and the repository of social ideals. The power of government would be extensive, but it would also, as the outgrowth of expressly affirming the right of the individual to change his society, be extensible. In contrast, southern Populists made the restorative conception of America a structural paradigm in its own right. There would not be a reversion to a prior stage, but the present stage, taking in the changes which have resulted in agriculture and industry, nevertheless would be statically rendered. In southern Populist thought, the proneness to laissez-faire is partly explained by this desire to accept, and at the same time neutralize the cultural and institutional consequences of, modernization. To paraphrase my earlier observation, monetarism was not the road to public ownership (and, in strict terms, it could obviate its use), which, in this context, meant that southern Populists had developed a line of attack that would seek maximum effectiveness from the manipulation of existing givens. The revitalization of the market mechanism, the exhortation to individual self-reliance, the magnification (in words alone) of dissent, all of these betrayed a more rigid interpretation of the formative context of rights. The future was not an informing feature of the present; man's reason was seldom remarked on; social ideals had been largely individuated rather than given a collective identity.

Southern Populists felt dimly menaced by the concept of

government as having potentially extensible powers and an expanding jurisdiction. The financial sector, as their area of greatest concern and involvement, had the one presumed virtue of being the most circumscribed area for the implementation of public policy. If the dominance of private bankers were shattered as a result, the damage to the wider configuration of the institutions and values of capitalism would still be readily contained. And within the financial sector, because southern Populists had generally distanced themselves from a notion of the efficacy of government, the massive intervention which they proposed had an air of unreality about it. They waxed enthusiastic about specific grants of power in a single area, and yet they disemboweled the state as an active, penetrating force in the political culture which might transform the social order. They proposed that government issue legal-tender notes, manage the currency, and make credit widely available, and even used the theme of sovereign power to justify the public assumption of these functions, but they nevertheless viewed the functions themselves in discrete terms. Although the control of banking would have been a special case of public ownership, analogous to the nationalization of railroads, they perceived the interconnection between the two demands, but refrained from conceiving the banking question, in its myriad forms, as an avowed test of the public principle. It is the public principle which I would like to explore further in this chapter.

The questions I began with—the determination of where power resided in society, of whether economic processes could be subject to public governance, and of what underlying principles would define the nation's forward course—received more explicit attention at the hands of western than southern Populists. The belief in a human-centered political universe, and its corollary, the infusion of ethics into structure, provided a signpost through these areas of concern. Government was the expression of a sovereign people. It was the instrument for securing and implementing elemental rights. Western Populists viewed the state itself as the embodiment of human rationality. Although the state would safeguard the right of property, the human right, because it was affirmed largely in a social or community setting, effectively readjusted Lockean postulates: Political sovereignty was freed from the traditional constraints of an anterior property right and could address the general welfare. These Populists could entertain the idea of potentially extensible powers because, they reasoned, the source of final authority, antecedent even to property and the law, lay in the people themselves. The state was a man-made instrument of human welfare.

1. The Challenge of Human Progress

The writings of Ignatius Donnelly expressed the human-welfare dimensions of the state, and the Populists' receptivity to a human-centered political universe. Donnelly, migrating from Philadelphia to Minnesota before the Civil War, had been a conventional Republican congressman during the 1860s; in the next two decades, he described a deepening reform progression, which carried him through the Granger and Greenback movements to the Northern Alliance, and finally the leader of Minnesota Populism. He was a man of astonishing, if perhaps frequently misdirected, intellectual powers. His quasi-scientific and literary battles of the 1880s, which led to books on the origins of the earth, the lost continent of Atlantis, and the discovery of the cipher which presumably demonstrated Francis Bacon's authorship of the plays of Shakespeare, may have suggested to contemporaries an erratic quality which harmed his later political credibility as a Populist. Donnelly was loved and respected but never taken seriously as a national leader. He was an outstanding party orator, an extraordinary publicist of the cause, but not a candidate. He published four political novels from 1890 through 1895 (we will consider the first three of these), and despite their apparent sensationalism, they reflected in the subtext if not the text of the argument standard Populist doctrine. Indeed, this is a key to the man: However far his imagination took flight to the ends of the universe, in *this* world he was supremely political and invariably planted both feet solidly on the ground. More than anyone I have examined here (including Frank Doster), Donnelly was a nineteenth-century American of a vanishing type: a practical visionary, the metaphorical blacksmith with a book in his hand. He could attempt (not too successfully) the role of power-broker, as his prodigious correspondence makes clear, or he could somewhat innocently hunger for office or preferment, as his diary reveals, but it is the novels which show Donnelly in his true political element. Here he fantasized about becoming the selfless leader performing good works in the service of humanity. More realistically, as his biographer Martin Ridge describes in detail, he had a long record of actual involvement in the reform politics of the upper Midwest.[1]

It would be mistaken to identify Donnelly with a millenarian image of the movement. Such a characterization exaggerates both his own political transcendence of the existing framework and Populism's inner vitality in areas which fell outside of its organization and relatively well defined ideology. The existence of subterranean currents of discontent was antithetical to his and the Populists' essentially rational conception of the state. It was precisely in the way the Populists had integrated mankind with political structure which demonstrated their cerebral protest and the social immediacy of ethics. The view of government was specifically rooted in the current setting. It was based on the perception of an existent oppressive state. There was not a retreat from reality, either backward or forward in time. Donnelly's exploration in the novels of alternative temporal and spatial frameworks was always a literary device which enabled him to develop unrestrainedly ideas of contemporary significance. In the 1890s, he mirrored, admittedly on a grander scale, the basic contours of Populist thought. His was not a voice in the wilderness. He wrote the much publicized preamble of the Omaha Platform, which gave the nation its first glimpse of unadorned Populism; the authenticity of his distillation of Populist views can be explained by his own thorough familiarity with them. When Donnelly stated, "We believe that the powers of government—in other words, of the people—should be expanded (as in the case of the postal service) as rapidly and as far as the good sense of an intelligent people and the teachings of experience shall justify, to the end that oppression, injustice, and poverty shall eventually cease in the land," [2] he was covering orthodox Populist territory. He was also succinctly formulating the human-centered character of the state.

In this discussion, I am providing a political commentary rather than a literary analysis. It is true that Donnelly's novels may therefore become empty husks in this rendering, because I have extracted ideological matter from the contextual setting of narrative, plot, and characterization, but I feel that for my purpose it is the political subtext—the inner dialogue between the author and the dissident groups of his own time—which is most significant here. In the case of *Caesar's Column* (1890) we have already had a hint (chapter 2, section 3) of the book's apocalyptic framework, a horrendously destructive revolution mounted by a secret brotherhood against world plutocracy, but we have already seen as well Donnelly's endeavor to prevent the very cataclysmic struggle he has prophesied. The novel, if it was melodramatic, was hardly nihilistic. Coming before the full impact of Populism, it reflected a positive doctrine of government. Donnelly was out of step with contemporary opinion, and he directly repudiated the existing structure of society. For him, the state would not be merely a summary of its available powers which had not been utilized; rather, he posited the state as comprising a new factor: It would be the guardian of popular rights, which was intended to have a transformative effect. He did not find it sufficient to propose remedial solutions within the prevailing social system. Such an approach would have glossed the seriousness of the perceived crisis. Instead, Donnelly began with the wider condition of disrepair (his penetrating analysis of the prevalent mood of alienation and feelings of futility), and he made this condition the basis for what he contended was an imperative need to extend the powers of government, if the path were to be broken for a more completed, fulfilled, nonalienated humanity.

When Donnelly's political formulations have been removed from the problems he planned to address, they may seem overly sanguine, for such was the trust he placed in a fully activated state. Yet when the background has been restored (his apparent utopian projection one hundred years into the future contained what were already discernible social conditions and cultural values), one comes to see the rational nature of his endeavor. The state would represent social man as a historical actor, asserting his powers of control over society. As the inversion of social Darwinist ideology and practice, it could achieve the elimination of poverty and reestablish human wholeness through cooperatively surmounting the stage of economic necessity. Privation had been created by, and was the responsibility of, society. The potential abundance of the productive system could be realized, and then democratized. Only a publicly oriented framework of government would integrate the political and economic communities. This unity of structure, and of purpose, was predicated on the inclusion of lower social groups in both communities. If Donnelly's argument became a means of forestalling social revolution, it nonetheless had compelling force in its own right and could stand alone. His concern was social betterment. His plea for a "renewal of the bond of brotherhood between the classes" had equal importance as the ethical assault on the existence of struggle per se, including the struggle of man for a bare subsistence.

In presenting his affirmation of the state, Donnelly threaded his way through a veritable wasteland. America had become a Stygian world. Suicide was commonplace. Appearances of material splendor disguised a rotting internal core of society. A brutalized underclass existed without hope. The novel's location a century in the future was to warn of the world toward which the nation was heading or in which it might have already arrived. In particular, suicide symbolized the negation of the sacredness of human life, which Donnelly placed within social contours that engendered self-respect and the capacity to experience meaning. He believed that blind materialism depersonalized the individual and deadened his life-sustaining impulses.

One of the principal characters, who spoke for Donnelly, revealed the efficiency and emptiness of modern society when he discussed the problem of suicide:

That, as it was, they polluted the rivers, and even the reservoirs of drinking-water, with their dead bodies, and put the city to great expense and trouble to recover and identify them. Then came the humanitarians, who said that many persons, intent on suicide, but knowing nothing of the best means of effecting their object, tore themselves to pieces with cruel pistol shots or knife wounds, or took corrosive poisons, which subjected them to agonizing tortures for hours before death came to their relief; and they argued that if a man had determined to leave the world it was a matter of humanity to help him out of it by the pleasantest means possible. These views at length prevailed, and now in all the public squares or parks they have erected handsome houses, beautifully furnished, with baths and bedrooms. If a man has decided to die, he goes there.

Donnelly did not relent in his indictment of what we might today call the rationalization of humanitarianism; there was medical supervision, pills, music, cremation, all considered by "authorities" to be "a marked improvement over the old-fashioned methods"—and by the character, "a shocking combination of impiety and mock-philanthropy." What rescued the statement from morbidity was not its overdrawn character (although this affords us partial release), but the immediately succeeding sentence, so plaintively worded as to leave no doubt about the perception of a compelling need for change: "The truth is, that, in this vast, overcrowded city, man is a drug,—a superfluity,—and I think many men and women end their lives out of an overwhelming sense of their own insignificance;—in other words, from a mere weariness of feeling that they are nothing, they become nothing."[3]

Donnelly was not expressing an agrarian suspicion of urban life. The city, like one of Melville's sailing vessels, became representative of the whole of society. Consider this exchange between the two main characters, prompted by the comment one had made about mankind's advances:

"Yes; it is the greatest of pities that so noble and beautiful a civilization should have become so hollow and rotten at the core."

"Rotten at the core!" I exclaimed, in astonishment; "what do you mean?"

"What I mean is that our civilization has grown to be a gorgeous shell; a mere mockery; a sham; outwardly fair and lovely, but inwardly full of dead men's bones and all uncleanness. To think that mankind is so capable of good, and now so cultured and polished, and yet all above is cruelty, craft and destruction, and all below is suffering, wretchedness, sin and shame."

"What do you mean?" I asked.

"That civilization is a gross and dreadful failure for seven-tenths of the human family. . . . It is pitiful to think what society is, and then to think what it might have been if our ancestors had not cast away their magnificent opportunities—had not thrown them into the pens of the swine of greed and gluttony."[4]

Donnelly's many-sided questioning of progress originated in his sense of the deceptiveness of material and industrial development. He was suggesting that an intensification of misery had served, under principles of greed, to shape social advancement.

The issue was not the constructive possibilities of technology. Donnelly, throughout his writings, held a positive view of the mastery of nature. Rather, he argued that the political formula for the accumulation of wealth was based on the cheapening of human labor. A framework of dominance had perverted the use of technology to antisocial ends. Donnelly believed a momentous historical departure to be occurring. Despite an apparent surface of undisturbed social growth, the concentration of wealth and an unresponsive system of government marked a progressive deterioration in society, which was borne most acutely by the laboring poor. His condemnation involved a total social system. There was an inward barrenness of society which defined, deformed, and destroyed the quality of life of all social classes.

The dominant groups in their "gorgeous shell" experienced on a different level the costs of pervasive emptiness. There was a corrosion of all knowledge, values, and beauty; in addition, these groups shared a tacit complicity in the practice of deprivation to secure their own well-being. Our first character, a visitor from Uganda, was still incredulous. Continuing his recitation of man's triumphs, he was chided by his American friend: "[B]ut you see only the surface, the shell, the crust of life in this great metropolis. To-morrow we will go out together, and I shall show you the fruits of our modern civilization." Suddenly, the vaster range of society's division appeared in view. Donnelly had more in mind than the evident hardship of working people. He saw a self-destructive factor operating in society, which was based on the elites' insouciance for the suffering they caused to others: "I shall take you, not upon the upper deck of society, where the flags are flying, the breeze blowing, and the music playing, but down into the dark and stuffy depths of the hold of the great vessel, where the sweating gnomes, in the glare of the furnace-heat, furnish the power which drives the mighty ship resplendent through the seas of time. We will visit the *Under-World*."[5]

This was an unlovely, but not, I think, a contemptuous portrayal of men in the final stage of degradation: "What struck me most was their incalculable multitude and their silence. It seemed to me that I was witnessing the resurrection of the dead; and that these vast, streaming, endless swarms were the condemned, marching noiselessly as shades to unavoidable and everlasting misery." If Donnelly harbored any fear toward an underclass, the more important point is that he identified one. He viewed it not as a fabrication, since it had enough similarity to contemporary accounts, but as a logical prediction based on current industrial trends. According to Donnelly, the future, in this case the laborer's complete alienation, had practically arrived. It was a future of unrelieved drudgery, where even aspiration would wither: "They seemed to me merely automata, in the hands of some ruthless and unrelenting destiny. They lived and moved, but they were without heart or hope. The illusions of the imagination, which beckon all of us forward, even over the roughest paths and through the darkest valleys and shadows of life, had departed from the scope of their vision. They knew that to-morrow could bring them nothing better than to-day—the same shameful, pitiable, contemptible, sordid struggle for a mere existence." Indeed, he discarded the future mask to reveal in a biting criticism of laissez-faire the economic foundation of alienation: "Here we saw exemplified, in its full perfection, that 'iron law of wages' which the old economists spoke of, that is to say, the reduction, by competition, of the wages of the worker to the least sum that will maintain life and muscular strength enough to do the work required, with such little surplus of vitality as might be necessary to perpetuate the wretched race; so that the world's work should not end with the death of one starved generation."[6]

Donnelly feared an underclass because it was the vehicle of revolution. Yet it became clear, as he proceeded to a statement of the role of government, that he was more fearful of the context of economic and social abuse which generated a violent response. His was an antinihilist plea for fundamental corrections directed to the removal of revolutionary premises. One goal of democratic state-building was to obviate the need for drastic solutions, which seemed to Donnelly destructive of civilization itself. But a second goal, rooted in the same devotion to civilization, was to emancipate an individual's intrinsic humanity, that which alone—because it restored meaning to the universe— had been historically worth conserving. Donnelly did not adopt a Wilsonian view of civilization, which equated order with constitutional processes and the maintenance of property rights; nor did he adopt a Sumnerian view of civilization, which utilized a more hard-bitten materialism to render capitalist development as the measure of society's welfare. Rather, Donnelly provided a more compassionate reading of civilization. He defined it almost purely by scientific and creative efforts, and thus he equated it specifically (this was a cosmopolitanism going beyond the particulars of nationhood) with human forces. Government could give body to a people's aspirations; it could help to fill out what Donnelly deplored as the hollowness of society, which was created through contemporary (and prospective) arrangements. It could enhance human possibilities so that not only revolution would be avoided but also the very notion of progress would be rendered meaningful.

The foregoing line of reasoning had been carefully traced in the novel by Donnelly's alter ego. He ascribed responsibility for the context of abuse to the intransigence of dominant groups: "There is no bigotry so blind or intense as that of caste; and long established wrongs are only to be rooted out by fire and sword. And hence the future looks so black to me." Donnelly's pessimism was grounded in the belief that class differences were hardening. He had no illusions about the easiness of a peaceful accommodation of interests. The outcome was perfectly understandable, even if it was strongly to be regretted: "The upper classes might reform the world, but they will not; the lower classes would, but they cannot; and for a generation or more these latter have settled down into a sullen and unanimous conviction that the only remedy is world-wide destruction." Significantly, Donnelly had not thrown up his hands in despair. He did not wish for a vindictive and thorough cleansing to break through the impasse. For Donnelly, even a rotten core could ultimately be salvaged. His position indicated a faith in man's redemptive powers (and his own essential reformism). Destruction had to be avoided: "We can say, as one said at the opening of the Cromwellian struggle, 'God help the land where ruin must reform!' "[7]

Donnelly unquestionably had an intense abhorrence of revolution. This was no uncommon fear. In personifying revolution in animalistic terms, he seemed to be emphasizing unlimited brute force, a caricature of evil itself, in an assault on an unsuspecting and defenseless society: "I tremble with horror when I think of what is crawling toward us, with noiseless steps; couchant, silent, treacherous, pard-like; scarce rustling the dry leaves as it moves, and yet with bloodshot, glaring eyes and tense-drawn limbs of steel, ready for the fatal spring." It was not, however, existing society which Donnelly wanted to protect, but something more precious and, as he conceived it, more perishable—civilization itself.

The remarkable point about his entire discussion is the way he drew sustenance from his vision of man. Man's human divinity and tremendous potentialities for goodness were reason enough not to give up the struggle to re-create the basis of social existence. Fear had to be channeled into constructive action: "And the thought forever presses on me, Can I do nothing to avert this catastrophe? Is there no hope? For mankind is in itself so noble, so beautiful, so full of all graces and capacities; with aspirations fitted to sing among the angels; with comprehension fitted to embrace the universe!"[8]

Donnelly may unconsciously have constructed a duality of struggle between the forces of good and evil. There often was a Manichean element in his perspective of the world, but this was generally expressed as speculation, in more fanciful moments, about the interplay of cosmic forces. Here the possible duality has an unexpected result. Donnelly did not place revolution in opposition to the existing structure of society; rather, he placed the perfectibility of man in opposition to both of these factors. Like Populists in general, he demonstrated a flexibility in one important regard: His fear of revolution did not drive him into the arms of the status quo. If he unequivocally rejected revolution (and perhaps socialism as well), he would not draw a line at some advanced point which necessitated choosing an either-or position. The prevention of revolution did not provide the pretext for the support of reaction. Nor did his fear of revolution blind him to the desirability of reform. Donnelly's spokesman attempted to reason with the secret revolutionary organization: "More than once I have spoken to them in these dim halls; and while full of sympathy for their sufferings, and indignant as they themselves can be against their oppressors, I have pleaded with them to stay their hands, to seek not to destroy, but to reform."[9] While sympathy hardly implied agreement, it was intended as more than a means to stifle change. Nevertheless, in any confrontation, Donnelly would accord greater value to civilization, which, because of its fragile character, could be preserved only by a reformist process.

Donnelly's reverence for civilization was derived from his broad historical sense of the cumulative growth of human intelligence. But more, he had an appreciation of the common bond between man and civilization, which was based on the perishability of each.

It was this sense of their mutual dependence and destinies which transformed a potentially Burkean argument into a ringing endorsement of the state. The connecting link between the continuing march of civilization and the expanding powers of government was the mutually shared purpose of emancipating the individual's intrinsic humanity. Civilization was man developing freely, and government was the collective life of society protecting his development. In this light, all forms of destructiveness would mark a possibly irreversible decline of man, human knowledge, and society:

I preach to them of the glories of civilization; I trace its history backward through a dozen eras and many nations; I show them how slowly it grew, and by what small and gradual accretions; I tell them how radiantly it has burst forth in these latter centuries, with such magnificent effulgence, until to-day man has all nature at his feet, shackled and gyved, his patient logman. I tell them that a ruffian, with one blow of his club, can destroy the life of a man; and that all the doctors and scientists and philosophers of the world, working together for ages, could not restore that which he has so rudely extinguished. And so, I say to them, the civilization which it has taken ten thousand years to create may be swept away in an hour; and there shall be no power in the wit or wisdom of man to re-establish it.[10]

Clearly, the presumption was against revolution; here, the "ruffian" came from the lower classes. But Donnelly's more basic contention was that all life-promoting forces had to be supported. In the long run, these forces were also threatened by the influences of a dominating caste. After Donnelly had established the importance of the conflict between civilization and the pressures which menaced it from above and below, his pronouncements on the nature of the state lost any trace of inflated rhetoric. He had the confidence of one who stood on familiar, and perhaps self-evident, ground.

Donnelly's changed mood reflected his more precise fixing of the existing context of society. Actually, his analysis proceeded on surprisingly moderate lines; for the most part, the capitalistic foundations of society were left in place. In coming to his basic formulation of the state, I first have to consider certain preliminaries of his argument. Although it was presented in a utopian form, the argument was meant to apply to contemporary society. Donnelly had revealed a tacit acceptance of the property right exactly when he introduced the discussion of governmental powers. Significantly, he had shown a curious indifference to the question of capitalism. In part, this relative neglect can be explained by the predefined, analytic set to Donnelly's framework, which minimized specifically capitalistic factors in favor of the emphasis on broader institutional decay, when he criticized the prevailing social order. He was reluctant to think in structural terms. His notion of a "rotten core" was conceived in essentially political and cultural rather than economic terms. He was also indifferent to capitalism because he believed that systemic difficulties, even when he identified them as systemic, could be confronted, flanked, or *absorbed* by means of a moral transformation. This approach favored an emphasis on ethical progressions of consciousness.

Further, Donnelly viewed as a fundamental purpose of government the achievement of the conditions of security and dignity for the individual. He projected from this baseline the goal of the liberation of human capacities. For Donnelly, the systemic context was quite immaterial, so long as this goal was achieved. He never questioned whether capitalism was compatible with its achievement. He could attack capitalism and at the same time remain remarkably oblivious to how much of the structure he allowed to stand. Even when he condemned certain social traits, as in his discussion of "cunning," he preserved them intact and channeled them into presumably constructive purposes. Finally, if other Populists tended to treat monopoly as separate from capitalism, making their criticism of monopoly sufficient to itself, Donnelly performed a similar exonerative function when he used interest rather than monopoly as the defining test. One has to be aware, therefore, of the capitalist dimension of his thought. The presence of capitalism did not qualify the moral emphasis; in Donnelly, the two happily coexisted. Nor did it deny the notion of the extensibility of government power, which he continued to hold in principle. But it did serve to demonstrate that such extensibility had boundaries, as well as did his economic framework.

In preparing the way for government, Donnelly began: "I should do away with all interest on money. Interest on money is the root and ground of the world's troubles. It puts one man in a position of safety, while another is in a condition of insecurity, and thereby it at once creates a radical distinction in human society." He traced the blighting effects of interest. The merchant was included along with the farmer and mechanic as alike disadvantaged, while "behind all these risks stands the money-lender, in perfect security," continually increasing his advantage, and also increasing the disparities of wealth in the community.[11]

But, asked the character's interlocutor, what of the necessity to borrow? In response to the query, Donnelly tied the abolition of interest to a defense of productive capitalism. The passage epitomized the self-deceptiveness of Populist economics. He identified a central internal category of capitalism (interest) which in fact had a far-reaching effect on capitalist operations. But then he returned the analysis to the essentials of a premonopolistic framework. One also sees an underlying theme noted in passing in our study, the connection between economic growth and general well-being. The factor of interest provided a self-enclosed mechanism of economic concentration: "The necessity to borrow is one of the results of borrowing. The disease produces the symptoms. The men who are enriched by borrowing are infinitely less in number than those who are ruined by it; and every disaster to the middle class swells the number and decreases the opportunities of the helplessly poor." This was followed by his implicit tribute to productive capitalism, once capitalism itself had been freed from the incubus of interest:

Money in itself is valueless. It becomes valuable only by use—by exchange for things needful for life or comfort. If money could not be loaned, it would have to be put out by the owner of it in business enterprises, which would employ labor; and as the enterprise would not then have to support a double burden—to wit, the man engaged in it and the usurer who sits securely upon his back—but would have to maintain only the former—that is, the present employer—its success would be more certain; the general prosperity of the community would be increased thereby, and there would be therefore more enterprises, more demand for labor, and consequently higher wages.[12]

Interest became very like a bottleneck in the economy, that point at which wealth was redirected to questionable ends. Wealth, when it was properly utilized, was not at issue. Indeed, the economic conversion of usurer into employer satisfied an important condition of growth and might be said to rectify the larger situation of deprivation. Donnelly joined his concern over

the expropriation of the middle class to a tacitly Algeresque promise of opportunity and mobility for the laboring poor, and in the
succeeding sentence, he yielded further ground to capitalism; the
employer became the pivot around which the welfare of the community turned: "Usury kills off the enterprising members of a
community by bankrupting them, and leaves only the very rich
and the very poor; for every dollar the employers of labor pay to
the lenders of money has to come eventually out of the pockets of
the laborers." Donnelly assumed the presence of owners and laborers as basic categories of society. He also made the laborers
dependent on the good working order of the whole. Donnelly
completed the passage by presenting interest as the explanation
for the concentration of wealth. Again, he employed a seemingly
radical context (the critique of ruling groups) which left important features of capitalism unexamined: "Usury is therefore the
cause of the first aristocracy, and out of this grow all the other ar-
istocracies. Inquire where the money came from that now op-
presses mankind, in the shape of great corporations, combinations, etc., and in nine cases out of ten you will trace it back to
the fountain of interest on money loaned."[13]

After he called for the abolition of interest, Donnelly next
would abolish all laws and customs which bore unequally on the
citizenry and which tended to the concentration of wealth. At this
point, the interlocutor noted: "Men differ in every detail. Some
have more industry, or more strength, or more cunning, or more
foresight, or more acquisitiveness than others. How are you to
prevent these men from becoming richer than the rest?" If it were
not that Donnelly was writing both portions of the dialogue, one
would be silently cheering Donnelly/Gabriel on, hoping he would,
exactly here, make his stand, championing without reservation
some form of preventive equalitarianism. Yet the response, "I
should not try to," was capitulative to a fault: "These differences
in men are fundamental, and not to be abolished by legislation;
neither are the instincts you speak of in themselves injurious.
Civilization, in fact, rests upon them. It is only in their excess that
they become destructive."[14] His previous discussion of civilization
was not thereby contradicted, so much as it was amplified in light
of a doctrine of capitalistic social balance.

When the liberation of human potentialities was given specific economic meaning, one sees Donnelly's indifference to systemic modes of organization in favor of roughly drawn safeguards to security which he believed were still compatible with man's basic propensities. Government, among its important functions, would harness antisocial drives, which Donnelly viewed as forces of human energy, to social ends. His analysis did not require a bedrock reconstruction of social personality and values on the individual level. Instead, the mergence of structure and values would be effected through the state. Paradoxically, the state was heightened in importance as a positive instrument of man, which testified to his creative powers, at the same time that it exercised a check on his destructive impulses. Donnelly out-Federalized the Federalists in the process of inverting their philosophic intent.

Turning to the social balance within capitalism, he continued: "It is right and wise and proper for men to accumulate sufficient wealth to maintain their age in peace, dignity and plenty, and to be able to start their children into the arena of life sufficiently equipped. A thousand men in a community worth $10,000 or $50,000, or even $100,000 each, may be a benefit, perhaps a blessing; but one man worth fifty or one hundred millions, or, as we have them now-a-days, one thousand millions, is a threat against the safety and happiness of every man in the world. I should establish a maximum beyond which no man could own property."[15] Throughout the writings of Populists, a single sentence, such as the last one in this passage, may appear quite advanced when it has been taken in isolation. Yet Donnelly manifestly had countenanced, if not actively praised, economic differentials. Further, precisely because he provided for accumulation per se, the very establishment of a maximum was denied a specificity and any sort of cutting edge.

Moreover, Donnelly implicitly treated the problem of capital accumulation by stating a *public* conception of Carnegiean improvement. Government would aid the laboring classes at one step removed, performing a philanthropic role rather than a directly redistributive role. He did not reject the proposition that government could create a full range of social benefits, but in the present context he had made government, in order to conserve the right of accumulation, the framework through which private benefactions could take place. In this case, the result was to weaken the emancipating thrust of government:

I should not stop his accumulations when he had reached that point, for with many men accumulation is an instinct; but I should require him to invest the surplus, under the direction of a governmental board of management, in great works for the benefit of the laboring classes. He should establish schools, colleges, orphan asylums, hospitals, model residences, gardens, parks, libraries, baths, places of amusement, music-halls, seaside excursions in hot weather, fuel societies in cold weather, etc., etc. I should permit him to secure immortality by affixing his name to his benevolent works; and I should honor him still further by placing his statue in a great national gallery set apart to perpetuate forever the memory of the benefactors of the race.[16]

Donnelly essentially governmentalized underlying capitalistic traits, and he did this at a rather late stage of the accumulation process. He also left intact the honorific trappings of this process. The pronounced elitist assumptions about how social beneficence was to be carried forward are readily apparent.

Donnelly was now prepared to announce a far-reaching position on the state, which included its extensible powers. One reason his formulation could be bold was that he, like many Populists, would permit himself a wide latitude when he became convinced that the grounds of attack were, after all, within the acceptable bounds of capitalism. There was no hypocrisy in such an attitude, merely an intuition of safety—a venturing out only when it appeared certain that Populism's political association with, and structural relevance to, America had not been broken. He was emboldened to advance political and economic doctrines precisely because of his devotion to an American construct of democratic rights. The preceding context of economic and ideological moderation allowed his spokesman in the novel to deflate the attributes of government to instrumental size. Donnelly's confidence was reinforced by the programmatic quality of his orientation toward government and by his sense that Populist measures were realizable: "Government is only a machine to insure justice and help the people, and we have not yet developed half its powers."[17] He advisedly put forward the mechanistic guise of government. Nothing was to derogate from the service of these principles; nor could the servant be other than man's creation. Government was stripped of transcendent claims on its own behalf. In order to make the instrument responsive, the spirit of infinite tinkering would be encouraged.

Donnelly's vision became at once deductive *and* pragmatic. In the manner of Hobbes, he ascribed to the state a freely created sphere of competence. The state was not bound by preconceived ideas. At the same time, it was directed to the specifics of problem-solving: "And we are under no more necessity to limit ourselves to the governmental precedents of our ancestors than we are to confine ourselves to the narrow boundaries of their knowledge, or their inventive skill, or their theological beliefs. The trouble is that so many seem to regard government as a divine something which has fallen down upon us out of heaven, and therefore not to be improved upon or even criticised; while the truth is, it is simply a human device to secure human happiness, and in itself has no more sacredness than a wheelbarrow or a cooking-pot." His utilitarian perspective had demystified the nature and foundations of the state beyond the point of return to the merely conventional. One cannot venerate a "cooking-pot." Donnelly has shifted the bases of obligation to man himself as the creator of government and the source of political authority. His formulation purposely downgraded whatever detracted from the human factor. The succeeding sentence might have been Donnelly's keynote: "The end of everything earthly is the good of man; and there is nothing sacred on earth but man, because he alone shares the Divine conscience."[18]

Donnelly's character discussed further programmatic remedies, and his justification was that "government—national, state and municipal—is the key to the future of the human race." This idea also introduced the theme of perfecting civilization, which was intimately related to the activation of the state: "There was a time when the town simply represented cowering peasants, clustered under the shadow of the baron's castle for protection. It advanced slowly and reluctantly along the road of civic development, scourged forward by the whip of necessity. We have but to expand the powers of government to solve the enigma of the world. Man separated is man savage; man gregarious is man civilized. A higher development in society requires that this instrumentality of co-operation shall be heightened in its powers."[19] Government provided the historical matrix of social cooperation. Individuals, realizing the bonds of mutuality, became civilized. Civilization, by Donnelly's construction of the term, was incompatible with one's separation from another. That would be savagery. It would also be a political arrangement devoid of rights and guarantees of safety. It would be "cowering" subjects and authoritarian rulers. The "enigma" to be solved was how to ensure the cooperative life together, along rational and equitable lines. Donnelly was concerned, not with the extension of power but with its substance: the possibilities of achieving cooperation, which became the ratifying condition for his somewhat uncritical approval of government. He made power practically synonymous with civilization because it could supplant a competitive ethic with a political and social solidarity.

The very simplicity of his illustrations drove home the importance of government. Too, on Donnelly's part, there was an evident spirit of experimentation, even though its application involved far-reaching structural changes: "There was a time when every man provided, at great cost, for the carriage of his own letters. Now the government, for an infinitely small charge, takes the business off his hands. There was a time when each house had to provide itself with water. Now the municipality furnishes water to all. The same is true of light. At one time each family had to educate its own children; now the state educates them. Once every man went armed to protect himself. Now the city protects him by its armed police. These hints must be followed out." Like the maturation of the town, the performance of social functions evidenced the progression of civilization. Donnelly's character matter-of-factly added: "The city of the future must furnish doctors for all; lawyers for all; entertainments for all; business guidance for all. It will see to it that no man is plundered, and no man starved, who is willing to work."[20] Donnelly's reliance on government suggests an emphasis primarily on structure as the means of achieving social rationality and humaneness.

Manifestly, contemporary patterns of consumption were neither rational nor humane, but raised a false standard for defining human worth. Donnelly had anticipated Veblen's critique of pecuniary emulation. This theme complemented his emphasis on society's growing decadence and man's antagonistic relationships. While men labor "at first for a competence," once they have "reached that point, they go on laboring for vanity—one of the shallowest of the human passions." Donnelly argued that the spirit of caste expressed a materialism which encouraged social striving, accelerated the consolidation of wealth, and reduced man's self-image to the wealth he possessed. However great the individual's accumulation of capital, each one looked enviously to the next level, for the "display" he could not match, or the ability to make men "cringe lower" to him, "and so the childish emulation continues."[21]

Donnelly further observed: "Men are valued, not for themselves, but for their bank account. In the meantime these vast concentrations of capital are made at the expense of mankind." Not merely did the "emulation of waste and extravagance" divert the powers of the human mind, but the impulse toward emulation drove a wedge between the propertied self and the inner self within man. The propertied self came to stand for the whole of man: "A crowd of little creatures—men and women—are displayed upon a high platform, in the face of mankind, parading and strutting about, with their noses in the air, as tickled as a monkey with a string of beads, and covered with a glory which is not their own, but which they have been able to purchase; crying aloud: 'Behold what I *have got!*' not, 'Behold what I *am!*' "[22]

Yet, Donnelly's discussion of pecuniary emulation also brought out certain elitist assumptions. He had originally posited a totality of cultural shallowness; here he held the masses especially culpable for showing deference to the wealthy: "And then the inexpressible servility of those below them! The fools would not recognize Socrates if they fell over him in the street; but they can perceive Croesus a mile off; they can smell him a block away; and they will dislocate their vertebrae abasing themselves before him." He introduced satirical scenes as comparisons: "It reminds one of the time of Louis XIV. in France, when millions of people were in the extremist misery—even unto starvation; while great grandees thought it the acme of earthly bliss and honor to help put the king to bed, or take off his dirty socks. And if a common man, by any chance, caught a glimpse of royalty changing its shirt, he felt as if he had looked into heaven and beheld Divinity creating worlds. Oh, it is enough to make a man loathe his species."[23]

Donnelly, of course, wished to demystify the contemporary

gospel of wealth, but his latent condescension, here and elsewhere in the work, revealed antidemocratic traces. The masses, perhaps, were not entirely capable of self-rule (particularly if they were unable to recognize Socrates on the street). These antidemocratic traces were to be found, however, not in the structure and goals of his framework of government, but in its inspiration and administration. Donnelly exhibited a sense of benevolence from above, which was consistent with his view of philanthropy and, apparent from his third novel, the edictal quality he assigned to leadership. Superior intellect, which he did not ascribe to the general populace, was decisive to his thinking. At one point the character's interlocutor queried, "is it not right and necessary that the intellect of the world should rule the world?" The reply, again precisely where a stand might be taken, did not dispute the proposition. Donnelly merely qualified its impact by justifying intellect through the purposes it served. He equated intellect with critical intelligence in the service of humane ends: "Certainly, . . . but what is intellect? It is breadth of comprehension; and this implies gentleness and love. The man whose scope of thought takes in the created world, and apprehends man's place in nature, cannot be cruel to his fellows. Intellect, if it is selfish, is wisely selfish. It perceives clearly that such a shocking abomination as our present condition cannot endure. It knows that a few men cannot safely batten down the hatches over the starving crew and passengers, and then riot in drunken debauchery on the desk. . . . True intellect is broad, fore-sighted, wide-ranging, merciful, just."[24] In addition, true intellect, Donnelly implied, was selfless rather than self-enriching; he presented a non-Sumnerian elitism, which nevertheless could not escape the attraction of guardianship.

In the last chapter, Donnelly's spokesman observed: "For good purposes and honest instincts we may trust to the multitude; but for long-sighted thoughts of philanthropy, of statesmanship and statecraft, we must look to a few superior intellects. It is, however, rarely that the capacity to do good and the desire to do good are found united in one man." Donnelly so democratizes elitism (while leaving its features intact) that he failed to see any inconsistency between mankind's infinite possibilities and the potential corruption of exceptional individuals. His solution to the contradictions of the novel was characteristically American. When the small band fled the scene of revolutionary destruction to found an ideal community in the hills of Uganda, they drafted a constitution with an intricate system of checks and balances. One branch of government represented the popular element, but the second branch was made up of "the merchants and manufacturers, and all who are engaged in trade, or as employers of labor," while the third branch was composed of "the authors, newspaper writers, artists, scientists, philosophers and literary people generally," who were "expected to hold the balance of power" between the first two branches. The people were hemmed in as much as liberated. Each branch of government had equal power. Thus, if he rejected the hegemony of an intellectual aristocracy, he provided that popular governance would be refracted through successive layers of representation, including one layer which was avowedly reserved to capitalistic groups.[25]

Finally, I mention Donnelly's scathing, parodic attack on the values of social Darwinism. Although he emphasized the importance of structure as the locus of a social transformation, he was perhaps most impressive in his criticism of contemporary values. The setting was a religious materialistic sermon delivered to the privileged on the eve of catastrophic breakdown. The sermon complemented and extended the theme of pecuniary emulation: Individuals were raised to the highest power of selfishness. The minister extolled the virtues of total callousness as a way of life. Individuals owed nothing to one another. Nature was the arena of human existence (and social struggle). According to the minister, it represented an impersonal, amoral process of development in striking contrast to human powers of control and creativity. The sermon (Donnelly called it a twentieth-century sermon to indicate the direction of prevailing society) described how Nature had fitted out the field mouse for life and then had "formed another, larger creature, to watch for and spring upon this 'timorous little beastie,' even in its moments of unsuspecting happiness, and rend, tear, crush and mangle it to pieces."[26] The rule of life, of competitive struggle and the dominance of the strong over the weak, bore a close resemblance to revolutionary destruction, in its silence and swiftness. Donnelly, like Lewelling, viewed existing capitalism, because it appeared to exemplify a blueprint of mutual slaughter, as generating the forces of its own destruction if a reformation of values and structure were not quickly instituted.

Donnelly's criticism cut deeper than a concern about the inhumanity of Darwinian social practices. The legitimation of the power of upper groups rested on the supposed inevitability of prevailing arrangements. The minister asked: "And what lesson does this learned and cultured age draw from these facts? Simply this: that the plan of Nature necessarily involves cruelty, suffering, injustice, destruction, death." The entire rationale of reform was denied. Indeed, suffering was to the good, while all else was mere sentimentalism. In the sermon, efforts at amelioration were ridiculed: "We are told by a school of philanthropists more numerous in the old time, fortunately, than they are at present, that men should not be happy while their fellow-men are miserable; that we must decrease our own pleasures to make others comfortable; and much more of the same sort." The minister had only contempt for any kind of social mutuality: "But, my brethren, does Nature preach that gospel to the cat when it destroys the field-mouse? No; she equips it with special aptitudes for the work of slaughter."[27] The glorification both of strength and inequality had by design turned Donnelly's own cooperative ethic inside out. Through the use of the sermon, he demonstrated the logical outcome of a society where principles of governmental responsibility were disallowed.

Donnelly had effectively paraphrased the position of William Graham Sumner, which repudiated not only the concept of welfare but also the most elemental human obligation defining a just society. The sermon was not a gross caricature but a faithful rendering of the conventional thought of the period. When Sumner wrote that "before the tribunal of nature, a man has no more right to life than a rattlesnake," he was expressing the absence of warmth and human compassion which so understandably enraged Donnelly. The brutality of an uncaring age had produced a structural form of suicide; according to Donnelly, in both cases, society, by its failure to recognize and engender social bonds, had negated the value of human worth. The futility of existence became at one with the denial of the right to exist. The words of the sermon represented everything that Donnelly and Populism opposed: "If Nature, with her interminable fecundity, pours forth millions of human beings for whom there is no place on earth, and no means of subsistence, what affair is that of ours, my brethren? We did not make them; we did not ask Nature to make them. And it is Nature's business to feed them, not yours or mine." The minister had taken the final step; God was devalued as the murderous angel, the fountainhead of death and destruction: "Shall we rebuke the Great Mother by caring for those whom she has abandoned? If she intended that all men should be happy, why did she not make them so? She is omnipotent. She permits evil to exist, when with a breath of her mouth she could sweep it away forever. But it is part of her scheme of life. She is indifferent to the cries of distress which rise up to her, in one undying wail, from the face of the universe. . . . Her skirts are wet with blood; her creation is based on destruction; her lives live only by murder."[28]

Callousness was given natural license. Impoverishment had an integral place in the natural order. Indifference was raised to an absolute. The masses became a curse. They were to be utilized and discarded; kept alive, sustained, they were a brake on social progress. "Let the abyss groan. Why should we trouble ourselves. Let us close our ears to the cries of distress we are not able to relieve." Simply, the poor "are part of the everlasting economy of human society. Let us leave them in the hands of Nature." But more: "Let us rejoice that out of the misery of the universe *we* are reserved for happiness." The minister completely transmogrified Donnelly's cooperative sense of civilization into a positive delight in the misery of the poor: Let us "throw open our windows, that we may behold the swarming, starving multitudes who stream past our doors. Their pinched and ashy faces and hungry eyes, properly considered, will add a flavor to our viands."[29]

2. Children of God

I will look only briefly at the remaining two novels. In 1891, Donnelly published *Doctor Huguet,* which was a further if limited step in his attempt to clarify the prerequisites of human aspiration and dignity. In this case, the subtext of the novel concerned the violation of political democracy through the prevalence of racial degradation. There could not be a social ethic of mutuality when any group in society has been denied full membership in, or the benefits of, the political community. In the absence of such an ethic, the principles of justice, and civilization itself, will have been retarded and the human potential of all men further diminished. In the novel Donnelly did not entirely live up to his own profession of faith. But he came close, and he appeared to experience a deepening conviction of human rights as the novel progressed.

As a novelist, Donnelly posed for himself a staggering creative challenge. He willed himself into the thought processes and context of hardship and discrimination of a southern black. The problem, in its very conception, spoke to Donnelly's imaginative powers, their harnessing to ethical issues, and his ability to identify questions of contemporary significance.

Doctor Huguet was a potboiler in every way except one. It revealed an authentic probing into the institutional structure of society, and Donnelly's own conscience, which reinforced the moral dimensions of the political order he sought to achieve. If he was less racially enlightened than I once believed, Donnelly grasped fully the dehumanizing consequences of segregation. He also developed a unitary notion of humankind which undermined, if it did not abandon, distinctions based on racial superiority and inferiority. Huguet began as a moderate, an upper-class southern physician in the period after the Civil War, who, though believing in Negro rights, was suddenly punished by God for not pursuing his convictions. When his mind and soul were transposed into the body of a local black man, he commenced a journey of despair and realization of the blacks' plight which was ended only at the moment of his lynching as a militant black leader. Restored to his white body, Huguet devoted his life to the Negro's welfare and biracial understanding. In the stage before his transformation Huguet was more restrained than later, although even then he asked a question which suggested the oneness of man: "If the white man is but a bleached negro, what right has he to mock his dark progenitor?"[30]

Donnelly developed his conception of citizenry when Huguet in a spirited conversation with his white peers affirmed the universality of the ballot as essential to democratic government. Whether or not his disclaimer of social equality was a means to gain basic political rights for blacks, he insisted on these rights in terms which subtly rejected the pejorative connotations of the mere proximity between the two races. (It is instructive that Watson dwelt on the physical aspects of desegregation and betrayed a disgust, as in his comment on schoolchildren throwing spitballs in "mixed" schools of the North. This was altogether foreign to Donnelly.) Our concern here is not with race per se, but with the correlates of a human-centered political structure, tested at the point of greatest vulnerability for Donnelly's period. Thus, when he was asked whether blacks "should have the same political rights" as whites, Huguet replied:

Why not? Political equality does not imply social equality, or physical equality, or moral equality, or race equality. When you go to the ballot-box to vote you find a group assembled of white men, originally of different nationalities—Yankee, French, German, Irish, Scotch—of different complexions, conditions, mental power, education and knowledge. No two are alike; no two are equal in any respect, and yet they all peacefully unite in expressing their political preferences. The right to participate in the government, in a republic, is like the right to breathe the atmosphere. No man feels degraded because the air he inhales has already passed through the lungs of his fellow-man, differing from him in every respect and condition. We must all breathe to live, and we must all vote if the republic is to live.[31]

Implicitly, Donnelly has constructed the analogy between the life processes of the individual and government, and his purpose, clearly, was to deny the invidiousness of diversity. Blacks were fitted into existing patterns of ethnicity. The fact of multiple differences in society was not a hindrance to effective government. Participation had become the defining characteristic of democracy.

Indeed, Huguet poked fun at the obvious rationale for segregation, the racial domino theory: "Because a man votes beside me at the polling-place, it does not follow that I must take him into my house, or wed him to my daughter, any more than those results follow because we breathe the same air."[32] That Donnelly so readily anticipated counterthemes leads one to believe that he had command of the narrative. Huguet was engaged in a verbal duel with his white-supremacy opponents.

When Huguet was asked whether or not whites were superior, he granted that they were on grounds of "their tremendous achievements," calling them, however, in words that again invoke the unitary conception, "the most capable subdivision of mankind" in history. He then returned the question: "But are we to do justice only to our superiors, or our equals?" Whether or not a residue of the belief in biological inferiority clung to these words, the apparent diversion became the basis for a far-reaching statement about power. At worst, we see a more vital reading of noblesse oblige than was customary, but it is more likely that this was a specifically nonracial stance which sought to make government responsive, as did Lewelling, to the weak. One notes an implicit condescension (possibly present in Populism itself). Yet the assertion of man's part in the purposes of divinity, directly contrary to the twentieth-century sermon, indicates something of the peculiar gentleness, as distinguished from Realpolitik, and moral force that characterized Populist notions of the neutral state. Huguet replied to his own question: "If so, it yields us no honor, for our superiors and our equals are able to enforce justice from us. Generosity can only be exercised toward those less fortunate than ourselves. Power has no attribute grander than the god-like instinct to reach down and lift up the fallen. If we can plainly perceive in the progress of humanity the movement of a great Benevolence, every year adding to the comfort and happiness of mankind, why should we not, to the extent of our little powers, aid Him in His tremendous work? How divine a thought is it that we are participating in the purposes and work of the Almighty One!"[33] Donnelly shifted from racial considerations to a broader political proposition: a statement of "benevolence," directed to human welfare, in which blacks were a special case of the disadvantaged poor.

The mission orientation now apparent shattered the message of the sermon. It supplanted race by the more direct factor of hardship. Donnelly was arguing that inequity, not alleged inferiority, was plainly at issue: "That, as he has dragged man up from reptilian barbarism to this splendid, this august era of peace and love, we are able to help the flagging footsteps of the laggards and stragglers who have dropped behind in god's great march! In such a work we become the very children of God—fired with his zeal, illuminated by his smile. How base and brutal it would be if we were willing to be fed with all the countless fruits of God's beneficence, and, in the midst of our full content, commend only poison to the lips of those whose sole offense is that Heaven has not given them our blessings!"[34] "Laggards" and "stragglers" are hardly complimentary terms, but this was quite different from a defense of racism.

In the same conversation, Huguet was asked to state his views on the necessity of keeping blacks out of government and away from the polls. There was sufficient militance in the answer to mark off Donnelly from countless other white Americans in the late nineteenth century, because he had greater insight into the existence of repression as well as deeper sympathies in the matter. Huguet declared: "The present system, practiced in some places, of brutally killing a man because he attempts to peacefully exercise the right which the laws of the land confer upon him, is, to my mind, revolting and dreadful, and a disgrace to the Southern people. To fill a man with lead, to tear his vitals to pieces, simply because he attempts to put a piece of paper in the ballot-box, when the law says he shall have the right to do so, is a horrible travesty on our civilization and Christianity; and I am glad to know that our best people repudiate it."[35] For Donnelly, citing the supremacy of the law was not out of place. It was crucial to the determination of all rights.

Yet that ambiguity persisted, even in such a far-reaching general context, can be seen from a statement pages later. Nominally, the passage concerned the efficacy of education; but it is an education in which racial characteristics were physiologically altered as a result of putative elevation and brought into conformance with white features. This was a reformist Lamarckianism quite remarkable for its confused sense of universality: "If you had visited the Northern cities, as I have done, and seen how education and good living are modifying the very forms and features of the race, even where the skin retains its original blackness, you would see that America is to do some good even to the least fortunate of her inhabitants." At best, Donnelly glimpsed the élan of a multiracial society: "I have seen black men there with features as perfect and as regular as the most cultivated Caucasian; and the streets of a Northern city, of a Sunday afternoon, are as gay as a many-colored garden, with the handsome daughters of Ham, of all shades of complexion." But, in fact, his assumption that white traits were the norm is evident: "[T]he truth is, that when you refine the mind you refine the features. Take brutality out of the brain, and it leaves the lips. Raise the heart and soul of man, and the bridge of his nose rises."[36]

Finally, however, when his fiancée sought to commit him to white supremacy, Huguet, referring to racialist politicians, distilled in a single sentence the thesis on segregation that Oliver Cromwell Cox would employ a half-century later. Its purpose was not the elevation of whites, but the impersonalization of blacks, to ensure a cheapened labor force composed of the landless: "It is not white domination they seek, but negro degradation; they are not satisfied to rule the blacks—they must ruin them; not content to deny the colored people leadership, they would reduce them to beasts." Cox's *Caste, Class, and Race,* perhaps the most uncompromising formulation of the economics of color, is an instructive comparison. For precisely with the foregoing distinction lies the punitive component in race aggrandizement, in turn sustained through antidemocratic political structures. In Donnelly as well, discrimination carried beyond race to a more encompassing negation of human potential: "I do not speak of the whole people, but of a faction, who rise to office on the shoulders of public prejudice. They are not teachers of the people, but betrayers of humanity."[37]

The doctor's own education commenced in earnest with the sudden transformation, as in this soliloquy of despair: "The day darkened as I sat and thought, but it was nothing to the profound darkness that settled on my soul. . . . I seemed to cringe into myself, as if the very props of life had been withdrawn from within me. . . . Never before had I realized the glory of my *white life*. Never before had I understood what 'honor, love, obedience, troops of friends,' meant. Never before had I comprehended the dreadful burden of disqualification and disability borne by the colored people of America. . . . Oh, my white brethren! Little do you appreciate what a glory it is to belong to the dominant caste; what a hell it is to fall into the subject caste!"[38] This became the plight of the utterly depersonalized. The passage was a meditation not only on color but also on domination and subjection, a statement of political relationships which contradicted his very sense of reality.

Seeking employment, so that he might "lead the negroes to better things," Huguet found that he was rejected at every turn;

he continued: "The high hopes and aspirations with which I had started out in the morning were all blasted and withered. I began to lose confidence in my own theories. The Archimedean lever would not work. I could not find a fulcrum for it. It seemed to me that the eloquence of Daniel Webster or the learning of William E. Gladstone, wrapped up in a black hide, would amount to nothing." The "fulcrum" was the American democratic principle, in which man's intrinsic worthiness was respected; but it was nevertheless violated—Donnelly's more basic proposition— through a caste-stratified society. "The world is a wretched-looking object viewed from below, but grand and gaudy as stage scenery to him who can contemplate it from above."[39]

Blacks, as the choice of words implied, reflected the same dependent relation as the industrial workforce of *Caesar's Column*, an underclass within the tinseled whole. In this case, the mood perceptibly brightened. Fully one year before the party's formation in the South and nation, Donnelly recommended a biracial political movement, not to stave off revolution, but as a positive solution. The idea of shared objectives, identified with Watson in 1892, had already surfaced and with greater vibrancy. Before the lynching, Huguet, now a black minister, exhorted: *"Let the black men break ranks!* Let them dissolve into the community. Let them divide politically on other lines than those of color. Great economic questions are arising which have nothing to do with the old struggles." The "tidal wave" sweeping among southern whites "for justice, for prosperity, for liberation from the plunderers, for each man's share of happiness and the fruits of civilization" found its equivalent desires among blacks. By leaving the Republican party, blacks could unite with this progressive segment to establish a more just society, founded on mutual protection:

The black man's interests are the same as theirs. He needs prosperity, growth, opportunity, happiness. So do they. He wants to see the robbers struck down. So do they. He desires all that civilization can give him— all that belongs to him. So do they. . . . When he breaks his own ranks and moves, in solid column, with part, at least, of his white friends and neighbors, they will perceive that his ballots are bullets, as potent as their own to kill injustice. Their own interests will compel them to defend his rights. The day of persecution and cruelty will end. In every intelligent white man the intelligent black man will find a defender; and the reign of peace and love and brotherhood will begin in the South, yea, in the whole land.[40]

The foregoing passage (albeit from a northerner) contained a specificity of references not found in later statements of self-interest. For this reason, it moved the discussion from race to an encompassing view of government. Blacks had rightful claims at the hands of civilization. They would ally themselves with a segment of southern whites which provided a focused and possibly class orientation. The goal of such an alliance, unlike that in Watson's paradigm, would involve more than an easing of racial tensions. Self-interest, thus shared, referred to a sense of intertwining futures, which would bring about the elimination of persecution. The progression to the end of the passage suggested a democratic rebirth, which would be racially inclusive and pointed toward a commonwealth. Donnelly's next sentence denied racialist categories. Although he leaned toward classical notions of self-improvement, he clearly did not reject a vision of black attainments out of hand: "And if the negro does not then rise to the topmost heights of culture and education and material prosperity, it will be his own fault."[41]

When he had been returned to his white body, Huguet reflected on his experience. This led to an open-ended prospect for the breakdown of antipathy between races and also classes. The ethical infusion of thought helped to define the emergent social structure: "I understand now, as I never did before, the feelings of the proscribed and wretched. . . . I shall erect school-houses, I shall provide teachers, I shall employ good men and women to work goodness in the land. I shall labor to enlighten minds, to enkindle souls, to sweeten tempers, and to lift both races out of the slough of bigotry and intolerance. I shall preach mercy and good will and peace on earth to men, for the great Gospel of Brotherly Love is the true solvent in which must melt away forever the hates of races and the contentions of castes."[42]

3. Moral Contours of Political Society

The subtext of *The Golden Bottle* (1892), Donnelly's third novel in as many years, concerned the more sharply delineated features of power, including the moral imperatives which had to be observed if government were not to abuse the public trust. Here more than previously, Donnelly had made man the antecedent standard of all expressions of sovereign conduct. The novel itself, because of its hastiness and transparently political intent, uniquely revealed the spontaneous outpouring of the Populist imagination. His starting place was the flight from privation: the desperate need to conquer economic necessity, as the precondition for a human existence. The story took the form of a young Kansan's dream, occurring just when his family was faced with dispossession of their land. In the dream, Benezet discovered a magic bottle that converted ordinary metal into the finest gold, providing him unlimited sources of wealth. The plot, however fanciful, is less important for us than the content of his vision and its relationship to a conception of governmental power. If the novel was a People's party tract (Benezet used the Populist platform as a basis for reconstructing American and then world society), it also served to advance wider objectives: the abolition of poverty, the promotion of a cooperative ethic, and the achievement of universal religious toleration. Donnelly's emphasis was on the creation of greater equity in wealth-holdings.

This was a veritable psychic spree aimed at democratization. The notable point is not his largely unexceptionable goals (surely these were bold by contemporary standards, particularly as they applied to international politics in which a world government was empowered to maintain peace and hasten national self-determination), but the peculiarly impulsive and direct way in which they were to be realized. Although there was fantasy in Donnelly's writings, especially here, he typified the primarily western expression of Populism in his attitude toward the extensibility of power.

As my last-quoted passage from *Doctor Huguet* suggested, Donnelly's treatment of power had an edictal character. Whatever was ordained would come to pass, as though such commands were a direct application from the brain of man. The staccato-like declaration of powers and duties merits attention. Significantly, it drew sustenance from, and made sense only in terms of, the legato stream of moral conviction, brotherly love, toward which everything was moving. In one passage in *Golden Bottle,* Donnelly italicized: *"Love God with all thy heart and thy neighbor as thyself."*[43] What invested power with its matter-of-fact quality was not only the human-centered locus of sovereignty, emanating from the people. This quality received added reinforcement from an ethically suffused configuration of man and his intentions. This latter factor made obstructions appear intolerable, accorded to solutions an air of self-evidence, and, through the closer association to God which it implied, endowed men's works with a divine purpose.

Donnelly believed that the ultimate ground of government was the divinity of humanity. The effect of this belief was to authorize the exercise of power, because power would therefore be confined presumably to a framework which morally defined and tempered its own objectives. In a manner of speaking, Donnelly had fused Hobbes and Rousseau; his faith in humanity was intended as a safeguard against absolutism; rather than arbitrariness, which removed all restraints, he sought the moral binding of power. There would be a highly focused implementation, a fixing of power to prevent its extension outside the pursuits of democratic governance. When power was not placed in the service of human needs, it became despotic. To Populists, the obvious dangers of self-righteousness were more than outweighed by man's superseding claims to a just existence. The element of directness stemmed from this consideration, especially in the present context. For if the rapid-fire declarations contrasted with the very slowness of the political process to which Populists had committed themselves, there still was truth in such fantasy. It was the plane of incisive realization on which they would like to act but were not free to do so. What I termed a "psychic spree" was a safety valve which nonetheless faithfully reproduced prototypic demands. In heightened form, it revealed the mental processes and ethical premises that applied to the Populist thinking about power in more normal, that is, political, situations.

There is a striking parallel between his passage on blacks and this one from *Golden Bottle* on Jews. One finds not only the desire to treat dispossessed peoples fairly (they became implicitly linked through a common experience of persecution), but the same quickened assertion of power once it was directed to humane ends. Benezet "restored Palestine to the Jews," commenting: "It seemed to me that this great race, the Israelites, from whom we had derived our religion and so much of our literature, should have some share in the awakening of the world." He then proclaimed the Jewish state: "I gave orders that all Jewish emigrants to the Holy Land should be carried free, with their effects, over the government railroads; that the land should be divided among them; houses built; railroads and ships constructed; a national convention held at Jerusalem, and financial help extended to make them at once a great and prosperous people."[44]

Notwithstanding the earlier historiographic debate on the nature of Populism, this instance of Populist Zionism, instructive of its own accord, has further value in showing the self-commending dimension of power. Where the need was manifest, inaction required explanation. This went beyond impatience. It expressed the sense of government as a responsive instrument, which, even in the present example, also suggested that power was in part reflective of a social order founded on confidence. It was as though a breakthrough were needed—here, the formation of a Jewish state; and for America, the restoration of constitutional rights. Thereafter the natural flow of power could begin—in fantasy, from a gimmick, such as a golden bottle; in actual life, from a movement of political struggle. In both cases it led to the affirmation of a people's autonomy.

When Benezet posited the rise of natural leaders, he not only demonstrated respect for diversity in the world, but, closer to home, maintained that human society was capable of finding its bearings once the start was made: "And out from all the lands of hatred and persecution the poor afflicted Hebrews, with their wives and little ones, poured in a steady stream into the old lands of their race; wealthy Israelites helped them, and natural leaders sprang up among them; and it will be but a little time until the Jews, too, shall have a nation and a flag, illustrious and honored in the world; while the smoke of their steamers shall ascend from every sea and every harbor on the globe."[45] My interest is not with anti-Semitism or philo-Semitism, but with self-creation, for Populists simultaneously a wellspring of power and a mandate for action which was held needful and morally just.

Leadership was nevertheless given inordinate attention. It perhaps focalized peoples' energies. But also self-creation became linked with prime movers, men who had to clear and show the way. At best, the leader was mankind writ small, incarnating its aspirations. Donnelly so effortlessly reconciled elitism and democracy that one suspects he failed to appreciate the presence of the former, viewing such manifestations of leadership as extensions of the people and in their service. Therefore only departures from the standard of humanity were considered elitist. Early in the novel Benezet stated: "The 'Golden Bottle' was a tremendous trust placed in my hands for the good of humanity. I was an humble instrument in the hands of some incomprehensible, spiritual power, with benevolent purposes for the creature, man."[46]

As the work proceeded Donnelly honed the formula of nonexpediential priorities. The antecedent standard of man's welfare was so cleanly put as to reduce the political framework to its essential principle (stated by Benezet in an address to Congress before assuming the American presidency): "Statutes, ordinances, customs; banks, bonds, money; beliefs, theories, religions; philosophies, dogmas, and doctrines, are only valuable as they conserve the happiness of mankind. Whenever they conflict with it, they must fall to the ground. Man is the only thing worth considering in this great world. He is the climax of the creative force; the ultimate object for which this planet was made; a little god working out the purposes of the great God."[47] This sacredness not simply of man but of his potentiality, if a political and moral touchstone, did not invoke God to sanction all directions of policy. Human well-being was foremost. It alone provided evidence of divine attributes and purpose. Far from a simple arrogation of right, behind which Populists could hide and claim the authority of God, the stance became a challenge to *act* in conformity with ethical principles. The connection with divinity had to be earned, specifically through service to man.

For Donnelly, even the approach to God was based on earthly works: "To set up anything—any device or invention of man, any belief or form or theory, statute or custom, against the welfare, happiness, development, of man—is a species of horrible blasphemy against the Everlasting One, whose child and instrument man is." Armed with this premise, which had been secularized in the marrow of Populist thought concerning government (the state was the embodiment of social works, creatively determined by a free people), Donnelly hardly needed a fictive platform before

Congress or the fantasy setting itself. For the content of this speech remained orthodox Populist doctrine, that natural melding of political specificity and ethical principles. In catechistic form, Benezet maintained the edictal quality:

> *Keep the land in the hands of the many.* [Cheers.]
> Limit the amount that any man may own. [Cheers.]
> See to it that the working-men obtain homes. [Great cheers.]
> *Use the powers of government for the good of the governed.* [Cheers.]
> Open the post-offices as savings banks, as other countries have done. . . . There are now one billion and a half dollars in the savings banks of this country. Do this, and every dollar of it would in a short time be deposited in the post-offices, with billions more which the people do not dare to trust to the banks, but have hidden away or buried in the earth.
>
> But what will the government do with all this vast sum, many times larger than our whole national debt? The answer is plain. Lend it out to the farmers and working-men on real-estate security, at two per cent per annum, to enable them to save or obtain homes; to break the backs of the usurers, and prevent the transformation of this country from a republic into a despotism. [Tremendous applause.]
>
> Nay, go farther. Issue paper currency, legal-tender, to the amount of fifty dollars *per capita*. [Immense applause.]

What dignified this apparently random list was the succeeding sentence. The breathless enumeration of powers came to rest in a moral proposition. "Man is now a 'drug,' and money is a god." Donnelly (through Benezet's summation) recurred to the imbalance stated in the first novel: "Let us reverse it. Let us make money a 'drug' and man a god."[48]

In fact, randomness of application could not hide unified assumptions about man's well-being. There was the extensibility of power, of course, with government only a mechanism to register basic safeguards and social needs. But also one notes an underlying substance pertaining to fair entitlement, equitable distribution, and responsive institutions. These have been given concreteness around the security of the home.

Greater specificity was supplied at a later point, when Benezet established a model town. Donnelly's description of the experiment, and the purposes it was to serve, is quite revealing: a freshly created setting designed to foster productive capitalism in microcosm, now modified on cooperative lines to encourage both opportunity and security. The ocean was harnessed to generate electric power; industrial zones were created, surrounded by parks and gardens; acre lots were given to the workmen on advantageous terms. This was followed by Donnelly's peculiar mix of capitalism, philanthropy, civic amenities (for self-improvement), and welfare services:

I offered [Benezet recounts] free power to all manufacturers who would build mills and factories, on condition that the work was to be conducted on the cooperative plan, each worker having a share of all the profits. I offered the same terms to combinations of the men themselves, with bank credit to enable them to carry on business. I established a bank of deposit and discount in every circle. In the very centre of each circle was erected a great town-hall, for the free use of those contiguous to it. Here were reading-rooms, lecture-rooms, art-schools, bath-rooms (supplied with sea-water), and shops where all necessaries could be bought at a small advance on first cost. Here, too, was a physician, paid by taxation, for every five thousand of population, free dispensaries of medicine, and a board of arbitration for the settlement of disputes free of cost to litigants.[49]

For Donnelly, Benezet probably represented what government could in fact accomplish in its own capacity—if, in this instance, on a less dramatic scale. This was less a question of paternalism than of furnishing the preconditions for a decisive break with previous oppression. If leaders remained prime movers, the state had wider structural significance in removing social impediments to economic well-being. After commenting that working people had not received the benefits of a homestead law, Benezet superbly fused the elitist and democratic themes: "The poor man is, at first, like the new-born child, he is perfectly powerless; he needs protection if he would advance to the full stature of manhood. He has now fought his own way, by organization, a long distance; government must come to his help for the remainder of the path of progress he is to travel over."[50]

Reflecting the larger schema of competitive capitalism, governmental protection became a stimulus to, and enabled the continuance of, further self-help. Traditional concerns were manifest. "Every man who came wanted a home." Again, he stated: "When it became known that at 'Cooperation,' for so I called my new city, men could procure, not only homesteads, but *homes*—roofs to shelter wife and little ones from storms and heat and cold, the rush of applications was tremendous." What of cooperation itself?

Donnelly spoke of profit-sharing, and yet this was not intended to alter the structure of ownership; workers would be less inclined to strike, as meanwhile "the capitalist got a liberal return on his money and a just reward for his business capacity, and he found himself surrounded, not by enemies, but by a brotherhood of friends."[51]

Moreover, one glimpses the quiet virtuousness, as one aspect of an ascetic cast: "Labor was limited to eight hours a day, hoping that some day even this period would be shortened. There was not a drinking-place in the whole city; no man dispensed poison and slew his fellows for profit. The hours gained from toil were spent in the gardens, or with their families, or in the lecture-rooms, or in reading instructive books and newspapers in the reading-rooms, or in innocent sports and games."[52] Indeed, however peculiar his mix of elements, Donnelly came very close on the intangibles and everyday patterns of social life to reproducing faithfully the Populist perspective.

After viewing the results of Benezet's model town, politicians posed questions which integrated government's instrumentalism, its human-centered purpose, and man's own divine mission as successively widening circles: "Why should not government expand its powers with the necessities of its surroundings? Has government any higher function than the relief of the human estate? And does not earthly power seem likest God's when it lifts up man and makes him contented, virtuous, and happy?"[53] Despite the even flow of words, the term "virtuous" leaps out to suggest a key feature of what, in the century preceding, might have been termed a civic religion: a puritanic zeal, that mixture of chasteness and asceticism so indicative of the Populist character and temperament. Home itself was not only a primary Lockean notation but also the life cell of civil propriety. Man's closeness to God fortified the imagery of chasteness. But it still remained for government to enlarge the application of this trait as a mainspring of the social polity; there would be an unassuming, determined, *and* righteous people, projecting their needs onto the political environment.

When Donnelly called for the liberation of what was distinctively human, this implicitly entailed the responsibility to live the human life: "For what is man if not a creature of the spiritual world, temporarily loaned to the material world by its great Designer.

The man who proclaims himself a brother of the beast, and no more, abases himself, not humanity. Who is so blind that he cannot see the tremendous spirit of man shining through the clay? Can clay think, reason, worship? No; not in a million years. That which is within the clay is that which thinks, reasons, worships; it is man; nothing else can be."[54] Donnelly's focus on man (even the term lost its abstract Enlightenment quality, becoming concrete and serviceable) took the discussion of power beyond matters of law and formal structure.

The proposition deepened to include a transformation of the heart, that which alone gave institutions a social purpose. "Law can prevent crime and insure justice," Benezet stated, "but it has its limitations. It deals not with thoughts, but acts. It can regulate the opening and shutting of the doors of the temple of the soul, but it cannot enter in and purify the polluted chambers." The notion of a civic religion aptly fit this context. It inclined men to the realization of social mutuality, pivoted on the individual's sense of moral and political obligation: "Only that which connects man with the vast spiritual brotherhood around him can do that mighty work. No reform of legislation is complete which is based on a beast-world, without conscience. Besides a fair division of the rights and goods of the world there must be a something vaster and profounder—man's *love* for his fellow—not merely a willingness to give him a fair show and a fair divide, but an *affection* for him, reaching from heart to heart." Man's earthly divinity, expressed in works, and implemented through government, was succinctly put in a closing line: "Men worshipped God by helping their fellows."[55]

CHAPTER SEVEN

The Legitimation of Productive Wealth: Nugent

Western Populists, in particular, ascribed to government a theoretical supremacy in the creation of a democratic social order. The concept of sovereignty conveyed the right, as well as the power, of a self-governing people to exercise control of the reigning system of economy and to infuse the legal and political foundations of society with an ethical content appropriate to social mutuality and individual freedom. The American nation, Populists reasoned, had the philosophical tradition to realize this goal in thought and the technological potential to give it a material underpinning through the elimination of poverty. Their apparent stridency was nothing more than a recognition that a failure to act, to affirm the full possibilities of a sovereign people, would encourage prevailing trends of monopolism and the corporate usurpation of practical authority in political and social affairs.

In this phase of our discussion, Watson's conservative inclinations may be considered as a convenient baseline. Donnelly's concrete rendering of the idea of man's intrinsic humanity went beyond Watson and combined wider concepts, directly and indirectly dependent on the import of sovereignty, with the narrower programmatic underpinning of the ideology. This dual level of Populist analysis will also be seen in chapter 8, when we examine the political determinants of sovereignty. Peffer's treatment of the state's intercessory role, in which the mediation of capitalistic activities was to be downgraded or removed, placed the emphasis on program. Weaver's proposition, that the state in principle subsumed all internal elements, strengthened both aspects of the critical perspective and added the structural argument which differentiated Populism from a Smithian framework on lines of government's autonomy and its presumed orientation toward welfare. Seldom, even in Donnelly, did the abstract and practical elements in Populist thought exist in isolation. In fact, it was their dynamic union which allowed for, as well as sharpened, the focus on each. The Omaha Platform merely brought together what was already evident; it realized actual and implied rights within a structure which was capitalistic yet anticorporate, which protected property yet made provision for a public dimension in keeping with aspirations of security, opportunity, and the liberation of social and productive energies.

Turning to Thomas L. Nugent of Texas, one finds significant refinements of the foregoing pattern. First, it should be said that Nugent is particularly important to this discussion. He provides the sectional balance that might otherwise be lacking. His comparative neglect, and consequent obscurity, makes any textual analysis of his views the basis for further study of Populism in the South, and more especially the midroaders of Texas. He presents, I believe, a "best-case scenario" of midroad ideological radicalism, a social and moral vision that many readers would find personally attractive, and yet the evidence is unmistakable that greenbackism and laissez-faire fit well in his perspective. Thus, he serves to illustrate and extend the theoretical passages which began the previous chapter. He is also significant for us because he makes clear the role of religion as a factor informing Populist thought both with basic imagery and ethical content, although his Swedenborgian creed differed considerably from southern evangelical Protestantism in providing the doctrines if not the forms for articulating protest.

Nugent's refinements of the foregoing pattern can be stated briefly: In his understanding, there was a partial receding on the public factor, a surprisingly clear and explicit capitulation on fundamental tenets of ownership, and a soaring vision of human potentiality which occurred in creative tension with these other features. Comparisons of Nugent with Donnelly and Henry Demarest Lloyd (see chapter 8) are instructive, for each possessed a transcendent vision of reformism. Yet each elaborated the vision in quite distinct ways, with cultural development and the movement toward political community, in Donnelly and Lloyd, respectively, matched by an evolutionary individualism in Nugent. He seemed to strike a midpoint in the effort to fuse the dreamer and practitioner. Nugent, like Lloyd, displayed uncommon sophistication, and, not unlike Donnelly, enlivened his vision with a firm technical grasp of, and commitment to, governmental programs. But if he communicates greater contact with everyday reality on political matters, the overall synthesis which commands our attention, separating him from both men, reduced the transcendent conception to an emphatic acceptance of property in large and competitive capitalism in particular. Perhaps nowhere in Populism did high ideological promise have such ordinary effect, and that fact requires that we look more closely at the precise combination of factors.

Were "radical laissez-faire" a meaningful term, Nugent, more than most Populists, would approach more completely this complex fusion of public rights and individual activity. He was simultaneously mindful of both aspects, effecting a reconciliation in part through the heavy stress he assigned the moral basis of individualism, which was extended to include necessary social alterations consistent with man's unfolding powers. However, such valuation invested the total framework with a peculiar quality difficult to generalize beyond Nugent's own position. For other Populists, while antecedent human liberty was the grounds for the doctrines of law and community interest, he used the same grounds to sanction extensible powers. This placed him at the movement's front line. But he also retained the individualist complexion, which modified the purpose and scope of society's collective features. As he became more paternal, he became more avowedly antisocialist. Despite advanced statements of public welfare and interest, there was an unmistakable Smithian component at the heart of his system.

Here, it should be added, one cannot divorce Nugent from his philosophic roots. He came by his antisocialism honestly; it was not a circuitous means for disemboweling a prospectively radical formation. The strength of his perspective, enabling him in the first instance to entertain freely the idea of the enhanced role of the state, lay in his sweeping confidence in moral evolution, as if it were divinely guided in consociation with man's ethical strivings. One is perhaps rightfully wary in treating of saints. But such was the contemporary reputation he, almost alone in the movement, enjoyed. He was a largely sequestered, studious, selfless political figure, persevering, in spite of failing health, as the party's gubernatorial candidate in 1892 and 1894. He died the following year, when he was about to achieve national party prominence. What gave some credence to the legend of Thomas L. Nugent was the content of his views. More so than Donnelly and Lloyd, Nugent was a mystic in politics, not of course to the extent of losing touch with the rational premises of argument, but in asserting and then developing an essentially Swedenborgian faith in scriptural literalism. This position became a means to posit mankind's universality and quest for social betterment. Four speeches will be discussed from 1892 to 1895.[1]

1. Tradition and Moderation

The first speech, delivered during the 1892 campaign, suggested the merging of ethical and political strands. Here, his concern was to differentiate Populism, in spirit and program, from the existing major parties. This was an acute problem in the South, where Democratic affiliation had received the highest cultural sanctions. Nugent spoke, then, of the need to reexamine the standards on which such hegemony rested and to determine whether in fact parties had been responsive instruments of welfare:

A great thinker has said that "as institutions grow larger, men grow small." It is so. The "rule of the ring" has been supreme in this republic of ours for the past thirty years and he who can manipulate most skillfully the political machine secures the prizes of public life, the offices and spoils. Great men no longer lead the old parties because great men are men of soul, of humanity, of genius, of inspiration. They are never machine men. Fitted by nature to soar amid the stars, they cannot sprawl in the gutter or court companionship with slime. Capable men are no doubt working the party machines for the usual rewards, but the times demand great men to mould the elements of reform into proper shape, and they will come as the inspiration finds them amid the ranks of the common folk.

The passage was more than vague exhortation; it captured the tension in modern life between organizational rigidity and animated impulses toward social change. It reflected a fear, not unknown in Populist circles, that institutions had lost their founding purpose and had to be revitalized through an alert citizenry. Less socially prominent groups had a fitting role to play: "The farmer of to-day is a reasoning and thinking man, rejoicing in a new-found intellectual strength of which but lately he did not dream."[2]

Nugent's target was not rigidity per se. Although at times he seemed fascinated with the cosmic struggle of inertia and life principles, his interest lay in what he regarded as the politically contrived obstruction to democratization which accompanied business control of party organization. After the Civil War, both major parties had betrayed their initial teachings, employed diversionary rhetoric, and avoided basic issues, thus marshalling "their political hosts on the two sides of the sectional line where every four years they stand in solid array, glaring at each other with the old-time hate gleaming in their eyes." Reduced to essentials, he continued, "Wall Street must, at any cost, be appeased," so that "both parties have tacitly agreed to ignore the silver issue and leave the gold standard intact," meanwhile agitating on the tariff and bloody shirt, "of all issues, least of all hurtful to Wall street."[3]

The main body of the speech was standard Populist fare, taken up with an analysis of financial contraction, concentration of wealth, and the debates on silver coinage. The tariff as well received close attention, because it provided an initial context for the determination of issues that Nugent would later develop: "But the question of remedies should be considered in relation to the problem of the proper distribution of wealth. The production of wealth would doubtless be largely increased by free trade, but it could not secure an equitable distribution of wealth products. Tariff for revenue only, if practicable at all with half a billion dollars revenue to raise annually, would doubtless afford some relief, as would any reduction in import duties, but it would have no effect to distribute the wealth of the country more equitably than the system of high protection."[4] The burden for equitableness, no matter how intensified the generation of productive forces, had to rest with the framework of distribution. His proposition incisively discounted the contemporary reliance on growth as such, especially in its trickle-down form. It also introduced the ethical notion of "proper," to reinforce still further the necessity of solutions geared specifically to questions of apportionment. Finally on the matter of the tariff, it revealed a mistrust with any measure that was taken in isolation. Yet one also finds in the passage support for free trade in principle, if, all things being equal, it could be achieved.

While not sufficient, economic growth and a revenue tariff were not objects of scorn.

Nugent's reservations appear to concern the major parties' failure to implement such a free-trade configuration, a condition presumably realizable (this is evidence of the latent Smithian impulse) if the totality of Populist reforms were brought into being. Thus, he noted that free trade divorced from proper distribution was not a persuasive remedy: "In so-called free trade England the rich still grow richer and the poor, poorer—millionaires and paupers are the joint products of their economical and industrial system. There, as here, the hovel rests in the shadow of the palace, starvation overtakes thousands, and a large section of the humanity of the United Kingdom is literally rotting down in poverty and crime, in the very presence of the palaces which shelter the chiefs of finance, trade and the factory." Nor, in America, had Democratic professions of a revenue-only tariff carried conviction. The platform "does not specify what rate of duty would constitute such a tariff," or the rate needed "to maintain our national revenues as now fixed," and it does not "propose any reduction in the pension charges or in any other expenditures, so as to bring the annual revenues within the limits of a strictly revenue tariff." On the one hand, Nugent shrewdly observed, citing recent measures, "the free list under Democratic policy must be understood to include free raw material with high protective duties on the manufactured product," thus conferring immense benefits on industry. On the other, in addition to the problem of Democratic intransigence over reductions, a revenue tariff would be inadequate so long as expenditures were frivolously high (he cited rivers and harbors, as well as pensions) and the tariff, reflecting current wisdom, remained the chief source of government support. In sum, Nugent said: "Tariff for revenue only, under present conditions is only a question of schedules of greater or less protection."[5]

After excoriating the Democratic leadership as "not only opposed to silver but to greenbacks as well, friendly to national banks and identified by social and pecuniary interest with the classes who live and thrive on monopoly and legislative favoritism," Nugent furnished an implicit description of what he himself favored. The context was a criticism of the false hopes raised by a prominent Texan on this issue: "Senator Mills, with his fervid and highly imaginative nature, full of southern chivalry and eloquence, no doubt has persuaded himself that a revenue tariff will create and distribute wealth, destroy monopoly, open the vaults of the banks and bond holders and send the money so long hoarded there, in vitalizing streams, to every nook and corner of the country; but the difficulty of impressing such views upon the cold-blooded national leaders referred to stamps his undertaking as the task of the century."[6] As the phrase "in vitalizing streams" testified, Nugent was not adverse to the liberation of the economy, achieved largely, as he turned to Populist remedies, through overcoming monopolist restriction in the three main areas of the movement's platform.

This platform, "a far more comprehensive and reasonable plan of relief" than that of the Democrats, stood first "in undying opposition to land monopoly—to so shape the policy of the government that the public land shall be used only by the actual settler," reclaiming land from corporations "as far as practicable." Central to Nugent's acceptance of property was his conception of legitimate (productive) wealth, pertinent also to the land question: "This will prevent any monopolization of the public lands in the future for speculative purposes." Next, to assure equity on matters of taxation, protection would be removed "from our tariff as soon as it can be safely and properly done" with the additional revenues to be supplied by a graduated income tax. In Nugent, concreteness frequently was tantamount to moderation. Even here, in tracing the argument one finds that not only was implementation of programs cautiously expressed, but Smithian features were allowed to reemerge. In the words of the relevant plank, the income tax had been tied to limiting "all state and national revenues to the necessary expenses of government, economically and honestly administered," which in turn formed the basis for entering "upon the policy of 'progressive free trade,' " a phrase he borrowed and so identified from the 1856 Democratic platform ("free seas and progressive free trade throughout the world").[7]

More interesting than the reference to capitalism, and perhaps to laissez-faire, was the need, characteristic of southern Populism, to return to the Democratic party of the pre–Civil War past for the inspiration needed to articulate principles. After quickly listing other demands, including a safe, sound, flexible currency issued directly by the government, free coinage, increase of the circulating medium, and government ownership of railroads, Nugent remarked: "In advocating the free coinage of silver, we put ourselves in line with the traditions and teachings of the 'old democracy,' all of whose great leaders, from Jefferson down, believed in bi-metal[l]ism." He observed in a further passage: "It will be seen that our opposition to national banks is supported by the teachings of Jefferson, Calhoun and the other great leaders of democratic thought, as well as by the platforms, the traditions and history of the old democracy. Who can fail to admire the fight of the old party under the leadership of Jackson and his successors, in favor of free trade and against national banks?"[8]

Though a means of fostering party differentiation, through contrasting Democratic performance and earlier principles, the emphasis on Jefferson and supposedly puristic Democracy indicated an inward turn more basic than mere constitutional reaffirmations. Consciously, a political temperament was being subtly invoked. It was one which decried immoderate change. More broadly, it envisaged solutions which, although they included governmental intervention, were confined within previously reached categories that accented restoration, essential soundness, and the tacit observance of determinate cultural boundaries. This is not to say that Nugent had feet of clay. Rather, despite his pleas for transcendence, he not only carried forward the historical traditions of a past affiliation; he expressed the wider ambivalence which harnessed newly sanctioned activism to the potentially classical demands associated with competitive capitalism.

The issues were not thereby blurred, so much as established in a reformist mold. Thus, the financial question, in all of its ramifications, loomed considerably larger than was the case where the Democratic political tradition had been less pronounced. After dovetailing free trade and opposition to national banks, he added: "Complete separation of the government and its revenues from banking institutions was the old slogan of democracy until the civil war and the vicious conditions produced by it induced forgetfulness of the warnings of the fathers." To complete this portion of the discussion, Nugent continued his attack on Democratic favoritism to national banks (as in interest-free government deposits selectively placed). He cogently remarked on the nation's capacity to "absorb" a far higher per capita circulation, and stipulated that "the means of getting this money to the people must be determined by the government."[9]

The desire to move with restraint, though not at the sacrifice of Populist goals, can be seen from his recommendations on the railroad question: "[W]e favor a commission, with power to fix and maintain rates—looking to government ownership as the only final and adequate solution of the problem."[10] Nugent stated his preference carefully. He implied that public ownership was dictated by necessity and not by ideological choice. Regulation was seen as inadequate because, to remain consistent, it left intact a property right that, so long as it was in force, had to be respected. Either the framework had to be changed in this one particular, thus removing the conflict, or, in the absence of such alteration, the commission would be bound, both morally and legally, to honor all prerogatives of ownership save that of determining rate structures, a situation open to litigation. In this case, public ownership did not abrogate so much as step around the property right for the purpose of preserving the larger principle. Simply, while property retained its private form, there could not be fundamental tampering. Only when Nugent was convinced that in a specific area regulation did not resolve outstanding grievances, would he reluctantly press onward. Public ownership became a negative or last-resort solution. Unlike in Watson's thought, however, after the deed was accomplished, it stood as a self-contained act. It had been deflated to fit within the total program and was not invoked to satisfy laissez-faire or competitive ends. This process of reasoning merits attention.

Nugent began: "For myself, I believe in a strong commission law conferring full power upon a commission to regulate and control railroads and to fix and maintain rates." Yet regulation entailed safeguards inclusive of the public and railroads alike: "I believe, however, that a commission, organized under such a law, should proceed with great caution, seeking always to do 'equal and exact justice' to the people and all interests involved." Then, coming to the heart of the matter, he admitted that his proposal would be largely ineffectual because regard for entrepreneurial decision making (including the right to define a fair return on investment) often worked to perpetuate the conditions regulation was designed to correct. Clearly, Nugent was aware that he had tied his hands through a scrupulous observance of such safeguards:

In the nature of things, however, the commission can not take from production the burden which our system of railway transportation puts upon it. It concedes that railroads are the private property of the corporations and must necessarily leave to the latter to determine the number and kind of officers, agents and employes, their duties and compensation. Hence, in adjusting rates, so long as these roads remain private property the commission must concede to the owners the right to fix the amount of operating expenses, the amount to be expended in betterments, etc. Hence the burden of the present rates must very largely remain; and when, in fixing rates, the commission drops to a point at which the roads cease to produce a reasonable income, as viewed from the standpoint of the owners, litigation must inevitably result, or a struggle in some form with the commission—all calculated to weaken and impair this form of regulation, possibly to destroy its usefulness.[11]

Operational control followed from ownership. If the enterprises in question had been of a different complexion, the grounds of deprecation would have been removed. Not least important, the impasse created through respect for property might well have cast doubt on the desirability of regulation as a social instrument.

Throughout, the avoidance of conflict seems uppermost: "At best, in my judgement, the remedy is a partial one, liable to great abuse, and if thrust into politics, likely to engender periodical bitterness and strife—to bring on, in fact, a war between the railroads and the people not favorable to a just and reasonable settlement of the great question of regulation." With the foregoing established, Nugent devoted but a single sentence to the alternative: "Government ownership, I verily believe, will obviate all of these troubles."[12] Instead, he turned to a discussion of compensation, suggesting that the issuance of government securities would rest on the sound basis of the revenue produced. Here as elsewhere he wished to make clear that Populism opposed the blind creation of paper money. Indeed, he specifically viewed the public appropriation of railroads as outside the context of wasteful expenditure. The sense was more that of rational administration than of mere businesslike procedures. It was as if he were saying that the plan was workable, came within the state's purview, and was more than generous to railroad interests, which would otherwise be courting disaster. In Nugent, though concreteness bred moderation, his matter-of-factness concerning the costs of operation, the provision for a sinking fund, and the savings to be effected, also conveyed direct powers of accomplishment: Public ownership was a practicable solution.

However, in the last analysis, what bolstered his almost instinctive confidence was his strongly moral and religious perspective. "Nearly 1900 years ago," he immediately continued, "a wonderful man, well known to history, but not much talked of in political parties, made his appearance in an oriental country. He was an embodiment of truth. Plain people gathered around him and heard him speak with delight. . . . It is not written that he drew to him those in authority, the wealthy or the elite of society." Nugent then turned, as had Lloyd and numerous others, to the "golden rule," finding a historical connection between the values sought and the popular forces awakened in the two periods: "Social and industrial justice has since that time been denied to the toiling and suffering classes, because truth has been on the cross wearing the crown of thorns. But truth is abroad once again among the common people, as of old; it is calling its own and its own is hearing the call. They are crowding to the front as in that olden time and thank God that times are now more auspicious than they were then. The inspiration leads them. They do not threaten, but they demand justice." As the last sentence attested, the tone was one of disciplined moderation: a persistence which yet avoided overt confrontation. There was a becoming sentiment of mission, of determination not to be dissuaded, of ultimate rightness: "The burden of all the ages is now upon them—the heaped and piled up burden of injustice and wrong. To the idle thunderbolts of politicians, such men can only answer with a smile. The banner of right waves above them; they are moving to victory."[13]

2. Ethical Premises of Reform

Later in the campaign, Nugent elaborated the notion of social transcendence in an altogether remarkable performance on the hustings. Concomitantly, the second speech demonstrated how a far-reaching context of thought still buttressed fairly ordinary ideas on economics. This was a not infrequent paradigm in Populism, which gave rise to self-deception over the degree of advancement that was proposed. In one way, Nugent was similar to Watson. He spoke briefly of the persecution of those who work for change: "There have been reformers in every age of the world. History is full of their schemes, their successes and defeats, their heroic lives and martyr deaths." In laboring against every form of wrong, political, social, religious, "they have relinquished worldly honors, surrendered fortune and sacrificed life itself."[14] Though designed to console, this strand of thought was perhaps a sign of the regrettable toll exacted in waging an uphill struggle, as the accompaniment of mission. But it was seldom a dominant theme in other Populists or in Nugent himself.

Nugent next moved to a more pertinent analysis of the limitations of the reformer: "He sees the external wrong—the dark shadow upon the world's life. The injustice and suffering which evil conditions bring to the toiling multitude, the undeserved power and prestige which these same conditions bring to the favored few—poverty for the millions, vast, unearned wealth for the very few." Significantly, this plane of awareness was not sufficient, even though, as in the preceding sentence, it was addressed to a substantive question. Nugent was looking to an as yet undefined anterior condition which concerned spirit rather than structure: "His schemes of relief have, for the most part, been directed against superficial evils—evils of administration or policy which reappear in spite of all palliatives." Nor were those especially gifted with foresight, "noble men" who "by pure weight of character have wrought changes of a more or less radical character in existing institutions," wholly up to the mark. "But even such exalted characters have never pierced to the core and uncovered the hidden causes of social evils." They had enabled society to retain "its capacity to exist, to maintain its organic life and to receive and hold, through its crude and broken forms, the divine ideals which throughout the ages have been slowly but surely evolving," but, despite this, they "have not, in thought or action, been able to transcend their external environments."[15]

It was precisely at this point that he developed seminal ideas on the nature of social change and the reform process. At first glance, one expects only a conventional attack on cultural inertia, as important as that may be: "The reformations started by them have run in grooves worn by existing social and political systems. Heredity and habits of thought and life have determined the scope and character of their efforts, hence social abuses have, in spite of those efforts, been transmitted from age to age, and the lines in which men now think are very much those which shaped human thought hundreds of years ago." This criticism extended to the atrophying of institutions, a loss of vitality: "Men, from habit, become conservative. We learn to love what we are accustomed to, and misguided affection makes us cling with death-like tenacity to social and political institutions long after they have ceased to be useful or serviceable to the human race—yes, long after they have become the instruments of injustice and oppression."[16]

But Nugent also went on to delineate a larger conservation of structure. As in presumably epochal religious changes, the old became historically embedded in the new. The old system kept its identity while shaping the new formation's growth. The process signified a continuous reproduction, because it was not grounded in fresh beginnings: "Luther's reformation corrected many abuses in the Romish church, but the Protestantism which he left to the world carries in its bosom the tyranny of opinion which, while greatly mitigating the severity of former church discipline, is quite effective in deterring men from too liberal indulgence of independent thought in the construction of doctrinal standards." More subtle forms of repression replaced those which were overt, "but both methods answered the purpose" of circumscribing thought, and "both illustrate the tendency of institutions to perpetuate themselves by means of the veneration in which they are held and the dread which they inspire." For Nugent, historical progression (manifested as "non-essential modifications") nevertheless consolidated the potential for abuse: "Romanism reappears in Protestantism in a less severe form with apparently a larger tolerance and a more benignant spirit—but is still carrying in its bosom all of the possibilities of old Romanism as it existed in Luther's day." The difference, he added, is that "modern civilization has too many material interests at stake to permit an extreme indulgence of the propensity to persecute." A "staying hand" was placed on "the tendency to ecclesiastical domination," but it did not press "against the system itself."[17]

The trends of church history found their parallel in political parties. For in both, "the spirit of domination asserts itself and is made effective by means of an imperious public opinion," and "there is rulership that will not brook opposition." This parallelism of objectified structures which had been emptied of vital creedal elements defined in Nugent's mind the institutional shortcomings associated with all organizations devoted to self-perpetuation. For him, religion merely illumined the larger problem of social and spiritual unresponsiveness in the world. The present danger lay in the existing major parties. Even when reformers from this quarter "have felt themselves warmed and thrilled with strange sympathy for the suffering and stricken multitude," still "they have been overborne and trodden under foot by the sordid and selfish horde who bear the standards of the parties, dictate their policies and control the offices which they dispense as the spoils of victory." Nugent, seeing such men prepared, "as readily as Caesar, Alexander or Bonaparte," to "convert the world into a human slaughter pen, if that were necessary to the gratification of their lust for dominion," became positively enraged: "Reform from such source! Never, unless right is to be confounded with wrong and truth with fiction."[18]

Logically, he had reached an important juncture. So effective had been his presentation denying the historical existence of meaningful change that he had to either surrender to pessimism or raise the affirmative call for a transcendent vision of reform. He pursued the latter course: "But is there no hope of reform—no hope for the downtrodden and oppressed? Yes, there is hope; not 'hope deferred that maketh the heart sick,' but hope brightening and glowing with ever-increasing effulgence. Great, humane, cultured men have toiled through weary years of investigation, vainly endeavoring to solve the problem of human life, but few of them have ever penetrated beyond the mere physical basis of existence." The spiritual factor would be his leading edge, yet in the deeper, nonrational, if not libidinal, sense one associates with profound reverence. This force, pantheistic in its breadth, alone seemed capable of moving beyond existing grooves and eliciting the selfless devotion necessary to the apprehension of truth. Man became humanized by reorienting his quest for betterment: "Truth, lying within and above the existing order of things, only comes forth when conditions favor to stand in glorious transfiguration before men, and then only to men who win her as a bride. When the opportunity serves she reveals herself to those who reverently wait upon her coming—it may not be in full-orbed splendor, but it will always be in a vision of glory, although shadowed by human infirmities and circumscribed by human limitations. But truth is not found by mere searching; thinking alone does not disclose her. She is seen, loved, embraced as a bride, embodied in the spirit and the life."[19]

In contrast to Lloyd, Nugent does not allow us, even in the context of transcendence, to forget the presence of human limitations. This was perhaps a warning that perfection was unattainable; equally, it suggested that more moderate requirements were consistent with the search for truth. As it was, the entire flight above prevailing institutions never carried further than a literal Christianity. "In all ages the wise and learned have sought her with longings unutterable, unquenchable; but it was given only to certain wise men to see her perfect star in the east; and that star led them to the babe in the manger, the 'golden child' of promise. Since then men have been learning the law of human service." This relationship between Christianity and reform established the direction, and set the boundaries, of change. It represented a belief in service, supported on intuitive grounds, which denied any specific interest in theoretical or systemic questions: " 'He sleeps in God who wakes and toils with men,' says the rarest of modern reformers. Here is the lesson—the rule—and he who works out the rule in practical life will know truth by an interior recognition far more convincing than any process of human reasoning. The Christ of history was not an ecclesiastic, nor a politician, nor a cultured theorist. . . . Little cared he for the petty differences among men—for their creeds and dogmas and beliefs. He came and taught and labored, not to inaugurate a system, but to reach and cure the world's ills which he clearly saw."[20]

In the Populist literature, it is difficult to find a clearer instance of the idealization of Christ as a *historical* figure, who as such was worthy of emulation because he expressed pertinent reform objectives: "I am not a theologian, nor even a member of any church, yet in this wonderful man and his work I see the ideal reformer, the one single, complete and symmetrical character of human history, giving his life to the work of arresting the evil tendencies inherent in the world's social and political institutions, upbearing the rule of absolute right in the face of an age given over to superstitious veneration for dead forms and whose highest ideals never rose above the level of the merely technical or legal." If fundamental change had been too readily identified with emotive effusions and an animus to rigidities of organization, blurring the focus on the historically specifiable political economy of the present, there still remained the dynamism of a more unsublimated vision of truth. This latter aspect was a basic ingredient of the reform impulse: "But, as in the days when Christ preached reformation in Judea, the common people are beginning to hear the truth with gladness. The spirit of humanity which Christ left in the world has not departed, although periodically subjected to partial suppressions."[21]

With the Christ-imagery, Nugent emphatically stated a projective social ideal. It derived support from further observations on the cultural resistance to new modes of thought. Yet there was at best an undercurrent of ambivalence concerning his framework. The promise of a lofty ideological breakthrough (not to be discounted, even if cast in a sermonizing mold) had been combined with quite modest reform demands. One would expect more to follow than actually occurred. As with so much else in Populism, the seemingly most advanced pronouncements incorporated and passively accepted a propertied orientation. Nugent's aforementioned "grooves" have been retained in the act of discarding them.

In two connected sentences, Nugent dramatically highlighted the tension. The first, still referring to the spirit of humanity Christ had left in the world, approached the subterranean chiliasm that proved so volatile a factor in European peasant disturbances, and that was remarkably lacking in the Populist experience: "In the popular heart 'deep is calling unto deep,' and the social brotherhood is slowly evolving and growing among the people as breast after breast thrills responsively to the sound of that 'calling.' " Then, holding constant that magnificent notion of "social brotherhood," itself very close to Lloyd's idea of a patriotism of love, one is keenly disappointed at the practical edifice constructed. Salient elements of competitive capitalism were set in place:

For the present, so long as selfishness demands its law of competition, we can only hope to make a successful fight against monopoly—to give back to the people their ownership of public utilities, to enact the "initiative and referendum" by which the country's legislation shall be placed under the direct control of the voters, to recognize the supremacy of the individual in matters of private concern, to restore to the commercial and social world the lost ideas of equity and justice, thus to untrammel legitimate industries and skill and leave them to pursue in freedom the beneficent work of producing wealth; and this reform movement necessarily must, upon humane and economic grounds, include "free trade throughout the world" within its scheme of remedies.[22]

Even separating the two strands of thought leaves abundant complexity in the second sentence alone. Antimonopolism as a generalized stance had not been surrendered. But to probe further is to see that the operant notion is capitalist vitalization. This was not simply to be treated as compatible with antimonopolism; in part, it was to be viewed as the moral fruition of primitive Christian standards. When social brotherhood and globalized free trade are integrated into a single system with the emphasis on untrammeling legitimate industries and skill, one finds oneself walking a historical path somewhere between Gerrard Winstanley and Woodrow Wilson. The vector of forces is not terribly distant from the Smithian position.

To fuse the humane and economic as consciously as Nugent did, was inevitably to stamp the former with a less than transcendent purpose. It was also to invoke Christ's historical example and teachings in the endeavor to fix capitalism on a more equitable course. The outcome, he immediately added, remained in the area of speculation, a utopianism facing capitalist encirclement: "What may be beyond that which is here outlined, only He can know who holds the destinies of the world in the hollow of His hand. Human selfishness must, of necessity, place limitations upon every social or political movement." Socialism, were it not for human selfishness, might be a desirable and realizable goal, although it was suitably distanced from present attainment: "If it [selfishness] shall ever be transcended, the glorified industries will arise in orderly unity and harmony like the 'City of God,' and the dream of

Bellamy will be a realized fact in concrete social life. As yet, such a state can only, as the millennium, exist in hope."[23]

Finally, if Adam Smith did not appear, Jefferson—as the modernized political vision of Christ—did, providing further ideological anchorage to hold Nugent's view of transcendence within prescribed limits. Guidelines had been given: "Already Jeffersonian simplicity is transcended—composite age is dawning upon the world with its quickening and uplifting power." The fount of ideas, however, remained a constant for Nugent: "The transformations already effected and which yet impend are largely due to the fundamental, political truths taught by Jefferson." Past and future were connected through the uncritical acceptance of a source which had engendered distorted practices but could also be endowed—this was the key to Populism—with democratic possibilities: "A crude generation appropriated them only to the demands of an extreme, selfish individualism, but the opening epoch will appropriate them to the demands of social and political justice."[24]

3. The Vitalization of Economic Processes

Throughout, one perforce deals with a living, dynamic statement of purpose. In Nugent's case, this is measured not by a single speech, but by the convergence of several strands, defining one another, of a unified perspective. Hence, his belief in the re-creation of a system of justice, and in the basic soundness of the Jeffersonian matrix of ideas, received further elaboration two years later, in his opening speech of the 1894 campaign. Although continuities are apparent, amidst orthodox Populist antimonopolism, there was a still firmer plea for the classic tenets of capitalism and an explicit disavowal of socialism. Again, the moral-economic fusion was apparent (with the vision of Christ now replaced by a specifically Jeffersonian-Smithian configuration). The stress was on individual participation in a productive community of wealth. In this regard, unblocking the channels of trade had the express function of obviating the need for socialism. It was a conscious Populist alternative to both prevailing capitalist and socialist modalities.

With the Pullman strike in mind, Nugent presented a biting indictment of monopolistic capital. But his concern was as much the destruction of a market framework and the foreclosure of opportunity, as the manner in which accumulation proceeded, to the detriment of the public welfare: "These industrial paroxysms are, however, object lessons, and they have in large measure disclosed to the masses what has been for some time apparent to the philosophical student of recent history, viz., that the spirit of plutocratic capitalism is the dominating force in our organized social and industrial life. Yes, it gathers the fruits of industry and divides them at its will. It controls and manipulates with almost unbridled power and license, every function of trade and finance. Its speculative lust finds opportunities of gain in the tolls levied upon the right to occupy the earth." Nugent dwelled on the last of these: "It denies to the people the heritage which the Creator gave them 'without money and without price.' It gathers into its storehouse the bounties which nature designed for the common use of all. The treasures of soil and forest, of water, and air, and sunshine, are poured at its feet."[25] As before, land possessed a semisacred character. It represented that basis for an independent life which, in becoming subjected to monopolistic appropriation, denied the principle of propertied individualism.

Yet though Nugent's view of the land was essentially Lockean, the associations with individual freedom raised the land factor to a public status. What was individual had to be rendered general or attainable to all. Opposition to capitalist encroachment was most concerted where private rights were endangered. By means of this seeming paradox, he could speak of the right of occupancy, common use, and nature's treasures, not in order to sanction collective ownership, but to indicate areas of transgressing corporation growth. The latter undermined the aspirations and legitimate claims of the individual.

Clearly, he regarded as odious "the spirit of plutocratic capitalism," which obliterated ethical standards and animalized man's character: "Thus it wipes out as with a sponge the distinction between right and wrong, makes merchandise of the noblest ideals, sets gain before the world as the highest end of life, and converts men into predatory human animals." The preceding indictment derived support from moral and political considerations:

"Fortunately, for our christian civilization, there are heroic men and women from whose minds the foul spirit of greed has not been able to drive the sweet ideals planted in the world's thought by the Son of the Galilean carpenter. But for these, spiritual hope would perish from the Earth. Capital could never have attained such ascendancy, but for the legislation which has given it unjust advantages and enabled it to monopolize both natural resources and public functions and utilities."[26] For Nugent, public functions and natural resources were pivotal, for, controlled by monopolies, they had a stranglehold on competitive enterprise.

Despite the forward ground it quickly occupied, this speech also illustrated the capitalist thrust of antimonopolism. It became less an incongruous amalgam of opposing trends than an intentional synthesis in which each component reinforced the other. Individual appropriation, the labor theory of value, equal opportunity, all taken together became synonymous with the achievement of social equity and just distribution. This state of affairs would be readily upset as soon as inroads were made into the scheme of private, individualistic entitlement, fostering in turn the organized accumulation of wealth. Safeguarding the public interest was crucial as a defense of the community, and of the individual's right to benefit from his labor. But more, it signified a recognition that the gains effected, where such interest was involved, became the principal leverage in a process of the concentration of wealth that multiplied corporate advantage and intensified economic disparities.

The passage was at once critical of and in resonance with an underlying Smithian doctrine:

Every person is entitled by the law of natural justice to possess and enjoy the fruits of his own skill and industry. Give to all equal opportunities, and under the operation of this law each would get his just share of the world's wealth; but give to any man the right to take not only the produce of his own labor but a portion of that which is derived from the labor of his neighbor, and you unjustly increase his opportunities of gain. Give to a few individuals organized into a corporation the right to dispense for a price services of a necessary and public character—services essential to the existence and well-being of organized society—and you arm them with the power to levy tribute upon the whole community, and acquire wealth almost without limit. You in other words provide for those consummate products of present economic conditions, the millionaire and the tramp.

The words "levy tribute," present also in other Populist writings, referred to the condition which perhaps best characterized the nature of intracapitalist differences. The conflict was not over property or even so much how it should be apportioned. Rather, it was over the presence of sanctioned expropriation *within* the propertied community. Aggregations of wealth signified a restriction placed on the growth and security of individual holdings, and monopolistic accumulation, pitting differentially powered segments of property against each other, represented a continuous flow from the whole of the community to a nucleus. Consolidation was realized at the expense of, and portended the destruction of, the independent producers of wealth: "By the telegraph, telephone and railway monopolies, the monopolies of money and land, it is easy to see that we have placed in the hands of individuals and corporations the power to levy toll upon the productive industry of the country—to virtually place all the labor of the country under tribute to a mere fraction of the population."[27]

The sense of the critique deepened at this point (while still holding firm to capitalist essentials). It was not simply the public character of monopolies which concerned Nugent, but the magnetic field by which wealth was drawn off from the generality of society. Therefore, he added: "And when we consider the vast and all pervading power and influence acquired by means of industries thus brought under the dominion of the few, every intelligent mind must see at a glance, that we could not in any other way have provided conditions so favorable to the undue concentration of wealth." This observation led him to the yet more evident point, recurring to an earlier theme: "And let it be remembered, that it is not the excessive production of wealth, but its unequal distribution, which constitutes the menacing evil of the times."[28] It was not simply that power and concentration had an adverse effect on proper distribution. For as a previous remark suggested, there was little to fear from the idea of productive industry.

Quite to the contrary, Nugent was explicit about the positive relationship between economic growth and political democracy, when restrictions and privileges had been stripped away. He saw in production the potential for society to bestow the natural advantages inhering in the modernization process, which were otherwise stifled by monopolistic controls: "Under normal conditions, the greater the production of wealth, the more widely diffused would be its benefits. As population increases and society becomes more highly organized, so ought the means and facilities of civilized life to be more and more within the reach of the great body of the people, and the comforts and conveniences of life to more and more abound. The point ought to be thus reached at which poverty would disappear."[29] The normalization of economic processes represented more than a defense of the small propertyholder (though he, in the final analysis, was the one presumably to be liberated). Nugent imparted to competitive capitalism— actually bordering now on a traditional view of laissez-faire— a more inclusive, vibrant reading. Fair opportunity became the distributive mechanism of justice, and individual production, the basic contribution to community well-being.

In Smithian fashion, the labor of each redounded to society's composite product. This yielded in turn (and here there was a departure from Adam Smith) the prospects of greater internal democratization. Nugent moved beyond an industrial equilibrium of forces to the predication of enhanced social benefits, growing out of freely developing production: "Such a condition [disappearance of poverty] could only be brought about, however, in a community all of whose members were afforded fair opportunity for the exertion of their faculties; for thus only could each be enabled to produce a proportion of the common stock of wealth and participate in the general enrichment derived from the cooperating efforts of all." And, more familiarly, normalized growth tokened rational production, liberated energies, and an end to artificial brakes on development: "In such a community there could be no material waste, no check in production, no limitation to the aggregate wealth by means of monopoly or the possession of unjust advantages."[30]

Nugent's ethical underpinnings fostered greater participation among lower economic groups than was to be found in Adam Smith. Yet in bare economic terms, he reached similar conclusions: "To produce results of this kind, nothing is needed but to destroy monopoly in those things which productive industry must have for practical use." In one encompassing sentence, he unequivocally stated the full case for competitive capitalism: "Protect these from the speculative greed of men, disembarrass trade of arbitrary legal interference, give free play to competition within the proper sphere of individual effort and investment, and steadily oppose those extreme socialistic schemes which seek by the outside pressure of mere enactments or systems, to accomplish what can only come from the free activities of men—do these things, and you will have achieved the real, genuine and lasting reforms which labor and capital equally need, and which in fact are the only practical reforms lying within the range of party action."[31] The faith in productive industry as a generative factor in social welfare was reaffirmed, thus furthering the larger Populist argument for the desirability of the internal generation of productive forces. Additionally, the specific requirements of laissez-faire, such as the rejection of outside pressure, were endorsed. When Nugent spoke of the "free activities of men," again repeating the moral-economic fusion, his reference was hardly to a nonpropertied context. Rather, he was speaking of unrestricted trade, freely operating competition, and initiatives in the private sector.

More revealing was his treatment of socialism. For it had been cast as the antithesis of such freedom in the economy, and although it was in a different form, the threat was very like that from monopoly. Moreover, socialism had unacceptable political implications, running afoul of Nugent's prescriptions for social change. There was a bias against "mere enactments or systems." This raised directly the question of what degree of structural alteration would be favored (or even tolerated). As in the previous remark, "nothing is needed but to destroy monopoly," one senses more clearly here the implicit limits to be placed on any transformation. Solutions remained effectively individualistic, if not also spiritual, in nature. Most important, public ownership, which he had approved on numerous occasions, became integrated within a competitive formation. This gave to the collective element a moderate construction that set it apart from socialism and "outside pressures." Indeed, in this passage, socialism contrasted sharply with more deeply conservative themes which were associated with internal generation. Notably, the test of reform was to what extent it addressed the needs of labor and capital alike and impartially: a reconciliatory goal which tacitly suggested the consent of both parties. Reform was further subject to confinement. Emphasis was given to its practical character. There was also the insistence that it properly emanate from the political process. These aspects together ruled out both a theoretical and systemic conception, and more direct steps of protest, such as strikes, because they were contrary to "party action."

In none of the foregoing did Nugent relinquish his critical perspective. But that, of course, was just the point. For Nugent, as for other Populists, reservations about how far to proceed, and, in a more positive vein, the affirmation of propertied values and institutions, had been blended into the antimonopolist critique. While the attack on prevailing capitalism was thought to be entirely deserved, there was no consequent progression to the analysis of capitalism in its competitive form. Monopoly and property remained separable categories. Criticism of the former tended to confer sanctification on the latter.

Stating that efficacious reform hinged on the removal of constraints, Nugent continued in a heated condemnation of the concentration of wealth in general and the Pullman Company in particular. "Millionaires are so common and wealth accumulations so rapid," he commented, "that it seems only a question of a few years when Billionaires will make their appearance. Inevitably, as the concentration of wealth goes on, pauperism must continue to grow and spread among the people." He cited Benjamin Flower's book on conditions of impoverishment in Boston, adding that such "wretchedness" was "so utterly squalid and hopeless that one with the horrible picture before his mental vision is almost tempted to doubt whether justice has any place in the affairs of men." This was an unusually pessimistic utterance from Nugent. Then, having the Pullman strike in mind, he warned of the opening of a capitalist offensive against labor: "Wages have only been maintained by labor organizations; but recent events convey the warning, that the apprehension of strikes will soon have spent its force, and then corporate wealth, no longer under its spell, will boldly throw off the mask behind which it has been masquerading as the friend of labor, and freely cut wages to enhance the gains of capital."[32]

The company's "monopoly from the standpoint of capital, is simply ideal," for besides its manufacturing facilities it controlled in detail, especially through company housing, the lives of its workers. It cut wages at will "to continue its periodical dividend payments" on grossly watered stock; meanwhile rents were maintained at a constant rate. The compounded pressure was aptly described: "Here the laborer is both tenant and employe—the victim at once of both usury and rent. He is dependent upon Pullman for work, for the opportunity to earn wages, to feed and clothe his family—he is dependent upon Pullman for standing-place on the earth." Wages returned to Pullman as rent. The result of this imposed circularity was stark intimidation:

When wages cease, rent ceases; but eviction follows the cessation of rent. Thus the apprehension of eviction which means loss of home to the laborer and his family, hangs perpetually over the latter to enforce silence and submission, when wages are cut to make dividends for fictitious stock. . . . Who will contend that the employe of Pullman, working under such conditions, is a free-man. . . . Extend the two-fold scheme of monopoly and spoliation so cunningly devised by the Pullman Company to all the corporations handling large investments in mining, manufacturing and mechanical pursuits, and the condition of the wage-worker and artisan would become utterly hopeless and helpless.

The evident feeling stemmed largely from his concern that Pullman might represent the wave of the future in corporate strategies. Nugent saw as reinforcement of company dominance over the laborer a new pattern of government suppression emerging in response to the strike. "And that our public policies must rapidly carry us in this direction has been made more evident by the recent injection of the element of force into the settlement of labor disputes." His capsule summary of the episode was as good as any: "Heretofore, controversies between railroad companies and their employes, although accompanied by the incidental stoppage of the mails and the interruption of interstate commerce, have not been regarded as presenting conditions of violence justifying the use of the regular army."[33]

Whether concerning the tendency of society toward pauperism and concentration, or the setting of compulsion in employment, or the state's complemental suppression, or the denial of freedoms associated with the land (he noted that "Pullman holds a monopoly of the land which is nature's divinely given opportunity to work"), the criticisms were not mere symbolic gestures in the direction of reform. Rather, they demonstrated a broadly gauged rejection of monopolistic practice and structure. Yet the counter phase, a sanctification of property, was also present. Nugent appreciated the role of labor orgainzations in maintaining wages, and understood the significance of, and conditions provoking, strikes. Notwithstanding this, he opposed strikes themselves: "The power with which the corporations are now armed cannot be overcome by strikes, which at best are unwise and oftentimes unjustifiable. Besides, the conditions they leave behind are frequently worse than those which aroused and provoked them."[34] This was not a tactical judgment. As will become clear, his paramount concern was with moderation and the political process.

Still more basic, the element of reconciliation, affecting not only strikes but also the stance toward social change, indicated a certain generosity to the presumed oppressor. Nugent resolutely refused to think in class terms or, when the pinch was on, to accept the structural impersonality of the corporation. For the potentially and actually moral individual in whatever walk of life had to continue to be the fulcrum on which justice and vitalization turned. Almost Rooseveltian in tone, his discussion employed the earlier, often quite astute analysis of cultural inertia (in which men were seen as products of their own institutional context and hence unable to glimpse the whole of society) in order now to exonerate the contemporary entrepreneur for his limited vision. This became something of a face-saving device in the presence of the implications of class:

In addition to all of this, it must be remembered, that corporations are but aggregations of individuals, and individuals are very much alike in whatever business or pursuit they may be engaged. Unfortunately the laboring man is not always unselfish, but, fortunately, the capitalist is not always sordid. It is a fact that calls for grateful recognition, that among all classes, in every trade, business, or calling, there are noble, humane, fair-minded men, whose sympathies quickly respond to the demands of justice, whose hearts are deeply affected by wrongful conditions, and who are not practical reformers battling for the people's rights because, involved in the general movement and organized social life of the times, the view-point from which they regard economic questions prevents them from recognizing fundamental truths which are now rapidly coming forth into the common thought of the people.[35]

This spirit of good will, rendered suitably concrete, removed confrontation from the reform agenda. It also permitted an orientation toward capitalism which left undisturbed the primary relations of property. As part of an educational process, attitudes had to be brought into conformance with the gathering forces of truth. Once more, the outcome was to rest questions of social betterment on conduct rather than structure. As one moves to the end of the speech, it becomes apparent that the root acceptance of property and its inevitable corollary, an accommodation between capital and labor, grew logically out of the paradigm of reform already described.

We see what might be thought astonishing declarations, which are perfectly consistent not only with Nugent's but also with Populism's central assumptions on productive capital and democratic political harmony. First, there was the statement which, among several others, prompted this reevaluation of Populist thought: "Wealth acquired in legitimate ways, by the exercise of the industry and skill and the investment of capital, cannot hurt either its possessor or the community. It is the spirit of gain run to riot in monopolies, that poisons and corrupts the fountains of individual and social life: and against this spirit must the efforts of populists be directed."[36] Were one to begin with this succinct formulation, as if it were discovered centuries hence as a lone surviving fragment of a vanished creed, the temptation would be great to dismiss Populism as a mildly reformist, ideological appendage of the dominant political culture. Even the qualification on monopoly, coming so fast on the heels of the legitimation of property, might be viewed merely as protest over an intensification of accepted beliefs concerning wealth.

Of course, the situation was more complicated. On its face, the preceding quotation depends on references which Populists had themselves given to the salient terms to render them part of a working vocabulary of protest. Thus if legitimation of wealth was present as the arresting fact, it was also carefully hedged about. This is precisely what a distant observer would fail to appreciate. Wealth was at best a conditional virtue, not an end in itself. In Populism, it was subject to two interrelated provisos. It had to comport with the dictates of fair entitlement, founded on the individual's direct and productive economic contribution. And, in the mode of its utilization as well as acquisition, it could not restrict others' rights of opportunity, whether by monopoly, spoliation, or privileges unjustly conferred under government.

Nugent could speak of a nonharmful complexion of capital accumulation because he supposed a standard in which individual
and community interests had been merged. In like manner, the
phrase "run to riot in monopolies" represented not the mere
excesses of legitimate wealth, but, for Nugent, a qualitatively different formation. It was one which was based on the negation of
the moral and economic principles he both espoused and found
practicable in the operations of capitalism. This negation became
total in its impact in that again it affected individual and social life.
Monopoly was less a scare word than a concrete embodiment of
the denial of politically and divinely sanctioned liberties.

The foregoing discussion points to a rounded contextual meaning which simultaneously conservatized and slightly radicalized
the Populist perspective: The uncritical acceptance of primal capitalist categories, though confined to a competitive stage, is obvious in the passage; but there is also the neglected, antimonopolist
underside of such acceptance. In differing treatments, the antimonopolist factor alternated between the development of competitive, nonpoliticized economic processes, and the conscious
strengthening of the public sector to achieve similar results
through the augmented role of the state. In either case, one returns to divergent capitalist political economies. It is this fruitful
source of conflict motivating Populism which would be likely to
go unnoticed by our hypothetical observer.

Nugent's value lies in forcing us to reckon with the conservatism in the movement's supposed radicalism. These elements of
Populist thought composed not a syncretic whole so much as
facets of a consistently applied ideology of propertied democracy.
His own preoccupation with moderation illumines sentiments
which were latent but nevertheless present in the broader range of
discourse. Thus, he continued, after stating that the spirit of gain
must be opposed: "But in combatting monopoly, let us never forget that neither force nor infringement of individual liberty is
justifiable or safe. Let us remember that we ought above all others
to set ourselves against anarchy in every form, against every measure calculated to break down the security which the laws afford
to private property, and in favor only of those lawful and orderly
methods which can always be successfully defended, and the ob-

servance of which will never fail to enlist for the workingman the sympathies of the good and worthy people of every class."[37] Nugent's abhorrence of violence did not reflect an abstract moralism. Instead, it resulted from the specific, manifold linkages which prompted gradualistic change and comprised what can be termed the Populist reverence for law.

Law implicitly underpinned a framework susceptible to moral suasion and rejuvenation. For this reason, structural features did not need to be dismantled, save when demonstrably impervious to correction, and Populists did not believe society had reached that point. The logical corollary was that class initiatives, frequently tantamount in the eyes of the movement to a segmentation of the legal norm of universal intent and application, were manifestly denied. For these became potentially eruptive, socially divisive, and, from every direction, antithetical to the individualistic emphasis. Infringement upon liberty was perhaps as great an evil as the continued existence of monopoly, though fortunately he did not feel compelled to choose. *That,* in reality, was the burden of his statement. It was a plea for remaining within the law, so that the cause of antimonopolism would have moral standing.

On one level, this was his most categorical defense of property. Law was particularized, rather blatantly, in the single function of security. More, protest itself was severely handicapped whenever the charge of anarchy was made, and in this case, Nugent himself raised that charge. There was a brittle quality to the discussion. Populists must wait upon the good opinion of a propertied social order, walking on eggs, as it were, lest they fail to generate the sympathies of a broader public not limited by class. On a second level, however, themes of property became easily reconciled, and without loss of their power, with the somewhat contrasting strand of Populist exceptionalism. The self-imposed mandate for promoting change carried the passage beyond its narrow concern over the security to private property. The phrase "above all others" recalled the dedication to mission, which here invested the movement with a special commission to bring means into alignment with democratic goals. In this light, the stress on lawfulness did not tie the movement's hands. Rather, it tended to reinforce its propertied sentiments, while at the same time activating its determination to gather support.

Paradoxically, toeing the mark restrained and steeled at once. Even enlisting nonclass sympathies, which had a dampening effect, also had the conscious objective, inhering in the idea of mission, of reaching outward through open recruitment, and engendering feelings of confidence and self-respect. Unquestionably though, the net result would be no more than a disciplined striving toward the configuration of law, property, and democracy already favored. The sense of mission registered only the acceleration of will and could not of itself produce a change of direction. The preceding rejection of violence led not unexpectedly to a confinement within the political system: "Let us cultivate the duty of submission to lawful authority, and in times of civil commotion, be first to give it support in its conflicts with the lawless. A good cause committed to violent methods inevitably finds in them its grave. An intelligent ballot is the only refuge of justice and liberty."[38]

In his concluding words, Nugent discussed the labor-capital balance, but his assertiveness was checked by his construction of equality. The "labor question," Nugent observed, was "at the center of the social difficulties into which our country has been led." Yet if denoting to contemporary society the prospect of class warfare, the labor question became in his hands a vehicle for restating producer values, weighted on behalf of self-appropriated profits: "Solve this question, so that the man who produces wealth shall own a just proportion of it, and those difficulties will vanish as mists before the rising sun." What followed might be best described as a mock, or shadow, confrontation. Improvement in labor's status had no bearing on, nor was it to be gained at the expense of, capital. The advocacy of equality thus became a halfway position, eschewing all claims of class dominance, pleading for accommodation, and claiming a rightful portion which also conferred respect to the portion specifically reserved for capital. For Nugent, entitlement was clearly a two-way street: "Labor, slowly rising from the dust of ages, stands at last erect upon its feet. Already it confronts capital, not to provoke strife, but for reconciliation and peace. It does not ask charity, it demands justice. It does not ask that capital be enslaved, but that it, the age-old burden-bearer be made free. It demands for itself, not superiority, but equality; and it knows by a wise instinct that, in the opening epoch now dawning upon the world, equality is coming to it in the sure unfoldings of God's providence."[39]

There was not the sense of forboding, concerning the future, that one sometimes finds in Populism. Yet a Jacksonian mustiness was retained, despite the motion forward. Equal rights, applied throughout the social structure, were defined primarily by the absence of sanctioned privilege rather than by equalization of condition or power: "This it knows; and it rejoices that in that day of deliverance the doom of 'special privileges' shall be pronounced, and 'equal rights' shall come to all alike."[40]

4. A Monetarist Defense of Property

The fourth speech, delivered before a state convention of the Farmers' Alliance in 1895, presented a technical analysis of the financial system in order to argue for the stimulation of economic processes. Nugent decried the use of a gold-redemption fund as the base for a circulating currency, for this unduly restricted the volume needed to keep pace with expanding productive development. It also encouraged insider raids on the treasury reserves, further increasing the government's dependence, in the form of interest-bearing bonds, on the banking community. Behind these practical matters lay the note-issue function of banks themselves, according the private sector a decisive role in controlling the money supply, as well as the relation between money and all other commodities and property. For Nugent, the latter were cheapened, to the detriment of agricultural products and investment in general, in favor of an appreciating dollar. He opposed this long-term deflationary context in its own right, arguing it led to stagnation and concentrated monetary power. It took on added significance as part of the expropriation process. It is striking that Nugent drew antimonopolist conclusions from thoroughly capitalistic considerations.

He spoke first of practical silver demonetization, contrary to historical and constitutional precedent, following the Civil War. Gold did not thereby "go into actual, bodily circulation, and do money duty in the channels of trade," but rather, served as the standard for the redemption of currency. Yet "larger and more far reaching even than the question of what the redemption money of the country shall be," he continued, was that of "what shall be the permanent financial system of the United States." The Cleveland administration's intention to withdraw government-issued paper currency, foster bank paper, and make gold "a redemption fund or base for bank paper," would therefore "virtually delegate to the banks the money-issuing power of the government, and compel the people to look to private corporations for their money supply." In the meantime, such gold coinage "will do duty simply as reserves in the vaults of the banks as a fund kept hoarded and out of circulation, to serve as a basis to hold up bank credits." Gold advocates recognized the need for paper (solely in the form of bank notes rather than government paper), but feared the enlargement of the specie base which supported its issuance. Here Nugent introduced the views of Frank Taussig of Harvard. According to Taussig, a broadened base would give rise to a proportionate " 'expansion of credit machinery.' " This was unacceptable to the gold-standard forces on the putative ground that stable values were threatened. Conversely, for Taussig, a diminished base through the elimination of silver that was " 'massed in fewer hands' " would provide " 'tone' " to the currency, thus making the foundation " 'more effective in sustaining the superstructure.' "[41]

Nugent deserved high marks for not losing his temper at this point. "Now, so far, populists can have no serious quarrel with the system. They have been for years saying what these gold advocates now admit, viz: that the world's business cannot be done with gold and silver alone, and that resort must be had to paper currency to supplement these metals." He also conceded "the utility of banks as business agencies," for "they do an important and useful work in affording the trading world the means of rapid and effective exchange, and in keeping its financial books." Though Nugent made distinctions concerning banking functions, he treated instruments of capital in a matter-of-fact way. Speaking of Populists, Nugent added: "They are willing that banks of discount and exchange shall, with proper safe-guards, remain until the advance in social thought shall enable the government to take charge very largely of the country's banking."[42]

However, beyond these areas of possible agreement, he repudiated outright the factor of private control, its monopolistic implications, and the consequent monetary stringency:

> But they will not consent that the purely public and social function of dispensing money to the people shall be turned over to private banking corporations, whose sole motive in discharging such a function can only be the ordinary human desire for gain. Here, therefore, they part company with the gold men. Narrow the base of circulation by limiting it to gold—strengthen the base by massing the gold in the vaults of the banks; then give to the bankers the monopoly of the business of supplying the country with paper money thus based! The policy implied in this scheme is to limit rather than inflate the currency; in fact, it proposes to provide against inflation except in so far as the bankers themselves may come to see the necessity of increasing the money supply.

An additional concern was the unsuitability of this financial system for the developmental energies then being expressed, coming "at a time when the productive capacity of our population is growing as never before."[43]

Certainly, Nugent's rhapsodizing of economic growth spoke to a positive industrial perspective. But it also had reference to the capacities of a capitalistic framework, when shaped by competitive principles, to sustain both such acceleration and a high level of social welfare. The critical element appeared to be financial reorganization as the principal liberating force. This centered on greenbacks, as inconvertible government paper, no longer dependent on specie redemption. Monetary theory became the ideological centerpiece that, in major segments of western Populism, comprehensive antimonopolism had been. Although one need not pass judgment here on the comparative degrees of radicalism in the respective sections, it should be said that on the matter of inconvertible paper, Nugent represented Texas midroadism at its most economically advanced. Even so, the context remained capitalist, and possibly more intensely competitive in inspiration because of the emphasis on money and banking. For in practice, these areas lent themselves directly to economic stimulation. As will be seen, Nugent was at pains to separate Populism from agitation over silver. But the issue that had been raised concerned the base of circulation and of itself hardly brought into question broader, systemic alternatives. Intracapitalist differences remained the focus of attention.

Discussing economic growth, Nugent listed numerous indices of achievement, as in this introductory portion of a lengthy sentence: "Consider the fact that, by the invention and application of labor-saving machinery, the capacity of our seventy millions of people to produce wealth has been augmented tenfold over that of the same number of people a hundred years ago—that, to express it more plainly, these seventy millions of progressive, energetic and speculative people can, by means of their mastery of natural and mechanical forces, which the inventive genius of the age has given them, produce more wealth within a given time than could have been produced a hundred years ago by 700 millions of people similarly endowed with mental and physical capacity; . . ." He asked his audience to consider further that "this immense productive capacity, under the spur of constantly improving facilities for intercommunication, and the exchange of wealth has developed a commensurate volume of trade," leading to "annual commercial transactions" of an astronomical sum; that population increases augmented the "volume of transactions," as did also the "improvements in the means of transportation and the transmission of intelligence," which brought "widely separated communities and nations close together," quickening the processes of trade; and that the "protection afforded by quarantine and improved scientific sanitation against the spread of infectious or contagious diseases," accompanied by "longer intervals between great wars," had "practically fixed" the population increase "as permanent wealth producers in the world's industrial system," regularizing the entire growth pattern. In contrast, "the supply of gold for monetary use" could not keep pace with this expansion. Gold itself was finding other uses. The situation was fraught with grave difficulty: There would not be the necessary "increase in the circulating medium" to carry forward the process; negatively, the successful limiting of "the world's primary money to gold alone" would result in still tighter concentrations of power and dominance, as well as untold misery. If economic growth held a certain fascination for Nugent, its juxtaposition with a gold-based currency (what he termed an "absolute atrocity") and the contrasting possibilities thought to follow dignified the argument as considerably more than an apologia for production and trade.[44]

Gold barely circulated; it was "not doing money duty among the masses," and it entailed the preservation of the national banking system. The latter was directed by men acting in "unity" through "national and state associations," and determined "to control the financial and currency legislation of the country." This aspect marked what I have termed the antimonopolist underside. It served as a precondition for any positive breakthrough on the economic front: "Backed as these people are by any amount of money, by the metropolitan press, by the shrewdest politicians and the ablest lawyers in the country, the amount of political influence they can bring to bear in effectuating their purpose must be seen to be perilous in the extreme to our free institutions. The fact that individual bankers are honest, upright gentlemen, is of small account. As a class they are inspired by the single selfish purpose of gain. . . . The national banking system, like Carthage of old, must be destroyed, and the national government must no longer be permitted to farm out its credit to corporations to be used for private gain."[45]

More pertinent was the theme of gold-induced social misery. It was the immediate setting that in some measure powered Nugent's vision of economic growth. He observed that "we present to people of other countries a seeming of general prosperity," because, despite the existence of poverty "in the dense centers of population in most aggravated and alarming forms," the territorial spread had afforded access, "though to a constantly diminishing extent," to the land. Whatever the appearance, he continued, "as the general aggregate wealth of the nation increases, so the hungry mouths and ill clad bodies increase, so grow upon us poverty, insanity and crime." To have reached this point, and to have said as well, "we are erecting, apparently, a splendid civilization, and yet its heart is being eaten out by the insatiate spirit of greed," suggested a depth of concern that he had seldom evidenced before.[46]

Although one year earlier Nugent had occasion to criticize the use of strikes, the present attack on currency and banking prompted a more sympathetic if still noncommittal treatment. A major argument for the gold standard was that "the laboring man's dollar will buy more than at any time in our history," a contention he vigorously disputed through this series of questions: "Why, then, are so many men struggling for the same dollar? Why the Pullman strike of last year, the outpourings of thousands of penniless working men, the marshaling of military forces, the declaration of martial law, the unseemly haste in resorting to courts for injunctions against the striking laborers, the quick condemnation and imprisonment of Debs, the labor leader? Why all these labor organizations—these combinations formed to keep up wages? Why does discontent pervade the ranks of laboring men throughout the whole country?" Rather than leading to "increased purchasing power," the appreciated dollar, for the worker, had meant widespread unemployment and insecurity. Gold became the financial mechanism supporting, if not also creating, broader trends of labor repression. Under this alleged "boon to the laboring man," the working classes "live constantly under the apprehension both of wage reduction and the loss of jobs." Here he cautioned, "the high wages paid skilled workmen in certain lines of production afford no test of the situation," and then he added, "it is the fact, rather, that there are millions of laborers skilled and unskilled, who get no jobs and hence no wages at all." His denial of workers' contentment and objective well-being was succinctly put: "No financial or economic system can be good which tolerates such conditions of idleness and poverty as prevail in this country."[47] With this, the criticism, perhaps because geared so closely to monetary relief, diminished in force.

For Nugent, the gold standard became virtually the functional equivalent of the monopolistic framework in its socially destructive and economically retardatory aspects. Introducing a reformation of the monetary structure was sufficient to liberalize basic energies already present in, though distorted by, the productive system. As an ultimate solution, a freely operating economy could provide the laborer with employment and a fair return, as well as maintain conditions of general prosperity. While Nugent did not thereby abandon the broader program of public ownership and perhaps even conveniently assumed it as a given, he nonetheless omitted from the discussion a positive role for government. In fact, he discounted any ordinary aid to be secured from this quarter. Given the monetary emphasis, one detects an animus toward any government intervention beyond the duties that were held to be necessary, and consistent with sovereignty. One is also brought forcibly back to the proposition that competitive capitalism was of overriding importance. An emancipating context of production became the principal means of overcoming social difficulties.

Thus, after deploring the conditions which prevailed, Nugent stated: "The demand which labor makes is, not that it be fed by the charity of government or individuals, but that it be given fair opportunities to exert itself; that social and economic conditions be so adjusted that every laboring man will find, not a job artificially created for him by a makeshift of legislation, but employment freely coming to him from the liberated, enlarged and revivified productive forces—coming to him in fact under such beneficent changes in our laws and public policies that he can hold in his firm and honest grasp all of the fruits of his labor."[48] Curiously, he jousted with a hypothetic left and totally ignored the ever-present right. For artificially created jobs and legislative makeshifts refer, of course, to governmental action. These were singled out, one supposes, as symbolic of precisely the alternative held to be unnecessary if the forces of production were only allowed to assume their normal course. "Liberated, enlarged and revivified" are the adjectival banners of a quasi-laissez-faire flagship, ready to do battle with formations on either ideological side of itself.

Even the laborer's welfare became a notation for the healthfulness of the general economy. The latter was perhaps a more imperative objective in Nugent's mind, particularly in light of his nonclass social vision; and, in any case, it was predicated on an adequate money supply to facilitate exchanges. Circulation more than underconsumption seemed to represent the nub of the problem: "But again, an honest dollar that would bring benefits and blessings to the laboring man ought equally to benefit all other classes. Labor in its various forms produces the nation's wealth. This is the ultimate truth. The exchange of this wealth constitutes all of the diversified business of the country. The vast throng of busy thousands who produce this wealth also in large measure consume it. If they are now in possession of an ample supply of sound money, they must exchange it for this wealth." Actually, in describing what ideally should be the case, his use of "honest dollar" and "sound money," propagandistic terms for the gold standard, was intended to show *why* this exchange of productive wealth had not occurred. For he went on to ask: "How is it, then, that all men of all classes complain of hard times, and chiefly of the difficulty of obtaining money with which to gratify their wants or carry on business? Why is it that so much of this wealth cannot be exchanged at all? Why, to specialize a little, does the farmer find it so difficult to sell his horse, his corn, his hogs, his crops, in fact, any part of his personal property except at ruinously low prices?"[49]

Nugent came to an underlying contention of Populism, whenever currency was thoroughly discussed. The purpose of these questions about the nature of money was to identify a still more critical issue than that involving sheer volume or velocity of circulation. Money was difficult to obtain, wealth could not be exchanged, sales were at ruinously low prices, all for the same reason: The prevailing monetary system depressed every other form of property in relation to the appreciated dollar. By this reasoning, money sought only narrow channels of maximal profitability, that pertaining to interest, speculation, government bonds, mortgages, or, in fine, whatever specifically financial arrangements begot more of itself. Nugent was not alone among Populists in maintaining that, under contemporary practice, money tended to inhabit its own realm. This is to say, there had not simply been a pervasive depreciation of values, to the detriment of the propertied community (for the monetarist the most egregious case of expropriation), but, with the comparative advantage enjoyed, there was no incentive to pursue more normal, that is, productive, investments. Capital was busy elsewhere. It was not only scarce but also largely indifferent to the promotion of exchanges.

He made his point with three consecutive questions: "Why is it, when property enters into competition with money, it inevitably goes to the wall? Why is it that the money owner does not care to buy property and cannot be induced to invest his money in productive enterprises? Is it not that money is enormously valuable as compared with property and commodities?" One takes in at a glance the coagulated processes, and beyond that economic depression, in which investment was not forthcoming. The still more fundamental, if elusive, theme, showing once again the nature and importance of intracapitalist differences, was the defenselessness of property at the hands of aggregated wealth. In a final

question, Nugent summarized the foregoing discussion of circulation, ascendancy over property, impediments to trade, coagula-
tion, and the implied need to abolish restrictions on behalf of
internal economic generation: "And, as money has value in proportion to the quantity of it out, do not such conditions show
beyond question that the monetary circulation is insufficient, and
that the dollar which buys so much of the products of labor, is
dwarfing and stinting trade and preventing the free and rapid exchange of commodities?"[50]

Finally, in regard to currency, Nugent proposed the use of inconvertible paper, primarily as a way to strengthen the circulation
base and hence to supply the requirements of increasing trade. But
also this became part of the larger political effort to reduce the
power of banking as a vital sector in the promotion of economic
concentration. The silver Democrats proceeded quite far in meeting Populist objections to the current system: paper money, direct
government issuance, a broadened circulation base through the
addition of silver. "In other words," he continued, "they want free
coinage of gold and silver at the present ratio, and government
treasury notes, or promises to pay, convertible into coin (gold and
silver)." The last-named feature, however, despite an acceptance of
paper money, defined the area of disagreement:

But their kind of paper money does not suit populists. It creates a public
debt to be paid off in some way and at some time. So long as it exists it
will constantly invite attacks from the people who now so clamorously
assert that the greenbacks constitute the weak element in our financial
system. The money power of this country will not let go its hold upon
the government so long as the financial legislation of this country affords
it the opportunity to make gain by the manipulation of the public funds
or money. So long as government notes redeemable in coin are in circulation, they will always find it practicable to deplete the national treasury
of its coin reserve.[51]

More was at issue than the presence of a national debt, based on
the government's obligation to redeem its notes in coin. For the
treasury raids and consequent reliance on banking syndicates to
preserve the gold reserve (through a flotation of government
bonds) signified a never-ending chain of depletion. This both
jeopardized the existence of any kind of firm reserve system and,
by making correctives banker-sponsored, further heightened
private financial controls. The Populist designation of a "money

power" may appear less simplistic than commonly thought, conveying as it does, in addition to concentration, this political and structural dimension.

If silver Democrats had been in power, the situation would not have materially changed: "The banks and syndicates will not stand by them—on the contrary, will hold themselves aloof, watching for the opportunity to go in and gather the spoils. . . . They will not let go so long as convertible paper exists to induce speculative raids on the metal[l]ic reserves, or invite efforts in favor of some funding schemes from which they may gain profit." The silver Democrats furnished no satisfactory way, given convertible paper, to retain an adequate coinage base for the enlarged volume of currency needed in trade. Current revenues and bond sales would not answer for the increase desired. If kept "within the limits of safe banking," then by this Democratic program "the supply of treasury notes must be limited to a sum greatly below the wants of the country." On the other hand, should the government "with impunity extend its credit beyond the limits of safe banking and therefore issue its notes to any amount," this would only, he contended, afford the "money-getters" wider scope for enrichment: "[T]hey understand that as the volume of credit paper expands, the facilities for making raids upon the coin base will proportionately increase, and they will not be slow to avail themselves of such favorable opportunities for gain at the expense of the public funds."[52]

The root of the difference lay in this. Under silver Democrats, "it is not proposed to put us on a paper basis, but to maintain specie payments." Nugent believed the former to be entirely feasible. In fact, this had occurred after the Civil War. With the suspension of specie payments, "greenbacks circulated freely, and there was no fear of a corner on a redemption fund." Only with resumption of specie payments in 1875 "have withdrawals of gold from the treasury been possible by means of the control of government paper." As for the latter, he repeated that because this paper was "payable on demand," reserves could not be held intact under a large flotation of convertible notes; hence, "the small reserve of coin must either restrict the paper issues below the wants of trade, or imperil those issues if enlarged sufficiently to afford a just supply of circulation to the country."[53]

This nuts-and-bolts financial discussion indicated that Populists by and large did not subscribe to a narrow silver doctrine. As in Nugent's case, they were quite sensible of the need to formulate a program of sufficient breadth to encompass the internal workings of the currency system. Yet notwithstanding basic differences with silver Democrats as well as with gold advocates, Populists had not departed the capitalist scene. By his own admission, in concluding the analysis, Nugent envisaged inconvertible paper as essentially correcting for an omission. It supplemented the base, in order to accelerate the conditions of exchange: "There is in fact no compromise between the paper system of the gold men and that of the populists. Populists favor the free and unlimited coinage of gold and silver at the present ratio, and the emission of inconvertible paper to supply any lack of circulation, thus to make the entire volume of money sufficient to supply the demands of trade. We cannot compromise on the perilous plan proposed by silver democrats."[54]

At best, this monetary approach indirectly made inroads into the structure of monopolistic capital, and that, only by invigorating the financial base, to pump the lifeblood of enterprise throughout the economic system. The disparities of wealth could be treated as deplorable. But, particularly for Nugent, the distinction between increased production and proper distribution still had reference, concerning the latter, not only to more equitable portions but also to the mechanisms capable of providing a solution. There was no direct, structural line between the monetarist vision and the equalitarian apportionment that was ostensibly sought. Rather, there was only a somewhat pious hope (itself based largely on competitive rejuvenation). For differential shares were not in themselves disputed. More relevant, capitalism in America was misconceived as being wholly under banker dominance. Nonmonetarists hardly found this finance capitalism central; they recognized, with varying degrees of awareness, that it diverted attention from specifically industrial consolidation.

Nugent stated with feeling that wealth increased, no matter how poorly labor was compensated: "Reduce it to a bare living, and compel it to serve in rags and filth, and it will still produce wealth rather than starve." And he added, in a memorable sentence: "The structure of wealth must still rise, even if the prostrate and tortured form of labor lies beneath its gilded foundation." A dark shadow was cast toward the close of the discussion. We see that he was very much aware of what lay beneath the positive urgings of enterprise and opportunity—a state of economic dependence which, as the real and first priority, had to be overcome. The shift in emphasis placed the still retained capitalist dream in a soberer light: "It is not that the world grows more wealthy as the years pass, which gives labor its cause of complaint—it is rather the fact, that labor can only, under its present conditions, have such a portion of that which it creates as suffices to forever keep it dependent and enslaved—that, in fact, it must sit like Lazarus beneath the tables of the world's robbers, to pick up the crumbs and have the sores upon its body licked by the dogs."[55]

Like other Populists, Nugent dealt with elemental propositions: "There is wealth enough and to spare, but it goes to the pampered few." The analysis stopped short of, and perhaps failed even to contemplate, a basic redistribution. Yet Nugent apparently welcomed competitive capitalism for *humanity's,* as well as capitalism's, sake: "Let us not forget that the millions of toilers are in more pressing need of remedy that shall prevent the unjust concentration of wealth, than they are for one which only can insure the increased production of wealth."[56]

CHAPTER EIGHT

Political Sovereignty: Lloyd, Peffer, and Weaver

The Populists' receptivity to the enlargement of government powers, which originated in their fusion of moral and structural elements, can be traced back to what I might term a jurisprudential domain of liberty. Populists maintained that government could not be separated from basic law, and that the law, to fulfill its promise, had to be transfused with democratic content. As a consequence, they insisted upon the priority of ethical and social factors in defining society's legal and political moorings. In Donnelly's thought and in varying measure most of the other Populists I have examined, only a moral leavening of the social order could prevent the excessive aridity or hardening of structures. This set the stage for man's introduction into what might be called a Populist credo: To safeguard each individual's rights, it was essential to protect and honor all others as fully human beings. The correlates of sovereignty I have identified include the popular foundations, autonomous character, and potentially extensible powers of the state (still within a capitalistic frame). Government was the responsive instrument of a people's will and creative strength.

The democratic transfusion of law was supplied by ethics. One notes a specific form of political moralism, focused upon equitable social relations and structural traits, which was sufficiently uncommon to furnish a clue to Populism's differentiated character. The Populist conception of sovereignty admitted a critical dimension to the evaluation of existing society. Ordinarily, moral force in America was reserved to the institutional framework, uncritically examined. It did not become, as it did for Populism, the superseding criterion by which to *judge* the efficacy and performance of that framework. Asserting the primacy of man, or more concretely, the authority of the governed, provided an alternative track back to the foundations of sovereignty in which property was not exclusively affirmed. Hence, there was also the more important detachment, if slight, which permitted criticism of the prevailing structure in moral, as well as other, terms.

In this light, the Populists' view of government had a direct bearing on and became indivisible from their broader rationale for protesting. If Populism were only concerned with the economy and society in a more conventional frame of reference, a statement of sovereignty presenting these moral and legal features would fail to materialize, and the potential for generating an alternative model of social development would not be realized. Protest would then have been reduced to a strictly quantitative affair having to do with an increased money supply, higher crop prices, and the marginalia of human betterment. It can be said, therefore, that ethics became the lifeblood of the movement's separate identity. Denied the underpinning of political values, Populism would have been transformed into what in reality it never became, namely, a mainstream, readily absorbable expression of discontent.

The moral dimensions of political sovereignty, particularly as expressed by the interrelated themes of human welfare, a social vision of mutuality, and the potentialities for individual and collective freedom of a constitutional democracy, have been nobly stated in Henry Demarest Lloyd's masterwork *Wealth Against Commonwealth* (1894). In presenting a concise summary of the philosophical sections of this book, I seek to refine still further a core of ideas found in the preceding authors. Lloyd was a veritable Mount Everest of Populist thought; he was hardly typical of the movement, but his value for present purposes lies in the clarity and relative advancement of his intellectual framework, enabling one to see the inner possibilities of Populist discourse. Even when historians refuse to concede his credentials as a Populist (he does not fit the stereotype of Populism as exclusively agricultural in origin and, more important, intention), surely they must recognize that interpretive differences among the scholars of Populism are less consequential than is the vitality of the ideas themselves broadly associated with the movement. I do not plead here for Lloyd's proper inclusion in my study, I simply assume his rightful presence because of his activities on behalf of Populism, the common intellectual ground and social values he shared with the other writers, and the vast panorama of human rights he has set before us.

Only after having established the significance of the moral factor can one proceed to the specifically political determinants of sovereignty. Peffer and Weaver, alike, operated on this more direct level, where power was treated in terms of contemporary realities. Yet even their analyses have a legal and philosophical complexion. Neither man, of course, was impervious to ethical considerations as witness their respective emphases on fair entitlement and public duty. But the thrust of the argument, in both cases, derived from the context of corporate abuse. This focused attention on the more traditional question of government's rights and jurisdiction. To move from human divinity to people's government is a difference of level and not of kind. Following the examination of Lloyd, I turn to a brief discussion of Peffer and Weaver, specifically on the authority of the state, which will serve to recapitulate and perhaps extend the meaning of Populist views in the political realm already found in these pages. Then, in conclusion, I will look at the Omaha Platform.

1. The Modern Commonwealth Man

Nugent has been helpful in marking a return passage to Lloyd. When Nugent referred to the conversion of "men into predatory human animals," and, still more, when he described the inner decay of institutional forms, he stated themes that figured prominently in Lloyd's writings; but on a fundamental point, the distinction between capitalism and monopolism, the two men had separate views. Lloyd attempted the difficult intellectual task of criticizing capitalism as a total political, cultural, and economic system—considering monopolism as the logical result of its evolution—by using, and at the same time transvaluing, key concepts such as self-interest that were a part of the system itself. More than any other Populist, he had developed a comprehensive and refined moral calculus in arriving at the principles of social organization. This thought centered on the tension between and the respective claims assigned to the individual and community, but he nonetheless could not work his way cleanly past the outer limits of capitalism. He redefined laissez-faire, collectivized the golden rule, and even liberated self-interest from its individualistic moorings, but the very effort suggested a reluctance to abandon outright a vision of the industrial and political democracy inherent in the existing framework of society.

From the opening line of *Wealth Against Commonwealth,* it is apparent that Lloyd viewed contemporary society as being in a state of fundamental contradiction: "Nature is rich; but everywhere man, the heir of nature, is poor." The difficulty was caused by the corporate appropriation of the productive system; this created an economy of contrived scarcity that was governed "not by the needs of humanity, but by the desires of a few for dividends." The result was a deeper paradox, in which the philosophic tradition had been used to defeat its own purposes: "Liberty produces wealth, and wealth destroys liberty." The prevailing order expressed "the obesities of an age gluttonous beyond its powers of digestion," a callousness in the world of production that was motivated by "ideals of mutual deglutition." Here Lloyd made clear that monopolism was part of the developmental process, rather than an exogenous factor: "What we call Monopoly is Business at the end of its journey. The concentration of wealth, the wiping out of the middle classes, are other names for it. To get it is, in the world of affairs, the chief end of man." If his definition of monopoly was centered on class expropriation and pervasive materialism, it also called attention to the altered character of property itself, for he later noted that through corporate hegemony "the naked issue of our time is with property becoming master instead of servant, property in many necessaries of life becoming monopoly of the necessaries of life."[1] This critical distinction, however, tended to exonerate property as such from the baleful consequences of monopolism, partly denying the historical connection he initially specified. Throughout the analysis, Lloyd declined to repudiate private ownership when it was successfully divorced from the powers of political and economic domination.

Instead, he concentrated his criticism on the value system in which property had been embedded, an unrestrained laissez-faire that he pronounced "one of the historic mistakes of humanity." Property was a matter of secondary concern. Unlike Sumner or

Locke, Lloyd did not seek to construct an ideological system for its defense, but to indicate the way in which the forces of production had become organized on antisocial lines. This search for the origins of monopolism led him directly to Adam Smith. His contention that the Smithian framework was merely transitory not only prevented a facile acceptance of laissez-faire but also encouraged an endeavor to include the needs of the community in any doctrine of property: "Institutions stand or fall by their philosophy, and the main doctrine of industry since Adam Smith has been the fallacy that the self-interest of the individual was a sufficient guide to the welfare of the individual and society. Heralded as a final truth of 'science' this proves to have been nothing higher than a temporary formula for a passing problem. It was a reflection in words of the policy of the day." Since the advent of capitalism, "every one has been scurrying about to get what he could," an exploitation of new opportunities on no "broader basis than private enterprise, personal adventure." These centuries were marked by competition, hostility, fragmentation, all in opposition to an ethically founded mutuality based on the rule of and humane precepts of law: "In trade men have not yet risen to the level of the family life of the animals. The true law of business is that all must pursue the interest of all. In the law, the highest product of civilization, this has long been a commonplace. The safety of the people is the supreme law. We are in travail to bring industry up to this." Contrariwise, under unrestrained individualism, the law had been drained of its moral standing, leaving only arbitrariness: "Our century of the caprice of the individual as the law-giver of the common toil, to employ or disemploy, to start or stop, to open or close, to compete or combine, has been the disorder of the school while the master slept." Lloyd regarded the dichotomy between individual and social principles as not only false ("In the ultimate which the mathematician, the poet, the reformer projects the two will coincide"), but harmful, because it represented a profounder structural disjunction of the industrial and political spheres of society: "As gods we are but half-grown. For a hundred years or so our economic theory has been one of industrial government by the self-interest of the individual. Political government by the self-interest of the individual we call anarchy. It is one of the paradoxes of public opinion that the people of

America, least tolerant of this theory of anarchy in political government, lead in practising it in industry. Politically, we are civilized; industrially, not yet."[2] His aphoristic conclusion spoke volumes about the grounds for his intended reconstruction of the social order.

First, it was imperative to reconceptualize the nature of self-interest so as to include the interests of the community, in order both to ensure the welfare of the masses and to correct the imbalance of industrial and political institutions. Lloyd observed: "We have not been able to see the people for the persons in it. But there is a people, and it is as different from a mere juxtaposition of persons as a globe of glass from the handful of sand out of which it was melted." Society had been endowed with a collective personality, not to obliterate the individual but to preserve each person's rights through a common structure of reciprocal obligations. This idea was initially stated in the form of a new and wider definition of laissez-faire that conformed to the requirements of a two-tiered framework, philosophical as well as economic in character. "The true *laissez-faire* is, let the individual do what the individual can do best, and let the community do what the community can do best. The *laissez-faire* of social self-interest, if true, cannot conflict with the individual self-interest, if true, but it must outrank it always." Lloyd was confident of the fusion of individual and social purposes because of the meaning he ascribed to civilization: "the process of making men citizens in their relations to each other, by exacting of each that he give to all that which he receives from all," thereby fixing the individual's fulfillment in a social matrix of rights. In contrast, the prevailing form of individualism had bred "that mêlée of injunctions, bayonets, idle men and idle machinery, rich man's fear of poor man and poor man's fear of starvation, we call trade and industry." This anarchic system of production was responsible for the contradictions found in society: "A partial truth universally applied as this of self-interest has been is a universal error. Everything goes to defeat. Highways are used to prevent travel and traffic. Ownership of the means of production is sought in order to 'shut down' production, and the means of plenty make famine." The "intolerabilities" of the age, as in "factory and mine where childhood is forbidden to become manhood and manhood is forbidden to die a natural death," reflected "the rule of private self-interest arrived at its destination."[3] Like monopoly, individual self-interest expressed a final stage of capitalism, in this case culminating in social cruelty and irrationality.

This principle was destructive to the process of capital accumulation as well. Lloyd turned to the anatomy of wealth as further illustration of uncontrollable power if not also criminality in the contemporary make-up of capitalism. His cryptic remark, "the lean kine of self-interest devour the fat kine," designed to show, as in urban decay and the failure to introduce safety equipment on railroads, the refusal to place human lives before "the scramble for private gain," equally applied to a broader set of dynamics in which wealth corrupted rather than enhanced social development: "We are very poor. The striking feature of our economic condition is our poverty, not our wealth. We make ourselves 'rich' by appropriating the property of others by methods which lessen the total property of all. Spain took such riches from America and grew poor. Modern wealth more and more resembles the winnings of speculators in bread during famine—worse, for to make the money it makes the famine." Material gain, especially when it was a product of despoliation, was not an index of achievement; the term "rich" had to have a wider referent, societal well-being, if it was to be compatible with economic vitality and political democracy. "What we call cheapness," Lloyd further noted, in obvious reference to the presumed benefits of the economy, "shows itself to be unnatural fortunes for a very few, monstrous luxury for them and proportionate deprivation for the people. . . . " This led to a whole train of abuses and "the progressive extinction of the independence of laboring men, and all business men except the very rich, and their reduction to a state of vassalage to lords or squires in each department of trade and industry." The class subordination attendant on the private concentration of wealth had clear political meaning: "If this be cheapness, it comes by the grace of the seller, and that is the first shape of dearness, as security in society by the grace of the ruler is the first form of insecurity." The vast extension of absentee ownership in which "all the profits flow to men who know nothing of the real business out of which they are made" only aggravated the problem of concentration, while rendering exploitation more impersonal. For Lloyd, such ownership typified the arbitrary nature of concentrated power—individuals "defying, though private citizens, all the forces and authorities of a whole people"—as well as the converse situation of the defenselessness of the community: "The dream of the king who wished that all his people had but one neck that he might decapitate them at one blow is realized to-day in this industrial garrote. The syndicate has but to turn its screw, and every neck begins to break." The imagery of absolutism was present; indeed, a reference to Captain Kidd represented the piratical character of existing practices, and there was also the sense of a criminal process at work: "Prices paid to such intercepters are not an exchange of service; they are ransom paid by the people for their lives."[4]

While Lloyd had not broken from capitalism, he developed an alternative conception of human betterment, primarily ethical, that elevated the principle of community over mere acquisitiveness through a notion of welfare as undivided: "Our nascent common-sense begins to see that the many must always lose where all spend their lives trying to get more than they give, and that all lose when any lose. The welfare of all is more than the welfare of the many, the few, or the one." The critical point was not that social benefits decreased when the profit motive operated (although for Lloyd this was a matrix of transactions in which mutual obligation had been denied), but that a just social order could not exist unless the framework of rights included *every* individual. Only through arrangements of strict equitableness, having universal application, could there be a common source of enforceable rights—a condition effectively nullified by the competitive pursuit of individual advantage and privilege. Lloyd's concern was not equalitarianism (although he tended toward this position); instead, he proposed a mutuality in social relations, insisting on the literal identity of interests of all the members of society and any single member as the practicable basis for the distribution and the security of rights. In its ethical guise, this formula of benefits had the sanction of history: "If all will sacrifice themselves, none need be sacrificed. But if one may sacrifice another, all are sacrificed. That is the difference between self-interest and other-self interest. In industry we have been substituting all the mean passions that can set man against man in place of the irresistible power of brotherhood. To tell us of the progressive sway of brotherhood in all human affairs is the sole message of history." Industry had to be brought within the cultural flow of political development. The deeper social process, occurring even "in the worst governments and societies," was "the ability of men to lead the life together," itself signifying the vitality of the cooperative impulses and their partial transcendence of stultifying forms that were at the base of the industrial experience: "It makes this fair world more fair to consider the loyalties, intelligences, docilities of the multitudes who are guarding, developing, operating with the faithfulness of brothers and the keen interest of owners properties and industries in which brotherhood is not known and their title is not more than a tenancy at will." Lloyd, in ascribing to workers the conduct of the productive system, not only questioned the role of owners in the economic process but also affirmed the potential liberation of energies under the rule of socially oriented values: "If mankind, driven by their fears and the greed of others, can do so well, what will be their productivity and cheer when the 'interest of all' sings them to their work?"[5]

Indeed, the more Lloyd probed the internal features of the prevailing structure, the greater the ethical division between self-interest and "other-self interest" appeared, and the more aware he became of the inability of a system founded on self-interest to satisfy the goal of a human community. He firmly stated the general proposition: "The man for himself destroys himself and all men; only society can foster him and them." But he also advanced to higher ground, castigating "the model merchant"—his term for the prototypic businessman—as "the cruelest fanatic in history," "the high-priest of the latest idolatry, the self-worship of self-interest," whose obsession with gain introduced "the poison of enmity" into trade, established rules of exchange to control "the ground we move on, the bodies we work with, and the necessaries we live by," and complicated economic procedures to prevent a "general comprehension and the general good." This emblematic figure defined the main features of the existing stage of society, a conjunction of the individual and the social structure indicative of mental deformity and systemic decay: "Business colors the modern world as war reddened the ancient world. Out of such delirium monsters are bred, and their excesses destroy the system that brought them forth. There is a strong suggestion of moral insanity in the unrelieved sameness of mood and unvarying repetition of one act in the life of the model merchant. . . . Only a lunatic is always smiling or always weeping or always clamoring for dividends. Eras show their last stages by producing men who sum up individually the morbid characteristics of the mass." Lloyd's term "moral insanity" was directed not to pathological but to intrinsic factors, a compulsive repetitiousness originating from the structure and values of society that revealed rigid defense mechanisms that shut out whatever did not conduce to materialistic striving. "The righteous indignation that other men feel against sin these men feel against that which withstands them." He did not caricature businessmen so much as identify an underlying characteristic of the prevailing social sensibility, an incapacity to experience human feelings, and a barrenness of ego that was expressed as ordinariness: "Sincere as rattlesnakes, they are selfish with the unconsciousness possible to only the entirely commonplace, without the curiosity to question their times or the imagination to conceive the pain they inflict, and their every ideal is satisfied by the conventionalities of church, parlor, and counting-room." Fittingly, he inverted Macaulay's warning on the danger of the lower classes, "Our barbarians come from above," to suggest both the recent origins of capitalist upper groups and their rejection of the limits of cultural restraint. More particularly, modern life had been drained of meaning: "To them science is but a never-ending répertoire of investments stored up by nature for the syndicates, government but a fountain of franchises, the nations but customers in squads, and a million the unit of a new arithmetic of wealth written for them." The political consequences, including the threat of repression, were inescapable: "They claim a power without control, exercised through forms which make it secret, anonymous, and perpetual. . . . They are gluttons of luxury and power, rough, unsocialized, believing that mankind must be kept terrorized."[6]

Following this comprehensive indictment of the existing order, a procedure that was essential to his articulation of a positive course, Lloyd turned from the individual to the systemic plane, largely remaining within capitalistic confines, to pursue his analysis of the integration of man and community, which he increasingly viewed in terms of industry and the political framework. Because he regarded political democracy as axiomatic—"a policy which, with whatever defects, is better than that which can be evolved by narrower or more selfish or less multitudinous influences of persons or classes"—he contended that in such a system power logically and ethically "should be taken up by the people." The literalism of Populist constructions was enlarged in meaning and scope to provide a more categorical statement of a people's government than was implied by the idea of pluralism or the several forms of a labor theory of value contained in the movement. As the primal base of the polity and economy, the people had to be confirmed in their rulership: "That which is must also seem. It is the people from whom come the forces with which kings and millionaires ride the world, and until the people take their proper place in the seat of sovereignty, these pseudo owners—mere claimants and usurpers—will, by the very falsity and iniquity of their position, be pushed into deceit, tyranny, and cruelty, ending in downfall." Unlike Donnelly, Lloyd did not fear the prospect of social breakdown, at least not in the same way. The pressing question was the locus of power, and if upper groups remained unbending—"Already the leader is unable to lead, and has begun to drive with judges armed with bayonets and Gatling guns"—there would still have to be a resolution of the conflict between "form and substance," the people and their just claims of governance. If some kind of clash was not inevitable, Lloyd nonetheless regarded the prevailing situation as untenable and concluded that force might be the necessary vehicle for realizing democratic change: "Unless we reform of our own free will, nature will reform us by force, as nature does." Of course, his preference was for the former way: "Has not man, who has in personal reform risen above the brute method, come to the height at which he can achieve social reform in masses and by nations? We must learn; we can learn by reason. Why wait for the crueler teacher?" But, precisely because of his evolutionary vision, he would not be deterred; the progressive historical development of humanity gave promise of further improvement: "The secret of the history we are about to make is not that the world is poorer or worse. It is richer and better. Its new wealth is too great for the old forms. The success and beauties of our old mutualities have made us ready for new mutualities." In a protosocialist vein,

Lloyd had blended structural and ethical principles in adjusting productive forces to new forms of organization: "The wonder of to-day is the modern multiplication of products by the union of forces; the marvel of to-morrow will be the greater product which will follow when that which is co-operatively produced is co-operatively enjoyed."[7]

Lloyd's purpose, at one with his specifically humanistic contribution, was the translation of ethical precepts into social practice, an institutionalization of love within the structure of society. He did not want pious platitudes ("All the runs and trills and transpositions have been done to death"), but "epigrams of practice." The individual was to be more directly incorporated into a context favoring the development of collective human potentialities: " 'Regenerate the individual' is a half-truth; the reorganization of the society which he makes and which makes him is the other half. . . . Love is a half-truth, and kissing is a good deal less than half of that. We need not kiss all our fellow-men, but we must do for them all we ask them to do for us—nothing less than the fullest performance of every power. To love our neighbor is to submit to the discipline and arrangement which make his life reach its best, and so do we best love ourselves." Whether or not the words "fullest performance" referred to the powers of government as well as to human potential, Lloyd was clear about the need for a concrete situation in which to embody social ideals: "History has taught us nothing if not that men can continue to associate only by the laws of association."[8]

More particularly, the role of the people, already considered to be fundamental in political society, had to be given the same importance in industry. "The new self-interest will remain unenforced in business until we invent the forms by which the vast multitudes who have been gathered together in modern production can organize themselves into a people there as in government." Unless "this institutionalization," tantamount to the achievement of (a not clearly specified) industrial democracy, occurred, the people could not be prevented "from being scattered away from each other again," destroying the mutuality so essential to a reconstruction of the total polity. On the structural level, the prerequisite for realizing "a people in industry" was the absolute denial of private encroachment in the public sphere, not least because this intrusion could shatter the unity, the shared identity gained through collective endeavors, of the new system: "There must be no private use of public power or public property. These are created by the common sacrifices of all, and can be rightfully used only for the common good of all—from all, by all, for all. All the grants and franchises that have been given to private hands for private profit are void in morals and void in that higher law which sets the copy for the laggard pens of legislatures and judges." The terms were expressly political in character and even restorative, as is clear when Lloyd observed concerning the evolutionary progression of rights: "In nothing has liberty justified itself more thoroughly than in the resolute determination spreading among the American people to add industrial to political independence."[9]

What was distinctive, however, was the additional prerequisite for "a people in industry," a principle of *social* individuation that was far in advance of American, if not also European, thought at that time. Law would provide the framework in which man's multiform responsibilities would engender a higher development of the self: "We can become individual only by submitting to be bound to others. We extend our freedom only by finding new laws to obey. Life outside the law is slavery on as many sides as there are disregarded laws. The locomotive off its tracks is not free. The more relations, ties, duties, the more 'individual.' " His vision of mutual obligation, as the social complement of cooperative production, led to what might be termed a modern commonwealth man, enriched for having experienced "the life together": "The isolated man is the mere rudiment of an individual. But he who has become citizen, neighbor, friend, brother, son, husband, father, fellow-member, in one, is just by so many times individualized."[10]

Lloyd concluded his prescription for democratic social change by reaffirming the institutional possibilities that he located in America's exceptionalism. The arbitrary power of monopolism "has found a people so disciplined by the aspiration and achievement of political and religious rights that they are already possessed of a body of doctrine capable, by an easy extension, of refuting all the pretensions of the new absolutism." Although he here cited Hamilton as an authority who recognized the need to align industrial with political and religious liberty, the point took on a more subtle meaning. America had exhibited "an acuter and extremer" form of capitalist development than other nations; this fact both revealed glaring systemic abuses to "a free people" and placed the society "at the front of the forward line of evolution."[11] This conscious awareness of political and social deprivation and objective consolidation of monopolism were bringing matters to a head.

For Lloyd, the disjunction between the industrial and political spheres, because it was based on the unrestrained and accelerated growth of industry, inspired the hope of finding the solution partly in an optimistic reading of the evolutionary course itself: "The hope is that the old economic system we inherited has ripened so much more rapidly than the society and government we have created that the dead matter it deposits can be thrown off by our vigorous youth and health." Paradoxically, the traditional elements of culture became the source of rejuvenation. This was a necessary conclusion for him to reach because of the ethical primacy of his argument, in which political and religious rights *were* the historical agents of democracy, and because of the manifest inadequacy of internal capitalist features in themselves to serve as the basis for change. Stating that "bad wealth" (a term taken from Emerson) had assumed "its monstrous forms so fast that the dullest eye can separate it from the Commonwealth," Lloyd merged evolution and ethics in a pattern of institutional development for the future: "In making themselves free of arbitrary and corrupt power in government the Americans prepared themselves to be free in all else, and because foremost in political liberty they have the promise of being the first to realize industrial liberty—the trunk of a tree of which political liberty is the seed, and without which political liberty shrinks back into nothingness."[12]

The notion of welfare as undivided had now been applied to liberty, which was its implementing force. Lloyd thus returned to the political and legal matrix as a means of affirming man's capabilities for self-government through a process of disciplined sharing: "Infinite is the fountain of our rights. We can have all the rights we will create. All the rights we will give we can have. The American people will save the liberties they have inherited by winning new ones to bequeath." This dynamic sense of social advancement, having less to do with evolution than human volition (the other side of finding the solution), lay in the attraction of America as an idealized heritage of basic rights. "Those who love the liberties already won must open the door to the new, unless they wish to see them all take flight together. There can be no single liberty." With the rise of a new social consciousness, penetrating all areas of life, the ethical permeation of economic structure would be accomplished: "Generals were, merchants are, brothers will be, humanity's representative men." Asserting that "the only true guidance comes from those who are led, and the only valid titles from those who create," Lloyd distilled the essence of, and perhaps took a step beyond, the Populist vision of man *in* community: "There is to be a people in industry, as in government."[13]

2. Prerogatives of Nationhood

Lloyd provided the basis for the idea of a people's government. Peffer and Weaver gave this idea a concrete meaning. Peffer's analysis was a response to the economic setting of pervasive hardship, financial contraction, and concentrated holdings, matters which he viewed as crucial to the broader statement of political sovereignty. On the farmers' subordination to dominant economic groups, he noted: "They toiled while others took the increase; they sowed, but others reaped the harvest. It is avarice that despoiled the farmer. Usury absorbed his substance. He sweat gold, and the money changers coined it. And now, when misfortunes gather about and calamity overtakes him, he appeals to those he has enriched only to learn how poor and helpless he is alone." Even the sober-minded Peffer had reserves of untapped anger. He went on to speak of a monied upper class as a group of gamblers dignified by social standing, men "with millions of dollars at their call, governments at their command, and a loyal people in their service," individuals, then, "whose acquisitions are only what their fellows have lost," and who, "without conscience," believe themselves "specially commissioned to prey upon the people," or, in fine, a "pampered aristocracy living off the wreakage of commerce, who rake in a railroad, a state, or a nation with equal complacency. . . ." The sentence rolled thunderously on, denouncing men "masquerading as philanthropists and patriots while they are despoiling a nation," pointing anew to the Populist contention that private sovereignty had displaced public sovereignty. The financial core of business appeared particularly egregious to Peffer: "Every trust and combine made to rob the people had its origin in the example of Wall Street dealers. Touch any spring along the keyboard of commercial gambling and a Wall Street sign appears. This dangerous power which money gives is fast undermining the liberties of the people."[14]

While in the 1950s the mention of Wall Street was regarded as evidence of Populist dementia, one can presently entertain the wider import of the term and recognize its utterly realistic usage. It was intended as an ideological notation to signify a fully realized structure of power in America. This conception further pointed to nonproductive capitalism as the defining systemic trait, and, more particularly in Peffer than in many western Populists, it was directed to monetary and banking policies as the principal leverage for achieving national control. "Money is the great issue—all others pale into insignificance before this, the father of them." Many within Populism indicted the corporate structure, as Peffer did elsewhere in his book, but what was representative was his emphasis on the usurpation of power which derived from private dominance, whether it was rooted in the financial sector or the comprehensive economic system. From a detailed case study of Treasury efforts to counteract a "stringency in the money market," a phrase he placed in quotations to indicate banker-created disturbances, Peffer showed through reports of the Secretary on the extent of bond purchases that an informal partnership of government and business already existed. Peffer moved the money issue outside a conspiratorial framework to the more specific ground of state partiality toward upper groups, which fostered the process of capital accumulation. Private activism and government complicity, as interrelated determinants of the financial question, furnished the baseline for his commentary on the nature of sovereignty. Even here, he ascribed a significance to money beyond its nominal meaning; in Populism basic issues of whatever character usually returned the discussion to political fundamentals: "This brings us to where we can understand what the real function of money is— namely, *to serve a public use*."[15]

Peffer assumed a capitalistic economy. He also relied on the constitutional setting for his definition of government powers and to a surprising extent, in building the case for a paramount authority, appropriated the original Federalist argument for conferring to the state that specific power which acts directly on the people. Equally instructive, though, is the transmutation of this potentially conservative articulation of forces into a vital antimonopolist perspective. This was accomplished by emphasizing the principle of a literal construction of the Constitution: Notwithstanding his premise of capitalism, the power to regulate commerce extended Federalist notions to unrecognizable lengths. The prerogatives of sovereignty, centered on regulation, in behalf of the public's well-being, promoted a decidedly extracapitalist conclusion. The state, because it was charged with the authority to act directly, did not require (and it would be derelict in allowing) capitalistic intermediaries to perform government functions in its place. Insisting that money be endowed with a public character, and placed under the commerce power, opened the pathway to a noninhibitory declaration, just as the similar conception of public ownership of railroads led to a wide-ranging statement of sovereign rights in relation to capitalism. Where government had jurisdiction, it had to act. On the level now under consideration, this too was part of the movement's credo. It had particular relevance to the way in which a capitalist political economy should be administered in its public aspects.

Thus, Peffer established the context for the analysis of money: "What the highway and its moving vehicles laden with produce do in the movement of commodities, money in circulation does in exchange of values; as it is with the highways, so it is with money—the function of both is to serve a public use." He continued, "let it be understood, to begin with, that the underlying proposition involved is that *money is a necessary instrument of commerce*."[16] Capitalist transactions were normalized, and hence assumed and fit into place. Meanwhile, Peffer directed attention simultaneously to the state's precedent claims of supervision and to monopolistic restrictive practices which interrupted the ordinary flow of commerce. To reflect capitalist premises did not ensure against structural criticisms. Indeed, at the heart of the Populist amalgam of ideas, this seemed actually to generate confidence that modifications of capitalism were entirely legitimate.

Peffer turned next to this dimension of the Populist argument.

It represented a confluence of constitutional literalism and faith in America, which was intended not to fend off opposition but to affirm the sources from which the movement drew in sanctioning change: "This proposition is not a new one. It has been suggested many times by economists, by statesmen, by lawyers in their briefs, and by courts in judicial decisions. Daniel Webster, in some of his most memorable speeches, asserted the doctrine. The Supreme Court of the United States has affirmed it, and it probably will not be disputed by any person claiming to have thought upon the subject. It is well that this be kept in mind." The tone, if partly chiding, was matter-of-fact. It was as though the neglected truth of public sovereignty needed only to be returned to the present agenda. The political didacticism evident here was the more explosive for its textbook-civics character; a laborious, inch-by-inch case was presented to buttress *existing* constitutional authority: "Money is a *necessary* instrument of commerce—not simply an instrument, but a NECESSARY instrument. Let it be inquired at this point why the people empowered Congress to regulate commerce among the several States? What is it to have such a thing as a regulation of commerce? Why is Congress authorized to levy duties upon imports? Why is Congress authorized to levy taxes upon the people? There is but one answer. All of these things are public functions, and besides being public functions they are classed among the prerogatives of sovereignty."[17]

By regularizing procedures in this manner, Peffer, through an emphasis on public functions, conveyed the unmistakable impression of the neutral state. Yet by that reasoning, the state had not been commissioned in the service of capitalism. Sovereignty, as a principle, was brought forward. But so also was the conjunction of people and nationhood, which Peffer stated with stunning simplicity: "The people of the United States constitute a nation." These words would be by turns nonessential, laughable, redundant, if one were unprepared to listen. As the basis for the state's popular foundations, their effect, to Populists at least, was incalculable. After taking note of the three branches, which "combined are called the 'Government,' " he proceeded with the lesson to exactly that end: "Acting in harmony they are an agent of the people for the purpose of executing the popular will."[18]

Peffer democratized Hamilton, or rather, to distinguish his own effort from that of Herbert Croly two decades later, he eviscerated the Hamiltonian economic premises at the same time that he retained the formal political framework. Meanwhile, he also conserved the Federalist logic on the ratification of the Constitution so as to assure, unlike Hamilton *or* Croly, the preponderance of democratic social elements. That Peffer again treated capitalism in such stringent terms (as a paradigm of exchange per se) shifted the priorities to the state in its mass-political dimensions:

The reason why Congress was authorized to take charge of the commerce of the people is that when the people of the several States undertook to regulate commercial affairs among themselves it was found to be utterly impracticable. One of the principal reasons for adopting the Constitution and organizing a new government under it was that there might be a central authority somewhere to exercise the sovereign power of the people. Commerce means simply trading among the people, selling and buying, buying and selling, carrying property, exchanging values, moving things from place to place. The people are all alike interested in this matter, and for that reason chiefly the Government is empowered to take charge of it and to regulate it—not to please the Government, but in the interest of the people.[19]

The state had been partially extricated from its mandate of servicing capitalism. It was to become the facilitator of economic circulation rather than a structural harbinger of the new corporate order. Most appropriately, Peffer turned next to the place where the community most conveniently (in theory) asserted itself, the right of eminent domain. In this regard, the state's role of facilitation was not surrendered, nor, of course, was confiscation remotely mentioned. Yet a subtle alteration occurred. The emphasis was given to "eminent" as opposed to "domain" or the two words in combination, signifying governmental supremacy in its real and potential application (with specific reference to property), rather than indicating the concrete steps of expediential clearing-away. The difference was between the announcement of a sovereign power, connoting guardianship and responsibility for the whole of society, and the technical, pragmatic rules invoked to remove obstacles to current projects.

Following the statement on government's being empowered to take charge of and regulate commerce, he continued, using "power" and "public" as his operative words: "From that comes the power to open and maintain thoroughfares; from that comes the power to take away lands belonging to the people; to move their houses and their fixed improvements in order that a highway may be opened there, that a canal may be cut through, or a railway constructed. These things are done in the public interest, for the common good. The land is taken because the public demands it; the property is used because the public wants it; it is all done to promote the general welfare." Though Peffer had not quite said so, he intended that the principle of eminent domain would confer the same public character on the objectives served in its execution. Thus, he added: "The railroad is as much a need of commerce as the common highway—indeed, it is much more important now, if such a thing could be, than the common highway, because producer and consumer are many miles apart." After reflecting on this distance, as affecting both markets and production, and noting further the staggering volume of America's "internal trade," he also included within this frame of reference a second basic factor related to commerce: "One of the essential parts of this vast system of trade, absolutely necessary for transacting it, is money. Without money commerce would cease; without money all movement of trade would stop; without money there would be no business; all exchange would be barter, and that would take us back to barbarism."[20]

There was nothing Machiavellian about including both factors. After all, it was not eminent domain that concerned him, but the larger authorization of power of which it was a special and highly illustrative case. On this ground, because all were "alike interested," the "common good" was involved, and the "general welfare" was promoted, regulation subsumed the effective means (here railroads and the money-system) for its faithful and efficient performance. What began as a formalistic diagram of capitalist requirements gave place, once their necessary character was made plain, to a statement and structure of public superintendence. The role of conservation was conversely one of control. The assumption of capitalism encouraged, more than it discouraged, the independent formation that, in the name of lubricous economic processes, nevertheless curtailed the ultimate political influence of the capitalistic starting point.

In fusing Hamilton and John Marshall, Peffer produced a characteristic Populist hybrid: a literalism of eminent domain, which permitted the specification in detail of whatever conduced to the implementation of the enumerated powers. The caption sentence may be taken as the accepted standard: "If, then, Congress is authorized to regulate *commerce* among the several States, it is also authorized to regulate the *instruments of* commerce." The field of implementation, however, was another matter. In constitutional form, it gave rise to un-Marshallian substantive rights. The mantle of sovereign prerogatives was thrown around public ownership itself, as the logical and practical corollary of eminent domain. In the process, Marshall's (and Hamilton's) safeguarding of the entrepreneurial function, presumably the immanent goal in the enlargement of national power, was downgraded as obstructing, through capitalist intermediaries, the state's rightful sphere of competence, as well as its authority to act directly on the people:

It may prescribe what kinds of roads and ways shall be opened; what kinds of vehicles shall be run on them; what shall be the rate of toll; whether, indeed, any person other than authorized agents of the Government shall be permitted to manage and to control the ways. The same power which authorizes the Government to open and maintain highways, post roads, and the like authorizes it to build roads for the people without the intervention of any corporation whatever; to build the roads, to own them, to manage them in the interest of the people; and this right to regulate commerce includes necessarily—not only impliedly, but *necessarily*—every function essential to the work.[21]

A clearer statement of Populist constitutionalism could not be asked. Once the enumeration of powers has been literalized, it became the charter right for undiluted, as well as extensive *and* extensible, powers. Corporate intervention was not wanted. Nor could government be restricted from translating the ground plan of regulation into the concrete services which went beyond implementation to the actual public displacement of private operations. The initial blueprint supposed basic areas of jurisdiction. But it also complemented the mere pronouncement of a public mandate. The state's performance, under the criterion of essentiality, was such that functions were now broadly conceived to mean the appropriation of specific modes which satisfied the purpose and spirit of regulation. Where powers were applicable, the means themselves, Peffer reasoned, should take on a public character.

Instruments of commerce had tangibleness as mechanisms, physical objects, rights-of-way. They had not been abstracted as residues of power but rather became the direct material embodiment of sovereignty. The construction he put upon railroads was equally clear in his discussion of the money system: "That makes it plain that it is not only within the province and power of the people through their agent, the Government, to regulate money as an instrument of commerce, but to regulate its quantity, to regulate the manner of its issuance, to dictate the material out of which it shall be made, to prescribe the form, the inscriptions, and devices which shall appear upon it, to prescribe the amount which shall be issued, the channels through which it shall reach the people, and to regulate the charges for its use."[22] What has been termed a "specification in detail" signified more: responsibilities which were indivisible from the originating power. This no longer referred to the process of circulation alone, but to the content of the political structure in which the instruments of commerce were to operate. The financial question implied a reconstitution of governing authority. If conservation had led to control, facilitation, while leaving capitalism intact, had denied to the political economy principal sources of enrichment and the sinews of corporate aggrandizement. For the banking structure as then privately constituted was bypassed.

Paradoxically, the Populist dedication to capitalism stimulated Populists to attempt the removal of capitalism's ideological and structural leading edge, an uncontested property right which had reached fruition in concentrated wealth (particularly within the public sector, as Peffer defined it). A specific capitalist formation had been affirmed, founded on antimonopolist principles which of themselves incorporated significant provision for government's intercessory role. Monetary and banking policy became the test of sovereignty. For Peffer, the specific traits of money (material, form, inscriptions) were clearly secondary to the wide swath of governmental power cut into current private operations. This affected not only the volume and velocity of money but also the source of authority and the nature of the goals to be served: whether government or the banking system would define monetary values, create the institutional framework for the issuance and circulation of currency, determine the availability and particular means of credit, and more concretely (the function to which Peffer was leading) regulate the rate of interest as well as the forms of acceptable security.

If only the test of sovereignty were involved, however, the outcome might well have been that which would result from the Federal Reserve System a quarter-century later. Formalistic state authority would preside over a privately rationalized and dominated banking structure, with government providing the imprimatur, centralizing apparatus, and public resources to foster stability in and copartnership with the financial community. But Peffer's discussion extended further. In principle, he already assumed the foregoing powers in regulating money and banking. He then actualized sovereignty by calling for direct government-to-people arrangements. This moved the entire range of functions under state auspices: "If, then, the Government may not only make the money as it is doing now—that is to say, performing the mechanical work—and dictate the material out of which it shall be made and regulate its value, but also regulate the manner of its issuance and provide the ways and means by which it shall reach the people, and may also regulate the rate of charges to be exacted for its use among the people, there is no reason why the Government should not do for the people directly what it is now doing for them indirectly through banking institutions, and permitting the banks to charge a very high percentage for their services."[23]

This was what was intended by the elimination of intermediaries. Categories of regulation had sanctioned in the past the private conduct of fundamental affairs. These categories were nevertheless intact, available, and only waited upon the restoration of a guiding public authority. The general interest could theoretically be implemented. This principle was indirectly lent credence by the way in which the private sector had thus far preempted (and all but destroyed) governmental functions. The general interest could also be practically realized, on sounder and more consistent grounds, through the state's fulfillment of its public obligations, rooted in its sovereign, constitutional make-up. For Peffer, this was particularly true of the necessity for cheap credit, which was perhaps the key feature, in his analysis, to democratizing the financial structure. The provision of credit had wider political moment in reversing the processes of wealth-concentration and the consequent impoverishment of producing groups: "If the Government may issue a hundred million dollars in bank notes to banking corporations upon deposit of Government bonds as security and then permit the banks to lend that money to the people at 10 per cent interest, what is to hinder the Government from lending the money directly to the people and taking their property as security, just as the banks do?"[24]

Sometimes the immediate purpose of the discussion was rudimentary, which was an unpromising context for the statement of high principle. Yet what distinguished Populists in this regard was that their arguments combined general propositions and concrete demands as interrelated thrusts. The issue of sovereignty was in part used deductively. It became a means to identify concrete areas in which governmental responsibility was held to be deficient. It served as well to demonstrate that economic questions were ultimately political questions, affecting the very character and prospects of popularly founded authority. But the specific nature of Populist grievances contributed to a flow in both directions. In Peffer's case, the question of interest rates prompted an inductive chain of criticisms leading to public governance, because practices which reflected state abdication and private encroachment were in dispute. When Populists established that a basis for the violation of rights was present, focused generalizations were possible: "So, we see, we now have all the necessary machinery ready for the inauguration and management of a system by which the people can control their own financial affairs in their own way."[25]

3. An Indivisible Sovereign Power

Weaver's political analysis was likewise a response to the economic setting, chiefly, the powers which had been bestowed on the corporate form:

The corporation and the wealth which it brings have become the chief concern of society and the State. The man and the family have been driven to the wall, the weak trampled under foot and the choicest opportunities of the century showered upon chartered combinations. Wealth, already posssessing great advantages, is not satisfied, and incorporates in order that it may have still greater power. Every class of business, every calling, everything except poverty, operates under a charter. . . . Competition and personal responsibility, except with the remaining multitude of the poor, are literally and absolutely annihilated by these monstrous combinations.

Again, Populism's implicit dedication to capitalism was expressed through its opposition to the prevailing form of capitalism; the "choicest opportunities" had been "showered upon chartered combinations." Structural restrictiveness and the loss of moral obligation figured alongside the more evident governmental favoritism signaled in the use of charters. More to the point was the factor of power itself. The unmolested private organization of power represented an increasing regularization of the social order on lines which were patterned after monopolism. Only the poor were purposefully excluded, or as Weaver stated: "The poor must defend themselves as best they can, single-handed and alone."[26]

He presumed that the state should be protective as well as independent. The insistence on independence was telling in that it was counterpoised to corporate features of anonymity that tended to maximize private controls while minimizing customary elements of restraint. As preliminary ground for the treatment of sovereignty, he spoke of the "supplimentary [*sic*] harvest of injustice and wrong doing which results from the creation of a horde of artificial persons, who are void of the feelings of pity and the compunctions of conscience," in substance, excess repression beyond the normal workings of mankind that were subject to "moral and legal accountability,"[27] and betraying the callousness associated with irresponsible power that the state had to curb. Indeed in its own right, the state had to reflect the opposite, a synthesis of responsibility and compassion.

The documentation of concentrated wealth, landlordism, railroad-mining pools, lobbying of unsavory kinds, jobbery affecting public lands, and the human devastation attendant on employers' lockouts and coercion had stimulated Weaver to outbursts which were uncharacteristically heated. On one occasion, he observed: "How completely do these statements and figures demonstrate the truth that our economic troubles are the results of puerile and vicious systems—systems born of avarice and upheld for plunder." On another, he stated: "But let us see if we are not traveling with frightful velocity along the same road which led

Rome to the grave." And again, following the analysis of income distribution, he warned: "These colossal fortunes have no parallel in the annals of the world. Unless the causes which have produced them be speedily removed they foreshadow the utter destruction of republican institutions and the inauguration of another tragic era in the history of civilization." Finally, at the heart of Weaver's indictment was a tremendous and enlarging discrepancy between America's productive and natural wealth, and the realities of mass impoverishment. This prompted him to ask: "By what evil genius are we controlled? Is there some fell spirit at the helm determined to drive our bark upon the rocks?"[28]

The inner motif concerned systemic dislocation. There was a shabbiness of private greed, intensified by the opportunities afforded by a government which had neither exercised checks nor provided definite guidance. The corporation, filling this vacuum, extended not only the range of possibilities for gain but also its direct influences upon the state. Private sovereignty cast a lengthening shadow. As the last question implied, the ship of state was endangered and needlessly floundering. This highlighted once more the importance attached to a proper framework of governance. Resuming his characteristic evenness, Weaver asserted the necessity of expansive public powers: "We submit that it is the duty of the American people to immediately search out the causes of these conceded evils and this growing discontent; and we must apply, and apply quickly, the amplest remedies which good hearts and wise heads can devise."[29]

As further preliminary ground in the context of the silver issue, Weaver again took note of the massive discrepancy between productive wealth and existing poverty. He tacitly posed a standard of what *might* be, were potential and actual performances matched. The exhilaration but added to a sense of needless and indeed anachronistic deprivation; in sum, the lack of fulfillment was correctible:

The Government of the United States is in its youth. Our resources of every description necessary to human comfort and advancement, are without a parallel. Our population, when compared with our inhabitable area and generous resources of soil, climate and products, is but meagre. With such surroundings as these it is right that we should look for happiness and contentment among the people. Instead, however, we find that discontent, debt and destitution exist throughout every state and territory in the Union. . . . We find millions of people homeless and out of employment; millions more in danger of losing their homes, and still more millions working for wages scarcely sufficient to sustain life and respectability and so meager as to shut out hope for the future.

The situation was correctible, and it was imperative that it be corrected; the initial positive accent rendered more plausible a turning to government, as the logical beneficiary of a nation's trust and affirmation of its democratic heritage. But more, the existent social misery, which openly violated reasonable expectations of popular contentment, self-evidently heightened the contrast between potentiality and actuality, compounded the perception of wrong, and reinforced the turning toward government for relief and rectification. Having shown the harshness of business practice through much of the book, Weaver then dealt in masterful under-statement: "These things result neither from pestilence nor fam-ine. The situation is full of the most aggravating contradictions."[30]

Singular in Weaver was the feeling of newness, vastness, oppor-tunity, and underlying this, the conviction that a challenge await-ed the nation. This once more enlivened the receptive attitude to-ward government:

This destitution, low condition of wages, idleness, debt, and this home-less condition among so many people—all of these distressing things—exist along side of abundant crops, within sight of millions of acres of unoccupied land and in spite of the fact that three-fourths of our country is still in the rough, new, unfinished and sadly in need of labor. . . . It is certainly the duty of statesmen, philosophers, philanthropists and chris-tian people to search out the real causes of these distressing evils. And having ascertained the cause or causes, it is their duty to remove the sources of irritation if within the range of human power.[31]

If, clearly, those thoughtful persons to whom fell the burden of discovering causes indicated Weaver's essential moderation, it is also true that "within the range of human power" bespoke a disposition that would entertain more fully realized conceptions of sovereignty than was the wont of Americans generally.

It was the highly specific discussion of the national debt that furnished the departure for his commentary. Defying conventional wisdom, he started by rejecting the analogy between the individ-ual and the state (as though each must balance a household ac-count in the same way). The importance of the distinction rested on the ability not only to confer collective rights on the state, but to ascribe to it paramount authority over all internal elements. Weaver did as much, without reifying the state as a separable force above its social base:

> When misfortune befalls an individual and he is forced to make expenditures which exceed both his store of money and available resources, he is likely to become the victim of avarice and fall into the clutches of those who possess that which he does not—ready cash. Few men under such circumstances are strong enough to avoid this common fate. An individual can simply direct his own actions and is only partially Sovereign over himself. As to all other persons he must control them, if at all, by contract or persuasion. But an independent and powerful Nation, if wisely governed, is not subject to such limitations and vicissitudes. The Nation is supreme and rules over the whole body as an individual controls his own person. It commands and every member, the head, the eye, the ear, the tongue, the hands, the feet—the whole organic structure must obey.[32]

If he has questioned budgetary maxims which persist even today, his purpose was not to make a case for deficit spending. Instead, he pressed for the more inclusive principle of autonomous governmental control regarding not simply the financial structure but all realms of political relationships and affairs.

Power becomes so astonishingly sweeping, by the logic of an undivided sovereignty, that Weaver had to start with the parenthetic insertion "if wisely governed" to establish from the outset some form of self-braking device or norm. Here, the matter-of-factness that was typical of Populism, when combined with the cogency of the preliminary ground, produced an apparently categorical formulation very like that of Hobbes: "No member of the body politic can become so great as to rise above, none so insignificant as to fall below the control of the Sovereign will. If circumstances warrant, the Sovereign hand can be laid upon the persons, the property, the commerce, and even the lives of its subjects."[33] In capitalizing "sovereign," Weaver, assessing the needs of the twentieth century, betrayed a nice eighteenth-century sensibility on fundamental matters. In the powers claimed for it, his "Sovereign hand" displayed little resemblance to Adam Smith's more invisible variety, still less, to John Locke's natural-state primordialities.

Technically, no social compact was specified; again, interestingly, this was in the same vein as Hobbes (as I see the latter's compact theory). In both, the reason was that the supremacy of the governing structure had to be demonstrated, if necessary, even at the expense, as Weaver explicitly stated, of property. "If circumstances warrant" was quite un-Lockean, however, on the still more compelling ground that the positive impetus had been supplied to state activism. The only construction that allowed a semblance of compact (since Hobbes and Weaver both rejected formal assent) was the presumed obligation of sovereign power to perform those functions mandated by its creation, in Weaver's case, those affecting and benefiting the general interest. Neither man was a lover of despotism, though a Lockean bias in present-day social analysis would have us believe this of Hobbes (largely because he had the preliberal temerity to set up claims which antecede that of property). Weaver, despite the breadth of the power he assigned to government, made abundantly clear that, as in Hobbes's case, sovereignty must observe internal sources of restraint. There was a moral obligation of responsible expression, which at the same time could not be permitted to limit powers exercised within the sphere of proper activities. Thus, Weaver stated: "That power so vast should be exercised with prudence and caution none will gainsay. But Government was created to meet and master emergencies with which individual powers and capacities are inadequate to cope."[34]

This was a more logically tight and extended statement of Lewelling's meliorative doctrine (an injunction to protect the weak). It also denied the latter's release from the compact as presented in his Kansas inaugural. But Weaver was at pains to be strict, not to deprive individuals of rights, but on the contrary, to insist that sovereignty should in fact act to its fullest capabilities and not surrender its jurisdiction to the private sphere. Actually, for him despotism lay with the reverse situation of inaction. To the degree that sovereignty incorporated and represented the people's will, a refrainment from acting was an obvious violation of the public trust. It signified the consequent undermining of confidence in government's potentialities, thus positively encouraging the rise of forces of usurpation, because they were private in character.

In himself mentioning despotism, Weaver assumed the initiative in arguing that public functions could not be privately administered. This was a more rigorous path to common Populist doctrine. Differently stated, sovereign power was most consistent when most utilized (a proposition Hobbes could have lived with comfortably):

Each individual member of society consented to the full exercise of this power when his citizenship began, and this consent can neither be withdrawn nor ignored; neither can the primal functions of Government ever be rightfully surrendered. What moral right have the rulers and lawmakers of a Sovereign and Independant [*sic*] Nation to refuse to exercise the legitimate powers entrusted to their care? What right have they to dethrone their Sovereign and send him forth into the market as an individual to beg where he should command, or to borrow where he should create? It is worse than the sale of the purple to the highest bidder; it is equivalent to advertising for a despot, an offer in advance to present him with the purple gratis when he shall appear, and finally to put the people under tribute to him and his successors forever.[35]

Consent and primal functions became fused. They comprised a core of public sovereignty. It was clear that the "rulers and lawmakers" were not the nation, did not of themselves express sovereign power, and again as in standard Populist doctrine, only represented an antecedent structure of fundamental rights. These rights could not be surrendered if independence for the state and freedom for its individuals were to be retained. For Weaver, as for the generality of Populists, extensible powers were profoundly linked with constitutionalism, focused in the government's charge to act on the people's behalf.

Weaver's illustration indicated the wider implications of the preceding passage. The sovereign being sent forth "into the market as an individual" meant that not only was governmental independence nullified (as self-creative power and authority), but the state as such was reduced to the characteristic uncertainty and powerlessness found in individuals, especially when placed at the mercy of stronger parties. The market of course signified exactly that, for in the context of national debt the state had to beg and borrow, not create and command. It had to depend on capitalist financial groups for its economic survival rather than in its own name determining the fiscal and monetary policies suitable to its needs and autonomy. Moreover, for Weaver the phrase "to him and his successors forever" expressed the ultimate negation of sovereignty in that it suggested the fear of a permanent reversal of democracy. Private forces, by gaining control of the vital processes of the state, would establish and perpetuate their rulership in a qualitatively different, that is, nondemocratic, formation.

Throughout, the specificity of these concerns made his framework of philsophic inquiry the more remarkable. Beyond the patent abrogation of sovereignty, under private influences, Weaver was protesting the movement toward an inverted compact in which government was the consenting and subordinative element and business the new locus of authority: a *dethronement* treated in literal fashion. He continued on the related trends of abdication and reversal: "The policy of public borrowing is subversive of sovereignty and is as illogical as it is full of evil consequences. No other system could possibly be devised that is so well calculated to enthrone the capitalistic classes among the nations of the earth." The structural shaping of the inverted compact issued from what he termed the refusal "to exercise the legitimate powers entrusted to their [policymakers] care" and raised the specter, with the creation of a new regime, of none other than private sovereignty: an accelerating counterlogic, founded on control of the nation's finances:

If a Nation becomes involved in war when its current revenues and available resources, as ordinarily understood, are inadequate to meet the strain, it must, nevertheless, have money or perish from the face of the earth. Resort is generally had to borrowing, either from its own citizens or from foreign capitalists. This implies a contract into which the capitalist, of his own volition, may or may not enter. It implies the right on his part to prescribe the terms on which the loan shall be made and the right to refuse the loan altogether. It places the life of the Nation at his mercy and the relation of Sovereign and subject is lost sight of completely. In fact, the Sovereign becomes the subject, and the subject the Sovereign. They exchange places and a new *regime* follows as certainly as if one king should abdicate and another be enthroned.[36]

Yet in Weaver's mind, utmost sovereign prerogatives were compatible with an essential if latent conservatism of purpose. Although the rearrangement of the sovereign-subject relationship became imperative both to state autonomy and the checkmate of antidemocratic political development, its final import lay in the redemptive powers held to inhere in constitutionalism—the belief in reformation, in the last analysis, to stave off revolution: "When the sovereignty of the people is thus displaced, either by voluntary surrender or by the gradual and cunning usurpation of capital, it is rarely ever regained—never except by upheavals which convulse society from center to circumference."[37]

4. The Mission of Public Service

The Omaha Platform serves as a notable example of the accuracy of the foregoing discussion. The Platform marked not only the general receptivity to government, but the narrower, explicit expression of power: the political and structural tasks to be accomplished. This latter area went beyond moral underpinnings and reasoned defenses of sovereignty to encompass virtually all discussion of antimonopolism and concrete demands. It might be summarized by an earlier quotation from the Topeka *Advocate* in which "a proper use of the instrumentalities of modern production and distribution" represented the common supposition of a public standard to define, coordinate, and implement a humanly fulfilling political economy. Throughout, government was not an adventitious element, but an integral component of the perspective on change and democracy, a catalyst for the positive re-creation of the social framework.

The Platform conveniently distilled basic thought which already had emerged out of the Alliance's educational ferment. A position was not boldly adopted so much as directly pronounced, as the rendering of all which had gained widespread political acceptance. One reason broad corrective measures could be declared without ideological misgivings was that Populism had a patriotic sense of identity with the American past. Donnelly noted in the preamble, "we seek to restore the government of the Republic to the hands of 'the plain people,' with whose class it originated," this after paying tribute to the Declaration of Independence (Populists chose July Fourth to promulgate the platform) and George Washington. Such allusions fairly abounded. Donnelly stated, "we ask all men to first help us to determine whether we are to have a republic to administer before we differ as to the conditions upon which it is to be administered." From the statement of principles, the first, calling for "the union of the labor forces," continued, "may its spirit enter all hearts for the salvation of the republic and the uplifting of mankind!" Every demand of the Platform (as opposed to several of the accompanying resolutions) entailed some degree of governmental intervention. The Populist trinity of concerns—money, transportation, land—mapped not merely legislative areas requiring corrective measures, but control zones to be occupied on behalf of public principles, lest integrated private power alter or reverse the complexion of democratic society.

Government became a neutral tool for accomplishing implicitly class-laden specific objectives having structural import. The second principle stated a conception of producer values which militated against unrestricted accumulation and partially qualified the profit motive. "Wealth belongs to him who creates it, and every dollar taken from industry without an equivalent is robbery." This pointed up the Platform's adversative character. Yet one notes from the third principle that a critical stance lent itself to the reconciliation of neutrality and class. Governmental action, however imperative, should not lead to a self-aggrandizing state. The distinction permitted the enlargement of public powers because it was founded on the confidence of a nonpolitical administration in areas of responsibility: "We believe that the time has come when the railroad corporations will either own the people or the people must own the railroads; and, should the government enter upon the work of owning and managing all railroads, we should favor an amendment to the Constitution by which all persons engaged in the government service shall be placed under a civil service regulation of the most rigid character, so as to prevent the increase of the power of the national administration by the use of such additional government employees." Civil service here represented the deflation not of state activism, but of partisan uses. As in the resolution favoring "a constitutional provision limiting the office of President and Vice-President to one term," the focus was on the improvement of structure to counter the inaccessible levers of decision making on party lines. This was a scrupulous rejection of partial implementation and political centralization divorced from public needs. Neutrality bespoke purposeful conduct as well as the absence of government favoritism. For the succeeding resolution was, "That we oppose any subsidy or national aid to any private corporation for any purpose."

Turning to the demands, one finds significant modifications of the contemporary structure voiced at every turn. There was a pragmatic crispness, an unselfconscious contemplation of governmental extension, which transposed entire, important segments of the private sector into public hands. Consider the main body of the financial plank. Banking functions had been drastically reduced, especially those involving control of the money supply, issuance of notes, and the availability of credit. This became tantamount to the creation of a new national banking system directed to public ends: "First, *Money*. We demand a national currency, safe, sound, and flexible, issued by the general government only, a full legal tender for all debts, public and private, and that, without the use of banking corporations, a just, equitable, and efficient means of distribution direct to the people, at a tax not to exceed two per cent per annum, to be provided as set forth in the sub-treasury plan of the Farmers' Alliance, or a better system; also, by payments in discharge of its obligations for public improvements."

Only from this baseline were ancillary points introduced: free coinage of silver, a circulating medium "not less than fifty dollars per capita," the graduated income tax, and postal savings banks. Singly and together, these comprised a basic addition to state power. Not inconsistently, sandwiched between income tax and postal savings was an injunction against wasteful expenditures. Once again it can be noted that the principle of extensible power became distinctly focused. The principle was charged with dedication to a mission of public service, and offered little encouragement to statist pretensions: "We believe that the money of the country should be kept as much as possible in the hands of the people, and hence we demand that all state and national revenues shall be limited to the necessary expenses of the government economically and honestly administered."

The statement on transportation was simplicity itself. It blended the commerce power and broad sovereign prerogatives: "Transportation being a means of exchange and a public necessity, the government should own and operate the railroads in the interest of the people." In this initiative, perhaps the boldest in Populism, one notes the mergence of matter-of-factness and neutrality. A paradigm for public ownership was justified by the primal ground of constitutional obligation, as in the addendum, where the post office became the archetypal form of government activity and public service: "The telegraph and telephone, like the post-office system, being a necessity for the transmission of news, should be owned and operated by the government in the interest of the people."

Power invariably had an antimonopolistic referent, as both the condition for its justification and the purpose for its use. This was true for the land plank as well. The term "alien ownership" is sometimes wrongly identified with nativist pursuits (when, in reality, emphasis lay with capitalist syndicates which withheld the land from use, exploited mineral rights, or contributed to the incidence of tenantry). The demand was on behalf of farming farmers, and was quite prescient on corporate trends in agriculture: "The land, including all the natural sources of wealth, is the heritage of the people, and should not be monopolized for speculative purposes, and alien ownership of land should be prohibited. All land now held by railroads and other corporations in excess of their actual needs, and all lands now owned by aliens, should be reclaimed by the government and held for actual settlers only."[38] The heritage of the people, in this case the land, but, in large, the system of democratic governance, had to be reclaimed. This was an implicit constitutional birthright.

Conclusion

Populists conceived a paradigm of capitalist democracy that had affinities with the economic order of Adam Smith in its concept of internally stimulated growth, but that, in confining the self-adjusting mechanism to an intermediate range of economic activity, sought, through an autonomous state, to keep intact the foundations of political authority and the doctrine of public sovereignty. A faith in man's power to order the polity through reason and cooperation, so that capital would not pose the danger of political and social usurpation, was central to the Populist formation. The guarantees of law to restore the precedent rights of personal security, independence, and contentment formed an indispensable corollary. By incorporating a moral-legal influence into the structure of society, Populists believed it would be possible for capitalism to realize the potential for abundance within reach in America.

Yet the activation of latent economic energies also required more equitable wealth distribution. Populists fused ethical and technical considerations that began from their basic premise that material hardship revealed a profounder loss of liberties reaching to the expropriation of a freely determined political and economic existence—and, even further, to the residual claims of human welfare that expressed society's reason for being. If the attributes of sovereignty were transferred to the corporate order, the result would be to alter irremediably the complexion of political development. Populists asserted that a failure to soften the intensity of capitalism through the regenerative forces of a democratically structured government would lead to an absolutist, self-determined economy and value system in which the normative standard would be maximum profitableness and the means of stabilization would be repression.

Law was an alternative historical path to the fount of governance that could free society from its contemporary ideological and structural encirclement, because it not only antedated the private appropriation of political values but also contained the reigning categories of popular rule. The principle of public supremacy in economic affairs, as an independent standard for evaluating the performance of capitalism, fostered a more cautious attitude toward property. This was an affirmation of property in defiance of monopolist organization that meant it could not be readily assimilated into the dominant political economy. This somewhat detached view of capitalism, in which its modifiable nature was associated with the position of antimonopolism, riveted the attention of Populists on performance—not only economic, but political and moral—as a critical test. The imbalance of structure brought on by private concentration had to be set right. If capitalism had been perceived as permanently encased in monopolism, the consent given to such a formation would have been reluctant at best.

Populists had placed capitalism on trial in the act of affirming its tenets of property, and more painful for them, they had placed America on trial by affirming traditional rights that bore little correspondence to existing conditions. From both quarters, capitalism and America, this resulted in a struggle that had a sobering effect on them, although it was America that became the ultimate barrier to their realization of a transcendent consciousness and program of structural change. By idealizing America as a political and historical construct that was inseparable from a democratic birthright, Populists could simultaneously proclaim the transformative possibilities of a property-based society and attack its excrescent features. The notion of excrescence implied the intrinsic soundness of what remained: the component of property. The more trenchant their reformism, the more Populists became attached to property. While playing off one part against another of the same developing structure might lead to a democratization of its internal content, it did not provide the political and ideological impetus—nor was this desired—to go beyond the existing systemic limits.

The incompleteness of Populist transcendence, however, must not obscure the nobility of the general effort, for Populists, under trying conditions, commenced a rational discussion of democracy that issued in, for an all too brief season, the vision of a people's government. America was not to be a setting of monopolist dominion, but the moral-legal source, fusing property, community, and human welfare, of a still viable democratic process that was capable of infinite replenishment when it had been returned to a free people. Protest marked a journey of rediscovery in which Populists summoned what was best in the American past; for having done so, they were treated as subversive to America in their own time, testifying to more than a devotion to a property-based society. In 1894, Ignatius Donnelly stated: "This People's party is fighting the battle of mankind. If American liberty dies, the liberty of the world is dead, for there are no more Americas on earth." The tragedy was that America, as Populists conceived it, so rich in promise, had probably departed, even as he was speaking, only to reemerge in caricatured form with twentieth-century liberalism.

Notes

Chapter One. Consciousness and Restraint

1. Theodore Saloutos, *Farmer Movements in the South, 1865–1933* (Berkeley and Los Angeles, 1960), esp. viii, 118. In the preface the author stated, "I have deliberately chosen to emphasize the manner by which the Populists undermined the faith of the farmers in the economic formula by preaching a doctrine of direct political action," and, by updating John D. Hicks, "explaining how the Populists sapped the general organizations of their strength and left them battered and bleeding to die." He added that Populists "literally disemboweled the organization from which they received so many of their ideas and gained so much of their inspiration." The animus toward Populism sought to repudiate class in favor of interest-group politics, crop diversification, restricted production, and a nonmilitant course, exactly the recommendations of contemporary opponents of the Alliance who sought to neutralize its influence.

2. Lawrence Goodwyn, *Democratic Promise* (New York, 1976). For a brief critical review, see *Historian,* 40 (Nov., 1977), 132–134. The book was a proscriptive reinterpretation of Populism that condemned all of the currents falling outside of a narrow, Texas-based, monetarist-cooperative framework. In this persecution-ridden account, the diverse claims of betrayal and the dilution of purity (Populism had been cut off even before it began its political stage, an ideologically impoverished replica of its former self because it departed from, or was incapable of further activating, the primal monetary doctrines) are reminiscent of European stab-in-the-back legends.

3. Robert C. McMath, *Populist Vanguard* (Chapel Hill, 1975), esp. 110, 122, 154. In addition to his emphasis on the Alliance's educational and communal features, the author drew the important distinction between the weakening of "*institutional* viability" and a corresponding push of "the Alliance *movement* toward insurgency," suggesting that the Alliance had in fact declined in the South before the ascendancy of Populism. McMath correctly observed: "The argument that the Alliance destroyed itself by shifting from economic cooperation to radical political action is not supported by the evidence, particularly in the South." See also my review in *North Carolina Historical Review,* 54 (Oct., 1977), 431–432.

4. John D. Hicks, *The Populist Revolt* (Minneapolis, 1931). Hicks's basic contribution was to provide the indispensable narrative structure of Populism; it is not a mark of disrespect to say that he failed to consider the dimension of ideology, or to entertain whether or not a process of radicalization had occurred. The pattern of protest and ideas of a political culture of dissent were outside of his analytic ken, even though the sources he examined provided ample clues. Because he did not treat the national foundations of power, he also could not assess

the import of the Populist challenge or define the range of grievances, further blurring the vitality and consecutiveness of ideological growth. One wants a systematic analysis of Populist reform in relation to capitalism as well as the framework and limits of antimonopolism. While the factor of class was on the agenda of historical discussion in 1930–1931, it is difficult to discern in the book, positively or negatively stated.

5. The collection of essays and documents of Chester McArthur Destler, *American Radicalism, 1865–1901* (New London, 1946), was an early and important attempt to fix more precisely the ideological roots of Populism, and also broke new ground in identifying labor and urban-reform components of the movement. For more recent works that go beyond narrative political history, see: Stanley B. Parsons, *The Populist Context* (Westport, 1973), J. Morgan Kousser, *The Shaping of Southern Politics* (New Haven, 1974), James M. Young-dale, *Populism: A Psychohistorical Perspective* (Port Washington, 1975), and Michael Schwartz, *Radical Protest and Social Structure* (New York, 1976).

6. The more recent social history springs from well-cultivated soil, in particular the writings of J. L. and Barbara Hammond, R. H. Tawney, and Marc Bloch. Among the newer works, I am indebted to Eric J. Hobsbawm, *Primitive Rebels* (Manchester, 1959), George Rudé, *The Crowd in the French Revolution* (Oxford, 1959), E. P. Thompson, *The Making of the English Working Class* (London, 1963), and Albert Soboul, *The Sans-Culottes* (New York, 1972). For America, Jesse Lemisch, in essays, articles, and reviews, has provided a nucleus for seeing the lower classes as prime historical actors. The writings of Herbert Gutman and David Montgomery, and the studies in labor radicalism and working-class history they have inspired, have also been valuable.

7. Barrington Moore, *Social Origins of Dictatorship and Democracy* (Boston, 1966). In Moore's analysis, the comparability of the three revolutionary epochs—whether in terms of origins, social alignments, or long-term consequences—was essential if the capitalist-democracy formation, particularly as applied to America, were to be demonstrated. The bourgeoisie, as an independent force, was the historical carrier of democratic political and economic institutions, as in the formulation, "No bourgeoisie, no democracy" (418). Further, capitalist revolution, at a decisive stage, cleared away premodern obstacles to subsequent democratic gradualism. Taking the measure of the major societal transitions, he also maintained that capitalist modernization without revolution has carried the historical conditions of fascism in the twentieth century, as in Germany and Japan. I do not quarrel with, and in later writings I will build on, this analytic framework. But what remains open to question is America's own historical pattern of development and its inclusion within the variant of capitalist democracy, given the significance of a bourgeoisie that did not have to dismantle an *ancien régime* to establish its political and economic dominance.

Moore was uneasy in this book about precisely such an inclusion, noting the halting character of the political and structural transformative energies following the Civil War, which was putatively America's social revolution: "To the extent that subsequent movements toward extending the boundaries and meanings of freedom have faced obstacles since the end of the Civil War, they have done so in large measure because of the incomplete character of the victory won in 1865 and subsequent tendencies toward a conservative coalition between propertied interests in the North and the South. This incompleteness was built into the structure of industrial capitalism. Much of the old repression returned to the South in new and more purely economic guises, while new forms appeared there and in the rest of the United States as industrial capitalism grew and spread" (153–154). The process of dismantling an old order, which alone could have engendered a vital democratization, did not proceed very far (I believe this helps to explain the severity of repression in the latter nineteenth century, in which cultural restraints on business practices and power were virtually unknown), suggesting a marriage of iron and cotton analogous to the marriage of iron and rye that Moore dwelt on in Germany.

8. Although Louis Hartz's *The Liberal Tradition in America* (New York, 1955) is widely regarded as the apogee of the consensus framework in American historical writing, with the attendant conservatism thus implied, this judgment misconceives the level of analysis that the book attained and the potentialities for a serious criticism of America that its perspective could support. Hartz's ideological portrait, even when it tended to dissociate liberalism from its specifically capitalist foundations, was not flattering: a pervasive Lockeanism that reached absolutist proportions, and that required a like rigidness of response for its conservation. The context of thought was one of unrelieved drabness, reflecting an equally static pattern of history and conception of time. Hartz described liberalism as follows: "Here is a doctrine which everywhere in the West has been a glorious symbol of individual liberty, yet in America its compulsive power has been so great that it has posed a threat to liberty itself" (11). A comparative perspective, like in Moore's case, sharpens one's focus on the nature of America.

Further quotations substantiate the critical possibilities of the analysis. Hartz found a political complacency rooted in uncontested dominance: "Frustration produces the social passion, ease does not. A triumphant middle class, unassailed by the agonies that Beaumarchais described, can take itself for granted" (52). He also found a narrow range of ideology, in which liberal premises had been gained without the experience of struggle: "This then is the mood of America's absolutism: the somber faith that its norms are self-evident. It is one of the most powerful absolutisms in the world, more powerful even than the messianic spirit of the continental liberals which . . . the Americans were able to reject. That spirit arose out of contact with an opposing way of life, and its very intensity betrayed an inescapable element of doubt. But the American absolutism, flowing from an honest experience with universality, lacked even the passion that doubt might give" (58). Throughout his analysis, he emphasized the absence of a politically and historically variegated pattern of growth, which makes it difficult to consider the American bourgeoisie as a progressive social force. There was not an adequate basis for the release of positive energies leading to a social transformation: "It is this business of destruction and creation which goes to the heart of the problem. For the point of departure of great revolutionary thought everywhere else in the world has been the effort to build a new society on the ruins of an old one, and this is an experience America has never had" (66). The moment one substitutes a propertied consciousness for the more vaguely defined liberalism (something Hartz was reticent about doing), the full dimensions of internal restraint, affecting both the forces of order and of change, become evident.

In these pages, I frequently return to his insight on the near monolithic character of Lockeanism in America, accepting the challenge he has laid down in the implicit query: Did Populism transcend the Liberal Community? Though my reply is not quite his own, it begins from an appreciation of what I am terming the American construct to indicate a political and ideological sensibility that has been mediated through the categories and institutions of property. An immersion in America, which consciously and unconsciously stood for an affirmation of the property right, formed the epistemological foundation of protest, strengthening its resolve while circumscribing its scope and effects.

9. One passage from E. H. Carr's *What Is History?* (New York, 1962) can be taken to summarize the dynamic relationships at the heart of the interpretative process: "The relation of man to his environment is the relation of the historian to his theme. The historian is neither the humble slave, nor the tyrannical master, of his facts. The relation between the historian and his facts is one of equality, of give-and-take. As any working historian knows, if he stops to reflect what he is doing as he thinks and writes, the historian is engaged on a continuous process of moulding his facts to his interpretation and his interpretation to his facts. It is impossible to assign primacy to one over the other. . . . And this reciprocal action also involves reciprocity between present and past, since the historian is part of the present and the facts belong to the past." History thus becomes "a continuous process of interaction between the historian and his facts, an unending dialogue between the present and the past" (34–35). I commend the entire discussion to younger scholars who may be wary of the role of interpretation.

10. Susan Orcutt to Lorenzo D. Lewelling, June 29, 1894, Lewelling Papers, Kansas State Historical Society, and contained in Norman Pollack, ed., *The Populist Mind* (Indianapolis, 1967), 36.

11. Thomas E. Watson, *The People's Party Campaign Book* (Thomson, Ga., 1892), 220.

12. Catherine Nugent (ed.),. *Life Work of Thomas L. Nugent* (Stephenville, Tex., 1896), 195–196.

13. Lorenzo D. Lewelling, manuscript of speech of July 28, 1894, Kansas State Historical Society.

14. Ignatius Donnelly (Edmund Boisgilbert, *pseud.*), *Caesar's Column* (Chicago, 1890), 122.

15. James B. Weaver, *A Call to Action* (Des Moines, 1892), 445.

16. Nugent, *Life Work of Thomas L. Nugent*, 176.

17. McMath, *Populist Vanguard*, 66, and Appendix A, for the varied social composition of the Farmers' Alliance in the South, particularly in the case of the leadership.

18. Halvor Harris to Ignatius Donnelly, Jan. 29, 1891, Donnelly Papers, Minnesota Historical Society.

19. *Farmers' Alliance* (Lincoln), Sept. 6, 1890, Nebraska Historical Society.

20. James H. Davis, *A Political Revelation* (Dallas, 1894), 251.

21. W. Scott Morgan, *History of the Wheel and Alliance, and the Impending Revolution* (Fort Scott, Kan., 1889), 16–17.

22. *Farmers' Alliance* (Lincoln), Sept. 6, 1890, Nebraska Historical Society.

23. *Platte County Argus* (Columbus, Neb.), Oct. 15, 1896, Nebraska Historical Society.

24. For the dissipative effects of emotionality in politics, see Franz Neumann, "Anxiety and Politics," in *The Democratic and the Authoritarian State* (Glencoe, 1957), 270–300.

25. This account is based on my study of Marion Butler's politics and ideology, drawn from his editorials, speeches in the United States Senate, and role as the national chairman of the People's party in the 1896 campaign. Until recently, Butler has remained a cipher in the historical literature of Populism. C. Vann Woodward's *Tom Watson* (New York, 1938) uncritically passed on Watson's charge that Butler was politically treacherous in 1896, an impression that has been corrected by two studies making extensive use of the Marion Butler Papers, Southern Historical Collection, University of North Carolina. See Stanley L. Jones, *The Presidential Election of 1896* (Madison, 1964), for a detailed account of the larger campaign, including the Populists' role, and Robert F. Durden, *The Climax of Populism* (Lexington, 1965), for an emphasis on Butler and the construction of joint-electoral tickets. These works began the necessary analysis of the complexities of Butler's position in 1896, and in the process they have altered the conventional picture of the Watson-Butler feud during the campaign. They have also helped to reveal Watson's antisocialism, acutely southern underpinning, and obsessive regard for personal vindication, in contrast to Butler's national orientation and steady, if also bold, management of the party organization under difficult circumstances.

The charge of political treachery, in addition, implicitly came to signify the further allegations of conservatism and racism, as though Butler was the opposite of everything that Watson represented. In both respects, a corrective is needed. Butler was more able, driving, internally secure, and given to systematic probing than was common of the leadership, especially in the South. He merits a careful treatment in his own right, beyond the disputes of historians, as a disciplined theorist and political strategist. Butler struck a balance in the national movement on economic and political issues that formed a bridge to the more ideologically advanced western portion, and particularly on public ownership as well as race he occupied a forward place in the South.

26. Butler traveled an agonizing path. Even to declare membership in an independent party in the South was to oppose the political foundations of the existing order. Then to identify racism as this order's central stablizing mechanism resulted in a further questioning of cherished assumptions, a critical step in widening his economic vision as well. By the late summer of 1892, Butler pierced to the heart of the region's politics: Racial agitation prevented the formation of independent movements, obscured the discussion of economic issues, and denied the legitimacy of an alternative political formula, in which class might displace race as a basis for resolving grievances. In order to combat the political and psychological intimidation of the dissenting forces, he called for the neutralization of the race issue in politics as the condition of Populism's survival. Butler did not explicitly reject segregation, but he began to address issues as they affected the poor directly rather than by racial categories, leading to a general loosening of the ties of orthodoxy across the range of nonracial concerns. A specificity of criticism, pertinent to economic deprivation and the organization of power, was now possible.

27. Butler's developing awareness, a process initiated through the questioning of racial assumptions of order, required much soul-searching, and was accompanied by the exposure to ridicule. The temporary achievement of fair elections in North Carolina in 1894 made practicable the biracial coalition that assumed power in that year and led to a democratization of local and state

government. The ideological growth he registered from 1890–1891 through 1895 took the form of a clearing away of cultural debris, a negative and yet an indispensable phase (for other Populists as well) in converting Populist ideology from surface propositions that still were incompletely absorbed to fully comprehended statements that had become shaped into an integrated program. A latent, imperfectly recognized class dimension could be extricated from the framework of one-party, business-oriented government and the political culture of white domination in order to create a sense of new structural and economic possibilities: Butler's support of public ownership, in the United States Senate in 1896, had turned his pre-Populist New South framework upside down. By finally confronting the meaning of demands that had been contained in the movement's platform and discussion from the start, he, like other Populists, had made the mental leap from rote acceptances, usually as the segmentation of reform, to an alternative perspective on, and within, capitalism.

28. See Woodward, *Tom Watson,* 277, for a brief description of the demoralization that had set in among Tom Watson's constituents, by 1895, when it became apparent that the political channels were blocked.

29. See Moore, *Social Origins,* esp. 275–313, for an excellent discussion of the Meiji Settlement and the consequent patterns of domestic repression and foreign expansion. The purposeful creation of a "surplus" body of laborers, the methods for extracting a larger return from agriculture, and the failure to build a strong internal market suggest important structural parallels between Japan and America in a decisive period of industrial development. Japanese workers hardly benefited from changes on the land or from the alignment of landlord and industrialist. In a statement that has significance for a comparative historical analysis, Moore wrote concerning the political foundations of underconsumption: "To raise the standard of living of the peasants and workers and to create an internal market would have been a dangerous undertaking from the standpoint of the upper classes. It would have threatened the exploitative paternalism upon which their authority rested in the factory and which was one of the main mechanisms for profit-making. For the landlords, the consequences would have been more serious still. A prosperous peasantry in a genuine political democracy would have deprived them of their rents. That in turn would have meant the liquidation of their entire position" (290–291).

30. In England, traditional cultural boundaries, although they did not mitigate economic harshness, discouraged the recourse to a more explicit political repression. A political space was opened for the working class to develop its separate consciousness, not only in relation to landed upper groups, but also in relation to a rising commercial and industrial middle class. The political and social variegation of English historical development, reflected in the welter of competing social forces, made impracticable a systematic atomizing of lower groups. If the predominant ideological themes reflected a commitment to order, they nevertheless did not divert the gaze of the masses through the representation of a promised mobility and fluidity of class and social structure. To a lesser degree, this competition among landed and bourgeois elements, in a class setting that did not offer false hopes to the working class, extended to the Continent.

31. G. G. Eggert, *Railroad Labor Disputes* (Ann Arbor, 1967), has developed the contemporary emphasis on insurrection and its legal-political implications

for the suppression of labor. The discussion of federal Judge Thomas S. Drummond, in which the strikes against railroads were considered to be a "war upon society," is particularly good.

32. Even apart from the monographic literature currently appearing, frequently inspired by the writings of David Montgomery and Herbert Gutman, the conventional accounts of major episodes provide support for this overview of labor disturbances. See Robert V. Bruce, *1877* (Indianapolis, 1959), Henry David, *The History of the Haymarket Affair* (New York, 1936), Ruth A. Allen, *The Great Southwest Strike* (Austin, 1942), Leon Wolff, *Lockout* (New York, 1965), and Almont Lindsey, *The Pullman Strike* (Chicago, 1942). A useful survey is Joseph G. Rayback, *A History of American Labor* (New York, 1959). For an intensive look at the vitality of working class political culture, and the ideological tensions (derived in part from Haymarket) that shattered its development, see Richard Oestreicher, "Solidarity and Fragmentation: Working People and Class Consciousness in Detroit, 1877–1895," Ph.D. diss., Michigan State University, 1979.

33. C. Vann Woodward's *Origins of the New South* (Baton Rouge, 1951) is the finest analysis of the region's development, a pattern of internal colonialism that was maintained through a one-party government and exploitative racial arrangements. His treatment of the conservative nature of Redemption, patterns of social control, and inter-regional relations of capitalist power comprises the foundation of all subsequent historical inquiry. See also chapter 3, note 28, below, for additional commentary on *Origins*. For recent qualifications of the complexion of indigenous elites, see Jonathan M. Wiener, *Social Origins of the New South: Alabama, 1860–1885* (Baton Rouge, 1978), and Dwight B. Billings, *Planters and the Making of a "New South": Class, Politics, and Development in North Carolina, 1865–1900* (Chapel Hill, 1979).

34. Moore, *Social Origins*, 111, note 1, recognizes the application of the term "peasantry" to southern conditions, although he overlooks its biracial character.

35. To avoid simplifying the character of repression in America in the latter nineteenth century it is necessary to recognize its diffusive quality, an intensity of application that nevertheless reflected a decentralized structure of force. The pattern of coercion was largely economic: an undisputed control of the workplace, the prevention of unionization, and a reliance on private armies to enforce corporate decisions. Key industrial sectors, such as iron and steel, had the look of forced-labor camps, while southern textile mills and tobacco factories resembled Oriental satrapies in their supposed quaintness. However, one must be cautious in delineating the larger system. If ownership exercised detailed supervision over living conditions and social discipline, this was not the same as a police state under government auspices. To regiment the entire populace was beyond the means of a still weakened, undeveloped, and inept federal bureaucracy. Nor had large-scale enterprise achieved the coordination in labor policy to effect such a goal, except possibly in railroads (and then, only on an industry-wide basis). Yet it was not necessary to establish a national police force in order for repression to have significance, although Thomas A. Scott of the Pennsylvania Railroad made this recommendation in response to the 1877 strikes. See Gabriel Kolko, *Railroads and Regulation* (Princeton, 1965), 14–15. Instead, the comparative absence of a national role—not entirely, as in the interventions of 1877 and 1894—provided an area of free grace for the local use

of force, breeding a sense of immunity which contributed to its swiftness. Through privately subscribed armories, the rise of agencies specializing in the control of labor, and the readiness of state militias to comply with the requests of capital, corporate policies became invested with an authoritative standing, especially since the appropriation of force was one of the basic prerogatives of sovereignty.

36. Norman Pollack, *The Populist Response to Industrial America* (Cambridge, 1962), 1–2.

Chapter Two. The Corporate Order: Peffer and Weaver

1. William A. Peffer, *The Farmer's Side* (New York, 1891), 8–9. Fritz Pappenheim's *The Alienation of Modern Man* (New York, 1959), treats in a moving way this problem of the basic expropriation of the human personality.

2. *Ibid.*, 29.

3. *Ibid.*, 42.

4. *Ibid.*, 47, 50.

5. *Ibid.*, 50–51.

6. *Ibid.*, 51.

7. See, for example, E. P. Thompson, "Time, Work-discipline, and Industrial Capitalism," *Past and Present*, 38 (1967). Herbert Gutman's *Work, Culture, and Society in Industrializing America* (New York, 1977), chap. 2, also discusses the implications of alternative time-frameworks for heightening a separate consciousness of rights.

8. The historical pattern of subordinating the landed sector to the requirements of accelerated industrial growth, which was inseparable from the creation of a modern capitalistic infrastructure following the Civil War, was similar to the larger dynamics of penetration into colonial and dependent economies of a later day. This suggests what some Populists, correctly, I believe, identified as an *imposed* condition of backwardness on rural elements that had little to do with "inevitable" transitions to modernity. As with so much else, comparative analysis becomes helpful on this point; see, especially, Paul Baran, *The Political Economy of Growth* (New York, 1957), chaps, 6 and 7, appropriately entitled "Towards a Morphology of Backwardness."

9. Peffer, *Farmer's Side*, 51–52.

10. Among his many comments on the subject, here in the context of international trade, Thorstein Veblen, in *Imperial Germany and the Industrial Revolution* (New York, 1915), superbly illuminated the social mechanism of what he termed group solidarity: "[T]he sense of group solidarity coalesces with the pride of achievement to such effect that the members of the group at large are elated with the exploits of any member of the group in good standing. So far will this sentimental sophistry carry, that the community not only looks with approval and elation on the successful self-aggrandisement of a given individual member at the cost of outsiders, but it will also unreflectingly further such enterprises at a palpable cost to itself and with the certainty of getting no gain from the venture,— as, *e.g.*, in exploits of loyalty" (49).

11. Peffer, *Farmer's Side*, 52.

12. *Ibid.*

13. *Ibid.*, 52–53.

14. *Ibid.*, 53–54.

15. *Ibid.*, 54.

16. In 1934, Hans Speier analyzed the fear of proletarization as concerned the German salaried employee, though without fully grasping the ideological portentousness of this bedrock frustration. This article, which is still valuable in that it illumines the dynamics of a perceived collapse of status, is reprinted in his *Social Order and the Risks of War* (New York, 1952), 68–85.

17. Peffer, *Farmer's Side*, 54–55.

18. Quite apart from the use of an implied loyalty oath to apply exclusionary definitions of membership in Populism, which is the burden of Lawrence Goodwyn's *Democratic Promise* (New York, 1976), I find that such categorizing becomes a simplistic reading of internal currents because it fails to examine the complexity and intentions of *either* grouping. Midroaders were not invariably more "radical" economically. They opposed not fusion per se but cooperation with the Democrats. Their opposition was a southern-centered manifestation, with perhaps excellent, but largely nonideological, reasons for such a stance. Fusionists, among them Weaver, often possessed impressive reform credentials, having identified comprehensive antimonopoly demands over a period of several years. In 1896, when the distinction had any real meaning in the movement's history, they perceived Bryan to be a necessary choice for the furtherance of reform unification. This decision was not for his sake or for the advancement of silver but to actuate forces Populism had helped to set in motion: the first step in successive reforms for which the alternatives appeared clear-cut. This is not to credit, or discredit, the wisdom of their political judgment. Rather, it is to suggest that: (a) there were few if any villains; (b) fusionists did not will the movement's destruction (nor did midroaders, though they for the most part sat out the campaign, were given to self-pity, and would not accept the difficult challenge of aggressively spreading the Populist ideology); (c) destruction in any case had deeper roots than the campaign setting, which merely located but did not explain the rapid demoralization occurring; and (d) most relevant here, short-term lines of cleavage, found on the convention floor in 1896, bear little correspondence to the longer-term patterns of ideological consistency. Fusionists in the campaign had not infrequently played a vanguard role previously. Some political discussion was unavoidable, so that Weaver's statements might be allowed to speak for themselves; in turn, these statements have value, beyond considerations of ideology, in clarifying the politics of Populism. My protracted study of Marion Butler (referred to in the introduction) analyzes the foregoing points; Butler was the Populist national chairman in the 1896 campaign. I have also examined closely the complete run of the Dallas *Southern Mercury* for subsequent incorporation in a monograph. This source, as the authoritative voice of midroadism, and, by conventional wisdom, of advanced radicalism, proves remarkably moderate in economic matters, particularly because it gave more attention to the financial question than such other areas as industrial concentration and public ownership. I am entirely mindful of the controversial nature of these remarks, but nowhere on the nuts-and-bolts level do I find Populist scholarship so wide of the mark as in the way it endows midroadism with a near-sacrosanct character.

19. James B. Weaver, *A Call to Action* (Des Moines, 1892), 5.

20. *Ibid.*, 5–6.

21. *Ibid.*, 27–28.

22. *Ibid.*, 28–29, 32.

23. Roberto Michels's *Political Parties* (Glencoe, 1949) early addressed the circulation process. In America the best known treatment is C. Wright Mills's *The Power Elite* (New York, 1956), which, despite its theoretic looseness, in holding for a tripartite structure of power, enabled one—in the midst of the Cold War—to resume the discussion of class. For a later statement, with solid empirical and conceptual underpinnings, see Gabriel Kolko, *The Roots of American Foreign Policy* (Boston, 1969), chaps. 1–2, and his precedent historical analysis, *The Triumph of Conservatism* (Glencoe, 1963), esp. chaps. 3–5 and 10.

24. Weaver, *Call to Action*, 32.

25. *Ibid.*, 32–33.

26. *Ibid.*, 33.

27. *Ibid.*

28. *Ibid.*, 35–36.

29. *Ibid.*, 79, 81.

30. For the changing conception of corporate prerogatives in this period, see Arnold M. Paul, *Conservative Crisis and the Rule of Law* (Ithaca, 1960), and for the corporate impact on the legal profession, see Jerold S. Auerbach, *Unequal Justice* (New York, 1976). Moreover, Weaver anticipates the outlines of Veblen's discussion concerning business influence on academic policy and recruitment in *The Higher Learning In America* (New York, 1918), as when Veblen noted that "the higher learning takes its character from the manner of life enforced on the group by the circumstances in which it is placed." He added: "Distinctive and dominant among the constituent factors of this current scheme of use and wont is the pursuit of business, with the outlook and predilections which that pursuit implies. Therefore any inquiry into the effect which recent institutional changes may have upon the pursuit of the higher learning will necessarily be taken up in a peculiar degree with the consequences which an habitual pursuit of business in modern times has had for the ideals, aims and methods of the scholars and schools devoted to the higher learning" (2–3).

31. Weaver, *Call to Action*, 81, 86.

32. Ignatius Donnelly (Edmund Boisgilbert, *pseud.*), *Caesar's Column* (Chicago, 1890), 3.

33. *Ibid.*, 4–5.

34. *Ibid.*, 5.

35. Weaver, *Call to Action*, 88.

36. *Ibid.*

37. *Ibid.*

38. *Ibid.*, 93–94.

39. *Ibid.*, 247–248.

40. *Ibid.*, 253.

41. *Ibid.*, 445.

Chapter Three. Public Rights and Individual Liberties: Morgan and Davis

1. W. Scott Morgan, *History of the Wheel and Alliance, and the Impending Revolution* (Fort Scott, Kansas, 1889), 15–16.

2. *Ibid.*, 16.

3. *Ibid.*

4. *Ibid.*, 16–17.

5. *Ibid.*, 17–18.

6. *Ibid.*, 21–22.

7. *Ibid.*, 22.

8. *Ibid.*

9. *Ibid.*

10. *Ibid.*, 22–23.

11. Louis Hartz, *The Liberal Tradition in America* (New York, 1955), esp. chap. 8. See above, chap. 1, note 8, for my comments on this extremely significant book. In the present context, the following quotation illustrates the conservative and propertied transvaluation of presumed democratic values in our general period: "And in the case of a man like Carnegie, who fled from the class 'stigma' of England as he called it, and flowered into an American millionaire, both the Old and the New Worlds meet in their worship of American opportunity. Whiggery, in other words, 'discovers America' in its use of America, and transforms into a conscious ideology the very conditions of its success: the death of Toryism, the peculiar language of Progressivism, and the isolation of Marx" (206).

12. Morgan, *History of the Wheel*, 23.

13. *Ibid.*, 23–24.

14. *Ibid.*, 24.

15. *Ibid.*

16. *Ibid.*

17. *Ibid.*, 24–25.

18. *Ibid.*, 25.

19. *Ibid.*, 26–27.

20. *Ibid.*, 29.

21. *Ibid.*, 29-30.

22. *Ibid.*, 52–53.

23. *Ibid.*, 54.

24. *Ibid.*, 560.

25. *Ibid.*, 560, 605.

26. *Ibid.*, 608.

27. *Ibid.*

28. C. Vann Woodward, in *Origins of the New South* (Baton Rouge, 1951), succinctly wrote: "Contrary to popular impression, the more radical wing of the agrarian revolt of the nineties was Southern rather than Western" (200). My reasons for dissenting are stated in the next several paragraphs of the text. For Woodward, heightened exploitation of the region promoted greater disaffection than in the West. While this is a plausible contention, it nevertheless underestimated the impact of the exploitation, and its nearly total cultural reinforcement through prevailing southern institutions and values. Woodward presented the most devastating analysis yet written on the pattern of southern modernization. It was a framework of internal colonialism. The success of northern penetration became dependent on the complicity of indigenous elites, a system of political closure, and a pervasive racialist ideology, which prevented biracial counterorganization and obscured the focus upon economic grievances. Yet, despite this considerable achievement, he had to hold in suspension such an untoward context, lest its full authoritarian dimensions reflect on the South per se. In its degradation, Populism was simultaneously an exonerative force. My feeling is that if Populism in the South tended to be more southern than Populist, this fact does

not detract from the movement's collective courage and accomplishments. It merely means that the regional imprint seriously circumscribed the range of ideological consciousness.

29. In his complex delineation, W. J. Cash, in *The Mind of the South* (New York, 1941), captured the tenor of an inclusive uniformity of culture. To that extent, as a native southerner, he dared to face the unpleasant truths at the heart of the region's psyche and institutions. Because initially fashionable, the book has not received the serious critical attention it deserves. Here, romanticism and fantasy took on the proportions of a mass neurosis, to obscure both social and economic reality and the bonds of guilt in maintaining degradative racial standards. See part 2, chap. 1 for the indispensable preliminaries to any discussion of the difficulties Populism labored under: a poisonous regimentation, realized in a one-party state, in which power shifted upward and all class needs had been shattered through the racial mechanism. Cash, precisely because he did not underestimate the context of repression, might be pardoned in the chapter following for not crediting the challenge that southern Populists had actually mounted. A breaking of the cultural surface appeared to him beyond hope of attainment, although he did note, of Populism and "common whites" that, "none the less, it did have in it, as I have said, that element of groping. . . . It did represent to a ponderable degree the flaring forth of an impulse to return to active concern with their economic and social status, and to make use of the political means to the end of its ratification" (169). Simply, focused thought on economics was itself a historical act of significance and of defiance.

30. Matters of interpretation aside, it must be averred that Woodward's *Origins* furnishes the most comprehensive scholarly account of political and structural cruelty. The pertinent discussion began with the retrenchment program of the Redeemer state governments, and moved forward to the construction of ideological diversions: "One of the most significant inventions of the New South was the 'Old South'—a new idea in the eighties, and a legend of incalculable potentialities" (154–155). The industrialization process had been founded on the labor of women and children, crop-lien peonage, as the agricultural system affecting the poor of both races, and the penalties attached to all modes of dissent. Woodward, on cultural suppression, is at his most moving when describing the plight of George W. Cable (163–164).

31. My study of Marion Butler investigates the process of political-cultural divestment as the precondition, consciously recognized and experienced, for mounting a protest movement. The Democratic party so monopolized the sources of political identity that merely to question one's affiliation became a painful act. Indeed, one must speak of Populists-to-be, who, in many cases, required some two or more years of constant soul-searching and stepped-up attacks on their former allegiance before the new party had sunk down roots in its own right. Populists, as I shall contend, were often more anti-Democratic than pro-Populist during this phase. One finds a series of discrete steps, tantamount to a backing into the movement, rather than an early and affirmative embracement of political independence. For a poignant expression of this deliberative aspect, see W. M. Walton to John H. Reagan, Feb. 25, 1896, Reagan Papers, The University of Texas Library, Texas Archives Division. The letter is reprinted in Norman Pollack, ed., *The Populist Mind* (Indianapolis, 1967), 55–56.

32. There was intellectual ferment in the South. This is made evident by

Robert C. McMath's *Populist Vanguard* (Chapel Hill, 1975), and Roscoe C. Martin's *The People's Party in Texas* (Austin, 1933), esp. chap. 7. But such ferment nonetheless failed to speak to matters of substantive breadth and the sheer cross-fertilization of ideas that one finds in western Populism. It would not be possible, for example, to write an analysis of ideological variegation and richness in southern Populism comparable to that found in Chester McArthur Destler, *American Radicalism, 1865—1901* (New London, 1946), chap. 1, on western currents.

33. James H. Davis, *A Political Revelation* (Dallas, 1894), 13.
34. *Ibid.*, 13–14.
35. *Ibid.*, 14.
36. *Ibid.*, 14–15.
37. *Ibid.*, 15.
38. *Ibid.*, 70–71.
39. *Ibid.*, 71.
40. *Ibid.*, 71, 72.
41. *Ibid.*, 72–73.
42. *Ibid.*, 73.
43. *Ibid.*, 74, 81, 82. Though summarizing a different set of historical and political dynamics, the phrase to "farm out," in prerevolutionary France, had much the same denotation as expressed here by Davis: the devolution or derogation of sovereign power. See Georges Lefebvre, *The Coming of the French Revolution* (Princeton, 1947), 10n, 36.
44. *Ibid.*, 83, 83–84.
45. *Ibid.*, 84–85, 86.
46. *Ibid.*, 92–93.
47. *Ibid.*, 95.
48. *Ibid.*, 95–96.
49. *Ibid.*, 96.
50. *Ibid.*
51. *Ibid.*, 96–97.
52. *Ibid.*, 97.
53. *Ibid.*, 97–98.
54. *Ibid.*, 98–99.
55. *Ibid.*, 99.
56. *Ibid.*
57. *Ibid.*, 99–100.
58. *Ibid.*, 100–101. With uncommon felicity, Davis closed by framing the distinction between democracy and aristocracy, that between Jefferson and Hamilton, or in terms made familiar by Parrington, that between human rights and property rights, as the basic cleavage thought to be still in effect. His introductory note, however, made clear that no drastic departure was intended: "The Populists are the defenders of the people and the Constitution, the upholders of liberty in its broader grander sense, consistent with our form of government, and we believe our forefathers formed our government with these things in view. Populists are the true Democrats, the true Republicans; the opposition are the real tories and aristocrats." Then he continued: "Public thought and discussion was divided between two general ideas of government in the beginning. One idea was to risk the people—give them all power and management of the interests of society or government through agents or

officers elected by themselves. . . . The other idea was that the people were unsafe; that they were not educated, were not competent; that they should have as little to do with government as possible; that the rich, who had better opportunities and were better educated, should have all the powers of government in their hands; that the wealthy classes should rule the masses; that an aristocracy should hold the offices and rule the people." Though Davis turned aside from overtly explosive content, by contending essentially for republicanism per se, he nevertheless ended with a defiant flourish: "We Populists are willing to trust the people, and they are not. They are the enemies to free government; we the friends of freedom" (264–265).

Chapter Four. The New Industrial Regimen: Kansas Populists

1. *Farmers' Alliance* (Lincoln), May 7, 1891, Nebraska Historical Society.
2. Lorenzo D. Lewelling, manuscript, speech of July 28, 1894, Kansas State Historical Society. For concise biographical information, see O. Gene Clanton, *Kansas Populism* (Lawrence 1969), 278, n. 1.
3. Quoted in Michael J. Brodhead, *Persevering Populist* (Reno, 1969), 87, 74, 88. Interpretation, mine throughout.
4. *Ibid.*, 60, 55.
5. *Ibid.*, 59, 59–60, 60.
6. *Ibid.*, 97–98.
7. *Ibid.*, 94, 102.
8. *Advocate* (Topeka), Sept. 19, 1894, Kansas State Historical Society.
9. See Clanton, *Kansas Populism,* 53, for the Diggs quote and brief sketch of McLallin's background.
10. *Advocate* (Topeka), Apr. 11, 1894, Kansas State Historical Society.
11. *Ibid.*, Nov. 22, 1893.
12. *Ibid.*, Mar. 29, 1893.
13. *Ibid.*, Feb. 14, 1894.
14. *Ibid.*, Aug. 15, 1894.
15. *Ibid.*, Nov. 14, 1894.
16. *Ibid.*, Apr. 10, 1895.
17. *Ibid.*, Dec. 6, 1893. Lewelling's "Tramp Circular," relevant to these pages, is found in the *Daily Capital* (Topeka), Dec. 5, 1893, Kansas State Historical Society, and is reprinted in Norman Pollack, ed., *The Populist Mind* (Indianapolis, 1967), 330–332.
18. *Ibid.*, Dec. 27, 1893.
19. *Ibid.*
20. *Ibid.*, July 20, 1892.
21. *Ibid.*, Aug. 17, 1892.
22. *Ibid.*, Sept. 20, 1893.
23. *Ibid.*, Feb. 7, 1894.
24. *Ibid.*, Apr. 11, 1894.
25. *Ibid.*, Apr. 25, 1894.
26. *Ibid.*, May 2, 1894.
27. *Ibid.*, July 18, 1894.
28. *Ibid.*, July 25, 1894.
29. *Ibid.*, Sept. 19, 1894. For a similar treatment of the Haymarket defendants, see *Ibid.*, Feb. 21 1894, occasioned by Governor Altgeld's pardon of those

who had not been executed in the first instance. Two sentences especially merit attention: "We know that the trial in question and the punishment inflicted upon those men was a most deadly blow to human liberty in America. They were persecuted by organized capital because they were prominent advocates of the rights of labor, and not because they were guilty of any act of violence."

30. *Ibid.,* Jan. 16, 1895.

31. *Ibid.,* Oct. 31, 1894. For a particularly strong editorial on Pinkertons, in connection with the breaking of a Brooklyn, New York, streetcar strike, see *ibid.,* Jan. 30, 1895.

32. *Ibid.,* Apr. 3, 1895.

33. *People's Party Paper* (Atlanta), Jan. 20, 1893, Library of Congress.

34. *Times* (Chicago), Nov. 4, 1894.

35. Henry D. Lloyd to Dr. W. G. Eggleston, Dec. 29, 1890, Lloyd to Samuel Bowles, July 11, 1892, Lloyd to B. Fay Mills, May 21, 1896, Lloyd Papers, Wisconsin State Historical Society.

36. Henry D. Lloyd to Edwin L. Shuman, May 28, 1896, Lloyd to Frederick H. Gillett, Nov. 30, 1896, Lloyd Papers, Wisconsin State Historical Society.

37. Henry D. Lloyd, *A Strike of Millionaires Against Miners* (Chicago, 1890), 15–16, 19, 32, 38.

38. *Ibid.,* 51–52, 58–59, 82, 96–97, 98–99, 112, 121.

Chapter Five. Alternative Views of Government: Nebraskans and Watson

1. *Farmers' Alliance* (Lincoln), Sept. 6, 1890, Nebraska Historical Society.

2. *Ibid.,* Feb. 28, 1891.

3. *Ibid.,* Oct. 22, 1891.

4. *Ibid.,* Mar. 3, 1892.

5. *Alliance* (Lincoln), June 26, 1889.

6. *Ibid.,* Oct. 12, 1889.

7. W. A. McKeighan to ed., *Farmers' Alliance* (Lincoln), Mar. 1, 1890.

8. *Farmers' Alliance* (Lincoln), Apr. 19, 1890.

9. W. A. McKeighan, "Wealth as a Political Power," *Farmers' Alliance* (Lincoln), Apr. 26, 1890.

10. John H. Powers, abstract of address, *Farmers' Alliance* (Lincoln), June 7, 1890.

11. *Farmers' Alliance* (Lincoln), Sept. 13, 1890.

12. *Ibid.,* Sept. 20, 1890.

13. *Ibid.,* Apr. 10, 1891.

14. *Ibid.,* June 18, 1891.

15. *Ibid.,* Nov. 19, 1891.

16. *Ibid.,* Mar. 10, 1892. For a similar analysis, taking note of contemporary events in Germany (and also praising the course of the German socialists), see this paper for Mar. 3, 1892.

17. *Alliance-Independent* (Lincoln), Mar. 2, 1893.

18. *Ibid.,* Aug. 24, 1893.,

19. Mrs. J. T. Kellie, in *Alliance-Independent* (Lincoln), Feb. 1, 1894.

20. *People's Party Paper* (Atlanta), Nov. 26, 1891, Library of Congress.

21. Thomas E. Watson, *The People's Party Campaign Book* (Author's edition [Thomson, Ga., 1892]), 40, 42–43.

22. *Ibid.,* 187.

23. *Ibid.,* 187, 188. For a similar statement by William Jennings Bryan, see p. 198; yet Bryan, at least, did not single out striking workers as an equal threat to society.

24. *Ibid.,* 210–211.

25. *Ibid.,* 211–212.

26. *Ibid.,* 212.

27. *Ibid.*

28. *Ibid.,* 212–213.

29. *Ibid.,* 215.

30. *Ibid.,* 216.

31. *Ibid.,* 216–217, 218. Watson had an excellent grasp of repression, which tied in here with his strain of pacifism: "This spirit of repression has a strong hold in this country. Strengthening of our Navy; building Forts, Arsenals, and Dock Yards has a deeper meaning lurking underneath. Let the people keep their eyes open and their vigilance unrelaxed" (218).

32. *Ibid.,* 219.

33. *Ibid.,* 219–220.

34. *Ibid.,* 220.

35. *Ibid.,* 220–221.

36. *Ibid.,* 221.

37. *Ibid.*

38. *Ibid.*

39. *Ibid.,* 222.

40. *Ibid.*

Chapter Six. Government and Human Welfare: Donnelly

1. See Martin Ridge, *Ignatius Donnelly* (Chicago, 1962), esp. chaps. 9–11, 13, 15, for the political context of Donnelly's social and ideological perspective.

2. Omaha Platform, July 4, 1892, reprinted widely, as in *National Economist* (Washington, D.C.), July 9, 1892, Library of Congress.

3. Ignatius Donnelly (Edmund Boisgilbert, *pseud.*), *Caesar's Column* (Chicago, 1890), 21–22.

4. *Ibid.,* 40.

5. *Ibid.,* 41.

6. *Ibid.,* 44–45, 46.

7. *Ibid.,* 79.

8. *Ibid.,* 82.

9. *Ibid.,* 83–84.

10. *Ibid.,* 84.

11. *Ibid.,* 116–117.

12. *Ibid.,* 118.

13. *Ibid.*

14. *Ibid.,* 119.

15. *Ibid.,* 119–120.

16. *Ibid.,* 120.

17. *Ibid.,* 122.

18. *Ibid.*

19. *Ibid.,* 129.

20. *Ibid.,* 129–130.
21. *Ibid.,* 131.
22. *Ibid.,* 131–132.
23. *Ibid.,* 132.
24. *Ibid.,* 125–126.
25. *Ibid.,* 353, 356–357.
26. *Ibid.,* 212–213.
27. *Ibid.,* 213–214.
28. *Ibid.,* 214. The Sumner quote is found in Sidney Fine, *Laissez Faire and the General-Welfare State* (Ann Arbor, 1956), 81.
29. *Ibid.,* 214–215, 216.
30. Ignatius Donnelly, *Doctor Huguet* (Chicago, 1891), 54.
31. *Ibid.,* 60–61. Though participation was never called into question, Donnelly seems more refreshingly direct in this book than in his preceding one in regard to the notion of self-government.
32. *Ibid.,* 61.
33. *Ibid.,* 63.
34. *Ibid.,* 63–64.
35. *Ibid.,* 65.
36. *Ibid.,* 68–69.
37. *Ibid.,* 80. See Oliver C. Cox, *Caste, Class, and Race* (Garden City, 1948), esp. 485–488, for the paradigm of racial-economic exploitation. As part of the larger process of reducing labor to a commodity, racialist ideology and practice was intended "to elicit a collective feeling of more or less ruthless antagonism against and contempt for the exploited race or class" (488).
38. *Ibid.,* 163, 166.
39. *Ibid.,* 200, 200–201.
40. *Ibid.,* 289, 289–290.
41. *Ibid.,* 290.
42. *Ibid.,* 308, 309.
43. Ignatius Donnelly, *The Golden Bottle* (New York and St. Paul, 1892), 269.
44. *Ibid.,* 280–281.
45. *Ibid.,* 281.
46. *Ibid.,* 69–70.
47. *Ibid.,* 125.
48. *Ibid.,* 125, 128.
49. *Ibid.,* 167–168.
50. *Ibid.,* 168–169.
51. *Ibid.,* 168, 169, 170.
52. *Ibid.,* 170.
53. *Ibid.,* 171.
54. *Ibid.,* 269.
55. *Ibid.,* 270–271, 291.

Chapter Seven. The Legitimation of Productive Wealth: Nugent

1. All references are taken from Catherine Nugent, ed., *Life Work of Thomas L. Nugent* (Catherine Nugent: Stephenville, Texas, 1896). In addition to the texts of several major speeches, this volume, published by his wife following Nugent's death, contains numerous testimonials and character sketches. Several of these

ring with an authenticity that carried beyond ritualized obeisance and achieved a more precise statement of underlying principles. The social dimension of Nugent's Swedenborgianism, as borne out by the political texts, is quite striking. One minister, W. F. Packard, wrote of Nugent as follows: "He had religious sensibility, but a sensibility which never rested until it had found its true perfection and manifestation in practice. . . . He was not satisfied with a superficial religion but was particularly interested in those instructions from the pulpit which enjoined a deep, living, all pervading sense of God's presence and authority, and an intimate union of the mind with its Creator. . . . It was a part of his faith that the highest happiness is found in that force of love and lofty principle through which a man surrenders himself wholly to the cause of right and of man; and he proved the truth in his own experience" (32, 33–34).

A second minister, A. B. Francisco, provided a still closer description, capturing Nugent's irreducible faith, but also, his distance from the masses while speaking in their name: "He stood in a more interior light than it was ever possible for him to reveal to the people. He spoke to a certain extent in parables. He, no doubt, felt at all times that he had many things to say to them that they could not yet hear. He was moved with compassion towards them. He sought to lead them by a way they knew not. . . . To him all things were but signs of the Lord's coming. All changes as but preparations for it. . . . He looked upon the whole human race as being conjoined to the Lord—and this conjunction he called the Divine Humanity. All things were to him a One. Each a part of an organic whole whose soul God is, and whose body is man. He looked, therefore, for a slow but certain redemption for all mankind; for the restitution of all things" (95–96).

2. *Ibid.*, 126.
3. *Ibid.*, 127.
4. *Ibid.*, 146.
5. *Ibid.*, 146–147, 148.
6. *Ibid.*, 148–149.
7. *Ibid.*, 149–150.
8. *Ibid.*, 151.
9. *Ibid.*, 151–152, 153, 154.
10. *Ibid.*, 154.
11. *Ibid.*, 154–155.
12. *Ibid.*, 155.
13. *Ibid.*, 156–157.
14. *Ibid.*, 159–160.
15. *Ibid.*, 160–161.
16. *Ibid.*, 161.
17. *Ibid.*, 161–162.
18. *Ibid.*, 162, 165. The parallel drawn is suggestive of Nugent's broader skepticism: "But I speak of the fact as one to be considered in testing the quality and possible effects of any reform movement." On the religious movements of John Wesley and Alexander Campbell, he noted: "No one can doubt the zeal, the philanthropy, or the good conscience of the membership of these religious organizations, but every dispassionate mind must see that so deeply involved in the affections of its members is each of these churches that any effort to change its simple customs or formulas would excite alarm and apprehension throughout the entire body. . . . Thus, in the course of time, even vital doctrines of the creed

might vanish, while the system itself would remain to circumscribe and dominate human thought and effort for many generations" (162, 163). He was not afraid to apply notions of institutional conservation to sensitive areas.

How much more was this true when it came to the Democratic party, his principal example of desiccated organization: "Democracy of to-day! What is it, but the shell from which the once juicy kernel has been extracted? The fire of patriotism that once burned in its bosom has been extinguished and the old political ideas wrought out through the brain of Thomas Jefferson and which the statesmen of Democracy, in the better ante-bellum days, guarded with unsurpassed devotion, no longer inspire its life or glorify its leadership. . . . And yet, vast multitudes of good men gather around this political body from which all real life has fled, and worship it because of the name it bears" (164–165). If concerned over the perishability of pure doctrine, he nonetheless remained somewhat uncritical of the original form, revealing, in the latter instance, a sense of betrayal as well as a restorative cast to his thought.

19. *Ibid.*, 165–166.

20. *Ibid.*, 166.

21. *Ibid.*, 168, 176. Nugent, in his loving attention to Christ, was projecting a vision of the complete reformer. First, Christ's knowledge was free from subterfuge or superficiality: "He was no sciolist—his words carrying a depth of meaning, a potency, a penetrating energy which words only bear when the spirit that fills them comes straight from the fountain of truth" (166). More basic was the identification of Christ with the aspirations of the lower classes (perhaps indicating Nugent's own deepest sentiments as well): "He was a carpenter, clad no doubt in coarse raiment and pursuing His vocation with diligence and skill. He was poor, very poor. . . . Ye tenants that labor and stint that landlords may flourish and grow and fatten upon your toil, behold your sympathizing brother—the landless Savior. . . . No, Christ was not a land monopolist. Neither was he a money monopolist. . . . Imagine Christ as a banker, a shaver of notes, a taker of usury! How horrible the thought. . . . But Christ did work—glorified industry—ennobled useful toil. . . . Yes, Christ's mission is especially to the landless, moneyless toilers. Hence the common people heard him gladly, congregated around him to listen, attracted by his strange but gracious words" (167, 168).

This was followed by a brief and essentially moral analysis of American historical development in which the role of capital was explicitly legitimated as an integral feature of producers' capitalism. Railroads, manufacturers, and retailers, each was a "producer" through adding value to the product. This conclusion prompted him to exclaim: "Capital! It is the hand maid of labor and the dispenser of blessings to all classes and conditions of humanity" (172). Or again, after tracing the stages of cotton production from the field to the finished garment, he declared: "Now in all these varied processes, capital has been present as a beneficent, useful factor, aiding labor in the creation of wealth for human service" (173). As will be evident shortly, Nugent's quarrel was not with capital per se. Rather, it was with capital's avaricious form, culminating in monopoly, that had come to characterize the recent period. This was the reason for my dwelling here on the moral dimension. The burden of the historical sketch was to suggest the departure from Christ's elemental principles, in turn leading Nugent to conceive of social redemption in moral and religious terms: "If the animating principle of that community life be greed, who can measure its power for evil, its destructive and devastating influence! If a sense of brotherhood dwells within and is diffused throughout it, is not this redeemed society? And what is redeemed society but redeemed and glorified industry?" (173–174).

The last question is critical to understanding his position. For, perhaps self-evidently, redemption was synonymous on the political-economic plane with reform. Christ need not have been invoked for justification, but the standard Nugent raised nevertheless took inspiration from this source. "Here, then, we stand upon this high ground of radical opposition to land monopoly, transportation monopoly and money monopoly—monopolies that have gradually grown up in and around our institutions and are gradually prostituting them to the purposes of mere private gain—enriching unduly the very few, impoverishing the many" (175).

22. *Ibid.*, 176.
23. *Ibid.*, 176–177.
24. *Ibid.*, 177.
25. *Ibid.*, 182. Nugent spoke with unaccustomed warmth on the wrongs committed against labor. As becomes clear, he did not sanction the use of strikes. Yet he recognized both the need for self-protection and the more basic expression of self-respect. Hence he stated less in the spirit of criticism than of resignation to inevitable social conflict: "Strikes are but a symptom of the deeper disease, which rankles at the heart of the body politic. Labor has long since learned that it produces the fund from which is derived its own compensation—nay, more, that it not only thus pays its own wages, but gives to capital a bonus for the privilege of doing so. Why should we wonder then, that it refuses to be satisfied with the dole which capital measures off to it, and resents the condition which forces it into the attitude of a mendicant? Why should we wonder, when labor is to-day in an agony to be free, to taste the sweets of independence, to find an open door to its lost opportunities? Why should we wonder, when labor, pressed to the wall, hunted like a wild beast, turns upon its oppressor in pure desperation and fights for its life—fights to maintain its standing place in the world's economic field? The fact that it realizes its dependence upon capital while conscious of its right to be free carries always the promises of conflict and peril" (181).

26. *Ibid.*, 182–183.
27. *Ibid.*, 183–184.
28. *Ibid.*, 184.
29. *Ibid.*, 184–185.
30. *Ibid.*, 185.
31. *Ibid.*
32. *Ibid.*, 185, 186.
33. *Ibid.*, 186–187.
34. *Ibid.*, 186–187, 195. Despite Nugent's general discountenancing of strikes, he strongly condemned President Cleveland's use of federal troops in the Pullman strike and expressed sympathy for Eugene V. Debs. In a reasoned constitutional treatment of the intervention, Nugent drew the distinction between localized disturbances and actual war or quasi-war. His response to the need for protecting property was less than panicked, even in the presence of violence. Not only were obstructions to commerce and mail stoppages incidental, rather than integral, to the strikers' purposes and conduct; they could not

justify the resort to national force (particularly when expressly against the wishes of state authority). The condition permitting national force was satisfied only under stringent definitions of the warmaking powers of Congress (187–191).

Hence he noted: "The standing army is raised for war, to cope with a public enemy in 'battle array,' not to quell civil disturbances, or mere local revolts, still less to suppress disorderly mobs of men and women, and least of all to guard and protect private property against thieves and incendiaries. Let it be understood, that the regular or standing army is but the instrument or weapon provided under the Constitution to give effect to the war-making power and that its use, therefore, is properly restricted to emergencies which call that power into exercise—let this be understood, and it can be seen at a glance how little there was in the emeute at Chicago to warrant the President in turning that community over to the tender mercies of General Miles and his battalions" (192). Nugent's references to "mobs" did not include strikers but only those who took advantage of the situation (188) after the army was ordered to Chicago (189). In still more marked contrast to modern practice, he also observed: "Justification for the use of the regular army can never arise under the Consitution upon any mere collateral or incidental effects likely to flow from domestic violence, nor upon a mere constructive infringement of national authority" (193).

Finally, after speculating on the influence of Attorney General Olney (a "corporation lawyer" serving as the president's legal adviser) in the decision, Nugent returned to the matter of a qualitative shift in business power: "But if this unwarranted use of the military arm of the government is dangerous when viewed as a question affecting the right of the States and the liberties of the citizen, the danger is greatly enhanced by the fact, that the precedent in effect commits the government to a policy of force extorted in behalf of organized capital in its conflicts with labor. Unless a civil revolt effected at the ballot box shall speedily drive the government back to strict constitutional methods, the advance of organized capital towards absolute dominion over labor must be greatly accelerated by the immense advantage thus acquired, since it is not to be presumed, that the monopolies which have been fostered and built up by vicious public policies will fail to grasp the full significance of this last step which the national government has taken in their behalf" (193, 194–195).

Nevertheless, to keep our perspective, it is important to remember that, as his phrase "civil revolt effected at the ballot box" suggested, he had not changed his mind on the long-term efficacy or the desirability of strikes: "Labor however can only hope to achieve a victory worthy of the name by strictly peaceable and orderly methods" (195).

35. *Ibid.*, 195.
36. *Ibid.*
37. *Ibid.*, 195–196.
38. *Ibid.*, 196.
39. *Ibid.*, 204–205. A more specifically economic analogue for the labor-capital balance can be seen in Nugent's discussion of the land question, preceding the quoted portions in the text, in which equalization of condition was explicitly denied. Nugent used the notion of productive capital as an obvious safeguard to property: "Now, no populist advocates the policy of destroying land titles, nor do they favor the subdivision of property: nor the limitation of

land ownership, but they recognize the fact, that the acquisition or monopolization of large bodies of land for speculative purposes only—that is to say, for the mere purpose of holding it out of use and finally disposing of it at enormously increased values to which the owner has not contributed by an hour's labor or the investment of a dollar in productive industry, is a great evil for which a remedy ought to be found." He then spoke of the possibilities of "the reclamation of unearned railway grants and the prevention of corporate ownership beyond the actual needs of the corporation's business." But in context it should be apparent that the antispeculative thrust, even with attendant remedies, failed to alter, and was not intended to alter, the capitalist basis on the land (202).

40. *Ibid.*, 205.
41. *Ibid.*, 209–213.
42. *Ibid.*, 213–214.
43. *Ibid.*, 214.
44. *Ibid.*, 214–216.
45. *Ibid.*, 216–218.
46. *Ibid.*, 221–222.
47. *Ibid.*, 222.
48. *Ibid.*, 222–223.
49. *Ibid.*, 223.
50. *Ibid.*
51. *Ibid.*, 227.
52. *Ibid.*, 228–229.
53. *Ibid.*, 229.
54. *Ibid.*
55. *Ibid.*, 235–236. The monetary approach, though not satisfactorily integrated, shared a place in Nugent's thought with the prevention of speculation on the land. In formal discussion, his acute attention to the latter factor was unique, even if it did not alter the broader outlines of the argument: "But I would be false to myself and the cause I represent to-day if I did not warn my populist friends that monetary reform, however sorely needed, will not bring the lasting and full relief which the country needs. It may lead to the production of wealth, but it will not afford the economic conditions necessary to the equitable distribution of wealth. It will bring increased prices for farm products, but it will greatly enhance the value of land and place land still further beyond the reach of labor. Even in our present distress we see land values getting beyond the reach of the laboring man. The scant money supply makes everything cheap but land. Population is ever growing—land cannot grow, except in value" (234).

For Nugent, land was in a profound sense the material and symbolic basis for opportunity. He noted further: "Brother Populists, look into this land question, for be assured that when settled on right lines it will forever solve the question of the equitable distribution of wealth" (235).

The preceding occurred just before the quoted portions on labor; following these portions he added with classic simplicity: "Thus only can conditions be so changed, that labor may live in contentment and peace, reaping that which it sows, dwelling beneath its own self-provided shelter, and enjoying evermore the sweetness of independence" (236).

56. *Ibid.*, 236.

Chapter Eight. Political Sovereignty: Lloyd, Peffer, and Weaver

1. Henry D. Lloyd, *Wealth Against Commonwealth* (New York, 1894), 1–2, 6–7, 494.

2. *Ibid.*, 494–495, 495–496, 496.

3. *Ibid.*, 497, 498, 498–499, 499.

4. *Ibid.*, 499–500, 500, 501, 502.

5. *Ibid.*, 503, 504–505, 505.

6. *Ibid.*, 506, 507–508, 508, 509, 510.

7. *Ibid.*, 516, 517, 518, 521–522.

8. *Ibid.*, 522.

9. *Ibid.*, 523, 523–524, 528.

10. *Ibid.*, 527.

11. *Ibid.*, 528–529, 529, 530.

12. *Ibid.*, 530.

13. *Ibid.*, 532, 535.

14. William A. Peffer, *The Farmer's Side* (New York, 1891), 74, 122–123.

15. *Ibid.*, 123, 162–167, 190.

16. *Ibid.*, 190.

17. *Ibid.*

18. *Ibid.*, 190–191.

19. *Ibid.*, 191.

20. *Ibid.*, 191–192.

21. *Ibid.*, 193.

22. *Ibid.*

23. *Ibid.*, 193–194.

24. *Ibid.*, 194.

25. *Ibid.*, 195.

26. James B. Weaver, *A Call to Action* (Des Moines, 1892), 248.

27. *Ibid.*, 267.

28. *Ibid.*, 282, 284, 292–293, 296.

29. *Ibid.*, 296.

30. *Ibid.*, 297–298.

31. *Ibid.*, 298.

32. *Ibid.*, 333.

33. *Ibid.*

34. *Ibid.*

35. *Ibid.*, 333–334.

36. *Ibid.*, 334.

37. *Ibid.*, 334–335.

38. Omaha Platform, in *National Economist*, July 9, 1892.

Bibliography

In my endeavor to study the mental landscape of Populism, I have adopted a principal method of other disciplines of learning: the textual exegesis of primary sources. The evidential field from which I have drawn is intentionally small, and yet it is conceivable that I have explored too many, rather than too few, Populists in these pages. I want still greater depth of focus, in order to demonstrate the appropriateness of an explication of texts, especially in my challenge here to reconstruct the public philosophy of the lower strata in American society. I have examined the following works, in the order of their appearance in the text: William A. Peffer, *The Farmer's Side, His Troubles and Their Remedy* (New York: D. Appleton and Co., 1891); James B. Weaver, *A Call to Action* (Des Moines: Iowa Printing Co., 1892); W. Scott Morgan, *History of the Wheel and Alliance, and the Impending Revolution* (Fort Scott, Kan.: J. H. Rice and Sons, 1889); James H. Davis, *A Political Revelation* (Dallas: The Advance Publishing Co., 1894); Thomas E. Watson, *The People's Party Campaign Book* (Author's edition: [Thomson, Ga., 1892]); Ignatius Donnelly (Edmund Boisgilbert, *pseud.*), *Caesar's Column* (Chicago: F. J. Schulte and Co., 1890); Donnelly, *Doctor Huguet* (Chicago: F. J. Schulte and Co., 1891); Donnelly, *The Golden Bottle* (New York and St. Paul: D. D. Merrill Co., 1892); and Catherine Nugent (ed.), *Life Work of Thomas L. Nugent* (Stephenville, Tex.: Catherine Nugent, 1896). I have also included a concise treatment of Henry D. Lloyd, *A Strike of Millionaires Against Miners* (Chicago: Belford-Clarke Co., 1890), and Henry D. Lloyd, *Wealth Against Commonwealth* (New York: Harper and Brothers, 1894), as well as letters from the Henry D. Lloyd Papers, State Historical Society of Wisconsin. In addition, I have used the files of the Topeka *Advocate* and the Lincoln *Farmers' Alliance;* two speeches were taken from the *People's Party Paper* in Atlanta.

The scholarship on Populism has provided both a firm narration of events (particularly on the state level) and sound coverage in such areas as political background, economic grievances, and social composition. It has produced several outstanding biographies as well. But it has been deficient in the systematic analysis of Populist ideas. While I have benefited from this scholarship, my primary indebtedness has been to the original sources, not only for my conceptual framework of Populism and interpretation of Populist thought, but also for my understanding of the movement's political, social, and economic features. I present here a compact list of readings on Populism and collateral topics. The secondary literature is of uneven quality (I will let the reader decide on the merits of the respective works), although among these writers I place C. Vann Woodward at the very top: Peter H. Argersinger, *Populism and Politics* (Lexington: University of Kentucky Press, 1974); Alex M. Arnett, *The Populist Movement in Georgia* (New York: Columbia University Press, 1922); Michael J. Brodhead, *Persevering Populist* (Reno: University of Nevada Press, 1969);

Robert P. Brooks, *The Agrarian Revolution in Georgia, 1865–1912* (Madison: University of Wisconsin Press, 1914); Allan G. Bogue, *From Prairie to Corn Belt* (Chicago: University of Chicago Press, 1963); O. Gene Clanton, *Kansas Populism* (Lawrence: University of Kansas Press, 1969); Thomas A. Clinch, *Urban Populism and Free Silver in Montana* (Missoula: University of Montana Press, 1970); Chester McArthur Destler, *American Radicalism, 1865–1901* (New London: Connecticut College Press, 1946), and *Henry Demarest Lloyd and the Empire of Reform* (Philadelphia: University of Pennsylvania Press, 1963); Robert F. Durden, *The Climax of Populism* (Lexington: University of Kentucky Press, 1965); Helen G. Edmonds, *The Negro and Fusion Politics in North Carolina, 1894–1901* (Chapel Hill: University of North Carolina Press, 1951); Gerald H. Gaither, *Blacks and the Populist Revolt* (University, Ala.: University of Alabama Press, 1977); Lawrence Goodwyn, *Democratic Promise* (New York: Oxford University Press, 1976); Sheldon Hackney, *Populism to Progressivism in Alabama* (Princeton: Princeton University Press, 1969); William I. Hair, *Bourbonism and Agrarian Protest* (Baton Rouge: Louisiana State University Press, 1969); John D. Hicks, *The Populist Revolt* (Minneapolis: University of Minnesota Press, 1931); Stanley L. Jones, *The Presidential Election of 1896* (Madison: University of Wisconsin Press, 1964); Albert D. Kirwan, *Revolt of the Rednecks* (Gloucester: Peter Smith, 1951); J. Morgan Kousser, *The Shaping of Southern Politics* (New Haven: Yale University Press, 1974); Robert C. McMath, *Populist Vanguard* (Chapel Hill: University of North Carolina Press, 1975); James C. Malin, *A Concern About Humanity* (Lawrence: Author, 1964); Roscoe C. Martin, *The People's Party in Texas* (Austin: University of Texas Press, 1933); Stuart Noblin, *Leonidas LaFayette Polk* (Chapel Hill: University of North Carolina Press, 1949); Walter T. K. Nugent, *The Tolerant Populists* (Chicago: University of Chicago Press, 1963); Bruce Palmer, *"Man Over Money"* (Chapel Hill: University of North Carolina Press, 1980); Stanley B. Parsons, *The Populist Context* (Westport: Greenwood Press, 1973); Norman Pollack, *The Populist Response to Industrial America* (Cambridge: Harvard University Press, 1962); Martin Ridge, *Ignatius Donnelly* (Chicago: University of Chicago Press, 1962); William W. Rogers, *The One-Gallused Rebellion* (Baton Rouge: Louisiana State University Press, 1970); Theodore Saloutos, *Farmer Movements in the South, 1865–1933* (Berkeley: University of California Press, 1960); Michael Schwartz, *Radical Protest and Social Structure* (New York: Academic Press, 1976); Roy V. Scott, *The Agrarian Movement in Illinois, 1880–1896* (Urbana: University of Illinois Press, 1962); Fred A. Shannon, *The Farmer's Last Frontier* (New York: Farrar and Rinehart, 1945); Barton C. Shaw, *The Wool-Hat Boys* (Baton Rouge: Louisiana State University Press, 1984); Vernon L. Wharton, *The Negro in Mississippi, 1865–1890* (Chapel Hill: University of North Carolina Press, 1947); C. Vann Woodward, *Tom Watson, Agrarian Rebel* (New York: Macmillan, 1938), and *Origins of the New South* (Baton Rouge: Louisiana State University Press, 1951); James E. Wright, *The Politics of Populism* (New Haven: Yale University Press, 1974); James M. Youngdale, *Populism, A Psychohistorical Perspective* (Port Washington: Kennikat Press, 1975). I would also mention my documentary collection *The Populist Mind* (Indianapolis: Bobbs-Merrill, 1967).

The following diverse works have helped to shape my analytical framework: Louis Hartz, *The Liberal Tradition in America* (New York: Harcourt, Brace and World, 1955); C. B. Macpherson, *The Political Theory of Possessive Individualism*

(Oxford: Clarendon Press, 1962); Herbert Marcuse, *Eros and Civilization* (Boston: Beacon Press, 1955); Barrington Moore, *Social Origins of Dictatorship and Democracy* (Boston: Beacon Press, 1966); Fritz Pappenheim, *The Alienation of Modern Man* (New York: Monthly Review Press, 1959); E. P. Thompson, *The Making of the English Working Class* (London: Victor Gollancz, 1963); and Thorstein Veblen, *Imperial Germany and the Industrial Revolution* (New York: Macmillan, 1915). Other writings which have furnished me guidelines include: Paul A. Baran, *The Political Economy of Growth* (New York: Monthly Review Press, 1957); E. H. Carr, *What is History?* (New York: Alfred A. Knopf, 1962); V. O. Key, *Southern Politics in State and Nation* (New York: Alfred A. Knopf, 1949); Gabriel Kolko, *The Triumph of Conservatism* (Glencoe: The Free Press, 1963); N. Gordon Levin, *Woodrow Wilson and World Politics* (New York: Oxford University Press, 1968); Robert G. McCloskey, *American Conservatism in the Age of Enterprise* (Cambridge: Harvard University Press, 1951); the historical and legal writings of Franz Neumann; the explorations of business structure and business ideology of Robert A. Brady; and the recent literature on the theory of the capitalist state, especially the books of Nicos Poulantzas. Finally, I take this opportunity to pay tribute to W. J. Cash's *The Mind of the South* (New York: Alfred A. Knopf, 1941) for the lasting impression it has made on me.

Index

This index attempts to reflect realistically the structure and material of the present book. I have emphasized the sequential ordering of ideas as they appear within the discussion of each of the writers, rather than providing separate entries for a multitude of terms. The following concepts and topics occur throughout these pages and hence do not lend themselves to ready itemization: *capitalism, democracy, ethics, government, human rights, law, monopolism, property, sovereignty,* and *the state.* The reader will be assisted in locating these broader themes by chapter titles and subheads.